Tank Warfare on the Eastern Front, 1941–1942

Tank Warfare on the Eastern Front, 1941–1942

Schwerpunkt

Robert A. Forczyk

Pen & Sword
MILITARY

First published in Great Britain in 2013 by
PEN & SWORD MILITARY
An imprint of
Pen & Sword Books Ltd
47 Church Street
Barnsley
South Yorkshire
S70 2AS

ISBN 978-1-78159-008-9

A CIP catalogue record for this book is available from the British Library.

Typeset by Concept, Huddersfield, West Yorkshire, HD4 5JL.
Printed and bound in England by CPI Group (UK) Ltd, Croydon CR0 4YY.

Pen & Sword Books Ltd incorporates the imprints of Pen & Sword Archaeology, Atlas, Aviation, Battleground, Discovery, Family History, History, Maritime, Military, Naval, Politics, Railways, Select, Social History, Transport, True Crime, and Claymore Press, Frontline Books, Leo Cooper, Praetorian Press, Remember When, Seaforth Publishing and Wharncliffe.

For a complete list of Pen & Sword titles please contact
PEN & SWORD BOOKS LIMITED
47 Church Street, Barnsley, South Yorkshire, S70 2AS, England
E-mail: enquiries@pen-and-sword.co.uk
Website: www.pen-and-sword.co.uk

Contents

List of Plates

A mixed German armoured Kampfgruppe begins the attack into the Soviet Union.

Abandoned Soviet T-26 light tanks from Oborin's 14th Mechanized Corps in Kobrin, 23 June 1941.

A knocked-out T-26 light tank and a victim of the early border battles.

A Pz.38(t) light tank from the 12.Panzer-Division, which was part of Hoth's Panzergruppe 3.

A German infantryman approaches a dead Soviet tanker next to his burning BT-7 fast tank, Ukraine, June 1941.

A 15cm sIG 33 (sf), probably from 1.Panzer-Division, passes an abandoned KV-2 heavy tank in June 1941.

During the Battle of Dubno on 26 June 1941, the Soviet 12th Tank Division attempted to attack the German-held village of Leshnev, but advancing into marshy terrain along the Syten'ka River they lost three T-34 tanks that got bogged down.

A T-34 Model 1941 which overran and crushed a German l.FH18 10.5cm howitzer.

A StuG III assault gun crossing a river in the early stages of Operation Barbarossa.

The hull of a KV-1 with at least four medium-caliber anti-tank round hits, which failed to penetrate, but a large-caliber artillery round, either 10.5cm or 15cm, has damaged the track.

A KV-1 heavy tank from the 124th Armored Brigade ambushed a German column northeast of Ivanovka on 9 October 1941.

Soviet tankers examine a Pz.38(t) light tank from the 7.Panzer-Division, abandoned near Yartsevo.

The onset of mud slowed down, but did not stop, German operations.

Soviet T-26 light tanks lead Timoshenko's counterattacks during the fighting near Smolensk in August 1941.

A Pz.III medium tank from 10.Panzer-Division, knocked out near Skirminova, east of Volokolamsk in mid-November 1941.

The last stage of Operation Typhoon began with German panzers attempting to batter their way through Rokossovsky's final layer of defense outside Moscow.

A Soviet white-washed T-34 in hull-down position awaits the German panzers, near Volokolamsk, November 1941.

Polkovnik Mikhail G. Sakhno's tanks from the Moscow Proletarian Motorized Rifle Division move to a new position in the vicinity of Naro-Fominsk, December 1941.

Two overturned Matilda II tanks near Volokolamsk, 1 December 1941.

A T-34 tank moving at speed in deep snow.

The crew of a Pz.III tank from the 14.Panzer-Division watch German infantry clearing a village, mid-1942.

The interior of Hube's command vehicle, 16.Panzer-Division.

A Pz.III tank from 11.Panzer-Division in action during the opening stages of Operation Blau, 28–30 June 1942.

An 8.8cm flak gun employing direct fire against Soviet armour.

A Pz.IV tank destroyed during the Second Battle of Kharkov in May 1942.

A Pz.III Ausf J with long 5cm gun.

An American-built Lend-Lease M3 Lee tank, shattered by 8.8cm anti-tank fire.

Tiger I heavy tank in August 1942.

A T-34 tank moving over rough terrain with infantry in *desant* role.

A Pz.IV Ausf G with long 7.5cm cannon in mid-1942.

A KV-1 heavy tank that overran a German reconnaissance car at the Battle of Ostrov.

A German Tauchpanzer III in testing.

List of Maps

Glossary

ABTU – *Auto-Bronetankovoe Upravlenie* (Main Tank Directorate), 1934–40.

AFV – Armoured Fighting Vehicle.

AOK – *Armeeoberkommando* (Army).

AP – Armour Piercing.

APBC – Armour Piercing Ballistic Cap.

APHE – Armour Piercing High Explosive.

C2 – Command and Control.

cbm – cubic meter of fuel, equivalent to 5,000 liters or 739kg.

DD – *Dal'noe deistvie* (long-range tanks).

DPP – *Dal'nia podderzhka pekhotny* (Distant infantry support tanks).

Fliegerverbindungsoffizier – *Flivo*, Luftwaffe liaison officer at Panzerarmee, created May 1942.

GABTU – *Glavnoe Avto-Brone-Tankovoe Upravlenie* (Chief Department of Autos and Armoured Vehicles), 1940–45.

Gefechtstroß – Combat trains, including ammunition trailers.

Gepäcktroß – Baggage train, including field kitchens.

GKO – *Gosudarstvennij Komitet Oboroniy* (State Defense Committee).

Großtransportraum – Large transport (GTR).

HEAT – High Explosive Anti-Tank.

HKL – *Hauptkampflinie* (main line of resistance).

Instandsetzungsgruppe – Repair group.

Kradschützen – Motorcycle infantry.

LSSAH – Leibstandarte SS Adolf Hitler.

MD – Military District.

NKO – *Narodnyi Kommisariat Oborony* (the People's Commissariat of Defense).

NKTP – *Narodnyi Kommissariat Tankovoy Promyslennosti* (the People's Commissariat of the Tank Industry).

NKVD – *Narodnyi Kommisariat Vneshnykh Del* (People's Commissariat of Internal Affairs).

NPP – *Neposredstvennaia podderzhka pekhoty* (direct infantry support tank).

OKH – *Oberkommando des Heeres* (German, Army High Command).

ОТВ – Отдельные танковые батальоны (Independent Tank Battalion).

OTTPP – *Otdelniy Tyazhelij Tankovij Polk Proriva* (Independent Heavy Tank Breakthrough Regiment).

PP – *podderzhka pekhoty* (infantry support tanks).

Pz.Regt – Panzer Regiment.

PZAOK – Panzerarmee.

RKKA – *Raboche-Krest'yanskaya Krasnaya Armiya* (the Army of Workers and Peasants/the Red Army).

RVGK – *Rezerv Verkhovnogo Glavnokomandovaniya* (Reserve of Supreme High Command).

SAP – *Samokhodno-Artillerijskij Polk* (Self-Propelled Artillery Regiment).

SR – Schützen-Regiment [Motorized Infantry].

StZ – Stalingrad Tank Factory.

TSAP – *Tyazhelij Samokhodno-Artillerijskij Polk* (Heavy Self-Propelled Artillery Regiment).

TTPP – *Tyazhelij Tankovij Polk Proriva* (Heavy Tank Breakthrough Regiment).

UMM – *Upravlenie Motorizatzii i Mekhanizatzii RKKA* (Directorate of Mechanization and Motorization of the Red Army), 1929–34. Re-named ABTU.

VAMM – *Voennaya Akademiya Mekhanizatzii i Motorizatzii RKKA* (Military Academy of Mechanization and Motorization of the Red Army).

V.S. – *Verbrauchssatz*. A basic load of fuel or amunition.

Vorausabteilung – Vanguard battalion (abbrev. V.A.).

Preface

In February 1986, amidst white-out conditions and sub-zero temperatures near the town of Yangpyeong in South Korea, I opened a wooden box that I was only supposed to open in the event of an emergency. Since my tank was alone on an independent reconnaissance mission with no other vehicles to assist, that emergency seemed to be at hand. In order to reach our battalion's assembly area at the railhead, we had to climb a mountain road with a 30° slope, but every attempt had failed because our tracks slid on the snow and ice. The box came from Germany and it contained snow cleats that could be attached to the tank's tracks for added traction on snow and ice. They were built by Rheinmetall, the same company which had rushed tank cleats to the Russian Front during the winter of 1941–42. Forty years later, the US Army bought a few sets for trials and I had been fortunate to receive one, but was instructed to use them only if absolutely necessary. My crew and I mounted the cleats on our tracks in less than an hour and started up the hill. The cleats dug into the snow and ice like teeth and we started to make progress up the slope. However, the temperature was around −23°C (−10°F) and the metal in the cleats grew increasingly fragile and started to shatter. Every 20–30 meters, another cleat would shatter, with pieces falling off the track. Eventually, our tank made it up the slope and back to the assembly area, but every tank cleat was broken by that point and the US Army decided not to purchase more sets of what appeared to be a one-time use item. Nevertheless, I was thankful that modern tankers could benefit from technology that had been developed as a result of the brutal experiences in armoured combat on the Eastern Front decades prior. Indeed, I came to appreciate that there are many lessons to be learned from the armoured operations of that conflict, which will be useful for some time to come.

This is not intended to be a day-by-day campaign narrative, although it may seem that way at times. Nor is it intended to be a 'guts and glory' compilation of tactical vignettes, although it will have some elements of that as well. Rather, this book will focus on the operational and tactical levels of combat in order to answer how and why the Red Army's tank units managed to defeat the heretofore undefeated panzer armies of the Third Reich. Issues that are tangential to armoured operations will only be addressed in passing or omitted altogether, but I do intend to touch upon many topics related to tank technology, production and maintenance that are usually left out of other histories. I also intend to tell this story, as much as the reference materials allow, from both sides' points of view rather than just one, which has unfortunately been the case in so many previous Eastern Front histories.

Introduction

'We are fifty or a hundred years behind the advanced countries. We must make good this distance in ten years. Either we do it, or they will crush us'.

Josef Stalin, 4 February 1931

Popular Mythology

The Russo-German War in general, and armoured combat on the Eastern Front in particular, have remained popular subjects in English-language historiography of the Second World War for the past six decades. However, much of what Anglo-American readers know or think they know about armoured warfare on the Eastern Front has been shaped by self-serving memoirs such as Guderian's *Panzer Leader* or von Mellenthin's *Panzer Battles*, or popular wargames such as SPI's *Panzerblitz* (1970) and a new generation of computer wargames. A cult of German tank-worshippers has arisen and its members are now firmly entrenched in their belief that all German tanks (meaning their beloved Tiger and Panther series) were better than any Soviet tanks and that the Red Army's tank forces only prevailed because of numerical superiority. There is a grain of truth in this argument, which was fostered by German veterans seeking to perpetuate the Third Reich's propaganda-line that the victory of the Red Army's 'barbarian hordes' was due to mass, not skill. However, the quantity over quality argument ignores a variety of critical factors encompassing the opposing war-fighting doctrines, strategic miscalculations and terrain/weather that significantly influenced the outcome of armoured operations in the East. Key facts, such as the German inability to develop a reliable diesel tank engine while the Soviets had one in production before Operation Barbarossa began, are often just ignored – even though it had a significant impact on the outcome of mechanized operations on the Eastern Front. Yet material factors were not the only influences upon armoured warfare on the Eastern Front. Napoleon's dictum that, 'in war, the moral is to the material as three is to one,' proved quite apt on the Eastern Front of 1941–45, with a host of moral and non-material factors influencing the outcome of battles and campaigns.

Looking across a hexagonal grid super-imposed over a two-dimensional map sheet, cardboard counters or plastic miniatures representing German Panthers or Tigers look so much more impressive than the opposing Soviet T-34s. The German tanks' strengths – long-range firepower and armoured protection – carry great weight in these kinds of simulations, while their main weaknesses – poor mobility and poor mechanical reliability – are only minor inconveniences, if depicted at all. For example, the oft-repeated canards about the Panther's 'teething problems' at Kursk are fobbed off as a temporary issue, costing a war-gamer a few movement points, without realizing that the Panther had persistent mobility issues throughout its career that prevented it from conducting the kind of wide-ranging mobile operations required by German maneuver warfare doctrine. The main strengths of the Soviet T-34 – reliable mobility over vast distances on its own tracks and suitability for mass production – are factors that lie outside most tactical-level simulations. Consequently, two generations of Anglo-American history buffs have been presented with numerous simulations that emphasize the superiority of German tanks and the cannon-fodder nature of Soviet tanks. The Cold War also played a role in shaping perceptions, with a large number of German veteran accounts that were often viewed uncritically, while there was a dearth of useful accounts from the Soviet side. When available, Soviet accounts were routinely discounted as lies or propaganda. After the collapse of the Soviet Union, fifty years after the onset of Operation Barbarossa, this ingrained Western perception began to change as previously unavailable historical material emerged from Soviet-era archives, but the balance of Eastern Front historiography in English is still heavily biased toward the German perspective. This book hopes to contribute to redressing that imbalance.

Another problem in evaluating armoured warfare on the Eastern Front is that much of the analysis to date has been fairly tactical in nature, focusing on a single campaign such as Stalingrad or Kursk, which tends to gloss over the impact of long-term trends that shaped each sides' combat performance. The Russo-German War lasted for forty-six and a half months. It was not decided by a single battle or campaign. This study intends to examine how Germany's panzer units performed against the Red Army's tank units during this entire period and why the Soviet Union prevailed. It is not my intent to provide a detailed chronology of every tank battle, but rather to discern the main trends emerging over time. I also intend to highlight actions that are often ignored or glossed over in other histories, which often suggest that nothing significant was happening on other parts of the Eastern Front when big battles were occurring around places like Stalingrad and Kursk. As a former tanker myself, commanding M60A3 TTS tanks in the U.S. Army in the Republic of Korea in the mid-1980s, I have an appreciation for how logistics, terrain and weather can affect armour operations and how seemingly minor deficiencies can have major consequences. Having felt the terror of sliding uncontrollably in a tank on an icy downgrade, or the difficulty of recovering tanks mired in deep mud, or fording a boulder-strewn river, I intend to offer an account of tank warfare that encompasses the oft-ignored, but critical, facets of armoured operations that have frequently been missing from other accounts.

Strategic Setting

Adolf Hitler intended to crush the Soviet Union and its inimical Communist ideology in one, swift campaign, using his battle-tested panzer divisions and Luftwaffe air fleets as his weapons of choice. In Führer Directive 21, issued on 18 December 1940, Hitler stated that, 'the bulk of the Russian Army in Western

Russia will be destroyed by daring operations led by deeply penetrating armoured spearheads.'[1] He deliberately chose to unleash a war of annihilation aimed not only at the destruction of the Red Army and Soviet state, but also at the eventual obliteration of the indigenous Slavic populations as a necessary precursor to German colonization in the East. Whereas previous operations in Poland, France and the Balkans had followed the methods of traditional German campaigning, Hitler intended Operation Barbarossa to be a crusade. Yet oddly, Hitler's grand strategic vision for the War in the East was not matched by sound strategic-level planning. Instead, the War in the East would be conducted primarily on the operational and even tactical levels, often on the basis of ad hoc or opportunistic decision-making, rather than sober assessment of ends and means.

The employment of Germany's armoured forces in the Soviet Union was shaped by three strategic assumptions made by Hitler and the *Oberkommando der Heer* (OKH). The first assumption was that the war in the Soviet Union would be a short campaign, resolved in a matter of a few months. Germany made no preparations for a protracted War in the East, including increasing tank production or training replacements, or stockpiling fuel and ammunition. The second German strategic assumption was that terrain and weather would have no significant impact on the conduct of the campaign. Hitler and the OKH regarded the Soviet Union as virtually flat, table-top steppe land that was perfect for rapid panzer operations, but ignored its numerous rivers, dense forests, immense distances and poor road networks. Previous German panzer operations had achieved victories after moving only 300–400km in fair weather over good roads. Indeed, no offensive in German military history had ever covered more than 500km in a single push. Since the first assumption of a short war expected a Soviet collapse well before the onset of the Russian winter, Hitler and the OKH completely disregarded the weather as a factor. The third strategic assumption was that the Red Army could be quickly and efficiently destroyed. Based on a combination of factors – the poor showing by the Red Army in the Russo-Finnish War, Stalin's purges of the officer corps and incomplete OKH intelligence assessments – Hitler and the OKH reckoned that they could destroy the best part of the Red Army in about six weeks of fast-moving campaigning. With the bulk of the Red Army smashed, including its tank forces, Hitler believed that the Soviet state would suffer a moral collapse akin to what happened in France in June 1940. These three strategic assumptions had a profound impact on German panzer operations in the Soviet Union and when each proved false in turn, they put the panzer divisions at a permanent disadvantage.

Stalin's immediate objective in mid-1941 was to deter German aggression until the Red Army was sufficiently prepared for him to take a more assertive tack with Hitler. He had foolishly ordered the disbanding of the Red Army's four existing tank corps in November 1939, only to order them re-formed as mechanized corps in July 1940 and their number doubled in response to the spectacular German victory over France. In order to give Soviet military power credibility in the eyes of Germany, Stalin also directed that the mechanized corps would be re-equipped with the new T-34 and KV-1 tanks to replace the lighter T-26 and

BT-series models. Soviet industry was ordered to produce over 5,000 of the new tanks and the mechanized corps were expected to be fully-equipped by mid-1942. However, Stalin became increasingly alarmed by reports that Germany was creating more panzer divisions, so in February 1941 he directed that twenty additional mechanized corps – requiring another 11,000 tanks – should be formed as quickly as possible. Even with the Stalingrad Tractor Plant (STZ) joining the Kharkov Plant (KhPZ) to produce T-34 tanks, it was unlikely that these twenty-eight mechanized corps could be fully-equipped before late 1943. Given these arbitrary changes in organization imposed by Stalin, the Red Army's twenty-eight mechanized corps were only partly equipped and in a state of fatal disarray in June 1941.

The deployment and employment of the Red Army's mechanized forces was based on three strategic assumptions made by Stalin and his General Staff. First, Stalin believed that there would be adequate early warning prior to any German aggression, giving Red Army units time to prepare and deploy for combat. Due to this assumption, Red Army leaders felt that they could defer measures to enhance combat readiness in favor of other organizational priorities. The second Soviet strategic assumption was that with adequate logistics, training and preparation, the Red Army could hold its own against the Wehrmacht. Tied to this assumption was an implicit belief that enemy incursions could be limited to the buffer zones in Poland and Lithuania acquired in 1939–40. The third Soviet strategic assumption was that industrial mobilization was the key to victory and that campaigns would be decided by the side that had the greater ability to sustain its forces in protracted operations, not by fancy maneuvers. Due to Stalin's ineptitude, the first Soviet strategic assumption was invalidated and undermined the validity of the second assumption as well. The cost of Stalin's strategic miscalculations was the loss of the bulk of the pre-war Soviet tank force in the first three months of the campaign. However, the third Soviet strategic assumption proved entirely correct and eventually provided the means for the second assumption to regain saliency by the second year of the war. In short, despite certain blindness to impending war, Stalin and the Soviet General Staff did a far better job laying the groundwork for protracted operations than the Germans, and this strategic calculus would provide the Red Army's tank forces with a valuable counterweight to the tactical skill of German panzer units. The Soviet numerical superiority in tanks for much of the War in the East – much bemoaned by German veterans – was not some sleight of hand trick, but the result of careful pre-war planning.

Hitler deployed four panzer groups with a total of seventeen panzer divisions and 3,106 tanks[2] for Operation Barbarossa, the invasion of the Soviet Union. In addition, two independent panzer battalions, Pz.Abt. 40 and Pz.Abt. 211, were deployed in Finland with 124 tanks (incl. twenty Pz.III). The 2 and 5.Panzer-Divisionen were refitting in Germany after the Greek Campaign in April 1941 and were in OKH reserve. Otherwise, the only other extant panzer units were the 15.Panzer-Division with Generalleutnant Erwin Rommel in Libya and two panzer brigades in France. No other panzer units were in the process of forming in Germany. Consequently, the OKH was committing virtually all of the available German panzer forces to Barbarossa, with negligible reserves and limited monthly production output to replace losses. In mid-1941, German industry was producing an average of 250 tanks per month, half of which were the Pz.III medium tank. Combat experience in France and Belgium in 1940 indicated that the Germans could expect to lose about one-third of their medium tanks even in a short six-week campaign, which Hitler regarded as acceptable losses. Furthermore, German industry had no tanks beyond the Pz.III or Pz.IV in advance development. The *Heereswaffenamt* (Army Weapons Office) only authorized Henschel and Porsche to begin working on prototypes for a new heavy tank four weeks before Operation Barbarossa began, and this program had no special priority until after the first encounters with the Soviet T-34 and KV-1 tanks in combat.

The primary operational objectives of the four German panzer groups were Leningrad in the north, Moscow in the center and Kiev and the Donbas region in the south. The distance from their starting positions to their operational objectives was 800km for Panzergruppe 4, 1,000km for Panzergruppe 2 and 3, and over 1,200km for Panzergruppe 1. Hitler expected these objectives to be reached within about ten weeks of the start of Barbarossa, an unprecedented rate of advance in modern military history. However, it was questionable whether German tanks could even move this far in this amount of time, even if much of the Red Army was destroyed on the border. As a general rule of thumb, about 5 per cent of tanks in a given unit will break down for mechanical reasons after a 100km road march, although most can be repaired within a few hours. Just three years before Barbarossa, nearly 30 per cent of the 2.Panzer-Division's tanks broke down on the unopposed 670km road march to Vienna, along good roads.[3] If the panzer divisions suffered a similar scale of combat losses as in the 1940 Western Campaign, no more than 10–20 per cent of the original panzers would be likely to reach their objectives.

Operation Barbarossa's bold scheme of maneuver was undermined by very poor intelligence preparation by German intelligence services. In actuality, the OKH intelligence staff had a faulty understanding of the strength and dispositions of the Red Army. German signals intelligence had not detected the reformation of Soviet mechanized corps in July 1940 and believed that the Red Army's armour was still deployed as independent tank and mechanized brigades.[4] In early June 1941, Oberst Eberhard Kinzel, head of the OKH's *Fremde Heere Ost* (Foreign Armies East), assessed that the Red Army would deploy forty-one mechanized brigades with about 9,500 tanks against the Wehrmacht.[5] Kinzel's shop produced a handbook on Soviet tanks for the panzer groups, which described the various models of the T-26, T-28, T-35 and BT-5/7 in detail. The handbook also included information about a new Soviet heavy tank equipped with 60mm-thick armour and 76.2mm main armament that had been used against the Finns in December 1939; this was the SMK prototype, which the Germans erroneously labeled as the T-35C. Although Kinzel was clearly aware that the Soviets had fielded a prototype heavy tank eighteen months prior to Barbarossa, he assessed that existing German anti-tank weapons could defeat it.[6]

Prior to the German invasion, Stalin wanted to keep his strategic options open, to gain territory when possible, but to avoid being dragged into a fight before he felt the Red Army was ready. He wanted a sizeable portion of the newly-forming mechanized corps positioned near the western borders to deter German attack, but the rest would be deployed further back in reserve. In the event of invasion, the Red Army's existing war plan directed that all available mechanized corps should be immediately committed to counterattack any German penetrations across the border. Unwittingly, this plan played into German hands, by forcing Soviet tank commanders to send unprepared units into battle piece-meal, directly into the face of on-coming German panzer *schwerpunkt* (main efforts). Indeed, the German panzer forces would be at their strongest in the border regions, where distance and logistics had not yet attenuated their combat power. However, the German planners in the OKH had no appreciation for the Soviet military philosophy of echeloned attack and defense, which meant that defeating the Red Army in a single campaign would prove far more difficult than the French Army in 1940. The entire essence of the so-called Blitzkrieg doctrine was in using concentrated armoured formations in short, powerful jabs to dislocate an enemy's defense by isolating his best forces. A reasonable enemy was then expected to sue for peace due to the sudden setback. However, neither Stalin nor the Red Army had any incentive to be reasonable once it became clear that Hitler's strategic objective was to exterminate them. By opting for a war of annihilation, Hitler made it impossible for the Wehrmacht to defeat the Red Army in a single campaign.

Terrain and Weather Factors

Between September 1939 and May 1941, German panzer divisions had encountered no serious difficulties in their campaigns due to either adverse terrain or weather conditions (other than the English Channel, which was conveniently ignored). In particular, Panzergruppe Kleist had been able to quickly pass through the 'impenetrable' Ardennes Forrest and then conduct successful opposed river crossings across the rivers Meuse and Somme in France. In April 1941, Kleist's panzers were able to overrun Yugoslavia and Greece in less than three weeks, despite numerous rivers and mountainous terrain. The overriding impression Hitler and the OKH leadership gained from the Wehrmacht's preceding campaigns was that terrain in itself was not a serious obstacle to the panzers. Nor did Hitler and the OKH have any useful experience with mechanized operations under winter conditions. In contrast, the Red Army had learned painful lessons about the limitations of mechanized units in forested terrain and winter conditions during the 1939–40 Russo-Finnish War and were in the process of incorporating some of the lessons learned.

Crossing rivers or large streams was an essential feature of military operations in the Soviet Union and the relative fording capabilities of tanks had a major impact on the tempo of armoured operations. Although both Germany and the

Soviet Union had a small number of tanks with amphibious capabilities, such as the Pz.III and Pz.IV *Tauchpanzer* and the T-37, T-38 and T-40 light amphibious tanks, the majority of tanks on both sides could not ford water that was deeper than one meter (i.e. chest deep on a man). The bridging capabilities of the 1941–42 panzer divisions were rather rudimentary – a Brückenkolonne B or K could construct a 50-meter long pontoon bridge in about twelve hours that could just support a Pz.III medium tank, but the Pz.IV and later Tiger and Panthers needed proper bridges to get across significant water obstacles. Indeed, the Wehrmacht lagged behind the Allies in assault bridging, having nothing like the British Bailey bridge. Soviet tank divisions of 1941 were supposed to have a pontoon bridge battalion, but most were never fully formed or quickly lost during the hectic retreats of 1941. While tanks could often cross smaller rivers at shallow fording sites, these critical locations were usually defended by anti-tank guns and mines. Larger rivers, such as the Dnieper or Volga, could not be crossed without substantial army-level engineer support. Pontoon rafts could be constructed to get small numbers of tanks across a large river, but this was usually only sufficient to defend a bridgehead against enemy counterattack. Thus, the capture of intact bridges – particularly railroad bridges, which could support the weight of tanks – was an important constant in Eastern Front armoured operations: both sides sought opportunities to seize poorly-defended bridges because they allowed tanks to do what they do best – move fast and use their shock effect to disrupt an enemy's defenses. When bridges or fording sites were not available, armoured operations came to a full stop.

Generally, you can try to go just about anywhere with a tank – at least once – but you may regret that you tried. Armoured operations on the Eastern Front were often impeded or channelized – forced into narrow mobility corridors – due to 'no-go' terrain such as marshes or dense forests. The marshlands between Leningrad and Ostashkov in northern Russia and the Pripet marshes were particularly hazardous for armoured operations. Tanks could easily become irretrievably bogged down in marshy terrain, or forced to move along narrow tracks that made them very vulnerable to anti-tank ambushes. In the early border battles in 1941, the Red Army foolishly lost a number of precious T-34 and KV-1 tanks in water-logged areas in the Pripet Marshes. The best tank country on the Eastern Front was the steppe country of the Ukraine, although this region also had the worst mud during the rainy periods. There were areas of 'slow-go' terrain in the Soviet Union, including urban areas and the ravines along the River Don, which could cause tanks to throw track. The Germans were particularly shocked by the almost total lack of decent all-weather roads in the Soviet Union, which increased the wear and tear on all vehicles and greatly reduced their mobility.

The Germans had totally discounted the severity of the weather in the Soviet Union and were shocked in turn by the summer heat, the autumn mud and the harsh winter cold. Mud in particular is the bane of the existence of all tankers, but the idea that it only interfered with German mobile operations and that it was only a problem during the autumn and spring *Rasputitsa* season is an oversimplification that has been accepted for too long in Western historiography about the Eastern Front. First of all, the Eastern Front stretched over 1,700km from Leningrad to the Crimea and the weather could vary considerably across regions; a typical rain system would cover a 400–500km wide area, but other areas received no rain (or snow). Weather fronts moved from west to east across Russia, meaning that bad weather would generally hit the Germans first. Second, the summer months of June–July tended to have the most rain, but April and May were the driest months. In 1941, Heeresgruppe Süd had twice as much rain in July as it did in September–October, and mud caused significant mobility problems in the summer as well. When mud occurred, the wheeled vehicles in armoured units and towed artillery pieces were likely to be the most affected, but tracked vehicles could generally move until the mud became so deep that the tank either scraped bottom or the roadwheels became too fouled with mud. When the supply trucks couldn't make it through the mud, armoured operations ground to a halt from lack of supplies and ammunition. Oftentimes, SPW half tracks had to be diverted from their primary combat tasks of transporting infantry to making supply runs through muddy areas or going to pull mired trucks out. Routine track maintenance became much more difficult when everything was caked in thick, gooey mud. Soviet tankers also complained about the mud and it significantly affected their operations as well. The main Soviet tanks in 1941 – the T-26 and BT-7 – had even narrower tracks and less engine power than the German Pz.III, meaning that most Red Army tank units in 1941 were more prone to being impeded by muddy roads. Since Soviet tank brigades in 1941–42 consisted of mixed vehicle types, the superior T-34s would still have to travel at the rate of the slower light tanks.

The first snow arrived over the Eastern Front in October 1941, but in most areas it consisted of only 5cm and turned to rain within twenty-four hours. There were only two or three days with snow in October, with more falling in the humid Ukraine than around Leningrad. Snowfall in November jumped to about 20cm in central Russia, but the heaviest snowfalls did not occur until December–February. German equipment was designed to operate in temperate areas and proved unsuited to cold-weather operations in Russia. Panzer crews were particularly shocked to find that their tracks could literally freeze to the ground in winter months or their batteries crack when the fluid inside froze. The Czech-built Pz.35(t) used a hydraulic system that literally froze in October 1941, bringing that vehicle's career to an abrupt end. When the German expectations of a short campaign were unfulfilled, the panzers were forced to conduct operations under all weather conditions, for which they were not psychologically or materially equipped.

Doctrinal and Technological Influences

During the interwar period, there were two contending schools of thought among major armies in regard to the proper employment of tanks. The dominant school was that tanks were best suited for the infantry support role and should be attached directly to infantry units. More revolutionary was the concept of armoured units that could operate independently, which was inspired in part by the theories of the British armour theorist, J.F.C. Fuller, and his Plan 1919. Fuller's theories of mechanization, expounded in his interwar writings, attracted followers in both the Reichswehr and the Red Army. The proponents of creating independent armour units argued for looking beyond the breakthrough battle and for using tanks in a long-distance, exploitation role. However, this kind of radical thinking ran head-on into the powerful cavalry lobbies in both Germany and the Soviet Union, who regarded tanks as a threat to the mounted branch's traditional use in the exploitation role. Both infantry and cavalry officers generally opposed the creation of independent tank units or tried to place limits on the kind of role they would serve. The infantry school argued for the development of infantry support tanks with a high level of armoured protection and had a howitzer-type weapon, but speed or range were not important requirements. Cavalry officers gradually accepted that tanks would be included in their country's armed forces, but preferred light, fast tanks that could assist the cavalry in reconnaissance and pursuit roles. These intra-service debates about tank design crossed national lines and shaped tank development in Britain, the United States, France, Germany and the Soviet Union in the 1920s and 1930s.

Armour theorists gradually recognized that in order to develop effective tanks, both the infantry support and cavalry exploitation missions needed to be reconciled in technical requirements. The utopian idea of a single 'universal tank' that could successfully accomplish all missions was quickly determined to be unfeasible and theorists recognized that more than one type of tank would be necessary in order to fulfill armour's potential on the battlefield. The infantry support mission required a tank that was equipped with weapons capable of engaging enemy infantry entrenched in fieldworks, bunkers or buildings. Given the high threat level from enemy artillery and anti-tank weapons, it would also be prudent for infantry support tanks to possess a high level of armoured protection. However, the exploitation mission suggested a tank with the primary requirements of speed and mobility. Most armies struggled with developing the right types of tanks, with the best characteristics and in the best mix to meet these mission requirements. Both the Red Army and the Reichswehr made choices about what tanks they wanted, based upon doctrinal and technological influences in the 1930s, which would shape battlefield outcomes in 1941–45.

Since Germany was not allowed to build or possess tanks due to the restrictions of the Treaty of Versailles after the First World War, the postwar Reichswehr made covert agreements with the Red Army to establish a tank training school at Kazan in 1929. The Red Army, which only had a handful of obsolete tanks left over from the First World War, was desperate to acquire foreign tank technology and willingly cooperated with the Reichswehr. During the four years that the Kazan school was operational, the Germans tested two different tank prototypes there and determined the necessity of mounting radios in every tank in order to exercise effective command and control over an armoured unit (the importance of this was further reinforced when German observers noted the successful use of radios in British pre-war tank exercises). German officers such as Erich von Manstein, Walter Model and Walter Nehring spent time in the Soviet Union and observed Soviet tank exercises, although this apparently did little to enhance their regard for the professionalism of Soviet tankers. As part of the deal for hosting the Kazan school, the Red Army acquired several 3.7cm Pak guns and the design for a 7.5cm anti-aircraft gun from the German firm Rheinmetall, which were used to bolster Soviet research on tank armament. The Soviets also acquired fuel-injection technology from Germany, which was used to enhance Konstantin F. Chelpan's development of an experimental diesel tank engine at the Kharkov Locomotive Works. However, the Soviet leadership believed that the Germans were not sharing their best technology and finally closed the school in September 1933.

Soviet military theorists such as Mikhail Tukhachevsky, Vladimir K. Triand-afillov and Georgy Isserson had been assiduously working on a new military doctrine since the late 1920s.[7,8] This doctrine, known as Deep Battle (*glubokiy boy*), was partly inspired by J.F.C. Fuller's Plan 1919 and mixed it with Marxist-Leninist thinking about protracted warfare. Early on, the Red Army leadership recognized the imperative need to develop a tank force, but was reluctant to choose between the infantry support and cavalry schools. Instead, the Red Army codified its basic tank doctrine in Field Regulations PU-29, issued in October 1929. These regulations specified that PP tanks would provide infantry support, while DD tanks would push deeper into enemy rear areas to destroy their artillery.[9] The Red Army cavalry lobby, in the form of Marshall Semyon Budyonny, also managed to retain enough influence that PU-29 was written to include joint tank-cavalry Deep Operations (*glubokaya operatsiya*). At the same time, the Red Army established the Office of Mechanization and Motorization (UMM) to develop the tanks necessary to fulfill the doctrine spelled out in PU-29, as well as train and organize all mechanized forces. The first head of the UMM, Innocent A. Khalepsky, decided that the Red Army also needed a heavy breakthrough tank to penetrate fortified areas, so he recommended a 60-ton tank with two 76.2mm howitzers and a 37mm cannon. From this point on, Red Army doctrine pushed Soviet industry to concurrently develop light, medium and heavy tanks.

At the start of the First Five Year Plan (1928–32), Soviet industry was unable to build indigenously-designed tank engines or tank guns and barely able to con-struct a few dozen light tankettes per year. Since Stalin and the Politburo were more concerned about falling behind Western tank developments than domestic economic consequences, they arbitrarily doubled the number of tanks required by the Red Army and rushed technical development in order to field the largest number of tanks possible. Three tank design bureaux were established under the plan: OKMO and SKB-2 in Leningrad and KhPZ at Kharkov. An artillery design bureau in Gorky was also tasked with developing new tank armament. At Stalin's behest, the UMM authorized numerous tank projects, many of which proved failures, but this also jump-started the Soviet tank industry. Between the pressure of fulfilling quotas established by the Five Year Plans and the personal con-sequences of 'obstructionism,' the Soviet tank design bureaux were forced to develop tanks that could be built quickly and in numbers, which would prove to be advantageous in a long war. Through ruthless effort, Stalin's regime was able to build up the Soviet Union's defense industrial base at an astonishing rate and succeeded in producing over 5,000 light tanks under the First Five Year Plan. A generation of young Soviet engineers proved adept at using off-the-shelf components and designs acquired legally and illegally from Britain and the United States, while Soviet engineers took the idea of sloped armour from John Walter Christie's innovative M1931 tank prototype and employed it on the BT-series light tanks. Soviet espionage was also successful in acquiring tank design information in Britain. Despite negligible experience in armoured vehicle design and fabrication, Soviet engineers were able to move from the prototype stage to series production of the T-26 and BT-series light tanks within less than two years. Although Soviet engineers were forced to use foreign-designed engine components and armament in their first generation of indigenous tanks, the design bureaux in Leningrad, Kharkov and Gorky were also given some of the best engineering talent in the Soviet Union, who were tasked with developing indigenous engines and cannon for the next generation of tanks. In particular, the talented Konstantin F. Chelpan made excellent progress – with the backing of Khalepsky, the head of UMM – in developing a practical diesel tank engine, which would have enormous implications for armoured warfare on the Eastern Front in the Second World War.

Due to the success of the First Five Year Plan, the Red Army had sufficient tanks by 1932 that it could afford to create both an independent tank force and separate tank brigades for direct infantry support. Two mechanized corps were formed – three years before the Germans fielded their first panzer divisions. The mechanized corps were intended for independent Deep Operations, up to 250km in three days. While the T-26 was intended to fulfill the NPP role, the BT-series fast tank (*Bystrokhodny* tank) was built for speed and mobility for the DD exploitation role. The Red Army formed separate heavy tank brigades with the new T-35 heavy tank and independent mechanized brigades to support the infantry and cavalry. During 1932–33, the Red Army began testing the Deep Battle concept in field maneuvers with the new tank units. When the Red Army had difficulty in actually conducting field exercises according to Deep Battle doctrine, the innovative Aleksandr I. Sediakin, deputy chief of the general staff, was put in charge of combat training and transforming the new doctrine into a practical reality. By 1934, Sediakin had developed a Deep Battle 'playbook' for Soviet commanders that instructed them how best to employ a combined arms attack using armour, mechanized infantry, artillery and airpower. Sediakin and his staff intensively studied and tested Deep Battle doctrine, using the mechanized corps as test beds, and one of his crucial findings was the logistical difficulties of getting fuel to tank units that achieved a deep penetration. The Military Academy of Mechanization and Motorization (VAMM) in Moscow also worked to train battalion and regimental-level armour leaders in the new doctrine. In 1936, Deep Battle became the official doctrine of the Red Army in Field Regulations PU-36. It is important to note, however, that Sediakin's 'playbook' approach to Deep Battle was in line with the Marxist preference for prescriptive training, which encouraged junior leaders to follow a checklist by rote, rather than employ initiative on the battlefield.

In contrast to the frenetic pace in the Soviet Union, tank development in Germany did not begin in earnest until 1934 due to the restrictions of the Treaty of Versailles. It took considerably longer for the German military leadership to develop a common picture of how best to use tanks, and even though Adolf Hitler became enamored of the potential of tanks, the creation of independent panzer units was initially opposed by a number of senior leaders, including Generaloberst Ludwig Beck, chief of the *Generalstab des Heeres*. Generalleutnant Oswald Lutz (Inspector of Motor Transport Troops) and his outspoken chief of staff, Oberst Heinz Guderian, became the primary advocates of an independent armoured force. Eventually, Lutz and Guderian successfully made their case and when Hitler authorized the re-branding of the Reichswehr as the Wehrmacht and expansion to thirty-six divisions in June 1935, three of the new units were designated as panzer divisions. Guderian, a former signal officer with no real command experience, was selected to command the 2.Panzer-Division. However, Beck and his operations officer, Oberst Erich von Manstein, maneuvered to create an alternative to the independent panzer divisions by recommending the creation of *sturmartillerie* units to provide direct support to the infantry. Manstein proposed providing each infantry division with a battalion of Sturmgeschütz (assault guns), based on a medium tank chassis. Thus, the Third Reich ended with its armoured assets divided between panzer and *sturmartillerie* units, plus the panzerjägers, who also eventually acquired self-propelled tank-destroyers.

Unlike Stalin, Hitler was unwilling to push excessive rearmament measures because he believed that his political legitimacy rested upon ensuring German economic recovery. Hitler wanted rearmament, but he wanted it on the cheap, so as not to place an undue burden on Germany's civilians. Armament factories thus continued to work single shifts and production output remained anemic. Amazingly, Hitler did not prioritize tank production before the invasion of the Soviet Union in June 1941 and allowed the manufacturing base to operate by peacetime standards even in the second year of the war. Consequently, German industry was not pushed and bullied along as Soviet industry was to quickly develop large numbers of new tanks. The cost of new tanks – not an issue in the Soviet Union – was an important one in a Germany that was still recovering from the Depression. Expensive luxuries, like heavy tanks, were deferred. Even developing a reliable medium tank proved to be a much greater challenge for German industry than it was for Soviet industry. While the Wehrmacht leadership wanted tanks that possessed sufficient firepower and mobility to execute the kind of mechanized warfare envisioned by Reichswehr doctrine of the late 1920s, they were initially forced to accept panzer divisions based mostly upon the Pz.I and Pz.II light tanks, and later ex-Czech Pz.35(t) and Pz.38(t) tanks. The Wehrmacht was slow to develop technical requirements for a new medium tank and ending up asking for two tanks: the Pz.III was intended to be the primary tank of the panzer divisions, with its high-velocity 3.7cm gun optimized for the anti-tank role, while the Pz.IV was intended as an infantry support tank, with its

7.5cm low-velocity howitzer. Both these programs proceeded at a snail's pace and whereas the Soviets were already demonstrating the ability to move from prototype to mass production in two years, both the Pz.III and Pz.IV programs required five years before they were ready for series production. Nor were German tank designs made with much regard to suitability for mass production, and fabrication was inefficiently spread across eight different firms. Due to a habit of continually introducing upgraded models, production output remained low. Even at the start of Operation Barbarossa, the production of Pz.III and Pz.IV medium tanks was still insufficient to even properly equip all the existing panzer divisions, never mind replace combat losses. Due to these design and production choices, the Third Reich's panzers were usually outnumbered by their Soviet opponents and their limited ability to replace tank losses shaped how German commanders employed their panzers.

The Pz.III and Pz.IV were both tentative and very conservative designs, and as it turned out, not terribly innovative. The main armament of the Pz.III was based on the existing 3.7cm Pak gun and eventually upgraded to the short-barreled 5cm KwK 38 L/42 in August 1940, which Hitler believed – rightly – was inadequate. He directed that a long-barreled 5cm gun be developed for the Pz.III, but the *Heereswaffenamt* (Army Weapons Department) failed to take any action on this. A tank is essentially based around its engine and both the Pz.III and Pz.IV were limited by their reliance on the 300hp Maybach HL120TR engine. Due to its low power output, German designers were forced to limit their medium tanks to the 19–22-ton range, which reduced the amount of armour and armament that the vehicles could carry. Reliance on a gasoline-powered engine also meant that fuel economy would be unsatisfactory, which would continue to haunt panzer leaders throughout the Second World War. Hitler expressed interest in developing a diesel tank engine – which he recognized offered savings in fuel and improved range – but German engineers fobbed off such ideas as 'too difficult and too time consuming,' so it was allowed to slide. If any word describes the state of German tank design at the start of Barbarossa, it is mediocrity. Furthermore, German tanks became less mobile after 1941, not more mobile, as weight was increased due to additional armour and heavier weapons. Indeed, during the entire period of the Third Reich, German industry never designed a tank specifically for long-distance mobile operations.

Most German officers believed that destroying enemy tanks was incidental to the primary missions of tanks and their preferred doctrinal and technical solution was to use small, easily-concealed anti-tank guns to ambush enemy tanks. High-velocity anti-tank guns such as the German 3.7cm Pak could penetrate 30–40mm of armour at ranges up to 500 meters, which was considered adequate to defeat most medium tanks. Given their small size, anti-tank guns were very likely to get the first shots off in an engagement, which suggested that they could achieve a very favorable kill-loss ratio on the battlefield. Even if enemy tanks won, it was easier to replace an anti-tank gun than an expensive tank. Yet mounting high-velocity guns on tanks such as the Pz.III detracted from their primary mission, since armour-piercing shells were not very useful in a breakthrough battle and were poorly suited to engaging the main threat – enemy anti-tank guns. Furthermore, tank versus tank combat was generally avoided throughout the early years of the Second World War, since it risked heavy losses even for the victor. At the Battle of Hannut in Belgium on 12–14 May 1940, the 3. and 4.Panzer-Divisionen tanks suffered 25 per cent losses in three days of combat with French tanks. Given the limited capacity of German industry to replace tank losses in 1940–41, the Germans had little enthusiasm for attrition-style tank combat. Consequently, the Germans assigned the primary anti-tank mission to their panzerjäger troops in order for the panzers to specialize in the breakthrough and exploitation missions. The development of German kampfgruppen tactics was based on this idea of combat specialization, with tanks forming only part of a combined arms team that also included motorized infantry, engineers, self-propelled artillery, panzerjägers, light flak and signals troops. German doctrine viewed the tank as a weapon system that acted as a 'combat multiplier' in the combined arms team, but dependent upon other branches for external support – including Luftwaffe close air support – to offset its limitations.

Unlike German tankers, Soviet tankers believed from their combat experience in Spain that tank versus tank combat was increasingly likely and they wanted tanks that could prevail in these conditions. General Dmitri Pavlov, who commanded a tank brigade during the Spanish Civil War in 1936–7, used his combat experience to shape Soviet tank doctrine as well as tank development in his next assignment as head of the ABTU.[10] Pavlov knew that in order to prevail in tank versus tank combat, Soviet tanks needed better firepower and better armoured protection. Soviet intelligence learned that the Germans were developing a 5cm anti-tank gun and fully expected them to deploy a high-velocity 7.5cm tank gun in the near future. The obvious solution, which Pavlov recommended, was to develop a new generation of dual-purpose medium-caliber guns that could fire both armour-piercing and high-explosive rounds. With ABTU's support, engineers on the Kirov Plant's SKB-4 team in Leningrad began developing the 76.2mm L-11 tank gun, which began testing in 1938, while Vasily G. Grabin's artillery design bureau in Gorky would be ready to begin testing its own 76.2mm F-32 gun in late 1939. Pavlov wanted whichever of these weapons proved itself superior in testing to be installed on the next generation of Soviet tanks. Pavlov also viewed the German 3.7cm Pak gun as a game-changer, since it made the T-26 and BT-series light tanks obsolete, so he pressed for the development of a 'shell-proof' medium tank that could withstand anti-tank fire from 5cm guns. He also lent his support to the development of Chelpan's 500hp V-2 diesel tank engine, which began testing in April 1938. Pavlov recommended that the new T-34 medium tank and KV-1 heavy tank under development should utilize sloped armour, the brand-new V-2 diesel engine and the L-11 gun in order to gain a significant advantage over Germany's first medium tank, the Pz.III. Although the KV-1 design was too advanced to incorporate sloped armour, the T-34 received the full benefit of the latest advances in Soviet tank technology. Thus, during the winter of 1940–41 the Red Army was receiving tanks that incorporated revolutionary design features and was gearing up for mass production, while the

Wehrmacht was content to rely upon conservatively-designed tanks that were built in totally inadequate quantities.

One of the prime reasons for this casual German attitude to tank development was that the OKH assumed that the Soviets were not capable of producing anything that could match German tanks. German technical exchanges during 1929–33 assessed Soviet tank technology as primitive and failed to detect the implications of the First Five Year Plan for Soviet tank-manufacturing capabilities. The Abwehr, German military intelligence, had very little insight into the Soviet Union and consistently underestimated the quantity and quality of Soviet tanks. Hitler, who was hell-bent on destroying the Soviet Union, accepted the Abwehr's flawed estimates of Soviet combat capabilities, since they were in line with his innate prejudices against Slavic culture and Communist ideology.

Despite a huge Soviet lead in doctrinal and technical developments in armour, Stalin squandered much of this advantage with his officer purges of 1937–41 and the abandonment of Deep Battle doctrine. Egged on by the NKVD, Stalin became convinced that mechanization and the desire for an independent tank force was a conspiracy by Tukhachevsky and his reformers to create a 'state within a state' in order to wrest control of the military from the Communist Party. Although the subsequent Stalinist purges of the Red Army are often cited as weakening the leadership cadre of the armed forces, it is less often noted that the purges specifically targeted the new mechanized units and the tank design bureaux that supported them. Kassian A. Tchaikovsky, commander of the 11th Mechanized Corps, was one of the first arrested and he died in prison. Marshal Tukhachevsky was executed in June 1937, followed by Sedyakin and Khalepsky in July 1938. Gregory Isserson managed to avoid arrest in the first round of the purges, but was arrested in 1941 and spent the entire Second World War in a labor camp. The NKVD then moved on to persecute the engineers building the tanks: Chelpan, developer of the V-2 diesel tank engine, was executed in March 1938, and the heads of the KhPZ and SKB-2 design bureaux were also executed. The purges continued from 1937 and extended for four years and continued even after the onset of Operation Barbarossa, claiming still more victims, including Pavlov. In addition to the elimination of Tukhachevsky and most of the higher-level tank leadership, the PU-36 Field Regulations and its doctrine of Deep Battle were suppressed. Further adding to the self-gutting process, Stalin ordered the disbanding of the mechanized corps in November 1939. This dealt a devastating blow to the Red Army's surviving tank forces, which greatly reduced their combat effectiveness for several years.

However, the Wehrmacht's stunning victory over France in June 1940 caused Stalin to reconsider, and he ordered the re-formation of eight mechanized corps in July 1940. This about-face only provided further organizational and training confusion for Red Army tankers and the new mechanized corps would not be able to participate in large-scale maneuver training until the late summer of 1941. Furthermore, Deep Battle was not reintroduced as official doctrine, so it was unclear how the new mechanized corps would be employed. In contrast, most

German tankers had gained valuable combat experience in the Polish, French and Balkan campaigns, and their maneuver-warfare doctrine had crystallized by June 1941. Whereas the largest German armoured formations in the Polish Campaign had been two corps-size formations with only a single panzer division and two motorized infantry divisions each, in the Western Campaign the Wehrmacht had fielded Panzergruppe Kleist with five panzer and three motorized infantry divisions. By June 1941, it had become standard practice for each German army group to have at least one Panzergruppe to lead its *schwerpunkt* (main effort) and rather than breakthrough attacks, the panzer divisions sought to conduct slashing pincer attacks that resulted in encirclement or *kessel* battles. The only positive Soviet combined arms experience to balance against this German tactical and operational skill was Georgy Zhukov's victory over the Japanese at Nomonhan in August 1939, but only a handful of Soviet tank units had been involved. By June 1941, the Wehrmacht held a clear advantage over the Red Army in terms of practical combined arms experience, which helped to conceal the technical limitations of German tanks.

Tanker Facts of Life

Tanks are complex weapon systems that require a number of sub-systems and the crew to function properly in order to provide the vehicle with its key characteristics: firepower, protection, mobility and communications. Tank crews vary in size, with 4–5 being the norm for a full-strength crew, but combat and non-combat casualties (as well as disease and sickness in winter months) could reduce crews. It is essential that each member of the crew perform his designated task well for the tank to achieve its full capability. A poorly-trained loader might be the lowest man in the tank crew hierarchy, but his inability to reload main gun rounds quickly in combat could easily lead to his tank losing a gunnery duel against a faster opponent. Likewise, the driver's ability to maneuver over rough terrain and use cover and concealed approaches is critical for the crew's survival. In June 1941, most Soviet tank drivers – particularly in battalions equipped with T-34 and KV-1 tanks – had very little practical experience, whereas the majority of German tank drivers had one or more campaigns under their belts. German tank driver training was also very thorough for new recruits, whereas this continued to be a weakness for the Red Army well into 1942.

The foremost fact of life as a tanker is the importance of maintenance and logistics. The track system and roadwheels take a great deal of abuse from large rocks, tree stumps and other assorted battlefield wreckage when the tank moves any significant distance. The track, held together by long pins, wants to fall apart and the crew must constantly monitor it for signs of damage. Most tanks carried a few spare track blocks, but extra track pins to hold them together were often scarce. Good crews check the track and roadwheels at every halt of more than a few minutes and conduct spot-tightening. If they fail to do so, crews can expect to routinely throw track (i.e. the track comes off the roadwheels), which immobilizes the vehicle. In tank platoons and companies, it is imperative that junior leaders force tank crews to conduct routine maintenance – even in extreme cold weather, muddy field conditions and during combat operations. Friction is a tank's worst enemy and river crossings tend to wash grease out of fittings on the running gear, which can cause roadwheel hubs to burn out if not tended to soon after fording. For example, a T-34 required a minimum of 1kg of grease for each 100km the tank moved on dry surface, but this would need to be replaced sooner if water obstacles were crossed. All tank engines and transmissions leak oil to some degree, particularly as filters and gaskets wear out. German tank engines often relied on rubber gaskets, which were prone to brittleness in the frigid Russian winters, leading to massive oil leaks if not promptly replaced. Turret systems including hydraulic reservoirs, optics and radios needed to be checked as well and the main gun needed to be bore-sighted again (usually by using string across the muzzle and a snake board target) after any significant move or firing. If the optical telescope and main gun went out of alignment due to hits on the turret or a very bumpy ride, then the tank's gunner would have a difficult time hitting targets. On a weekly basis, crews needed to check the engine and transmission for wear (often detected by tiny metal shavings in the engine compartment, indicating excessive wear), as well as the batteries, leaf springs or torsion bars and brake systems. Contrary to photos depicting the 'difficulty' of panzer crews in cleaning the gun tube with a cleaning rod (a five–ten-minute job), one of the worst tasks was replacing a snapped torsion bar, which necessitated pulling off multiple road wheels and plenty of sledgehammer work to get the broken pieces out (in typical field conditions, a four–six-hour job). If tanks were driven with one broken torsion bar, the shifting weight would likely break the next torsion bar as well. Both sides often pushed their tanks to operate in 'degraded mode', with broken or worn parts, but tanks in this condition were often little more than placeholders with decreased combat value. The most important vehicles at the tank battalion level are the recovery vehicles and fuel trucks, which are essential to keeping the unit functional.

The man standing in the cupola of the tank turret is usually divided into one of two types: a tank commander or a tank rider. The Wehrmacht was particularly adept in 1941–43 at putting the right officer or NCO in the cupola, a man with the training and proven leadership ability to aggressively lead his tank section, platoon or company into combat. A tank commander is bold and is trained to use the shock effect, firepower and mobility of armour to accomplish his mission. In contrast, the Red Army was very weak in junior officer and NCO training at the start of the war and few tank commanders displayed bold aggressiveness. A tank rider is a passive fellow, a follower, one who obeys orders but shows little initiative. Unfortunately, Stalin's purges had stifled initiative at lower levels and encouraged a great deal of passivity in the ranks, which greatly undermined the combat value of Red Army tank units in the first year of the war. A common mishap – other than sudden death – for tank riders was to allow their tank to ram its gun tube either into the ground, or trees or buildings while moving, damaging the weapon. Eventually, by 1943–44, the Red Army began to gain experienced, aggressive junior leaders who could excel at small unit leadership in combat, while the quality of German junior tank leaders declined steadily after 1942.

In combat, the crew became a closed-off entity, with only fleeting awareness of friendly tanks and infantry around them. German tank commanders were trained to move and fight 'unbuttoned' (i.e. cupola hatch open and head out), which gave them better situational awareness in battle, but exposed them to the risk of injury from artillery, snipers or machine-gun fire.[11] Soviet tank commanders were taught to fight 'buttoned-up' and to rely upon their vision blocks, which proved totally inadequate. For a system that placed so little value on the lives of its soldiers, it is odd that the Red Army enforced 'buttoned-up' tank operations, since this sacrificed situational awareness and often enabled small numbers of German tanks to outfight superior numbers of Soviet tanks. Many of the accounts that extol the lethality of German tank gunnery fail to note the contribution of 'buttoned-up' tactics to these kill tallies; better situational awareness allowed the Germans to shoot first and inflict massive damage before the surviving Soviet tanks could even detect them. Inside the tank turret, experiencing the main gun firing is akin to a small explosion inside a building, and the turret quickly fills with choking ammonia fumes. A good crew turns on the turret blower before firing, which reduces the noxious gases, but it was not unusual for novice Soviet crews to be vomiting inside their turrets after half a dozen rounds were fired. German tanks normally did not fire their main guns while on the move as it was too inaccurate; they preferred to seek out good defilade positions, where terrain obscured the hull but allowed the turret to fire at approaching enemies. In contrast, the Red Army had attempted to develop gun stabilization systems before the war and often encouraged crews to fire on the move. Very little tank fighting occurred at night, since tanks could not effectively engage targets at ranges much beyond 100 meters unless flares were fired, but this tended to aid the defender more than the attacker.

Aside from maintenance and combat, the rest of a tank crew's life was focused on getting adequate food and sleep. Compared to infantrymen, tankers are very comfort-oriented and this often led them to commit tactically imprudent actions. When panzers from Kampfgruppe Eberbach stormed into Orel in October 1941, one platoon from 6./Pz.Regt 35 left their vehicles unguarded so that they could go sleep in nearby buildings – and were then surprised when Soviet tanks counterattacked into the city during the night.[12] Semen L. Aria, a Soviet tanker, recalled that on a freezing night in the winter of 1942–43, his crew decided to sleep in a peasant hut without posting a guard over their T-34. In the morning, the tank had been stolen by another unit; Aria was sent to a penal unit.[13] During a big push, tank crews were usually given several days' rations, but these were soon consumed and it could take days or even weeks for normal supply services to catch up. Both German and Soviet tankers often had to rely upon appropriating food from local civilians during mobile operations. Soviet tankers called this 'Grandmother's rations'. German tankers called it looting. Tanks were often required to move at night to avoid enemy aerial observation and sleep-deprived crews were more prone to road accidents. In moving through wooded areas at night, it was not unusual for tank commanders standing in a cupola to be abruptly woken up by tree branches across the face. Commanders had to constantly talk to their drivers over the intercom during night road marches, lest they nod off.

In combat, only about one-quarter of tanks hit by enemy action actually caught fire and burned out. Both sides tended to claim every enemy tank hit as a 'kill', but a good percentage of hits either bounced off the armour or failed to penetrate. Based upon post-battle analysis of both sides' records, the Germans appear to have often exaggerated their tank 'kills' by up to 200 per cent and the Soviets by 500 per cent. Even those tanks that were considered 'knocked out' could often be repaired, since the damage inflicted by armour-piercing ammunition was usually not catastrophic. Crew casualties were usually limited to 0–2 fatalities per tank knocked out, with the rest of the crew wounded, so it was not unusual for a given crew to have been knocked out several times during the course of the war. In the early years of the war, Soviet tankers often abandoned their tanks if hit, and simply walked back to their own lines. The Red Army eventually issued a directive that tank crews that returned to their lines without their tanks would be sent to penal units, which forced Soviet tankers to stick with their damaged vehicles.

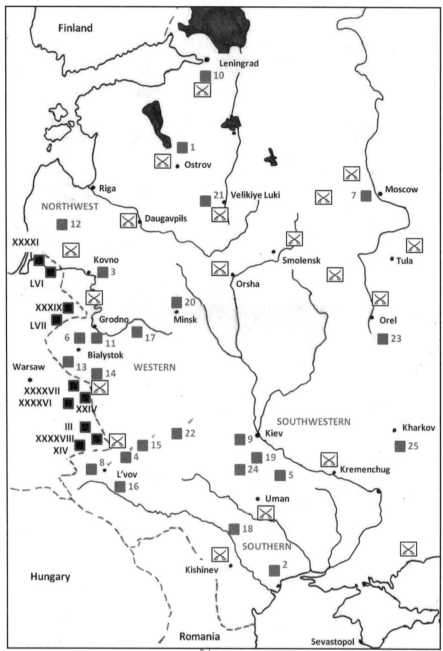

Overview – disposition of major German and Soviet armoured units at start of Barbarossa, 22 June 1941 and major battle sites, limit of German advance.

Chapter 1

The Opposing Armoured Forces in 1941

The German Panzerwaffe

The Wehrmacht initially deployed seventeen panzer divisions against the Soviet Union, organized into four Panzergruppen.[1] Nine of the panzer divisions were less than a year old, having been formed from other existing infantry units between August and November 1940, when Hitler decided to double the number of panzer divisions. In practical terms, this meant that nearly half the panzer divisions involved in Barbarossa had no previous campaign experience in their current role. Nor was the internal structure of the panzer divisions uniform: eight were organized with two panzer battalions and nine divisions had three panzer battalions. The Panzergruppen were further divided into ten Armeekorps (mot.), later redesignated in early 1942 as Panzerkorps, with each controlling up to two panzer divisions and up to two motorized infantry units. The Panzergruppe (or Panzerarmee after October 1941) would be the primary German operational-level armoured formation of 1941–42, while the Panzerkorps would be the primary tactical-level formation.[2] Previous campaigns had taught the Wehrmacht the value of concentrating armour, so it was rare for individual panzer divisions, brigades or regiments to operate independently in the first year of the war in the East.

The bulk of the Panzerwaffe was massed with Heeresgruppe Mitte in the center, with Generaloberst Heinz Guderian's Panzergruppe 2 and Generaloberst Hermann Hoth's Panzergruppe 3. These two Panzergruppen had nine panzer divisions with a total of 1,786 tanks, or 57 per cent of the total available for Barbarossa. Guderian, who had fought so hard to promote the concept of an independent panzer branch before the war, now used the credibility that he gained as a corps commander in Poland and France to ensure that he was given the strongest panzer divisions for Operation Barbarossa. Panzergruppe Guderian would start the campaign with nearly 1,000 tanks in thirteen panzer battalions and all five of his divisions were fully equipped with Pz.III medium tanks. In contrast, Hoth's Panzergruppe 3 had a total of twelve panzer battalions in four panzer divisions, none of which were equipped with Pz.III medium tanks. Instead, Hoth was provided with 507 Czech-made Pz.38(t) light tanks, equipped with the 3.7cm Skoda A7 cannon. The Pz.38(t) tanks were still in production by BMM in Prague and had better mobility than the Pz.III Aus F/G models, but significantly less armour and firepower. Indeed, Hoth's Panzergruppe was primarily configured as a pursuit force and had negligible anti-armour capability.

Generaloberst Guderian's Panzergruppe 2 (Heeresgruppe Mitte)

Formation	Pz.II	Pz.III	Pz.IV	Pz.Bef	Total
3.Panzer-Division	58	110	32	15	215
4.Panzer-Division	44	105	20	8	177
10.Panzer-Division	45	105	20	12	182
17.Panzer-Division	44	106	30	10	190
18.Panzer-Division	50	115	36	12	213
Total	241	541	138	57	977

Generaloberst Hoth's Panzergruppe 3 (Heeresgruppe Mitte)

Formation	Pz.II	Pz.IV	Pz.38(t)	Pz.Bef	Total
7.Panzer-Division	53	30	167	8	258
12.Panzer-Division	33	30	109	8	180
19.Panzer-Division	35	30	110	11	186
20.Panzer-Division	31	31	121	2	185
Total	152	121	507	29	809

Generaloberst Höpner's Panzergruppe 4, which was tasked to support Heeresgruppe Nord's advance toward Leningrad, was the smallest German armoured formation given an independent mission in Barbarossa. Höpner had three panzer divisions, comprising eight panzer battalions with 590 tanks. His panzer units were all veteran outfits, but equipped with a motley collection of German and Czech-made tanks. In particular, the 6.Panzer-Division was primarily equipped with obsolescent Czech Pz.35(t) light tanks, which had no spare parts available even at the start of the campaign. The Czech Pz.35(t) was not mechanically reliable enough for a protracted campaign and none would remain in front-line combat service after October 1941. The 1.Panzer-Division was particularly fortunate in having two out of its four Schützen Abteilung (rifle battalions) equipped with a total of nearly 200 Sd.Kfz.250 and Sd.Kfz.251 half tracks.

In southern Poland, Generaloberst von Kleist's Panzergruppe 1 was assembled to spearhead Heeresgruppe Süd's advance toward Kiev. Kleist was given the second-best equipped Panzergruppe after Guderian, with ten panzer battalions in five panzer divisions, with a total of 730 tanks. Kleist's command had no Czech-built tanks and a good number of Pz.III medium tanks, but he also had significantly more ground to cover in his objectives than the other Panzergruppen. Abwehr intelligence estimates on Soviet tank strength and dispositions were poor, but sufficient to indicate that Kleist would be up against some of the strongest formations available to the Red Army. Thus, it would come as little

Generaloberst Höpner's Panzergruppe 4 (Heeresgruppe Nord)

Formation	Pz.II	Pz.III	Pz.IV	Pz.35(t)	Pz.38(t)	Pz.Bef	Total
1.Panzer-Division	43	71	20	0	0	11	145
6.Panzer-Division	47	0	30	155	0	8	240
8.Panzer-Division	49	0	30	0	118	8	205
Total	139	71	80	155	118	27	590

Generaloberst von Kleist's Panzergruppe 1 (Heeresgruppe Süd)

Formation	Pz.II	Pz.III	Pz.IV	Pz.Bef	Total
9.Panzer-Division	32	71	20	12	135
11.Panzer-Division	44	71	20	8	143
13.Panzer-Division	45	71	20	13	149
14.Panzer-Division	45	71	20	11	147
16.Panzer-Division	45	71	20	10	146
Total	211	355	100	54	730

surprise that Kleist would need help from at least one other Panzergruppe to complete his mission.

The main combat elements of the 1941 Panzer Division were a panzer regiment (some divisions still had panzer brigade headquarters) with two or three panzer battalions; two *Schützen* (motorized infantry regiments) with a total of four battalions; a *Kradschützen* battalion (motorcycle infantry); an *Aufklärungs Abteilung* (reconnaissance battalion); a motorized artillery regiment with a total of thirty-six towed howitzers; a *Panzerjäger Abteilung* with towed 3.7cm and 5cm Pak guns and a motorized pioneer battalion. Most of the infantry rode in trucks, but panzer divisions were beginning to receive the excellent Sd.Kfz.250 and Sd.Kfz.251 half tracks; about 560 were available at the outset of Barbarossa. Altogether, the panzer division was authorized a total of 5,300 infantry in the five *Schützen* and *Kradschützen* battalions. A 1941 panzer division had a total of about 4,100 vehicles. The organization of a *Panzer Abteilung* (battalion) was far from standardized in June 1941, but its combat elements were authorized two or three light companies (equipped with Pz.III, Pz.35(t) or Pz.38(t)) and one medium company with Pz.IVs. All told, an ideal, full-strength *Panzer Abteilung* would have between sixty-six and eighty-eight tanks (fifteen to twenty Pz.II, thirty-five to fifty-two Pz.III, fourteen Pz.IV, two Pz.Bef) and 625–780 men.[3] Although a number of obsolete Pz.I light tanks were still in the panzer division, they were not in the panzer regiments but in the panzer *pionier-bataillon*, where they served as mine-clearing vehicles.

Major sub-units in the Panzer Division				
Subordinate Unit	*Troop Strength*	*Armored Cars*	*Trucks*	*Half Tracks*
Panzer-Regiment (2/3 Bns)	1,760/2,520	0	174/250	22/28
Kradschützen-Abteilung	1,032	2	74	0
Aufklärungs Abteilung	623	33	53	0
Schützen-Regiment	2,180	6	316	2
Panzer-Pionier Bataillon	852	1	120	10
Artillerie-Regiment	2,146	0	159	67
Panzerjäger-Abteilung	700	2	85	10

The main German battle tank employed in Operation Barbarossa was the Pz.III, with the newer Ausf G and H models representing the best available to the Panzerwaffe at that time. These models, both armed with the 5cm KwK 38 L/42 cannon, were better in terms of firepower and protection than the T-26 or BT-series light tanks which still comprised the bulk of the Red Army's tank forces. The Pz.III was intended to defeat enemy tanks and carried a typical basic load of eighty-five armour-piercing and fifteen high-explosive rounds. The standard 5cm Panzergranate 39 armour-piercing round could penetrate up to 47mm of armour at 500 meters, enabling the Pz.III Ausf G or H to defeat all Soviet light tanks at typical battlefield ranges. The Pz.III would even be able to inflict damage on the Soviet T-34, using Panzergranate 38 with flank or rear shots fired from ranges under 500 meters; difficult, but not impossible. The 5cm Panzergranate 40, which had much better armour-piercing capability due to its tungsten penetrator, entered production just before the start of Barbarossa and was available only in limited numbers; for example, Panzergruppe 4 had enough Panzergranate 40 available to equip each Pz.III with just five rounds.[4] While the Pz.III's anti-armour firepower was modest, its main limitation was its tactical range of barely 100km on a single load of fuel, which was not very impressive. The Pz.IV medium tanks, armed with the 7.5cm KwK 37 L/24 howitzer, were armed with a mix of fifty-two high explosive rounds, twenty-one armour-piercing rounds (k.Gr.rot.Pz. (APC) or Panzergranate) and seven smoke rounds at the start of Barbarossa.[5] While the 7.5cm k.Gr.rot.Pz. round could penetrate up to 39mm of armour at 500 meters, its low velocity made it poorly-suited for anti-tank combat against T-34 or KV tanks. In an effort to improve firepower, the Germans were developing a new type of High Explosive Anti-Tank (HEAT) rounds for the 7.5cm howitzers on Pz.IVs and StuG III assault guns, but they would not be available until the end of 1941. In actuality, both the Pz.IV and StuG III were only suited for the infantry support role in 1941, leaving the Pz.III as the sole effective dual-purpose tank employed by the Panzerwaffe in Barbarossa. In addition to the panzers, the Wehrmacht deployed twelve *Sturmgeschütz-Abteilung* with over 200 StuG III assault guns and five Army-Level *Panzerjäger-Abteilung* equipped with 135 Panzerjäger I tank destroyers. The Panzerjäger I was an improvisation, with the high-velocity Czech-made 4.7cm cannon mounted atop an obsolete Pz.I chassis; the 4.7cm was one of the best anti-tank weapons available to the Wehrmacht at the start of Barbarossa.

Nearly one-quarter of the German battle tanks heading into the Soviet Union were Pz.II light tanks, which were already obsolescent in the previous French campaign. Unlike the Pz.I, the Pz.II still played a major role in German tank platoons and companies. Although often used as a scouting tank, the Pz.II tank had better armoured protection than either the T-26 or BT-series light tanks and its rapid-firing 2cm KwK 30 cannon could penetrate their armour at ranges under 500 meters. The Pz.II would also play a useful role in escorting supply convoys through forested areas infested with Soviet partisans.

Despite much media publicity about Germany's so-called Blitzkrieg doctrine both during and after the war – which was intended to create the impression of short, successful campaigns – the Panzerwaffe had a relatively amorphous doctrine in 1941. One of the key components of this doctrine was a preference for combined-arms tactics in mixed kampfgruppen; tank-pure tactics were rejected as foolhardy and inefficient. As an example, the 4.Panzer-Division's Kampfgruppe Eberbach in early July 1941 was comprised of one *Panzer-Abteilung*, one *Kradschützen Kompanie* (motorcycle infantry), a *Schützen Kompanie* (Mechanized Infantry) in SPW half tracks, an artillery battalion (twelve towed 10.5-cm howitzers), two *Pioneer Kompanie*, part of a *Brückenkolonne*, one heavy flak battery (8.8cm) and one light flak battery (2cm). All told, Kampfgruppe Eberbach started with about 2,300 troops and 750 vehicles. Other variations included *Panzerjäger* and *Aufklärungs* (reconnaissance troops), as well as more infantry. Each panzer division would normally form three kampfgruppen, usually one that was tank-heavy and two that were infantry-heavy.

Another key component of the German doctrine was extensive use of radios in tactical vehicles to ensure effective command and control. German panzer units operated company, battalion, regiment and division-level radio networks, which enabled timely sharing of combat information and provided German commanders with excellent situational awareness. Using the Medium Frequency (MF) Fu-8 or Very High Frequency (VHF) Fu-6 radios mounted on a Panzerbefehls-wagen III (armoured command vehicle) or a Sd.Kfz.250/3 half track, a German panzer kampfgruppe commander could exercise command over a 40km radius while moving and up to 70km while stationary. German panzer platoon and company radio nets relied upon the VHF Fu-2 and Fu-5 radios, with a 2–4km radius of control. The mounting of radios in every panzer allowed the Germans to get the most out of their available armour and mass it where it was needed most. Furthermore, the use of the Enigma encryption device gave the Germans a secure means of communicating orders between divisions, corps and armies. Although German panzer units lacked direct air-ground communications with Luftwaffe units in June 1941, requests for air support could be passed from forward kampfgruppen up through the division radio net in a reasonable period of time.

German operational and tactical-level panzer doctrine incorporated elements of the *Stosstruppen* tactics of 1918, with a preference for infiltration and encircle-ment, rather than costly, frontal attacks. The Germans also learned first-hand in the streets of Warsaw on 8 September 1939 that panzer divisions fared poorly in cities, although this lesson would often be ignored during the Russo-German War. Instead, the panzer divisions were intended to create a breach in the enemy front on favorable terrain – with help from infantry, artillery and the Luftwaffe – and then advance rapidly to encircle the enemy's main body before they could react. The panzers would push boldly ahead of the non-motorized infantry divisions, who would have to rely upon assault-gun batteries for close support in completing the breakthrough battle. German doctrine assumed that once enemy units were encircled in a *kessel*, that they would either quickly surrender or be annihilated with concentric attacks. The doctrinal preference was to use pairs of panzer divisions or corps to encircle an enemy with double envelopments, rather than the riskier single-envelopment approach. Thus, the German doctrinal solu-tion to the Red Army was to conduct successive battles of encirclement until the best Soviet units were demolished. However, the doctrine employed by the German Panzerwaffe had two primary flaws, which had not appeared in previous campaigns. First, the Germans could not logistically sustain a series of panzer encirclements indefinitely; eventually fuel shortages and mechanical defects would bring the advance to a halt and that might give the enemy a chance to recover. Second, the doctrine was developed at a time when anti-tank defenses were relatively weak, which enabled panzer divisions to run roughshod over most infantry divisions caught in open terrain. Yet as Soviet anti-tank defenses steadily improved in 1942–43, German panzer leaders continued to believe that enemy infantry could not stop an envelopment from occurring.

The men leading the panzers into the Soviet Union were a well-trained and professional cadre, but nearly one-third had little or no direct experience with tanks. Indeed, many German senior armour leaders in 1941 were still learning their trade and not completely aware of the capabilities and limitations of tanks. Half of the top thirty-one panzer leaders came from the infantry branch and one-third from the cavalry. At the most senior level, Generaloberst Ewald von Kleist of Panzergruppe 1 had more experience with commanding large panzer forma-tions than any other officer in any army, although he had never actually served in a panzer unit. Generaloberst Heinz Guderian, commander of Panzergruppe 2, had commanded a panzer division and led his motorized corps in Poland and France, but was the only non-combat arms officer in command of panzer units in Operation Barbarossa. As a signal corps officer turned mechanization advocate, Guderian remained something of a dilettante throughout his career and had the impulsive, undisciplined nature of a military maverick – he was not a team player, but an individualist. Six of the ten commanders of motorized corps in June 1941 had previous battle command experience with a corps, but three – including General der Infanterie Erich von Manstein – had no personal experience with panzer units. Only three panzer corps commanders: General der Panzertruppen Georg-Hans Reinhardt, General der Panzertruppen Leo Freiherr Geyr von

Schweppenburg and General der Panzertruppe Rudolf Schmidt had both extensive corps command experience and had previously led a panzer division in battle.
Hitler's creation of ten new panzer divisions in late 1940 diluted the division
leadership pool somewhat and, by the start of Barbarossa, only eight of the seventeen panzer division commanders had previous division command experience and
five of the seventeen were new to the Panzerwaffe. A number of the new panzer
division commanders, such as Generalleutnant Walter Model, had primarily
been staff officers with limited command experience. The German officers
tended to be older than their Soviet counterparts due to Stalin's purge of the
Red Army, with the average age of the top thirty-one panzer commanders being
fifty-three.

At the platoon, company, battalion and regiment level, German tankers were
very well trained in operating their vehicles and there was a high proportion of
combat veterans. All had been trained at either Panzertruppen Schule I in
Munster or Panzertruppen Schule II in Wünsdorf, which helped to standardize
skill levels across the Panzerwaffe. Most panzer divisions passed the winter of
1940–41 in France or Germany, with considerable time spent in gunnery and
maneuver training. Units rotated through training areas such as Grafenwöhr or
Warthe, as well as gunnery training at the Putlos range on the Baltic. The
German tank crews were extremely well-trained in their basic tasks of driving,
loading and gunnery and were cross-trained in order to fill gaps created by
casualties. German tankers were also trained to conduct routine maintenance, but
they were not so handy at mending thrown track, conducting battlefield recovery
or repairing simple defects; they tended to wait for their I-Gruppe (*Instandset-
zungsgrupe*, Repair Group) mechanics to arrive. This type of casual attitude was
not an issue in the French campaign, but in Russia it often led to tanks being
abandoned. At the start of Barbarossa, most panzer commanders were proven
junior officers or NCOs. It is also important to note the role played by other
members of the panzer company and battalion, particularly the *Spieß* who played
the role of company first sergeant. The real strength of the German *Heer* (Army)
lay in its carefully groomed NCO corps, consisting of men who could easily
assume higher positions when necessary to fill gaps created by combat losses.
German training also put great stress on individual initiative and problem-
solving, which produced a very aggressive and dynamic quality in combat;
soldiers were encouraged to act quickly and not wait to be told. At the beginning
of Barbarossa, the German panzer soldiers in general also had very high morale:
they believed that they were on a winning team and that the campaign would be
over quickly, with the survivors being well-rewarded by a grateful Fatherland.
The Fascist philosophy of the Third Reich, replete with parades, medals, hero-
worship and neo-Gothic heraldry, helped to create a generation of over-achievers
who sought to gain recognition through dedicated service and self-sacrificing
behavior. As it turned out, excellent training, an aggressive spirit and high morale
were major factors in explaining the Panzerwaffe's successes in 1941–42, as well
as its subsequent defeats.

The ability of the panzer divisions to achieve decisive operational-level success in the Soviet Union rested squarely on the ability of the corps- and army-level logistical echelons to sustain the panzer spearheads with fuel and ammunition, as well as replacement crews and vehicles. However, the German logistical system was not robust enough to conduct a protracted campaign in the Soviet Union, over vast distances and in all weather conditions. A 1941 panzer division required one V.S. (*Verbrauchssatz*) of fuel, equivalent to 125cbm $(m^3)^6$ or 125,000 liters or 92.3 tons, to move all of its vehicles a distance of 100km on roads. German doctrine specified that each panzer division needed four V.S. of fuel stockpiled in order to begin an offensive, which would give it a theoretical range of 400km, although the poor state of Russian roads meant that one V.S. was often only sufficient to move a division 40–50km. In order to reach distant objectives such as Moscow or the eastern Ukraine, the Germans would require dozens of V.S. for each panzer division. However, the logistical capabilities of the Wehrmacht were grossly insufficient for an operation on this scale. The Third Reich perennially suffered from inadequate fuel production and even a short duration campaign on the scale of Operation Barbarossa would severely diminish the available fuel reserves. The Panzergruppen were allocated sufficient fuel for a two-month operation, with only limited reserves available to sustain any operations beyond the summer months. Even if the fuel was available, sustaining the armoured spearheads into the depths of the Soviet Union was nearly impossible, since the Panzergruppen lacked the organic transportation resources to efficiently move fuel more than 50km beyond a railhead. Each panzer division started with three organic fuel companies with a total of thirty trucks that could carry 75cbm of fuel or 0.6 V.S. Consequently, a panzer division could exhaust its entire fuel stockpile in a two-day advance and then become immobilized until more fuel was brought forward; this happened repeatedly during Operation Barbarossa in 1941 and Operation Blau in 1942. Rapid advances left the nearest railheads far in the rear, which made resupply far more time-consuming than anticipated. Armoured operations by both sides would be constrained by the slow progress of their rail repair units.

German fuel shortages were exacerbated by the general shortage of wheeled vehicles in the Wehrmacht, which was only temporarily made good by the use of thousands of captured British, French and Russian trucks. Unfortunately, these second-hand vehicles broke down at an alarming rate during Barbarossa, due to lack of spare parts and the poor condition of Russian roads. The panzer division's mobility was based just as much on the Opel 36S medium cargo truck as it was on its tanks, but German domestic production of this key vehicle was never enough to satisfy authorized levels, never mind combat and non-combat losses. Further adding to German logistic problems, Hitler was so confident of a Russian collapse that only three weeks after Barbarossa began he ordered German industry to curtail ammunition production for the army by autumn 1941.[7] When the campaign did not end as expected, the German army found itself running dangerously short of artillery and anti-tank ammunition in December 1941. In short,

Germany's panzer forces were powerful and well-led forces, moderately well-equipped, but fragile due to their unpreparedness for a protracted campaign.

The Red Army's Tank Force

In June 1941, the Red Army had the enormous total of 18,700 serviceable tanks available, plus another 4,500 tanks under repair. About 63 per cent of the available armour – over 14,000 tanks – were deployed in the twenty-eight mechanized corps authorized between July 1940 and March 1941. Another 1,700 tanks were included in five separate tank or mechanized divisions deployed in the Far East and Transbaikal and 6,000 were deployed with cavalry units, training schools, repair facilities and storage depots.[8] Soviet armour units were in the early stages of re-equipping with the KV-series heavy tanks and T-34 medium tank, but out of 385 KV-I and 185 KV-II built by mid-June 1941, only 433 had been issued to troop units. Similarly, about 1,000 T-34 tanks were built before the German invasion and 903 had arrived at units.

A total of eighteen of the Red Army's twenty-eight mechanized corps were stationed in the five border districts in the west, with a total of 10,688 tanks, of which roughly 83 per cent were serviceable. Four more mechanized corps were deployed in central Russia, as second echelon forces. None of these formations had existed for even a year and only one had been able to conduct division-level training before Barbarossa began. Consequently, the level of corps and division-level training and experience within these mechanized corps was negligible in June 1941 and severely reduced their combat effectiveness. Unlike the German panzer units, the structure of the Soviet mechanized corps and its component tank and mechanized divisions was fairly uniform in June 1941, even though many units were only partially-equipped skeletons. On paper, the Soviet mechanized corps was a powerful formation that could field two tank divisions, a mechanized division, a motorcycle regiment and a motorized engineer battalion; altogether an impressive total of nine–twelve tank, nine infantry and six artillery battalions, with over 37,000 men and 6,000 vehicles. Compared to the German panzer divisions, the Soviet mechanized corps was tank-heavy, with insufficient infantry and artillery. However, the various deficiencies of the mechanized corps and their constituent divisions rapidly became irrelevant as they were destroyed or disbanded within the first three weeks of the campaign. The Soviet Stavka disbanded all remaining mechanized corps on 15 July 1941 and converted their remnants into tank brigades, which became the de facto primary Soviet armoured formation for the rest of the year. Forced onto the defensive by the violence of the German invasion, the Red Army was forced to disperse its remaining armour and commit it in the infantry support role.

Initially, the Red Army's best armour was concentrated in the south near Kiev because that is where the Soviet general staff expected the Germans to make their main effort, but the remaining armour units were spread thinly in Lithuania and Byelorussia. The Northwestern Front's 8th Army defended a 155km-wide front along the Lithuanian-East Prussian border with five rifle divisions and General-major Nikolai M. Shestopalov's 12th Mechanized Corps, which had a total of

725 tanks and ninety-six armoured cars.[9] Shestopalov's corps had no modern tanks – BT-7s and T-26s – and it was dispersed across a 110km-wide area. Over 30 per cent of his tanks were non-operational.[10] The 12th Mechanized Corps had most of its artillery, but less than half its authorized trucks or radios, which made a war of movement or command and control difficult. On the other hand, the 12th Mechanized Corps had a fairly well-trained cadre, including Colonel Ivan Chernyakhovsky, commander of the 28th Tank Division. The remainder of the Lithuanian border was defended by the 11th Army, which had eight rifle divisions and General-major Aleksei V. Kurkin's 3rd Mechanized Corps. Kurkin's command had 630 tanks, including fifty-one KV heavy tanks and fifty T-34 medium tanks, but its constituent divisions were dispersed across a wide area. Altogether, the Red Army had a total of 1,355 tanks defending the Lithuanian border, although the majority were T-26 and BT-7 light tanks. In addition, the Northern Front had another 1,431 tanks available as reinforcements, with the 1st Mechanized Corps stationed near Pskov and the 10th Mechanized Corps near Leningrad; however, these were second-echelon formations equipped primarily with older light tanks, including BT-2 and BT-5s. The Red Army's armour force in the Baltic Special Military District was inadequate in quality and was poorly deployed from the start, but also enjoyed the advantage of terrain that favored the defender, with its numerous rivers, marshes and forests.

Although the Red Army concentrated six mechanized corps with 2,200 tanks in the Western Front to defend the Bialystok salient, the only formation with any real combat capability was General-major Mikhail G. Khatskilevich's 6th Mechanized Corps. Khatskilevich had nearly half the tanks in the Western Front under his command, including four heavy tank battalions with 114 KV heavy tanks and seven medium battalions with 238 T-34 tanks. In contrast, the 11th, 13th and 14th Mechanized Corps were at half strength or less and equipped primarily with T-26 light tanks. These four first-echelon corps – assigned to support the 3rd, 4th and 10th Armies – were arrayed in an arc from Grodno to Bialystok to Brest, and deployed 30–60km behind the border. Further back, between Baranovichi and Minsk, the Western Front had the 17th and 20th Mechanized Corps in second echelon, but these were both cadre formations with only 129 light tanks

Soviet Armour Forces in the Northwest and Northern Fronts, 22 June 1941						
Front Formation	*KV-I/II*	*T-34*	*T-28*	*T-26*	*BT*	*Total*
Northwestern						
3rd Mechanized Corps	51	50	57	41	431	630
12th Mechanized Corps	0	0	0	483	242	725
Northern						
1st Mechanized Corps	6	8	76	375	522	973
10th Mechanized Corps	0	0	0	177	281	458

Soviet Armour Forces in the Western Front, 22 June 1941					
Formation	*KV-I/II*	*T-34*	*T-26*	*BT-2/5/7*	*Total*
6th Mechanized Corps	92–114	70–238	83	53/67/350 470	1,021
11th Mechanized Corps	0–3	0–28	141–243	0/44/0	237–287
13th Mechanized Corps	0	0	263	15	294
14th Mechanized Corps	0	0	518	6	520
17th Mechanized Corps	0	0	1	24	36
20th Mechanized Corps	0	0	80	13	93

between them. General Dmitri Pavlov, who had been instrumental in guided Soviet tank developments in the late 1930s as head of the ABTU, was now in command of the Western Front and he had the four first echelon mechanized corps positioned to support his twelve front-line rifle divisions. Pavlov essentially committed all his armour to a positional infantry support role, leaving no room for maneuver options.

The Kiev Military District, soon to become the Western Front under General-Polkovnik Mikhail P. Kirponos, had a total of eight mechanized corps with over 4,400 tanks deployed in the region. Kirponos deployed the five strongest of these mechanized corps in his first echelon near the border, between Lvov and Rovno; these corps had between 45 and 90 per cent of their equipment. Among these, General-major Andrey Vlasov's[11] 4th Mechanized Corps was the best-equipped armoured formation in the Red Army of June 1941, with 101 KV heavy tanks and 313 T-34 tanks. On paper, Vlasov's corps was as strong as any German Panzergruppe and, in addition to its new tanks, had a full complement of artillery and over 2,000 trucks. Strikingly, the thirty-nine-year-old Vlasov had no previous experience with tanks, but was a rising star in the post-purge Red Army. Kirponos' second echelon of armour consisted of three cadre mechanized corps deployed west of Kiev; these formations were equipped solely with light tanks and had between 20 and 40 per cent of their equipment. Further south, the Odessa Military District had two partly-equipped mechanized corps defending the Romanian border with 700 light tanks and a single battalion of T-34s. In central Russia, in the Moscow, Orel and Volga military districts, there were four more partly-equipped mechanized corps, with 2,000 light tanks but no KV or T-34 tanks. Another 5,000 Soviet light tanks were beyond the reach of the Wehrmacht, located in the Caucasus, Transbaykal, Central Asian and Far Eastern military districts. Even more important were the 15,000–20,000 tankers in these districts, who would provide the Stavka with a ready reserve of at least partly-trained armour crewmen to form new tank brigades.

After mid-July 1941, the primary Soviet armoured formations were the tank regiment and the tank brigade. At the outset of the war in the East, each Soviet mechanized corps had five tank regiments: two in each of its two constituent

Soviet Armour Forces in the Southwest Front, 22 June 1941							
Formation	*KV-I/II*	*T-34*	*T-26*	*T-28*	*T-35*	*BT-2/5/7*	*Total*
4th Mechanized Corps	101	359	106	68	0	127	761
8th Mechanized Corps	71	100	298	0	48	276	793
9th Mechanized Corps	0	0	144	0	0	134	278
15th Mechanized Corps	64	72	44	51	0	439	670
16th Mechanized Corps	0	0	214	75	0	360	649
19th Mechanized Corps	6	2	291	0	0	0	450
22nd Mechanized Corps	31	0	464	0	0	163	658
24th Mechanized Corps	0	0	100	0	0	100	200

tank divisions and one in the mechanized division. The tank regiments were intended to function as part of a combined-arms structure within a division and were tank-pure formations with no organic infantry or artillery; each tank regiment in the tank divisions was authorized three tank battalions with a total of sixty-two tanks. However, once the mechanized corps began to disintegrate under the hammer blows of the German Panzergruppen, the Stavka opted to rely upon independent tank brigades both for expediency of formation and simplicity of command and control. The tank brigades authorized in late August 1941 were based upon the remnants of the mechanized corps and were supposed to have three tank battalions with a total of ninety-one tanks and a motorized infantry battalion. However, as Soviet losses mounted and industry could not yet replace them, the size of the tank brigade continued to shrink. In September, the tank brigade was reduced to two tank battalions with sixty-seven tanks and in December to only forty-six tanks and the infantry battalion was omitted.

Prior to the war, most Soviet tank battalions were usually comprised of only one tank model, but the number of tanks could vary from thirty to fifty. The new T-34 and KV-1 tanks were being fielded by battalions, so there was little integration with existing models prior to the German invasion. The Soviet tank battalion was much smaller than its German counterpart and grew increasingly leaner throughout 1941. Typically, the Soviet tank battalion had a headquarters, an eighty-man maintenance company, a reconnaissance platoon with three BA-10 or BA-20 armoured cars, a twenty-one-man medical section, some fuel and ammunition elements and three tank companies. The Red Army kept tinkering with the size of tank platoons prior to the war, trying out 3-, 4- and 5-tank platoon configurations. Heavy tanks were normally kept in 5-tank platoons, but the light and medium tanks quickly abandoned the pre-war 4-tank platoon and relied upon a 3-tank platoon structure for most of the war.

Although the new KV-I, KV-II and T-34 tanks attract much attention in estimates of the Red Army's relative combat power in June 1941, these tanks comprised barely 12 per cent of the available Soviet armoured forces at the outset of Barbarossa and were initially rendered nearly combat ineffective by a host of logistical and training defects. Many of these modern tanks had only arrived at their units a few weeks or months prior to Barbarossa and had been stored in warehouses, pending summer training in 1941. Very few crews had trained on either of these new tanks and they were so dissimilar to the earlier light tanks that even experienced tankers needed a transition course before they could effectively use these vehicles in combat. However, far more serious was the shortage of 76.2mm main-gun ammunition for the KV-I and T-34 and the almost complete absence of 152mm ammunition for the KV-II. The more fortunate T-34 tank battalions had a single basic load of ammunition – often with no armour-piercing rounds – while the less fortunate units had only been issued machine-gun ammunition. The fuel shortage was even worse, with most Soviet heavy and medium tanks having no more than one basic load of fuel, enough for a few days operation. Most of the fuel in forward depots was gasoline for the T-26 and BT-series light tanks, but diesel fuel for T-34s and KVs was still in short supply. Spare parts for the new tanks were virtually non-existent. Consequently, the only real advantage enjoyed by the T-34 and KV tanks at the outset of Barbarossa was the enormous effort required by the Germans to destroy them, but otherwise their innate firepower and mobility advantages were squandered by inadequate logistic readiness.

The main Soviet battle tanks employed in 1941 were the T-26 and the BT-7 light tanks, which comprised nearly 80 per cent of the available armour. The T-26 had been designed as an infantry support tank and reflected early-1930s thinking on tank design. About one-third of the operational T-26s in June 1941 were improved models built in 1939–40, but the rest were older models with negligible combat capability. Compared to the German Pz.III Ausf. G or H models, even the newer models of the T-26 were clearly inferior in mobility and protection. The T-26's greatest weakness was its powerplant, derived from a GAZ truck engine and lacking in mechanical reliability. Between 30 and 40 per cent of the available T-26 light tanks were inoperative at the start of the campaign and most of the remainder suffered mechanical breakdowns after a few weeks of operations. The BT-series light tanks were more capable opponents, particularly the upgraded BT-7M model which first appeared in 1939. The BT-7M employed the same V-2 diesel tank engine as the T-34, giving it greatly superior mobility and reliability over the Pz.III. Unlike the T-26, the BT-7M had thicker, sloped armour, making it closer in protection to the Pz.III. Unfortunately, the KhPZ had ceased manufacturing the BT-7M just before Barbarossa began, in order to concentrate on T-34 production. Both the T-26 and BT-7 mounted the 45mm 20K cannon which – at least on paper – was comparable to the 5cm KwK 38 L/42 on the Pz.III. Unfortunately, the 45mm gun was undermined by poor quality control in the manufacture of its BR-240 APBC rounds, with steel penetrators that shattered on impact and had difficulty penetrating the armour on the Pz.III and Pz.IV at ranges beyond a few hundred meters. The remaining Soviet armour, including the T-35 heavy tank, the T-28 medium tank, the older BT-2/5 series and the T-37/38/40 light tanks were too obsolescent and too few in number to matter much in the tank battles of 1941–42.

Doctrinally, the Soviet preference for armoured units throughout the war was to maintain three types of units: large formations for independent mobile operations, separate battalion, regiment or brigade-size formations for infantry support and separate RVGK (Reserve of Supreme High Command) units under direct Stavka control. After the dissolution of the mechanized corps in July 1941, the Red Army was left with only infantry support units until spring 1942. While the materiel-poor Red Army of late 1941 could not afford to set aside units for the RVGK until it was clear that Moscow would not fall, this became a priority in 1942 and would eventually provide the Stavka with an advantage that the OKH rarely enjoyed on the Eastern Front – an appreciable reserve of armour that could be shifted to critical fronts.

Soviet armoured tactics at the start of the war were very basic because the level of training was so low in most units. Tank platoons and companies were primarily taught to attack on line to simplify command and control, although wedge formations were also possible. Soviet tank platoons attacked in very dense formations, often with only five meters between vehicles. Soviet tank commanders usually lacked binoculars and were taught to operate 'buttoned-up' in combat – which drastically reduced their situational awareness versus German tankers. Since the Soviet Union had not developed an armoured personnel carrier analogous to the German Sd.Kfz.251 – a serious deficiency – Soviet tanks did not operate as closely with their attached motorized infantry as German panzer kampfgruppen did. Taken together, these bunched-up and nearly-blind Soviet tank-pure formations proved easy pickings for German panzer and panzerjäger units. Another tactical consideration was the tendency of the Red Army to substitute 'scripted' by-the-book methods for common sense; Soviet armoured tactics in 1941–42 were entirely proscriptive in nature. Indeed, the influence of Marxist dialectical materialism on Soviet military theory led to a slavish devotion to 'scientific approaches' to military problems. If an attack failed with heavy losses, Soviet political commissars blamed commanders for not following 'the playbook,' while refusing to admit that school-taught tactics needed to be modified to suit battlefield realities.

None of the officers who commanded the Red Army's mechanized corps in June 1941 had been in their position for more than a year when the German invasion began, and most only for a few months. Soviet mechanized corps commanders were considerably younger than their German counterparts – an average age of forty-four versus an average of fifty-three for the Germans – and less experienced. Some 58 per cent of the mechanized corps commanders had no prior experience with tank or mechanized units and 16 per cent had no prior experience with commanding large formations. After the purges gutted much of the original cadre of experienced Soviet tank officers and the original mechanized corps disbanded in 1939, the new mechanized corps recreated in 1940–41 were heavily staffed with cavalry officers; by June 1941, half the mechanized corps were commanded by cavalrymen. However, it would be a mistake to generalize all the Soviet tank commanders of 1941 as incapable. In particular, General-major Semen M. Krivoshein, commander of the 25th Mechanized Corps in the

Volga Military District (MD), was one of the most experienced tankers in the Red Army; he had successfully commanded tank units in Spain, the Far East, Finland and Poland. Indeed, Krivoshein was easily as experienced and capable as most of the German panzer division or corps commanders of 1941. Although only thirty-nine years old in 1941, General-major General Dmitri D. Lelyushenko, commander of the 21st Mechanized Corps, was another experienced and capable Soviet tanker. Most of the Soviet tank officers were graduates of the Frunze Military Academy or VAMM, but some, such as General-major Mikhail P. Petrov, had negligible civilian or military education (in his case, limited to a fourth-grade education), which put them at a huge disadvantage when matched against the Wehrmacht's Generalstab-trained panzer generals. Among the commanders with no tank experience was General-major Konstantin K. Rokossovsky, a cavalry officer who would quickly demonstrate an aptitude for combined-arms warfare. Overall, the Red Army's tank leadership in June 1941 was a mixed bag, with a few exceptional officers, a large batch of moderately-capable but inexperienced officers, and a healthy number of chair-warmers.

At the division, brigade, regiment and battalion levels, the situation was about the same, although there were far more unfilled vacancies, with many units still awaiting 25 to 50 per cent of their junior officers from training units. Pre-war officer training required between one and two years and the rapid formation of so many mechanized units temporarily overwhelmed the tank training schools administered by the GABTU. For example, the premier Orel Tank Training School (BTU) had begun training 800 junior officers in September 1940 to operate as T-34 platoon leaders, and the first would be available in the late summer of 1941. In the interim, the Red Army did have a number of outstanding mid-level tank officers, such as Polkovnik Pavel Rotmistrov and Polkovnik Mikhail E. Katukov, who were quite capable of handling a tank brigade or division-size force in combat, if given the opportunity. At the company and platoon level, most extant junior officers were the products of hasty training and few could read a map or direct more than their own tank in battle. Although the enlisted ranks had not been damaged by Stalin's purges, the rapid expansion of 1940–41 created a great shortage of trained drivers and gunners that had not yet been made good by June 1941. Thousands of conscripts had been sent to six-month tank training schools at Orel and Leningrad, but were still in the pipeline when the invasion began. Lacking a solid NCO corps like the Wehrmacht, the Red Army had few unit-level trainers and had to rely upon centralized training facilities, and there was no one in most tank units to enforce training standards. Few crewmen were cross-trained on other crew functions, which meant that it was difficult to replace casualties. Soviet driver training was particularly inadequate; before the invasion, the Soviet general staff training directorate had issued a directive that the obsolete T-27 tankette would be the primary vehicle used for training in order to save wear and tear on the Red Army's main battle tanks. Unfortunately, the handling characteristics of the 2.7-ton T-27 were so dissimilar that operating it in no way prepared novice drivers to operate the 32-ton T-34 or 45-ton KV-1. The number of hours allocated to driver training during the hectic re-formation of the mechanized corps was minimal, particularly for the newer tanks. Consequently, Soviet tank crews had numerous accidents during road movements in 1941, often resulting in the loss of tanks.

On the whole, Soviet tank training was overly mechanical in nature, geared to produce soldiers who performed tasks by rote, not by personal initiative. Gunnery training was also inadequate, with sub-caliber firing often substituted for actual main gun firing. In 1945, when the Red Army overran German gunnery ranges in East Prussia and Silesia, Soviet tankers were amazed to find tank gunnery ranges with pop-up targets and moving targets mounted on sleds – none of which existed in the Soviet Union even at the end of the war. Instead, most Soviet crews were fortunate if they had fired four shells at a stationary plywood target before heading off to their unit. In combat, Soviet tankers often fired off all their ammunition as fast as possible, since they had not been taught about the need to conserve rounds.[12] Stalinist-era paranoia also had a negative influence on maintenance training in Soviet tank units. During the purges, the NKVD had created the threat of internal 'wreckers', or counter-revolutionary saboteurs, so the RKKA general staff – not wanting to appear in collusion with anti-regime forces – issued a directive that forbade tank crews from conducting routine maintenance without proper (i.e. political officer) supervision. Concerned that soldiers might willfully contaminate the oil or fuel in their tank engines, political officers simply forbade most routine maintenance at unit level and directed that any work be conducted by supervised technicians at army-level depots.

Soviet armoured operations at the outset of the war were severely hampered by inadequate logistic preparations. Logistics was never a strong suit of the Red Army and operational planning was still tied to a reliance on railroads and fixed supply bases, which proved very vulnerable to the German style of Blitzkrieg. Tank ammunition, particularly 76.2mm armour-piercing rounds, was in short supply and few KV or T-34 tanks had more than one basic load in June 1941. About one-quarter of the available ammunition was stored in supply dumps near the western border, which were quickly overrun in the first weeks of Barbarossa. Even worse, most of the Red Army's fuel reserves were held back in depots around Moscow, Orel and Kharkov, leaving the forward units with only enough fuel for 1–2 weeks of operations.[13] Simply put, the superficial appearance of combat-readiness among even the best-equipped mechanized corps was quickly exposed as false when tank units were found to have only enough fuel and ammunition for brief combat operations. A Soviet 1941 tank division required one-third less fuel than a German panzer division, about 60–70 tons, but too few GAZ and ZIS-5 fuel tankers were available to move it with the tanks. The logistical infrastructure to enable true mechanized maneuver operations – which had often been identified as a key weakness in pre-war maneuvers – simply did not exist in June 1941.

Among the many deficiencies of the Red Army's mechanized forces in June 1941, the aspect that sealed the fate of the pre-war mechanized corps was the lack of effective radios. Most of the mechanized corps only had about half of their authorized radios and most of those available dated back to 1933–34. While

Soviet industry had pulled ahead of the Germans in terms of tank development, it had fallen behind in terms of communications technology.[14] Unlike the Germans, only tanks operated by company or battalion commanders were equipped with radios, although some platoon leaders were just getting them in June 1941. Soviet command tanks, usually a BT-5, BT-7 or T-34, mounted a HF 71-TK-3 Model 1939 radio set. The 3-watt output of the 71-TK-3 transmitter was weak compared to the 20 or 30-watt transmitters on German command tanks, and this Soviet radio had an effective range of only about 6km. Of course, radius becomes a moot point when only one tank in ten even carried a radio. Even the most modern Soviet tanks, such as the KV and the T-34, were saddled with these underpowered and obsolescent radios, with which only one or two tanks in a company were equipped. The failure of the Red Army leadership to insist on equipping all tanks with modern radios – as Guderian had done for the Panzerwaffe – rendered effective command and control over large Soviet armoured formations virtually impossible at the outset of the war. Lacking effective communications, Soviet armoured units were forced to rely upon flags, messengers and dangerous follow-the-leader formations.

Chapter 2

The Dynamic of Armoured Operations in 1941

'Surprise and then forward, forward, forward.'

6.Panzer-Division, Order of the Day, 22 June 1941[1]

Panzergruppe 4 versus the Northwest Front, 22-30 June

Nervous about the obvious German military build-up along the Lithuanian border, General-polkovnik Fyodor I. Kuznetsov, commander of the Baltic Military District (soon to be redesignated the Northwest Front) attempted to improve the readiness of his command, even without specific guidance from Moscow. Under the guise of an exercise, Kuznetsov decided to move General-major Nikolai M. Shestopalov's 12th Mechanized Corps forward from Riga and Liepaja and concentrate it around Siauliai on 19–20 June 1941. Kuznetsov wanted Shestopalov's armour within 60km of the border to support the three rifle divisions the 8th Army had deployed along the border. These three rifle divisions were required to screen a 155km-wide front along the border with units at only 60 per cent strength, which meant they were little more than a tripwire.[2] While Shestopalov's corps was in a better position at Siauliai to respond to a border incident, the hastily-conducted move consumed most of the unit's on-hand fuel and left the corps fuel depot in Riga 190km in the rear. Since the 12th Mechanized Corps had less than half its authorized number of fuel trucks, it would take multiple convoys back to Riga to refuel the tanks at Siauliai. Furthermore, a large number of tanks and other vehicles fell out on the march due to technical defects, so it would take a few days to bring the 12th Mechanized Corps up to readiness. Once the 12th Mechanized Corps was en route to Siauliai, Kuznetsov issued other orders to the 8th Army to begin laying minefields on the border and prepare bridges for demolition. When General Georgy Zhukov, chief of the Soviet general staff in Moscow, heard about Kuznetsov's unauthorized movements of armour and defense preparations he exploded with anger and ordered him to repeal the orders. Zhukov even stooped to calling Kuznetsov's efforts to evacuate family members 'an act of cowardice' and accused him of trying to 'spread panic among the people'. With no small amount of courage – and personal risk – Kuznetsov ignored Zhukov and established a tactical command post in the woods south of Dvinsk (Daugavpils).

At X-zeit (X-hour), 0400 hours (local time) on 22 June, Heeresgruppe Nord began crossing the Lithuanian border, with Generaloberst Höpner's Panzergruppe 4 and ten infantry divisions from 18.Armee. General der Panzertruppen

Georg-Hans Reinhardt's XXXXI Armeekorps (mot.) crossed the border just south of Taurogen with the 1.Panzer-Division on the left and the 6.Panzer-Division on the right, with the 36.Infanterie-Division (mot.) trailing. The 1.Panzer-Division attacked directly into the town of Taurogen with Kampfgruppe Westhoven, while Kampfgruppe Kruger enveloped the town and crossed the Jura River at an unguarded ford. Thanks to Kuznetsov's last-minute alerts, the 125th Rifle Division put up a tough fight for Taurogen and the panzers were slowed by mines and anti-tank fire; Taurogen was not secured until 2000 hours. In clearing the city, 1.Panzer-Division expended a great deal of ammunition and lost the better part of a day, while much of the 125th Rifle Division actually succeeded in escaping to the northeast. While the 1.Panzer-Division was clearing Taurogen, Generalmajor Franz Landgraf's 6.Panzer-Division moved past some anti-tank ditches on the east side of the town with Kampfgruppe Raus and Kampfgruppe Seckendorff and advanced northeast, directly toward Siauliai, although they had no knowledge of Soviet armour being there. The 48th Rifle Division, armed only with training ammunition as part of Kuznetsov's impromptu mobilization exercise, was easily brushed aside. Overall, Höpner's plan to use a panzer division to seize the border city of Taurogen was ill-conceived and ultimately limited the XXXXI Armeekorps (mot.) to a 30km penetration on the first day of Barbarossa, which merely pushed the enemy back rather than encircling them.

In contrast to Reinhardt's methodical attack through the Soviet border defenses, General der Infanterie Erich von Manstein's LVI Armeekorps (mot.) avoided Soviet resistance centers by advancing cross-country, almost due east, toward Kedainiai, with 8.Panzer-Division's Kampfgruppe Crissoli way out in front, followed at some distance by 3.Infanterie-Division (mot.) and 290.Infanterie-Division.[3] Manstein was focused on his objective – the bridges over the Dvina River 300km away – and essentially ignored Soviet forces that did not directly block his path. Consequently, Manstein's lead division advanced 70km through heavily wooded terrain on the first day and had no significant contact with Soviet forces.

The Soviet response to the invasion was sluggish and confused. Once Kuznetsov was sure that the Germans were across the border in force, around 0930 hours, he decided to commit his armour to counterattack. However, Luftwaffe air attacks seriously disrupted Soviet high-level communications and 8th Army did not issue its own counterattack order until 1400 hours.[4] Due to these communications problems, Kuznetsov's orders did not reach the 12th Mechanized Corps until 2340 hours. The orders directed Shestopalov to advance southward 70km and strike the left flank of the German invasion group. However, the 8th Army order temporarily diverted the 23rd Tank Division to assist the 10th Rifle Corps in restoring the border near Memel, which dispersed the counterstroke by the 12th Mechanized Corps; this indicated the divide within the Red Army between those who viewed mechanized forces as best used en masse as a shock force and those who wanted it dispersed for infantry support. Kuznetsov had also sent orders to General-major Aleksei V. Kurkin's

3rd Mechanized Corps, assembling west of Vilnius behind the 11th Army, instructing him to detach his 2nd Tank Division to attack the German right flank somewhere near Raseinai. In order to coordinate the attack, Kuznetsov sent Polkovnik Pavel P. Poluboiarov, the Northwest Front commander of tank and mechanized forces. Kuznetsov's concept of an armoured double pincer attack was not a bad plan, just not feasible under current conditions.

Shestopalov's corps began moving forward during the night of 22–23 June, but lacked the fuel to move all his tanks at once. Efforts to send supply convoys back to Riga for more fuel were frustrated by confusion and jammed roads. Kuznetsov wanted the armoured counterattack begun at dawn, but Poluboiarov was able to convince him to delay the operation until the bulk of the 3rd Mechanized Corps was ready. Polkovnik Ivan Chernyakhovsky, commander of the 28th Tank Division, made a forced march of 60km to reach the front, but at dawn the Luftwaffe detected the Soviet armoured columns and attacked, knocking out forty-four tanks and a large number of wheeled transport. Despite this, Chernyakhovsky's advance guard finally reached their assembly areas in the late afternoon of 23 June. Chernyakhovsky was supposed to wait for the rest of the corps, but instead decided to conduct a hasty attack with forty T-26 and BT-7 light tanks from Major Sergei F. Onischuk's 55th Tank Regiment. Moving forward to contact without infantry or artillery support, Onischuk ran straight into the German 21.Infanterie-Division around 2100 hours and lost two BT-7 and three T-26 tanks to German anti-tank guns. Chernyakhovsky followed Onischuk's mixed battalion in his own command BT-7TU and, according to Soviet accounts, personally engaged a German Pz.IV medium tank (possibly from the 1.Panzer-Division) at a range of 800 meters. When his 45mm AP rounds failed to penetrate at this range, Chernyakhovsky maneuvered his BT-7 closer and knocked out the Pz.IV with a flank shot from 400–500 meters.

Onischuk sent his deputy, Major Boris P. Popov, on a flanking maneuver through the woods with seventeen BT-7 light tanks and Popov succeeded in overrunning some German infantry and a couple of 3.7cm Pak guns. Popov, coming from a peasant background and with only a secondary education, lacked the training of his German panzer counterparts but was recklessly brave and steadfast. He pressed the attack even as the Germans began to rally and his BT-7 was struck repeatedly and set afire. When Popov attempted to exit his burning tank, he was shot and killed by German infantry; he would soon be posthumously decorated as a Hero of the Soviet Union (HSU). Although Chernyakhovsky's hasty attack inflicted some damage, three hours of fighting cost him seventeen of forty tanks engaged and he ordered Onischuk to disengage. Realizing that the Germans were too strong, Chernyakhovsky decided to regroup and wait for reinforcements.

While Shestopalov's corps was beginning a piecemeal attack on the supposed flank of Panzergruppe 4, there was considerable armoured activity occurring to the east around Raseiniai and Kedainiai. After easily overrunning the 48th Rifle Division northeast of Taroggen, the 6.Panzer-Division advanced 55km and occupied Raseiniai by the afternoon of 23 June. Generalmajor Landgraf's two panzer kampfgruppen secured separate bridgeheads over the Dubysa River and he paused the division in Raseiniai to refuel and re-arm. Meanwhile, General-major Egor N. Solyankin's 2nd Tank Division force-marched 100km from Kedainiai in order to retake Raseiniai. Solyankin's division included six different tank types, including thirty-two KV-I, nineteen KV-II and fifty T-34, further complicating combat logistics. The KV heavy tanks fared particularly poorly on the long road march due to clogged air filters and transmission malfunctions; nearly half broke down en route to the battlefield. However, Solyankin managed to get a good portion of his force near Raseiniai late on 23 June and he planned to attack at dawn the next morning.

Oddly, the 6.Panzer-Division was not expecting a major Soviet armoured counterattack, even though reconnaissance aircraft from Panzergruppe 4 had spotted tanks approaching from Kedainiai. Thus the Germans were doubly shocked on the morning of 24 June, when not only were they attacked by a large Soviet armoured group, but also by three different types of tanks that they did not even know existed. Solyankin directed his main effort – two tank regiments and part of a motor rifle regiment – against Kampfgruppe Seckendorff. The Soviet tanks attacked in waves, with the light BT and T-26 types out front, followed by T-34s and then the KV heavy tanks. Although shocked by the appearance of T-34, KV-I and KV-II tanks, the German panzerjäger followed doctrine and did not engage with their 3.7cm and 5cm Pak until the Soviet tanks were within 200 meters. The German AP rounds simply bounced off and then the Soviet heavy tanks overran the panzerjägers and part of Kradschützen-Abteilung 6. No German infantry had yet been overrun by enemy tanks in the Second World War and this was terrifying. After bashing their way through Kampfgruppe Seckendorff, three KV heavy tanks led by Major Dmitry I. Osadchy forded the Dubysa River and attacked part of Schützen-Regiment 114. The KV tanks managed to overrun part of a German artillery battery before being engaged by direct fire from 15cm howitzers. Although the howitzers could not penetrate the KV's thick armour, they managed to blow off the tracks, immobilizing them.

The 6.Panzer-Division was shocked by the violence of this attack. Most histories of the Battle of Raseiniai depend upon Erhard Raus' account, even though he was only lightly engaged in this action.[5] Raus' account focuses on his efforts to destroy a single KV-2 that managed to get behind his kampfgruppen and sever his supply line, but says little about the decimation of Kampfgruppe Seckendorff. The Soviet attack subsided when the commander of the 3rd Tank Regiment was killed by shell splinters and his tanks ran low on fuel and ammunition. The Soviet pause granted the Germans a short reprieve. Due to constant Soviet bomber attacks on the German supply columns crossing the Lithuanian border, Panzergruppe 4 had kept its available 8.8cm flak batteries in the rear and none were available near the front at Raseiniai. Reinhardt quickly ordered a flak battery to move forward to support 6.Panzer-Division and, in the meantime, Landgraf was on his own against Solyankin's tanks. Oberst Richard Koll, commander of Panzer-Regiment 11, led a counterattack with his diminutive Pz.35(t) light tanks and a handful of Pz.IV against the Soviet tanks pounding on Schützen-

Regiment 114, but this was a hopeless gesture and Koll broke off the attack after suffering significant losses. Another odd thing about the Battle of Raseiniai is the absence of the Luftwaffe; the arrival of Stukas might have tipped the balance, but they were nowhere in sight.

Solyankin launched six separate attacks on 24 June, which considerably upset the Germans, but Soviet armour power waned as fuel and ammunition were exhausted. Soviet combat logistics fell apart. Most of the T-26 and BT-7 light tanks, as well as the motorized infantry, were lost early in the battle, leaving the remaining KV and T-34 tanks unsupported. The Soviet heavy tanks made one last effort to break through to Raseiniai late in the day, but by this point an 8.8cm flak battery and a 10cm heavy howitzer battery had arrived and they succeeded in immobilizing several tanks, causing the attack to falter.

Although stunned by the Soviet counterattack at Raseiniai, Reinhardt spent the day skillfully directing the 1.Panzer-Division and 36.Infanterie-Division (mot.) around Solyankin's open flank. Meanwhile, Manstein's 8.Panzer-Division had marched almost unopposed into Kedainiai, overrunning Solyankin's rear area units. By nightfall on 24 June, Solyankin's 2nd Tank was enveloped on both flanks. The next morning, Solyankin attempted a breakout with his remaining heavy tanks in the lead, which caused 1.Panzer-Division some tense moments when Kampfgruppe Westhoven was attacked by KV heavy tanks near Vosiliskis. Once again, the panzerjägers were unable to stop the Soviet heavy tanks and the Germans were forced to use 8.8cm flak and 10cm howitzers in the anti-tank role. Afterwards, Reinhardt spent the next day reducing the encircled 2nd Tank Division and Solyankin was killed in action on 26 June. While the Battle of Raseiniai was a Soviet defeat, Solyankin's division had effectively held up Reinhardt's entire corps for three whole days.

By the time that the 2nd Tank Division was surrounded at Raseiniai, Shestopalov's 12th Mechanized Corps was nearly surrounded near Kaltinenai by German infantry from the I and XXVI Armeekorps. The Soviet 23rd and 28th Tank Divisions fought doggedly against the AOK 18 on 24–25 June, but their T-26 and BT-7 light tanks were rapidly picked off by German panzerjägers. After two days of combat, the corps exhausted its supplies and was reduced to about 20 per cent of its armour. Recognizing that his forces were too weak to hold Lithuania, never mind throw the Germans back across the border, Kuznetsov ordered Shestopalov and the remaining infantry from the 8th Army to withdraw north of the Dvina River. Chernyakhovsky conducted a skillful rearguard action with the remnants of his 28th Tank Division, enabling the bulk of the corps to escape. During the retreat, Shestopalov was wounded and then captured, dying soon afterward in German captivity.

By 0800 hours on 26 June, Manstein's advance guard from 8.Panzer-Division had seized both the rail and road bridges over the Dvina at Daugavpils intact after a 315km march. While Manstein had accomplished his intermediate objective in just four days, he was in no position to exploit it. His bold dash had consumed 5.5 V.S. of fuel (545 tons) and, as a result, the 8.Panzer-Division was now immobilized for lack of fuel. In addition, the long-distance road march caused twenty-four tanks from Panzer-Regiment 10 to fall out due to mechanical defects.[6] Reinhardt's corps was still engaged around Raseiniai, 165km to the rear, and not in a position to support Manstein for several days. Kuznetsov directed the 21st Airborne Brigade to try and retake Daugavpils, while the Stavka dispatched General-major Dmitri Lelyushenko's 21st Mechanized Corps from Idritsa to retake the bridges. Although Lelyushenko's corps was little more than a cadre formation with no tanks and few vehicles, the VAMM in Moscow provided Lelyushenko with two tank battalions crewed by instructors and students; this added 105 BT-7 and two T-34 tanks to the 21st Mechanized Corps. In addition, the Stavka reinforced his corps on 23–24 June with a large shipment of 45mm anti-tank guns and the new 76.2mm USV gun.

Lelyushenko quickly reorganized his incomplete corps into two combat groups, each with a tank battalion, a rifle battalion mounted on trucks and a mixed artillery/anti-tank battalion. He then set out on the 200km road march to Daugavpils on 25 June. Despite Luftwaffe attacks that destroyed some of his wheeled transport, Lelyushenko's lead group reached the vicinity of Daugavpils within two days. At 0800 hours on 28 June, Lelyushenko attacked the 8.Panzer-Division's forward positions northeast of Daugavpils with about sixty BT-7s, supported by some infantry and artillery. The German panzers were short of fuel but Lelyushenko's tanks started the battle with very little ammunition and could not get anywhere near the bridges. Lelyushenko kept attacking all day as the rest of his troops arrived, but this only served to erode his combat power in piecemeal attacks. After providing Manstein with a stressful day, Lelyushenko broke off the attack at nightfall and fell back to defensive positions north of the city. By 30 June, Lelyushenko's corps comprised only about 3,000 troops, seven BT-7s and forty-four artillery pieces.

By 28 June, the Northwest Front was in full retreat from Lithuania, although the German pursuit failed to catch any large units. Kuznetsov briefly tried to form a defense along the Dvina with the remnants of the 12th Mechanized Corps and the rifle divisions of the 27th Army, but Manstein had already breached the river line on 26 June and Reinhardt's corps crossed the Dvina near Jekabpils on 29 June. With the river line defense collapsing, Kuznetsov ordered his forces to fall back toward the Stalin Line positions at Pskov and Ostrov, but on 30 June he was relieved of command. The next day, Kampfgruppe Lasch from the 1.Infanterie-Division, supported by five StuG-III assault guns, entered Riga.

Höpner pushed Panzergruppe 4 north toward Ostrov, about 200km distant, with Reinhardt's corps on the left and Manstein's on the right. Despite the outward appearance of success, Panzergruppe 4's performance in Lithuania was sub-par. Aside from the 2nd Tank Division and parts of one rifle division, the bulk of the Northwest Front escaped. Time and again during Barbarossa, local German commanders became so impressed with seizing territory that they missed golden opportunities to encircle and eliminate Red Army units. One of the iron rules about armoured warfare on the Eastern Front was not to commit one's best armoured units until the enemy's strength had been located. Höpner went into Lithuania fairly ignorant about the location of opposing Soviet armoured units and then he mistakenly committed all three of his panzer divisions before any of Kuznetsov's armour had been located. He foolishly committed 1.Panzer-Division to a street battle for Taurogen, tying down his best mobile unit for a full day, and failed to coordinate the actions of Manstein's and Reinhardt's corps.

Panzergruppe 3 and the Crossing of the Neman, 22–24 June

Generalfeldmarschall Fedor von Bock, commander of Heeresgruppe Mitte, intended to pulverize the Soviet Western Front forces in the Bialystok salient with a powerful armoured pincer attack from both north and south, then continue on to finish any remnants around Minsk. The northern pincer was formed by Generaloberst Hoth's Panzergruppe 3, which fielded four panzer divisions and three motorized infantry divisions in the XXXIX and LVII Armeekorps (mot.). The initial objective for both corps was to crash through the Soviet 11th Army border defenses and advance 45–65km to seize crossings over the Neman River at Alytus and Merkine. Following this, both corps would drive due east across Lithuania and Belarus and then envelop Minsk from the north. Hoth's initial attack benefited from striking near the boundary between the Northwestern and Western Fronts, but the terrain was more heavily wooded than the area that Höpner had to traverse. The Luftwaffe's VIII Fliegerkorps, which included 158 Ju-87 Stuka dive-bombers from St.G. 1 and St.G. 2 and seventy-eight Bf-110 fighter-bombers from ZG 26, was assigned to provide close support to Hoth's Panzergruppe.

The Soviet 11th Army had eight infantry regiments screening a 170km-long sector along the southern Lithuanian border. Kurkin's 3rd Mechanized Corps was in reserve, on the east side of the Neman River. When Panzergruppe 3 attacked across the border at 0405 hours on 22 June, both German armoured corps advanced abreast and easily bypassed the bulk of the 128th Rifle Division and pushed on to the Neman. A strong kampfgruppe from 7.Panzer-Division, led by Oberst Karl Rothenburg, reached the outskirts of Alytus at 1240 hours and was soon able to seize the two bridges over the Neman intact from an unprepared NKVD guard detachment. Kuznetsov, the Northwest Front commander, had already stripped the 3rd Mechanized Corps of the 2nd Tank Division to support his counterattack at Raseiniai, leaving only Polkovnik Fedor Fedorov's 5th Tank Division in a position to stop Rothenburg's kampfgruppe.

Fedorov's tanks had to march 30km to reach Alytus and a number of tanks fell out due to mechanical problems, so by the time his lead elements reached Alytus, Rothenburg's Panzer-Regiment 25 was already crossing the Neman. Leytenant Ivan G. Verzhbitsky, leading the 2nd Battalion/9th Tank Regiment, was the first to arrive, with forty-four T-34 tanks. One T-34, commanded by a Sergeant Makogan, engaged the German column and destroyed a Pz.38(t) tank crossing the northern bridge. This action was the very first German contact with the T-34 – less than ten hours after the start of Barbarossa. Although the T-34 was vastly superior to the Pz.38(t), the Soviet tanks only had a few rounds of AP ammunition and the drivers had no experience with their new tanks. Verzhbitsky decided to deploy his tanks in defilade and await reinforcements, which soon arrived with the twenty-four T-28 medium tanks of the 1st Battalion/9th Tank Regiment. The German panzers could not close to effective range of their 3.7cm cannon and were effectively blocked by Federov's tanks. While Rothenburg was temporarily stymied, he called up the Luftwaffe, who blasted the Soviet positions with high explosive. Meanwhile, a smaller kampfgruppe from the 7.Panzer-Division seized the southern bridge, but was blocked by the Soviet 10th Tank Regiment, equipped with forty-five BT-7 tanks.

Fedorov launched three counterattacks during the day, which inflicted some damage on 7.Panzer-Division, but his own forces were rapidly depleted. Unlike the Germans, Federov had minimal infantry and artillery support and no air support, as well as far less fuel and ammunition for his tanks. Schmidt, the XXXIX Armeekorps (mot.) commander, directed the lead kampfgruppe from the 20.Panzer-Division toward the northern bridgehead and it arrived around 1930 hours.[7] With the III/Pz.Regt 25 in the lead, the 7.Panzer-Division broke out of the bridgehead and began to roll up Federov's tired tankers. By nightfall, Federov had to break off the action. The Battle of Alytus cost the 5th Tank Division seventy-three tanks (sixteen T-28, twenty-seven T-34 and thirty BT-7) against the 7.Panzer-Division's loss of eleven tanks (seven Pz.38(t) and four Pz.IV). Most of the T-34s were lost due to crew errors, including two sunk in the Nemen River and others toppled into ditches or craters. According to Soviet sources, German tank losses at Alytus numbered about thirty, but this included armoured cars and tanks that were only damaged. It also appears that a single Soviet T-34, commanded by Sergeant Makogan, may have been responsible for nearly half the German losses; in tank combat, it is not uncommon that much of the damage is inflicted by a few highly-skilled crews.

After seizing Alytus, the 7 and 20.Panzer-Division brushed aside the remnants of Federov's division on 23 June and advanced quickly upon Vilnius, while 12.Panzer-Division advanced from the Merkine bridgehead as well. Hoth's rapid exploitation from the Alytus bridgehead prevented the Soviet 11th Army from establishing a new front, so opposition in front of Panzergruppe 3 was weak and scattered. Amazingly, a 3,000-man battle group from the 5th Tank Division evaded pursuit and managed to escape toward Pskov. The 7.Panzer-Division's Kradschützen-Abteilung entered the outskirts of Vilna at dawn on 24 June. Hoth's defeat of the left wing of the Northwest Front put the neighboring Western Front forces in the Bialystok salient at risk of envelopment from the north.

The Destruction of Pavlov's Armour in the Bialystok Salient

General Dmitry Pavlov had not increased the alertness of his Western Front forces, as Kuznetsov had done, and he was committed to a virtually static defense of the Bialystok salient. Much of Pavlov's armour was still stationed in its peacetime garrisons and ill-prepared to transition immediately to mobile wartime operations. He did have more infantry on the border than Kuznetsov had, which

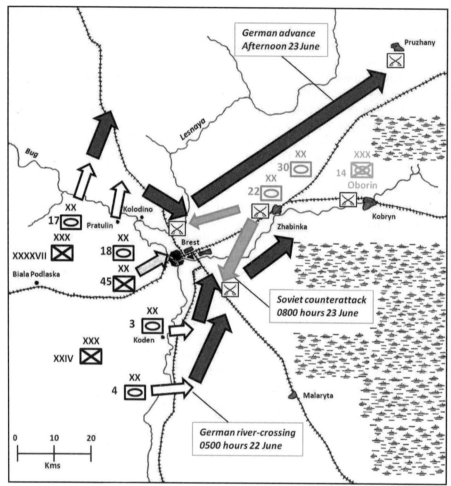

Von Schweppenburg's XXIV Armeekorps (mot.) crosses the Bug River and defeats Oborin's 14th Mechanized Corps, 22–23 June.

briefly gave him the illusion that a coherent defense could be established around Bialystok.

German intelligence estimates of the strength of Pavlov's armour were wildly inaccurate and assessed that the Red Army had about 1,000 tanks in the area, instead of the actual number of 2,251. The Germans had correctly identified the 6th Mechanized corps at Bialystok, but were unaware of the existence of the 11th and 14th Mechanized Corps on the flanks. However, the general excellence of the German operational plan for an armoured double envelopment of the Bialystok salient, along with Pavlov's failure at battle command, was sufficient to hand the Wehrmacht its first major victory on the Eastern Front.

At the same time as Hoth's Panzergruppe 3 attacked the Northwest Front's 11th Army along the Neman, 200km to the south, Generaloberst Heinz

Guderian's Panzergruppe 2 attacked the Western Front's 4th Army near the fortifications at Brest-Litovsk. Guderian decided to bypass Brest-Litovsk, with General der Artillerie Joachim Lemelsen's XXXXVII Armeekorps (mot.) to the northwest and General der Panzertruppen Leo Freiherr Geyr von Schweppenburg's XXIV Armeekorps (mot.) to the south. Both corps had to cross the 90-meter-wide Western Bug River, which represented a substantial obstacle. In addition to division-level pioneers, Heeresgruppe Mitte provided Guderian with substantial engineer support, including Sturmbootkommando 902, with eighty-one assault boats.[8] The Luftwaffe's II Fliegerkorps, which included 115 Ju-87 Stuka dive-bombers from St.G. 77 and eighty-three Bf-110 fighter-bombers from SKG 210, was assigned to provide close air support to Guderian's Panzergruppe.

Although Generalleutnant Walter Model's 3.Panzer-Division was able to seize the Koden bridge intact with a coup de main, there were no bridges in the area Lemelsen chose to cross the Western Bug. Instead, after 8.8cm flak guns were used to knock out Soviet bunkers on the eastern bank of the Western Bug near Pratulin with direct fire, the 18.Panzer-Division sent 120 infantrymen from its Kradschützen-Abteilung across in assault boats to secure the far side at 0415 hours.[9] German artillery and Stuka bombardments were used to suppress the Soviet defenders on the eastern bank. Thirty minutes later, Major Manfred Graf von Strachwitz led his I/Panzer-Regiment 18, equipped with submersible Pz.III and Pz.IV *tauchpanzer*, across the river by driving along the bottom. Model's Panzer-Regiment 6 was also equipped with *tauchpanzer*, but the capture of the Koden bridge obviated their use in this role. Once both corps had established bridgeheads on the opposite shore, German pioneers began to build a 16-ton pontoon bridge for each panzer division and improve the crossing sites. Yet aside from the *tauchpanzers* and Model's spearhead, the mass of Guderian's armour would not begin to cross the Western Bug until about 1220 hours on 22 June, and it would take about six hours for an entire panzer regiment to cross. Thus, the bulk of Guderian's combat power would not cross the bridges until the evening of the first day.

Across the river, the closest Soviet armoured formation was General-major Stepan I. Oborin's 14th Mechanized Corps. By chance, most of the units of the 14th Mechanized Corps had been engaged in training exercises on the night of 21–22 June, and General-major Vasiliy P. Puganov's 22nd Tank Division was 40km away from its normal garrison in Brest-Litovsk. Puganov, formerly in charge of combat training for the GABTU, had taken most of his T-26 tanks to gunnery ranges near Zabinka, while his artillery and rear services were still at Brest. The opening German artillery and air attacks on Brest-Litovsk demolished much of the 22nd Tank Division's ammunition and fuel stockpiles, as well as much of its artillery. Oborin's command post was bombed at 0500 hours, demolishing his communications links, so he was not able to alert his corps until after the Germans had already begun crossing the Bug River. Nevertheless, Puganov dispatched a tank battalion towards the river, but it was unable to seriously interfere with the German crossing. Despite continued Luftwaffe bombing, Oborin was gradually able to gather the combat elements of the 22nd and 30th Tank Divisions around Zabinka by late morning.

Neither Guderian nor Model waited for the pioneers to complete their work at the fording sites, but crossed to the eastern bank to lead their advance guards. Guderian moved with Strachwitz's *tauchpanzer* battalion to capture an intact bridge over the Lesnaya River, north of Brest, while Model jumped aboard an Sd.Kfz.231 (8-rad) armoured car and pushed toward Kobrin. Polkovnik Semyon I. Bogdanov, commander of the 30th Tank Division, responded by dispatching one of his tank regiments to counterattack Strachwitz's panzers at 1200 hours. However, Guderian requested Luftwaffe close air support sorties, which defeated the counterattack. Oborin decided to call off any further hasty attacks and issued an order at 1830 hours: the 14th Mechanized Corps would temporarily shift to the defensive, but launch an all-out three-division counterattack on the German bridgeheads at 0500 hours on 23 June. Puganov used the night to refuel and rearm his tanks from warehouses in Kobrin. Oborin was an artilleryman with no experience of armour and he opted for the safe, textbook approach taught at the Frunze military academy, but he also gave Guderian a quiet night to bring the bulk of his armour across the Bug.

Oborin's counterattack began around 0800 hours, consisting of 200 T-26s from Puganov's and Bogdanov's tank divisions, but with limited infantry and artillery support. Bogdanov's armour attacked the 18.Panzer-Division, while Puganov attacked 3.Panzer-Division. In a very one-sided action, German panzers and panzerjäger had little difficulty in destroying the unsupported enemy light tanks, although the Germans did lose a number of tanks as well. Once Oborin's armour was decimated, Guderian attacked with all four panzer divisions of the XXIV and XXXXVII Armeekorps (mot.) on line, pushing northeast. Puganov's 22nd Tank Division was demolished by Model's 3.Panzer-Division and Puganov was killed, while Bogdanov's 30th Tank Division was shoved aside.[10] Lemelsen's corps captured Pruzhany and advanced over 80km on 23 June, while von Schweppenburg's corps captured Kobrin. Oborin was wounded in the mêlée and, when he flew back to Moscow for treatment, he was arrested and later executed for desertion. Bogdanov took charge of the remnants of the corps and retired east toward Pinsk. The tank battles around Zhabinka, Kobrin and Pruzhany had failed to seriously delay Guderian's panzers and the defeat of the 14th Mechanized Corps sealed the fate of three Soviet armies in the Bialystok salient.

While Oborin's 14th Mechanized Corps was being taken apart by Guderian and the rest of the Bialystok salient was under attack from all directions, Pavlov was initially uncertain what to do with his armoured reserve – General-major Mikhail G. Khatskilevich's 6th Mechanized Corps – until others made the decision for him. On Pavlov's northern flank, the Soviet 4th Rifle Corps, defending a long stretch of the border north of Grodno, was virtually obliterated by the attack of the German VIII Armeekorps on the morning of 22 June. General-leytenant Vasily Kuznetsov, the 3rd Army commander, hastily decided to commit General-major Dmitri K. Mostovenko's 11th Mechanized Corps to counterattack the German 8.Jäger-Division, which was already on the outskirts of

Grodno. Only Polkovnik Nikolai P. Studnev's 29th Tank Division, stationed south of Grodno, was able to respond on short notice. By 1200 hours, Studnev had deployed his understrength 57th and 59th Tank Regiments on line, which had no more than two KV tanks, twenty-six T-34s and thirty-eight T-26 tanks. Interestingly, this was one of the rare occasions during the border battles where Red tank units were not exhausted by long marches and out of fuel, and they thus had real potential to inflict some damage on a German infantry formation. However, Studnev was not one of the rising stars of the Red Army; before the war he had twice been relieved of command and was only given a division command in 1941 because Stalin's purges had so thinned the ranks of senior tank officers. Southwest of Grodno, Studnev's two tank regiments bumped into a kampfgruppe from Infanterie-Regiment 84, supported by some assault guns from Sturmgeschütz-Abteilung 184. After advancing a few kilometers, Studnev mistook the handful of assault guns for tanks and quickly halted and decided to engage by fire, not maneuver, which handed the initiative to the Germans. Soviet tankers had not been trained in fire discipline and they rapidly fired off much of their ammunition, but hit little. While their short-barreled StuG-IIIs and 3.7-cm Pak guns were useless in a long-range gunnery duel against Studnev's T-34s, the Germans instead used their excellent radio communications to request close air support from the VIII Fliegerkorps, which promptly dispatched Ju-87 Stuka dive-bombers to the scene. For four hours, Studnev's semi-stationary tanks were pounded from the air and by German artillery, which knocked out virtually all his light tanks and some of his T-34s. Finally, Studnev ordered his survivors to pull back after his division operations officer was killed and both tank regiments became combat ineffective. For the loss of about half his sixty-six tanks, Studnev had inflicted only about fifty casualties on the 8.Jäger-Division.[11]

After the failure of Studnev's counterattack, the Soviet 3rd Army commander decided to abandon the city of Grodno (which had a pre-war population of 50,000), including its fuel depot. When Marshal Semyon K. Timoshenko, the People's Commissar for Defense and de facto commander-in-chief of the Red Army, learned of the loss of Grodno, he believed that Hoth's armour was responsible. Timoshenko immediately telexed an order to Pavlov at 2115 hours, directing him to send the 6th Mechanized Corps to eliminate the German forces threatening Grodno. Three hours later, Pavlov obediently issued the orders to Khatskilevich's Corps and sent his deputy, General-major Ivan S. Boldin, to co-ordinate the counteroffensive. At this point, Pavlov believed that the 13th Mechanized Corps supporting the 10th Army would be able to stabilize the situation south of Bialystok, where the German 4.Armee had crossed the border in force on Guderian's left.

Khatskilevich's 6th Mechanized Corps began moving from its deployment areas around Bialystok before dawn on 23 June. When the sun rose, German reconnaissance aircraft quickly detected the mass of Soviet armour moving toward Grodno and Fliegerkorps VIII delivered a series of punishing attacks on the packed columns; the 7th Tank Division lost sixty-three tanks to air attack. After a 90km road march, the combat elements of Khatskilevich's corps reached their assembly areas southwest of Grodno around 1400 hours, but since most of the KV tanks only had a quarter-load of fuel remaining, Boldin decided to postpone attack until the next morning. However, the Luftwaffe had destroyed the fuel depot in Bialystok and the nearest alternate fuel supply was in Volkovysk, 75km away. There was actually plenty of petrol for the T-26 and BT light tanks, but diesel was in short supply. On paper, Khatskilevich had one of the most powerful armoured groups in the Red Army, with over 100 KV and 200 T-34 tanks, but the shortage of diesel fuel greatly reduced their combat potential.

Boldin intended to attack with the 6th Mechanized Corps into the flank of the German XX Armeekorps at 1000 hours on 24 June. Due to lack of radios, Boldin was unable to coordinate with the 11th Mechanized Corps, which also intended to counterattack again on 24 June. Boldin had a very inaccurate picture of the enemy situation, which led to faulty deployments for the 6th Mechanized Corps. When Khatskilevich's tanks began advancing the next morning, they found that the enemy was still nearly 30km away and the long approach march gave the German XX Armeekorps plenty of time to establish an anti-tank defense with the II/Flak 4, equipped with twelve 8.8cm flak guns. Fliegerkorps VIII returned and the Stukas caused considerable damage with accurate dive-bombing. Still awaiting resupply of diesel fuel, Khatskilevich committed only his petrol-fueled BT and T-26 light tanks, which the 8.8cm flak guns of II/Flak 4 shot to pieces at ranges up to 800 meters; between twenty and forty Soviet tanks were lost.[12] Khatskilevich decided to break off his attack, apparently deciding to wait for his heavy tanks, infantry and artillery support to move up, rather than to conduct an attack with just unsupported light tanks. Pavlov had also promised air support, so Khatskilevich could expect better results if he waited. Likewise, the 11th Mechanized Corps continued to attack the 8.Jäger-Division on 24 June, but lost most of its remaining tanks. However, Khatskilevich's premature attack had alerted the Germans that a major Soviet armoured counterattack was forthcoming and the 256.Infanterie-Division had time to establish a robust anti-armour defense around the town of Kuznica, strengthened by a battery of 8.8cm flak guns, and two batteries of StuG III assault guns from Sturmgeschütz-Abteilung 210.[13]

On 25 June, Khatskilevich continued his attack with 150–200 tanks, but his artillery and air support failed to materialize. As before, the Soviet armour attacked in successive waves, with BA-10 and BA-20 armoured cars in the first wave as reconnaissance, followed by a second wave of T-26 and BT light tanks, to engage enemy positions. The T-34 and KV tanks appeared in the final third wave. When Khatskilevich's armour struck the 256.Infanterie-Division, the gunners in Panzerjäger-Abteilung 256 quickly found that their 3.7cm and 5cm anti-tank guns could not defeat the Soviet tanks at normal ranges of 500–600 meters. For a moment, the Germans were seized with panic at the sight of Soviet heavy tanks and it seemed that the Red Army might actually achieve a local victory. The second battery of StuG III assault guns from Sturmgeschütz-Abteilung 210 was dispatched to deal with the Soviet armour, but their short-barreled 7.5cm howitzers were equally ineffective. Horst Slesina, a German war correspondent, witnessed the combat against the KV and T-34 tanks near Grodno:

> Then more gun barrels grew along the horizon. A tall tank turret becomes visible followed by a gigantic tank chassis. Tanks! Giant tanks like we have never seen before! Russian 52-ton tanks with a 15-cm gun [KV-2]! Crippling fear strikes us. Then the Pak guns are swung around. Their fire barks from all barrels, but these light anti-tank weapons have no effect. The shots bounce off the mighty steel walls like rubber balls ... The panzerjäger fight with wild intensity. They let it come to the shortest ranges, firing cold-bloodedly, as they have learned, at its weakest points ... Shrill shouts beckon the assault guns ... They rush straight at the Russians ... A terrible duel is fought at the closest range. There is a hellish crash next to me – a direct hit on one of the assault guns![14]

At least two assault guns, a few Pak guns and two infantry guns were destroyed, but Khatskilevich's tanks failed to break the 256.Infanterie-Division's defenses because they attacked without significant infantry or artillery support. Instead, once the Germans recovered their composure they began to immobilize the Soviet heavy tanks by firing at their tracks. The 8.8cm flak guns from 9./Flak 4 had several crewmen wounded, but chalked up another dozen or more kills. German Panzerjägers soon discovered that the 5cm Pak 38 anti-tank could penetrate a KV-1 heavy tank's side armour with the Panzergranate 40's tungsten carbide penetrator at ranges up to 200 meters, but this required a very steady crew.[15] A few KV-1 tanks did succeed in plowing through the German line like elephants, causing more damage by crushing vehicles and equipment in their path, but then became mired in marshy terrain and were abandoned. Khatskilevich, trying to lead his corps from a T-34, was killed and the attack faltered. Nevertheless, the appearance of 150–200 Soviet tanks caused a panicked reaction from XX Armeekorps, which erroneously reported to Heeresgruppe Mitte that its infantry had been 'reduced to cinders.'[16]

By midday on 25 June, Pavlov was finally aware that the main threat to the Bialystok salient was not at Grodno, but that Hoth's and Guderian's panzer groups were advancing relentlessly toward Minsk on his flanks. At 1645 hours on 25 June, Pavlov ordered Boldin to take what was left of the 6th and 11th Mechanized Corps and immediately force-march toward Slonim to prevent German panzers from cutting the Minsk–Warsaw highway. However, the rearward movement rapidly became a rout that destroyed both corps, with much equipment abandoned along the way. Pavlov evacuated his Western Front headquarters to Mogilev on 26 June, further diminishing Soviet command and control over the Minsk–Bialystok fighting.

While the best of Pavlov's armour had been fixed at Grodno, Hoth's panzers had swept almost unopposed across southern Lithuania, occupying Vilna on 24 June. The only Soviet formation left standing between Hoth's panzers and Minsk was the understrength 21st Rifle Corps, stationed near Lida. Soviet pre-war military exercises had determined that Lida was a likely avenue of approach for enemy armour, so the 21st Rifle Corps and 8th Anti-tank Brigade had been positioned in this area to protect the boundary between the Western and North-west Fronts. However, both the rifle divisions and anti-tank brigade possessed only 40 per cent of their authorized strength and were in no position to stop the German LVII Panzerkorps. The 12.Panzer-Division skillfully slipped around the flank of the 21st Rifle Corps while the 19.Panzer-Division fought its way into Lida on 25 June. Hoth pushed the 12 and 20.Panzer-Divisionen towards Minsk, while the 7.Panzer-Division split off toward Borisov on the Berezina.

Meanwhile, after brutally shoving the remnants of Oborin's 14th Mechanized Corps out of the way, Guderian's Panzergruppe 2 achieved a clear breakthrough at Pruzhany and pushed rapidly northward toward a link-up with Hoth's panzers. With unusual alacrity, Pavlov managed to shift the 47th Rifle Corps over 160km to establish a blocking position at Slonim, while the cadre-strength 17th Mechanized Corps dug in at Baranovichi. When Generalleutnant Hans-Jürgen von Arnim reached Slonim with the vanguard of his 17.Panzer-Division late on 24 June, he found that the Soviets had burned the wooden bridge over the Shchara River and were entrenched on the far side. Guderian was faced with the daunting task of conducting an opposed river crossing against a foe with significant artillery support. Nevertheless, pioneers from the 17.Panzer-Division's Brücko B column were able to bridge the Shchara during the night, and the next day the XXXXVII Panzerkorps fought its way into Slonim and then Baranovichi. At this point, Guderian split his panzer group up into three sections, attempting to simultaneously accomplish multiple missions. He directed the 29.Infanterie-Division (mot.) to turn westward and establish a blocking position to prevent the escape of the Soviet 3rd and 10th Armies from the rapidly shrinking Bialystok pocket, while the rest of the XXXXVII Panzerkorps advanced northeast toward Minsk. Von Schweppenburg's XXIV Panzerkorps was sent due east toward Slutsk, which Model's 3.Panzer-Division overran on 26 June. Although Guderian clearly had the Red Army on the run, he also effectively dispersed his panzer group on divergent axes, which complicated his already tenuous logistic situation.

The second-echelon Soviet 13th Army made a futile last-ditch effort to defend Minsk with the understrength 20th Mechanized Corps and several reserve rifle divisions, but Hoth was able to concentrate the 12 and 20.Panzer-Divisionen on the northern outskirts of the city by 26 June. Minsk was surrounded by a pre-war Fortified Region that had 580 bunkers, including 45mm anti-tank casemates, but it was garrisoned by only four fortress battalions. The 13th Army managed to get two rifle divisions of the 44th Rifle Corps into position to reinforce the Minsk fortified line north of the city just before Hoth's panzers arrived, but they were spread thinly across a 50km-wide front. The Luftwaffe also bombed the city mercilessly, setting more than half of Minsk afire – which added to the defender's chaos. At 0300 hours on 27 June, both the 12 and 20.Panzer-Divisionen began assaulting the Minsk Fortified Region with their motorized infantry – a total of just eight battalions. A number of concrete bunkers with 76.2mm howitzers proved particularly troublesome. The Soviet troops fought tenaciously, but both German panzer divisions were gradually able to fight their way through the

2–3km-thick fortified belt by the end of the day. Interestingly, heavy rain was already creating mud and waterlogged roads around Minsk, hindering German mobility. On 28 June, Hoth resumed the attack and the Soviet defense crumbled; Generaloberst Josef Harpe's 12.Panzer-Division was able to reach the center of Minsk before noon. Once it became clear that Minsk could not be held, most of the Soviet 13th Army succeeded in escaping east to the Berezina river, where they began establishing a new line. The rapid seizure of a large city by panzers alone – repeated at Orel in October – gave the Germans the false impression that even larger urban areas, such as Moscow and later Stalingrad, could be seized by a bold armoured coup de main.

Thanks to the relentless advance of Hoth's and Guderian's panzers, the Wehrmacht had achieved a major victory that encircled and then smashed the bulk of Pavlov's Western Front within six days of Barbarossa's start. Boldin and Mostovenko managed to herd the remnants of the 6th and 11th Mechanized Corps into several semi-effective combat groups by gathering up all remaining fuel and operational vehicles, and ruthlessly abandoning everything else. Despite heavy losses in the fighting around Grodno, these armoured battle groups succeeded in evading the encroaching German dragnet for a time by moving eastward along forest tracks near Volkovysk. However, their luck ran out when they discovered the German 29.Infanterie-Division (mot.) blocking their escape route at the town of Zel'va. Several BT-7 tanks attempting to ford the Shchara River were shot up by German Pak guns, forcing the remainder to divert 10–15km south to cross the river near Klepachi. Although the Soviet armour managed to ford the river on 27 June, they found that the Germans had already established blocking positions near Klepachi and Ozernitsa as well. An anti-tank ambush quickly claimed four more Soviet tanks. Major Iosif G. Cheryapkin, commander of the 57th Tank Regiment, led a determined breakout attempt with ten tanks and, despite being wounded, succeeded in escaping the encirclement. Another group from the 13th Tank Regiment, with two T-34s and one KV-1 tank, made it as far as Slonim on the road to Minsk; both T-34s were immobilized by German panzerjäger but the KV-1 nearly escaped, until it fell off a wooden bridge into the Shchara River. Other Soviet tank crews and leaders escaped as well, including Boldin, Mostovenko and Polkovnik Mikhail Panov. As formations, all of Pavlov's mechanized corps were eliminated in just a week of combat and the road between Volkovysk and Zel'va was littered with tanks that had run out of fuel, but German claims about eliminating over 3,000 Soviet tanks in the Minsk-Bialystok pocket ignored the fact that a significant number of Soviet tankers had escaped the *kessel* and would soon participate in defeating the Panzerwaffe. The Minsk-Bialystok *kessel* battle provided the first indication that the limited amount of German motorized infantry in the panzer groups prevented them from forming airtight encirclements. Soviet troops were everywhere in the forested terrain and the Germans only succeeded in scooping up clumps of Red Army troops along roads and in towns. Those who took to back trails through marshes and forests often escaped, albeit without much equipment.

Hoth's and Guderian's panzers linked up again east of Minsk on 5 July, trapping still more troops from the Western Front. Reduction of Pavlov's encircled forces continued for several more days. Although Hoth seized a crossing over the Berezina at Borisov and Guderian had a bridgehead at Bobruisk, both panzer groups had to divert the bulk of their forces to holding and reducing the *kessel*, leaving little left for exploitation eastward toward their next objective – Smolensk. Until the roads through the pocket were cleared of resistance, it was also difficult for the panzer groups to receive fuel and ammunition resupply in quantity.

Both Panzer groups had achieved their initial objectives and were well-positioned to pursue their next objective – Smolensk – in early July. A number of modern historians, including David Stahel and David Glantz, have portrayed German losses in the Minsk-Bialystok *kesselschlact* (encirclement battle) as excessive, but these assessments are due to misinterpretation of statistics and over-reliance on biased Soviet-era accounts.[17] A number of sources fail to differentiate between '*totalausfall*' (total loss) and damaged but repairable tanks, most of which would be returned to service in a matter of days since the Germans held the battlefield. It is also a mistake to include Pz.I losses with German losses, since these obsolete light tanks were no longer included in German tank companies and were only being used in auxiliary roles. During the Minsk-Bialystok fighting between 22 June and 5 July, both Hoth's and Guderian's panzer groups lost about sixty-five main battle tanks each as total losses, or 12 and 7 per cent of their starting strength. In addition, about one-third of their tanks were not combat-ready due to battle damage and mechanical defects, although the 10.Panzer-Division had been in reserve for part of the battle and still had 84 per cent of its tanks operational. In comparison, all but a handful of Pavlov's armour were total losses in the battle, representing a lop-sided 16–1 exchange ratio of 130 German tanks for well over 2,000 Soviet tanks in the *kessel*. German personnel losses in the panzer groups were also far from debilitating at this point. For example, the heavily-engaged 18.Panzer-Division suffered 331 killed and missing in the battle, with total casualties about 6 per cent of the division's strength. The only significant panzer leader casualty in the battle was Oberst Rothenburg of 7.Panzer-Division, whereas the Red Army lost five of six mechanized corps commanders and most of the tank division and regimental commanders in the pocket. German victory in the Minsk-Bialystok *kesselschlacht* changed the equation for the rest of the 1941 campaign as far as the Moscow axis was concerned; the Germans went from numerical inferiority in armour to a position of strength even when attrition losses were factored in.

After losing virtually all his tanks – but not his tankers – Pavlov was relieved of command, recalled to Moscow and executed on 22 July. Timoshenko assumed direct control over the remnants of the Western Front, which were already forming a new front. While approximately 259,000 Soviet troops were lost in the catastrophe at Minsk-Bialystok, tens of thousands more escaped to fight another day.

Von Kleist's Panzergruppe 1 versus the Southwest Front

The situation facing Heeresgruppe Süd at X-hour on 22 June 1941 was far more disadvantageous than that faced by either of the other two German army groups. Von Kleist's Panzergruppe 1 had to conduct an opposed river crossing across the Western Bug into a heavily-defended fortified region, which meant the 6.Armee's infantry would first have to create a series of bridgeheads before German armour could be committed. Beginning at dawn on 22 June, the 6.Armee used five infantry divisions to conduct multiple crossings across the Western Bug River. The 298.Infanterie-Division, with the help of Brandenburg infiltration troops, managed to seize an intact bridge at Ustilug. German pioneers also succeed in capturing an intact bridge further south, at Sokal. Two Soviet rifle divisions opposed the crossing but were too thinly spread to seriously interfere with the initial bridge seizures. Wasting no time, 6.Armee immediately sent Sturmgeschütz-Abteilung 197 across the Sokal bridge at 0450 hours.[18] In order that von Kleist's panzers would not be delayed by the use of just two bridges, German pioneers immediately began building pontoon bridges across the river to provide multiple crossing points. Despite the successful crossing of the Western Bug, von Kleist could initially commit only three of his nine motorized divisions to exploit the bridgeheads due to the narrowness of the attack sector and congestion at the two bridges. General der Panzertruppen Ludwig Crüwell's 11.Panzer-Division crossed the Sokal bridge and pushed past weak resistance nearly 30km by the end of the first day. From Ustilug, the 6.Armee was able to seize the town of Vladimir Volynskii, which opened the way for General der Panzertruppen Friedrich Kühn's 14.Panzer-Division to push toward Lutsk – Panzergruppe 1's intermediate objective.

General Leytenant Mikhail P. Kirponos, in command of the Southwestern Front, hurried to his new wartime command post at Tarnopol, but once there he could barely communicate with any of his subordinate forces for the first two days of the war. His headquarters personnel were unable to establish a functioning radio command net (during peace-time, the Red Army tried to avoid use of radio communications in order to limit opportunities for adversary signals intercepts, but when war erupted suddenly, most units had neither the experience nor the correct code books to initiate secure communications) so he was forced to rely upon civilian phones to try and coordinate his forces. In this command vacuum, local commanders began making their own decisions on how to respond to the German invasion. The Soviet 5th Army, headquartered in Lutsk, directed General-major Semen M. Kondrusev's 22nd Mechanized Corps to counterattack the German forces threatening Vladimir Volynskii. Although most of this corps was about 100km from the border, by chance its most powerful formation, Polkovnik Petr Pavlov's 41st Tank Division, was conducting field training just north of Vladimir Volynskii. Pavlov had thirty-one KV-2 heavy tanks (which lacked 152mm ammunition) and 342 T-26 tanks, which were in an excellent position to counterattack the German 14.Panzer-Division as it marched over the bridge at Ustilug. Instead, Pavlov found himself in a quandary that was not uncommon in the Red Army of June 1941 – he was out of radio communications with Kondrusev's corps headquarters and his pre-war mobilization orders directed him to deploy to Kovel – away from the Germans at Ustilug. Pressured by local Soviet commanders to do something to help the crumbling border defenses, Pavlov split the difference by sending the bulk of his tanks on the road to Kovel, but detaching a tank battalion under Major Aleksandr S. Suin with fifty T-26 light tanks to support Soviet infantry at Vladimir Volynskii. Suin's battalion arrived just in time to be shot to pieces by German panzerjäger, who knocked out thirty of his T-26 tanks and forced him to abandon Vladimir Volynskii.

Only vaguely aware of the extent of German advances by the end of 22 June, Kirponos was able to get in touch with General-major Ignatii I. Karpezo's 15th Mechanized Corps, located near Brody, and order them to counterattack Crüwell's 11.Panzer-Division near Radekhov while the rest of Kondrusev's 22nd Mechanized Corps deployed to counterattack at Vladimir Volynskii. The 1st Anti-tank Brigade (RVGK) under General-major Kirill S. Moskalenko, which was fully motorized and equipped with forty-eight 76.2mm F-22 anti-tank guns and seventy-two 85mm M1939 anti-aircraft guns, was ordered to create a blocking position west of Lutsk. Moskalenko's anti-tank unit was one of the most powerful anti-armour formations in the Southwest Front and was also plentifully supplied with anti-tank mines. Kirponos had four other first-echelon mechanized corps in the Southwest Front, but the 4th and 8th Mechanized Corps spent the first few days of the war marching and counter-marching to no useful purpose. Rokossovsky's cadre-strength 9th Mechanized Corps was beginning a 200km march to Lutsk, but would not arrive for a few days. The 16th Mechanized Corps was even further away from the border. In short, although Kirponos had an overall 6–1 numerical superiority in tanks over von Kleist's Panzergruppe 1, the piecemeal arrival of Soviet armour on the battlefield meant that the Red Army's advantage was whittled down to a 2–1 local superiority, which was adequate for defense but not attack. Nevertheless, an order from the Stavka, signed by Georgy Zhukov, was received at Kirponos' command post at 2300 hours on 22 June, directing Kirponos to counterattack with five mechanized corps within less than forty-eight hours.

On 23 June, von Kleist's armour advanced eastward, with Kühn's spearhead in the north and Crüwell's spearhead in the south. They were advancing along very narrow frontages and not mutually supporting, as they were separated by a distance of over 50km. Under these circumstances, the Red Army should have been able to inflict heavy losses on these vanguard units. During the morning, the 13.Panzer-Division reinforced the 14.Panzer-Division across the Western Bug and, together with infantry from 6.Armee, they began to mop up the remaining Soviet border defenses. Crüwell's 11.Panzer-Division advanced to Radekhov with Kampfgruppe Riebel (Oberstleutnant Gustav-Adolf Riebel's Panzer-Regiment 15 and the Luftwaffe I/Flak Regiment General Göring, with twelve 8.8cm flak guns) and Kampfgruppe Angern (Oberst Günther von Angern's 11 Schutzen Brigade and the 119.Artillerie-Regiment).[19] Part of the Soviet 20th Tank Regiment, from General-major Sergei I. Ogurtsov's 10th Tank Division, was in the town, but they were apparently caught by surprise and hurriedly

abandoned Radekhov, along with twenty BT-7 and six T-34 tanks. After securing
the town, Riebel sent a tank platoon from Oberleutnant Edel Zachariae-
Lingenthal's 5./Panzer-Regiment 15 forward to reconnoiter to the south and this
platoon spotted a group of Soviet tanks in column approaching Radekhov from
the southwest along a road. The German tanks quickly occupied hull-down
ambush positions and waited until the Soviets – which were T-34 medium tanks
– were within 100 meters. Then the five Pz.IIIs opened fire with 3.7cm and 5cm
Panzergranate AP rounds.

> Even though at this short distance every shot was a hit, the Russians drove on
> without much visible effect ... Despite repeated hits, our fire had no effect.
> It appears as if shells are simply bouncing off. The enemy tanks disengaged
> without fighting and retreated.[20]

This Soviet probe merely alerted Riebel to the presence of an impending
Soviet armoured counterattack and he promptly deployed the I and II/Panzer-
Regiment 15 in a linear defense just west of Radekhov, with the Luftwaffe 8.8cm
flak guns in the center and Kampfgruppe Angern's artillery behind him.[21] Soon
thereafter, Ogurtsov conducted a sloppy, unsupported attack with just two tank
and two motorized infantry battalions across open terrain in broad daylight.
He refused to wait for reconnaissance to spot the German positions or his own
artillery to deploy, so his forces went into battle blind. Tank–infantry cooperation was virtually non-existent. The 100-odd Soviet tanks attacked in several
waves; first the light BT-7 and BA-10/20 armoured cars, then the medium T-28
and T-34 and finally the KV-1 heavy tanks. The German tankers opened fire at
about 400 meters and easily put paid to the first wave of Soviet light tanks, but the
T-34s began engaging the German tanks from 800–1,000 meters and knocked
out three Pz.III and two Pz.IV tanks. The 5cm KwK 39 L/42 was completely
ineffective at that range, but in desperation Oberleutnant Zachariae-Lingenthal
ordered his Pz.IVs to fire 7.5cm Sprenggranate 34 (HE) rounds at the T-34s.
Since the T-34s had been committed straight after a long approach march, they
were still carrying reserve fuel drums on their back decks, which could be set
alight by shell fragments. A lucky hit or two convinced the Soviets to pull back.[22]
Despite the near invulnerability of their armour to German 3.7cm and 5cm guns,
a number of T-34s and KV-1s were immobilized by hits on their tracks and then
abandoned by their crews. After suffering nearly 50 per cent losses, Ogurtsov
broke off his amateurish attack. The Soviet 10th Tank Division lost forty-six
tanks in their first battle with 11.Panzer-Division, but knocked out five German
tanks and several anti-tank guns.[23] After the action, Zachariae-Lingenthal
inspected some of the abandoned T-34 tanks, alarmed by its superior firepower
and armoured protection and later wrote, 'this was a shocking recognition to the
German panzer and panzerjäger units and our knees were weak for a time.'[24]
Meanwhile, Kirponos tried vainly to bring up more of his mechanized corps in
order to comply with the Stavka-directed counteroffensive on the morning of
24 June, but only the 15th and 22nd Mechanized Corps were in any position to
do anything. Von Kleist was gradually feeding more armour into the battle as the

Soviet border defenses were eliminated, but he initially held back the 9.Panzer-Division and his four motorized infantry divisions. This was an important command decision – throughout the Battle of Dubno, the Germans maintained strong mobile reserves, while Kirponos committed each formation as it arrived with nothing left in reserve to deal with enemy breakthroughs. Due to poor Soviet radio security at the division level and below, the German 3rd Radio Intercept Company was able to detect Soviet armour units moving toward the border. Although army and higher-level units used good encryption on their radio nets, the tank regiments and divisions employed simpler ciphers that the Germans could break and often failed to change frequencies and call signs for days after compromise. Soviet tank units also had a bad habit of calling for fuel supplies just before launching an attack, which provided German intelligence officers with a valuable indicator.[25] Thus poor Soviet radio procedures in tank units handed another advantage to the German panzer divisions.

Not surprisingly, no grand Soviet counteroffensive materialized on the morning of 24 June, since neither the 15th nor 22nd Mechanized Corps were ready to attack. Instead, Kühn's 14.Panzer-Division attacked eastward toward Lutsk at 0800 hours, supported by bombers from Fliegerkorps V. Kühn's panzers brusquely pushed aside a Soviet rifle division blocking the road to Lutsk, but then ran straight into Moskalenko's 1st Anti-tank Brigade west of Lutsk. Moskalenko's unit was caught with its guns still limbered in column, enabling the panzers to shoot up his lead battalion, but once the rest of his unit deployed on line, the German tanks were vulnerable in the open. The Soviet anti-tank gunners were easily capable of penetrating the Pz.III and Pz.IV tanks at 1,000 meters or more, and it was only the lack of supporting infantry or tanks that prevented Moskalenko from giving 14.Panzer-Division a very bloody nose. As it was, both sides suffered significant losses in this first major duel between panzers and Soviet anti-tank guns. It was not until 1400 hours that the 22nd Mechanized Corps was finally ready to attack, and then only with part of the 19th Tank Division. Bravely charging, a battalion of forty-five T-26 light tanks struck the left flank of the 14.Panzer-Division near Voinitsa and briefly regained some ground. However, the Germans were merely withdrawing to regroup and at 1800 hours they struck back with a combined-arms attack that shattered the 19th Tank Division. Not only were most of the division's light tanks lost, but the division commander was wounded and all three regimental commanders were killed or captured, as well as the artillery commander. The remnants of the Soviet division fell back in disorder toward Lutsk, along with Moskalenko's anti-tank brigade. During the retreat, Kondrusev was killed by German artillery fire, leaving the 22nd Mechanized Corps leaderless.

Nor had Karpezo's 15th Mechanized Corps been able to stop Crüwell's 11.Panzer-Division, which bypassed Soviet blocking positions east of Radekhov and advanced 55km to the outskirts of Dubno. Karpezo seemed to think that his mission was to defend Brody, and was content to sit almost immobile as Crüwell's division marched past him. Indeed, Crüwell took considerable liberty with Karpezo, leaving his right flank dangerously exposed – but nothing happened.

German panzer commanders were trained to accept risk and ignore their flanks, and in 1941 this often paid handsome dividends. Generaloberst Hans-Valentin Hube's 16.Panzer-Division followed in Crüwell's path, as well as two infantry divisions, to exploit the breakthrough. Zhukov, who had arrived as Stavka representative at Kirponos' command post at Tarnopol, ordered him to launch a counteroffensive into the flank of 11.Panzer-Division by 0700 hours on 25 June, even though this would be another piecemeal attack. While the German panzer corps commanders used radio to direct and maneuver their panzer-divisions in coordinated fashion, the Soviet mechanized corps operated with little or no coordination with other friendly formations at this point. Lack of C2-driven coordination prevented Kirponos from effectively massing his armour on the battlefield.

While the main armoured battle was developing around Dubno, Kirponos' strongest armoured formation – General-major Andrey Vlasov's 4th Mechanized Corps – was senselessly committed by the 6th Army commander to local counterattacks against the German 17.Armee approaching L'vov. Vlasov's counterattack did not go well, as his armour was also committed piecemeal and without artillery support. Polkovnik Petr S. Fotchenkov's 8th Tank Division lost nineteen of its 140 T-34s and the 32nd Tank Division lost sixteen tanks on 24–25 June fighting German infantry units. Vlasov did not report these heavy losses to Kirponos, but did claim the destruction of thirty-seven enemy tanks, even though no German armour was in this sector. Even worse, the tanks of the 4th Mechanized Corps were marched hither and yon by the 6th Army, which wanted tanks everywhere at once, but the result was that hundreds of tanks fell out due to mechanical defects.

25 June was a very good day for Panzergruppe 1. Generaloberst Eberhard von Mackensen had both 13 and 14.Panzer-Divisionen advancing toward Lutsk, and together they were strong enough to force Moskalenko's anti-tank brigade to withdraw. By the afternoon, German tanks from 13.Panzer-Division seized a bridgehead over the Styr River and occupied Lutsk.[26] The Soviet 9th and 19th Mechanized Corps, approaching from the east, were too late to save the city. Karpezo continued to sit immobile, ignoring Zhukov's attack order, and allowed Crüwell's 11.Panzer-Division to fight its way into Dubno by 1400 hours. Soviet infantry attempted to form a defensive line behind the Ik'va River, but Crüwell's fast-moving kampfgruppen defeated this effort. The easy capture of both Lutsk and Dubno effectively drove a wedge between the Soviet 5th and 6th Armies, making efforts to coordinate joint actions even more difficult. The only positive aspect of the day for the Soviets was that the 9th and 19th Mechanized Corps were assembling near Rovno and the 8th Mechanized Corps had arrived to reinforce Karpezo at Brody. On a map, it appeared to Zhukov that the Red Army could mount a powerful armoured pincer counterattack to cut off the vanguard of Panzergruppe 1 at Dubno.

However, Zhukov's efforts to jump-start a counteroffensive were no more successful on 26 June and only resulted in further diminishing Kirponos' armour. General-major Konstantin K. Rokossovsky established a fairly strong blocking position due east of Lutsk, which prevented either the 13 or 14.Panzer-

Divisionen from advancing directly on Rovno, but recognizing that his 100-odd light tanks stood no chance against Mackensen's III Armeekorps (mot.), he opted to make only a demonstration to comply with the letter of Zhukov's order and then shifted to the defense. General-major Nikolai V. Feklenko was less circumspect and obediently launched an attack with his 19th Mechanized Corps against 11.Panzer-Division at Dubno around 1400 hours. Feklenko attacked with about 200 tanks, but only two KV-1 and two T-34; the rest were either T-26 or T-37 scout tanks armed only with machine-guns. Crüwell easily repulsed Feklenko's counterattack and both KV-1 tanks were lost. Adding insult to injury, Crüwell boldly pushed his motorcycle battalion, Kradschützen-Bataillon 61, 30km eastward to the outskirts of Ostrog.[27]

On the southern side of the bulge produced by Panzergruppe 1's advance, Karpezo's 15th Mechanized Corps was joined by General-leytenant Dmitri I. Ryabyshev's 8th Mechanized Corps, which had just completed a 600km road march to the front. Ryabyshev's corps had lost almost half its tanks due to mechanical breakdown, including forty-four out of forty-eight T-35 heavy tanks. Ryabyshev's corps conducted a forward passage of lines early on 26 June, passing through Karpezo's disorganized corps. Karpezo opted to remain on the defensive, allowing Ryabyshev to make the main effort in assaulting the right flank of General der Panzertruppen Werner Kempf's XXXXVIII Armeekorps (mot.) between Leshnev and Kozyn. Ryabyshev began a premature attack with General-major Timofei A. Mishanin's 12th Tank Division at 0900 hours, but the rest of his corps could not be committed until the afternoon. Ryabyshev intended to capture the village of Leshnev, then push on to seize Berestichko, which would isolate the 11.Panzer-Division at Dubno. Ryabyshev was confident that Mishanin's division, which had a company of KV-1 tanks and a full battalion of T-34 tanks, could accomplish this mission.

Unfortunately, Mishanin's armour was committed nearly straight off the line of march, with no time to reconnoitre the unfamiliar terrain or for his artillery and engineers to arrive. Consequently, Mishanin conducted a nearly pure-armour attack with his two tank regiments, but only minimal infantry support. The tanks immediately encountered very marshy terrain along the Syten'ka River, which was little more than a stream, but the Soviet tank crews lacked the skill to negotiate even this minor obstacle. Three T-34 tanks were stuck in the marshy terrain and Mishanin was forced to look for an alternate crossing in full sight of the German troops from the 57.Infanterie-Division in Lishnev. As the Soviet tanks bunched up around the river, the Germans called for artillery fire, which pounded the massed armour. Eventually, Mishanin was able to get his tanks across the marshy terrain and assault into Leshnev. The German panzerjäger were overwhelmed by the T-34 and KV-1 tanks and a number of Pak guns were crushed under their tracks. The German infantry abandoned Leshnev and fell back. However, before Mishanin could consolidate on the objective, an armoured kampfgruppe from Hube's 16.Panzer-Division attempted to retake Leshnev. While the Pz.III and Pz.IV tanks were seriously out-gunned by the T-34 and

KV-1 tanks, the German panzers enjoyed artillery and air support, as well as better C2, which evened the odds considerably. German gunners concentrated on hitting the tracks on the bigger Soviet tanks and succeeded in immobilizing some of the T-34s. Eventually, the German panzers broke off the action and retreated. Mishanin had twenty-five tanks stuck in the marshes or knocked out around Leshnev and was in no position to continue the attack with his unsupported armour. Instead, he sent a company of KV-1 tanks forward to sever the Berestichko-Dublin road and to shoot up some of the German wheeled traffic along this route. Ryabyshev's other two divisions, the 34th Tank and 7th Mechanized, only got into the fight late in the day and achieved little or nothing.

Amazingly, one of the most powerful Soviet armoured units of June 1941 had failed to inflict significant damage on a single German infantry division. The Red Army's failure to use combined arms tactics – which was mostly due to impatience in the higher command – almost completely negated the superior capabilities of the T-34 and KV tanks. By the end of 26 June, it appeared that Ryabyshev and Karpezo were still in an excellent position to smash in von Kleist's right flank on the next day, but the Germans had their own surprise in store. German reconnaissance aircraft had been observing the mass of Soviet armour around Brody all day and they had spotted the GAZ-AAA radio trucks belonging to both the 8th and 15th Mechanized Corps command posts. Around 1800 hours, several groups of low-flying Ju-88 bombers from Fliegerkorps V came in and bombed both command posts. Karpezo was badly wounded but Ryabyshev survived, minus his radio truck, which was left burning. This one air strike – which was a result of poor operational security in the Red Army – seriously degraded Soviet C2 in the armoured battles around Dubno. On top of these difficulties, the Stavka reiterated its order at 2100 hours that Kirponos would continue attacking with all armoured forces and forbid even tactical retreats to prevent encirclements.

Despite Kirponos' intent to launch a pincer attack from Rovno and Brody to encircle the German forces in Dubno, the lack of coordination between the mechanized corps and other Red Army units resulted in a series of piecemeal battles throughout 27 June. The pincer from Rovno collapsed as Feklenko's and Rokossovsky's understrength corps dashed themselves to pieces against 14.Panzer-Division and two supporting infantry divisions. Von Kleist's panzers now had the benefit of infantry support, which had caught up with them, greatly increasing the staying power of the frontline units. Once the Soviet armour from the 9th and 19th Mechanized Corps was spent, the Germans committed their armour: both 13 and 14.Panzer-Divisionen attacked, threatening to envelop the remnants of Feklenko's and Rokossovsky's corps. Meanwhile, Crüwell's 11.Panzer-Division blasted its way through a thin blocking force of Soviet infantry and captured Ostrog. A counterattack by fifteen BT-7 light tanks against Panzer-Regiment 15 in Ostrog failed to budge the Germans. Kirponos was forced to cobble together Task Force Kukin, a small mechanized formation, to block Crüwell from pushing even further east.

In spite of the myriad problems afflicting the Red Army's armour units at the outset of the war, Ryabyshev's 8th Mechanized Corps came close to achieving a real success southwest of Dubno on 27 June. Assembling Mishanin's 12th Tank Division, Polkovnik Ivan V. Vasil'ev's 34th Tank Division and Colonel Aleksandr G. Gerasimov's 7th Motorized Division north of Brody, Ryabyshev was able to mount a fairly organized attack that managed to envelop and isolate the 11 and 16.Panzer-Divisionen, as well as part of the 75.Infanterie-Division, by midday on 27 June. A number of Soviet tanks were lost crossing the marshy terrain, but a mobile group with about 200 tanks succeeded in fighting its way to the outskirts of Dubno. Mishanin was wounded in the attack and Soviet losses were heavy, but the situation for Kempf's XXXXVIII Armeekorps (mot.) was equally desperate. By the end of the day, German and Soviet armour units were thoroughly inter-mixed southwest of Dubno and there was no distinct front line.

Although Zhukov abruptly returned to Moscow, he continued to hound Kirponos by teletype messages to continue the counter-offensive against von Kleist's Panzergruppe 1. Kirponos, intimidated by his commissars, complied and thereby sentenced much of the remainder of his armour to annihilation. Rokossovsky managed to scrape together a battle group with about fifty T-26 and BT light tanks, a handful of KV-2 heavy tanks and some infantry, which he used to attack into the northern flank of Panzergruppe 1's bulge on the morning of 28 June. However, by this point the infantry from 6.Armee had arrived in force to bolster von Kleist's exposed flanks and the panzerjägers from 299.Infanterie-Division stopped Rokossovsky's attack cold. Polkovnik Mikhail E. Katukov led his thirty-three BT-2 and BT-5 light tanks into battle and lost all of them.[28] As usual, Soviet armoured attacks went in with little or no reconnaissance support and negligible artillery support. Massed artillery, anti-tank fire and flak destroyed most of the Soviet armour, although a single damaged KV-2 limped away. Once the Soviet attack was spent, Generaloberst von Mackensen deftly coordinated the 13 and 14.Panzer-Divisionen into an all-out attack that smashed in the flanks of the Soviet 9th and 19th Mechanized Corps. The fragments of seven Soviet tank and motorized infantry divisions were routed and fled back behind the Goryn River. Feklenko abandoned Rovno, which was quickly occupied by the 13.Panzer-Division.

While disaster was striking the northern group of Soviet armour, Ryabyshev's 8th Mechanized Corps found itself being encircled. This was the first instance in the war in the East of Soviet armour achieving a significant penetration of German lines, and Ryabyshev set a precedent that would occur again and again over the next two years. First, no follow-on forces were available to support the breakthrough; the nearly leaderless 15th Mechanized Corps mounted only a demonstration attack against the infantry of the German XXXXIV Armeekorps which provided no help to Ryabyshev. Second, the Germans reacted quickly to sever the narrow penetration corridor used by the attacking Soviet armour, isolating the bulk of the 12th and 34th Tank Divisions in a *kessel* just west of Dubno. Third, morale and C2 within the trapped forces quickly disintegrated, resulting in rapid loss of any unit cohesion. The German 75.Infanterie-Division played a vital role in isolating the bulk of Ryabyshev's forces, which speaks volumes about the Soviet lack of battlefield situational awareness at this point. A foot-marching infantry unit could envelope fully motorized units. Once Ryabyshev's armour was encircled, Hube's 16.Panzer-Division began a series of attacks that quickly reduced the *kessel*. German heavy artillery and flak was brought up to finish off the trapped Soviet T-34 and KV-1 tanks, which were now low on fuel and ammunition; twenty-two tanks were knocked out. Ryabyshev, who was outside the *kessel*, personally led the 7th Motorized Infantry Division in an effort to break through to his two trapped tank divisions, but failed after crippling losses. By the end of 28 June, Ryabyshev's corps had been neutralized and von Kleist's Panzergruppe 1 had driven a deep wedge into the boundary of the Soviet 5th and 6th Armies. In just six days of battle, four of Kirponos' mechanized corps had been defeated and the remainder had been seriously reduced.

For the first six days of the battle, while Kirponos was grinding up his own armoured forces in piecemeal battles, von Kleist held back the 9.Panzer-Division and his four motorized divisions. Once the best Soviet armoured formations were spent, von Kleist began to commit his second-echelon motorized forces on 28–29 June. The 9.Panzer-Division attacked unexpectedly into the flank of the Soviet 6th Army north of L'vov and quickly broke through its infantry. The 16 and 25.Infanterie-Division (mot.) used their superior mobility to quickly reinforce the flanks of Panzergruppe 1 at Berestichko and Rovno, which enabled the panzer divisions to resume their attacks eastward. Von Mackensen's III Armeekorps (mot.) sliced into the fragments of Rokossovsky's forces and pushed them back. After heavy fighting with Hube's 16.Panzer-Division southwest of Dubno, Ryabyshev retreated with the remnants of his corps, reduced to 35 per cent of their initial tank strength, four infantry battalions and four batteries of artillery. The rest of his corps, roughly 10,000 troops and 200 tanks, were left in the *kessel* outside Dubno. With the Southwest Front's forces in retreat or faced with encirclement, the Stavka finally ordered Kirponos to withdraw to the Stalin Line on the old border.

In the final actions near Dubno, the trapped tankers of the 34th Tank Division took advantage of fog along the Ik'va to stage a breakout operation on the night of 30 June, which succeeded in saving some troops, but not much equipment. In a confused night action – rare on the Eastern Front – the Soviets massed their remaining tanks and punched through Hube's cordon. The Germans massed artillery, flak guns and tanks to destroy the fleeing Soviets, but some German troops panicked when T-34 and KV heavy tanks appeared out of the mist and overran their positions. Corps Commissar Nikolai Popel, leading the breakout, later wrote:

> One of our T-34s flared up like a torch, darting around a field. Over a dozen Pz.IVs ganged up at the same time on a KV-1. We were shooting German vehicles pointblank. When ammunition ran out, we rammed them ... Sytnik's KV-1 [Major A. P. Sytnik, commander 67th Tank Regiment], in the heat of battle, rushed ahead of the others. [He] rammed several Pz.IIIs. His

vehicle became a pile of shapeless metal. He began retreating with his crew deeper into the thickets.[29]

By 1 July, the Southwest Front was in full retreat and Panzergruppe 1 had achieved its initial objectives. The tank battles fought between Panzergruppe 1 and elements of seven Soviet mechanized corps around Lutsk–Rovno–Dubno–Brody in the first week of Barbarossa were the largest tank battles to date, involving over 600 German and 3,800 Soviet tanks. While it is true that von Kleist failed to encircle and destroy any Soviet mechanized corps, as occurred in the battle of the Bialystok-Minsk *kessel*, the 8th, 15th and 19th Mechanized Corps were badly mauled and three other mechanized corps lost at least half their strength. Approximately two-thirds of the Soviet armour, or 2,500 tanks, were lost in the battle between 22–30 June 1941; the majority of losses were caused by non-combat factors, including mechanical failure and lack of driver training. The technical superiority of the Soviet KV-1 and T-34 tanks counted for very little in the Battle of Dubno due to untrained crews and inept tactics. The Stavka's insistence on launching a premature counteroffensive resulted in the best Red Army armoured units being thrown into battle piecemeal, where they were chopped to ribbons by veteran panzer units. In addition to material losses, losses of senior armoured leaders included two of six mechanized corps commanders, six of eighteen division commanders and ten of thirty tank regiment commanders. The surviving formations were reduced to division-size battle groups with little artillery or support services left after the retreat to the Stalin Line. The one bright spot for the Red Army in the Ukraine was that second-echelon armoured units near Kiev and the 2nd and 18th Mechanized Corps, deployed with the Southern Front near Odessa, were too distant to be significantly affected by the initial German Blitzkrieg; these formations would greatly assist Kirponos in slowing Heeresgruppe Süd's advance upon Kiev in July–August.

In contrast to the damage suffered by Kirponos' first-echelon armour, the German panzer units in Panzergruppe 1 suffered very light losses in the first week of combat; no senior panzer leaders were casualties and total personnel losses were around 5 per cent or less. Excluding Pz.I and command tanks, no more than twenty-five tanks in Panzergruppe 1 were totally destroyed by 30 June, with about another 100 damaged or down for mechanical defects, but all five panzer-divisions were still fully combat-capable. German leadership, from von Kleist, to von Mackensen and Kempf at corps level, to Crüwell and Hube at division level, had demonstrated great flexibility and aggressiveness. Even when briefly isolated, the panzer divisions retained their cohesiveness and fought their way out of trouble. To be sure, the Pz.III tanks armed with the 3.7cm KwK 36 L/46 cannon had proven to be a liability in combat against Soviet tanks, but the German skill at combined arms warfare and air-ground coordination had carried the day against Soviet numerical superiority and technical advantages. As Heeresgruppe Süd continued its advance to the Stalin Line in early July 1941, von Kleist was still outnumbered but his forces were better handled and, thus, capable of achieving decisive local superiorities.

An Assessment of the June 1941 Border Battles

The last nine days of June 1941 had cost the Red Army about 25–30 per cent of its pre-war armour and, across the board, the mechanized corps had fared very poorly against the more experienced and better-trained panzer-divisions. Even worse, most of the available T-34 and KV heavy tanks were lost in the initial debacles and it would take months to replace these losses. Yet many second-echelon Soviet armoured formations in the interior of the USSR remained intact, and the Stavka began to move them forward as rapidly as possible to meet the panzer divisions head on. While the second-echelon mechanized corps were equipped mostly with light tanks, they were at least given the chance to properly fuel and arm their vehicles. Given that the best Red Army tank units had only turned in a mediocre performance against German infantry, it would have been wiser to avoid tank-on-tank battles until the playing field was more even, but Stalin was only concerned with results, not losses.

Operation Barbarossa consisted of offensive 'pulses', dictated by the ability of the panzer divisions to attack for a week or two, gain some ground, encircle some Soviet formations, then wait for resupply and their own infantry to catch up. Although it has become fashionable for some modern writers to insist that Barbarossa had clearly failed by either July or August because the Red Army was still undefeated, that is not how either side saw it at any point before the winter of 1941–42. As every professional soldier knows, no plan survives contact with the enemy and even Hitler and the OKH recognized that a quick, cheap victory over Russia was not in the cards after mid-July. However, Hitler believed that the Wehrmacht was accomplishing his intended objective – smashing the Red Army – even if not according to schedule. Throughout the summer and autumn of 1941, German forces held the strategic and operational initiative, with the Soviets only managing to mount counterattacks in between German offensive pulses.

The four German Panzergruppen suffered about 10,000 casualties and lost 106 tanks (including thirty-three Pz.38(t), forty-four Pz.III and fifteen Pz.IV) '*totalausfall*' in the first eight days of the invasion, but given the scale of destruction they were inflicting on the Red Army, these losses did not seem excessive. About another 200 tanks were damaged or down for repairs, meaning that most panzer divisions still had 100 or more operational tanks in early July. While it is true that operational tank strength in some divisions dropped as low as 30–35 per cent during the summer, the strength of most panzer divisions hovered at around 80–100 operational tanks until cold weather arrived. In contrast, Soviet armour was rapidly disappearing from all but critical sectors on the battlefield.

The first week in Russia revealed that German operational-level efficiency was far more at risk from logistical inadequacies than combat losses. German units quickly discovered that the poor condition of Russian roads greatly increased fuel consumption; one V.S. of fuel would suffice for only 70km of movement instead of 100km. Losses of trucks in panzer units due to a combination of enemy action, accidents and inadequate maintenance quickly resulted in heavy losses of supply vehicles, which put even greater strain on division and corps-level logistics. The

Wehrmacht was still essentially tied to the railheads for long-haul, bulk logistic shipments such as fuel (9,000 tons per day), ammunition and spare parts, but the Eisenbahntruppen could only repair and regauge the Soviet broad-gauge tracks at a slow rate.[30] Even once repaired, the railroads were only delivering half of the army's supply needs and fuel and ammunition were in short supply throughout most of the summer fighting. As the Panzergruppen advanced eastward, they quickly moved far beyond practical resupply range and were often forced to call upon the Luftwaffe for emergency resupply. Yet while aerial resupply could suffice in an emergency, it could never really take the place of ground resupply columns. Typically, a single Ju-52 could carry just 1,600 liters of fuel, sufficient to refuel a platoon of five Pz.III tanks. In order to refuel an armoured kampf-gruppe, the Luftwaffe would have to conduct about twenty-five Ju-52 sorties, and that does not include additional sorties required for food, ammunition and other supplies. Unless the Wehrmacht could improve its logistic capabilities – which was doubtful – the Panzergruppen would become increasingly depleted as they advanced further eastward.

Stopping Höpner's Advance on Leningrad, July–September 1941

Once Höpner got across the Dvina River in strength with Reinhardt's XXXXI Armeekorps (mot.) and von Manstein's LVI Armeekorps (mot.), there was nothing that the retreating Northwest Front could do to prevent the German panzers from racing across the Latvian countryside in the first days of July 1941. General-major Aleksei V. Kurkin's 3rd Mechanized Corps had virtually ceased to exist and the 12th Mechanized Corps had suffered 80 per cent losses, including its commander. General-major Dmitri D. Lelyushenko's 21st Mechanized Corps gamely conducted a fighting retreat from Daugavpils and tried to make a stand against von Manstein's SS *Totenkopf* Division at Rezekne, but was wrecked in the process. By the time he reached the Russian border near Ostrov, Lelyushenko had seven tanks and 3,000 troops left. All told, the Northwest Front had fewer than 100 tanks remaining, mostly T-26, to defend the approaches to Leningrad against Höpner's Panzergruppe 4, which had at least 300 operational tanks.

The Soviet general staff had not anticipated a direct threat to Leningrad from the southwest and the only remaining armour in the area belonged to General-leytenant Markian M. Popov's Northern Front, which was tasked with defending the city from the Finns. Popov had two armoured formations at his disposal: General-major Ivan G. Lazarev's 10th Mechanized Corps stationed around Leningrad, and General-major Mikhail L. Cherniavsky's 1st Mechanized Corps stationed near Pskov. Lazarev's corps was essentially a training command with some 450 light tanks and it was tasked to operate in Karelia against the Finns. By the time the Finns declared war on 25 June, the entire 10th Mechanized Corps was deployed on the Finnish front. Popov was more concerned about the Finns than the Germans and, just prior to the German invasion, he had ordered the 1st Mechanized Corps to transfer its 1st Tank Division by rail to the Soviet 14th Army at Kandalaksha, near the northern Finnish border. On the first day of the war, Popov decided to move the rest of Cherniavsky's 1st Mechanized Corps from Pskov back to Pushkin, where it could provide additional support against the Finns. Although Cherniavsky had no T-34 or KV tanks, he did have two full-strength mechanized divisions with a total of 550 tanks. If his corps had remained at Pskov, they would have been in an excellent position to block Höpner's panzers; instead, the 1st Mechanized Corps was moved away from the approaching German forces.

The march of Cherniavsky's 1st Mechanized Corps from Pskov toward Leningrad on 22–24 June was indicative of the dysfunctional nature of Soviet armoured operations at the start of the war, even when conducted without enemy resistance. Despite the lack of harassment from the Luftwaffe and the relatively good roads leading to Leningrad, the 1st Mechanized Corps road march was a debacle. Large numbers of tanks fell out from mechanical defects and traffic control was non-existent. No repair or recovery assets were attached to the convoys to deal with broken-down vehicles, which were simply abandoned at the roadside. A number of regimental, battalion and company commanders regarded the move to Pskov as an administrative rather than tactical movement and travelled separately from their troops. Left poorly supervised, Soviet tankers were undisciplined and left the march columns without permission. After two days on the road, the corps had barely moved 100km and was so thoroughly scattered that Popov ordered Cherniavsky to reassemble his corps at Krasnogvardeysk (Gatchina). Once there, Popov began to detach individual battalions and then the 163rd Motorized Division from the 21st Mechanized Corps, in order to support his operations against the Finns.

However, by late June it was obvious that the Northwestern Front had been defeated in Lithuania and that German panzer forces were racing across Latvia. On 29 June, Zhukov personally intervened by transferring the 1st Mechanized Corps from Popov's command to the Northwestern Front, and Cherniavsky was ordered to force-march back to Ostrov. Zhukov also wanted the 1st Tank Division returned from the Finnish front, but Popov managed to delay this for nearly three weeks. Instead, Cherniavsky marched to Ostrov to confront Höpner with the 3rd Tank Division, the only major unit still under his command. Once again, an administrative road march was plagued with difficulties and after five days Cherniavsky's armour was still about 60km from Ostrov. During this time, Kuznetsov was relieved of command on 3 July and General-major Petr P. Sobennikov took over command of the Northwestern Front.

While Cherniavsky was crawling toward Ostrov, Reinhardt's XXXXI Armeekorps (mot.) was racing toward the Russian border. Generalleutnant Friedrich Kirchner's 1.Panzer-Division easily penetrated through the Stalin Line fortifications on the border and Kampfgruppe Krüger fought its way into Ostrov late on 4 July. Krüger's troops even managed to capture the bridges in the city over the Velikaya River intact. Höpner's advance upon Ostrov was aided by the ability of Heeresgruppe Nord's quartermasters to move fuel and ammunition forward rapidly.

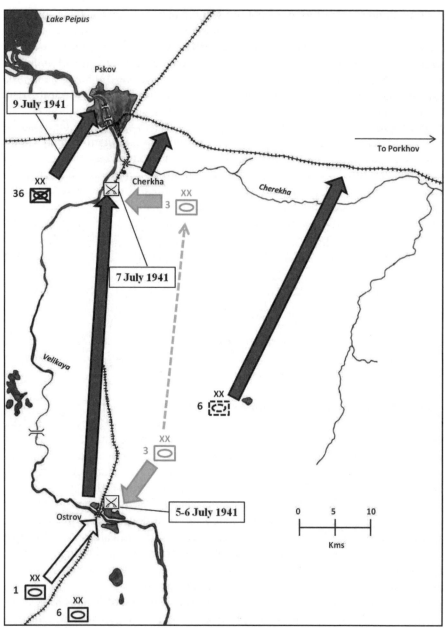

Cherniavsky's 1st Mechanized Corps versus Reinhardt's XXXXI Armeekorps (mot.); Soviet
3rd Tank Division counterattack against 1.Panzer-Division at Ostrov, 5–6 July and delay back to
Pskov, 7–9 July.

When Sobennikov learned that Ostrov had fallen, he ordered Cherniavsky to force-march his armour to the city and, in conjunction with the 41st Rifle Corps, attack early on 5 July. To reinforce the attack, Cherniavsky was provided with ten new KV heavy tanks straight from the factory in Leningrad and was promised air support.

After marching all night, Cherniavsky was able to begin his counterattack against 1.Panzer-Division in Ostrov at 0530 hours on 5 July. The Germans were dismayed by the appearance of more KV heavy tanks and 1./Panzerjäger-Abteilung 37 was overrun. German Pak guns and vehicles were crushed under the tracks of the KV tanks. Spearheaded by the KV tanks, one Soviet tank company managed to fight its way into Ostrov and nearly recaptured the bridge. Yet Cherniavsky was only able to get three tank battalions, with no substantial infantry or artillery support, into the battle and the German combined-arms kampf-gruppen displayed enormous resilience. A battery of 10cm s.K 18 howitzers engaged the KVs directly with Pzgr Rot (AP) ammunition and managed to knock out a KV-2 and several other tanks.[31] Cherniavsky pulled his armour back to wait for support units to arrive and he recommenced his attack with armour and two infantry regiments at 1525 hours after a thirty-minute artillery preparation. Although better prepared, this attack failed when the lead elements of the 6.Panzer-Division arrived to reinforce the German defense of Ostrov. A sudden German attack flung Cherniavsky's forces back in disorder. Altogether, Cherniavsky's corps suffered about 50 per cent losses, including eight of ten KV tanks and most of the light tanks.

Stalin got personally involved in the armoured counterattack at Ostrov and ordered Sobennikov to continue the operation no matter the cost. Cherniavsky attacked again on 6 July with his remaining forty tanks, as well as the remnants of the 21st Mechanized Corps. Reinhardt's two panzer divisions easily repulsed these feeble efforts and, by afternoon, the Soviets were in retreat. The Battle of Ostrov demonstrated that the Red Army's inability to implement combined arms warfare put their armour at a significant disadvantage in a stand-up fight against even a single panzer division.

After failing to stop Reinhardt's panzers at Ostrov, the 3rd Tank Division fought a delaying action back to Pskov, which was the first city in Russia proper that was threatened by German panzers. In an effort to stop the 6.Panzer-Division from crossing the Velikaya River and reaching the city, the 3rd Tank Division mounted a sacrificial counterattack at Cherekha at 1700 hours on 7 July with about 100 BT and T-26 light tanks. In this kind of tactical combat, the Pz.35(t) and Pz.IV tanks of Oberst Richard Koll's Panzer-Regiment 11 had the upper hand and they broke through and seized the bridge over the Velikaya intact. Prompt action by Podpolkovnik Gregory N. Pasynchuk's 5th Tank Regiment stopped Koll's tanks from exploiting the bridgehead, but Pasynchuk was captured in the scuffle at the bridge. Fighting continued for five hours, but by nightfall the 3rd Tank Division was down to about thirty-five BT tanks, while 1 and 6.Panzer-Divisionen still had a total of over 200 operational tanks remaining. On 9 July, Reinhardt's panzers fought their way into Pskov – again, this was non-doctrinal for tanks to fight into cities without substantial infantry support – and the remnants of the 3rd Tank Division retreated eastward.

While the tank battles at Ostrov and Pskov were occurring, on the Northwest Front the Soviets were frantically trying to establish a strong blocking position at Luga 140km south of Leningrad to prevent Höpner's panzers from advancing directly up the highway to Leningrad. Luftwaffe reconnaissance soon detected the Soviet concentration at Luga and Höpner decided to use Reinhardt's corps for a direct assault upon the town, while using von Manstein's LVI Armeekorps (mot.) to conduct a wide envelopment of Luga to the east. Manstein's corps had been lagging behind in the push across Latvia and did not reach Ostrov until five days after Reinhardt's panzers had captured the town. Höpner was partly at fault, having assigned von Manstein some of the worst marshy and wooded terrain to traverse, but von Manstein also made the kind of mistakes that someone who had never worked with tanks before would make – like mistaking 'no-go' terrain for 'slow-go' terrain. Generalmajor Erich Brandenberger's 8.Panzer-Division, which was von Manstein's only panzer unit, was turning in a very lackluster performance during the Russian campaign. Höpner's choice of assigning a very difficult mission to a two-division motorized corps with a commander who seemed to have lost his aggressive edge seems rather suspect, and one can only speculate about whether von Manstein's abrasive arrogance – he was not widely popular among other senior German officers – led to Höpner's command decision.

Von Manstein advanced directly toward Porkhov with 8.Panzer-Division and 3.Infanterie-Division (mot), pushing aside the wreckage of 3rd Tank Division. On 10 July he captured Porkhov and then advanced northeast toward Soltsy, with the intention of outflanking the Luga position. Reinhardt made his first probes against Luga on the same day, but the 1.Panzer-Division was repulsed. He sent 6.Panzer-Division on a flanking maneuver to the west, but their advance along forest tracks was slow and tortuous, the exact opposite of Blitzkrieg. Normally, the German instinct for envelopment over frontal attack was the correct one, but at Luga Höpner failed to recognize that he was in a race against time and that the *schwerpunkt* should have remained there, instead of trying lengthy flank marches through slow-go terrain.

On the Soviet side, the bulk of the 10th Mechanized Corps' 21st and 24th Tank Divisions had just returned by rail from Karelia and greatly stiffened this position, which was held by a rifle corps. The Soviet Northwest Front – now under the command of Marshal Kliment Voroshilov – became aware of the German outflanking efforts and realized that Reinhardt's decision to split Panzergruppe 4 into non-supporting corps offered the Red Army an ideal opportunity to defeat at least one of the German spearheads and thereby reduce the threat to Leningrad. General-leytenant Nikolai F. Vatutin, the talented and aggressive chief of staff of the Northwestern Front, recommended committing the 11th Army's reserve to encircle and destroy von Manstein's LVI Armeekorps (mot), which was furthest from any potential help. Vatutin requested and received the 21st Tank Division, as well as five rifle divisions, to establish an ambush position near Soltsy, along the forest trail that von Manstein would have to pass.

Von Manstein advanced up the sandy trail from Porkhov to Shimsk with Brandenberger's 8.Panzer-Division strung out in a long march column, with a one-tank front. Brandenberger's 8.Panzer-Division had not yet suffered significant losses and still had 163 operational tanks.[32] The Germans advanced without flank guards through the forest and the Luftwaffe failed to detect any Soviet concentrations in this area. On the morning of 15 July, Vatutin sprang his ambush, with the fresh 70th Rifle Division cutting the road behind 8.Panzer-Division's lead kampfgruppen, while another rifle division and the remaining thirty-five BT-7 tanks from 3rd Tank Division conducted a fixing attack against the 3.Infanterie-Division (mot). Von Manstein soon found that he had advanced into a linear ambush, with elements of five Soviet divisions attacking him from all directions. The next day, the 21st Tank Division attacked the flank of 8.Panzer-Division at Soltsy with 128 T-26 light tanks and a handful of KV heavy tanks against Pz.38(t) and Pz.IV tanks. Vatutin ensured that the attack was supported by Soviet bombers and artillery, although tank-infantry cooperation was still problematic. After three days of heavy fighting, the 8.Panzer-Division fought its way out of the encirclement, but was forced to abandon Soltsy and retreat all the way back to Dno. Reinhardt sent the SS-Division *Totenkopf* to assist von Manstein in breaking away, but the result was still a German tactical defeat, since they had to abandon damaged vehicles on the battlefield. The Soviets claimed to have destroyed seventy German tanks, but the actual number was twelve tanks as total losses (two Pz.II and ten Pz.38(t)) and twenty-seven damaged, although losses of wheeled vehicles were much heavier.[33] The Soviet 21st Tank Division lost fifty-four of its 128 tanks, but for once the heavy Soviet armoured losses were justified, since von Manstein's effort to outflank Luga had failed. After von Manstein extracted his corps from Vatutin's ambush, Höpner sent the shaken 8.Panzer-Division into reserve (although the division still had 124 operational tanks), leaving von Manstein with no armour.[34]

Despite the setback at Soltsy, Reinhardt succeeded in gaining a small bridgehead across the Luga at Poretsye with Kampfgruppe Raus from 6.Panzer-Division on 14 July, and then 1.Panzer-Division gained another bridgehead at Sabsk. Nearby Soviet militia units, supported by some tanks, immediately began counterattacking both bridgeheads with great ferocity. Raus, whose kampfgruppe was isolated from the rest of his division and virtually out of supply, was struck the hardest. A Russian militia company, supported by a single KV-1 heavy tank, managed to infiltrate through nearby forests and launched an attack that caught Kampfgruppe Raus by surprise:

> ... the KV-1 emerged from the forest and drove with such speed, and so close, past a well-camouflaged 10-cm gun that the crew had no opportunity to fire at it. The tank circled the church, crushing everything that appeared suspicious, including Oberst von Waldenfel's regimental headquarters. Our

Pz.35(t) were powerless – as at Raseiniai their fire had no effect on the monster. At long last, one particularly plucky NCO put an end to this critical situation. He jumped on the tank and kept firing his pistol into the driver's vision slot. The latter, wounded by bullet spatter and his vision obstructed, was compelled to turn back.[35]

Although there were far fewer T-34s and KV heavy tanks on the battlefield by mid-July 1941, the ones that did appear tended to be more dangerous since now they were fully armed and fueled, and had drivers with some experience. The Kirov plant in Leningrad was building more than forty KV tanks a week and the Northwest Front was receiving many of these. Furthermore, there were many re-called reservists with combat experience from the Russo-Finnish War and the best of these were used to form KV crews. The fact that Kampfgruppe Raus was forced to use such ad hoc desperation tactics to stop a single KV tank attack indicates the increasingly evident inadequacy of German tank and anti-tank weaponry.

After an advance of over 400km in less than three weeks, a combination of stiffening Soviet resistance, adverse terrain and supply problems brought Höpner's advance to a virtual halt. It would take almost three weeks for Reinhardt's corps to get sufficient supplies and reinforcements to break out of its Luga River bridgeheads. The stubborn Soviet defense at Luga bought Leningrad almost an additional month to prepare its defenses. After the Battle of Soltsy, both the 1st and 10th Mechanized Corps were dissolved, but part of the 1st Tank Division (minus one tank regiment and its motorized rifle regiment) was returned to Leningrad from the northern Finnish front on 17–19 July. The division remained in reserve near Krasnogvardeysk for the rest of July and into early August, receiving replacements and twelve new KV-1 tanks from the Kirov plant. By early August, the Northwest Front had about 250 operational tanks left: the 24th Tank Division at Luga (less than 100 BT-2 light tanks), a few tank detachments from the disbanded mechanized corps (about fifty–100 mixed BT and T-26) and the 1st Tank Division (sixty–eighty tanks).

Large-scale armoured warfare did not resume on the Leningrad front until 8 August. Reinhardt's XXXXI Armeekorps (mot.) began its breakout from its bridgehead near Kingisepp, while von Manstein's LVI Armeekorps (mot.) made a direct frontal assault on the Luga position. The 24th Tank Division committed individual platoons of light tanks to support the 41st Rifle Corps at Luga, but Voroshilov held most of his remaining armour back for the first few days, uncertain whether it would be needed to counterattack any German breakthroughs. In the breakthrough battle, Höpner's panzers were aided by the arrival of several German infantry divisions, but heavy fighting lasted along the Luga line for two weeks. Voroshilov began committing the 1st Tank Division in bits and pieces, but a detachment sent to aid the defense of Kingisepp was ambushed by Reinhardt's panzers and lost twenty-eight tanks on 11 August, including eleven KV heavy tanks. The Soviets claimed eleven German tanks in this action. However, the 1st Tank Division was able to make good some of its losses, including five more KV tanks and four of the new T-50 light tank (of which only sixty-nine were built).

The Luga position was gradually enveloped as Reinhardt enlarged his Kingisepp bridgehead in the west and other German forces captured Staraya Russa and Novgorod in the east. The Soviets briefly managed to divert German attention away from the main battleground by launching their own bold counter-attack at Staraya Russa, which encircled X Armeekorps on 16 August and forced Höpner to dispatch von Manstein to rescue the trapped German infantry. Meanwhile, Reinhardt's panzers finally crushed Soviet infantry around Kingisepp then pushed eastward toward Moloskovitsy, where there was a head-on clash between the 1.Panzer-Division and General-major Viktor I. Baranov's 1st Tank Division on 15 August. Baranov was one of the most experienced senior Soviet tank leaders, having commanded a tank battalion in the Spanish Civil War and then a tank brigade in the Russo-Finnish War, where he was awarded the Hero of the Soviet Union (HSU) for his role in breaking through the Mannerheim Line. However, the Battle of Moloskovitsy went badly for the Soviet tankers, who lost fifty-two of sixty-five tanks, including six KV, four T-28, thirty-two BT-7, six T-50 and four T-26, and the division was forced to retreat to Krasnogvardeysk. Baranov claimed that his tankers inflicted the loss of 103 tanks and forty-one anti-tank guns upon Reinhardt's corps, but the Germans were not seriously damaged. Once in Krasnogvardeysk, which was a strongly fortified position blocking access to Leningrad, the 1st Tank Division received additional new-built tanks and trained reservists to replace its losses. The division was reorganized into a three-battalion armoured group with a total of fifty-nine tanks. Baranov put the thirty-four-year-old Kapitan Iosif B. Spiller in command of his 1st Tank Battalion, which had twenty newly-built KV tanks. Spiller was another very experienced Soviet tanker, with prior combat experience against both the Japanese and the Finns. Contrary to the mass of English-language, German-influenced histori-ography which often depicts Soviet tankers as untrained and unskilled buffoons, the Red Army did in fact possess men who were every bit as experienced and capable as their opponents.

After the debacle at Moloskovitsy, Baranov decided to avoid large-scale battles with Höpner's panzers, since Red Army tank units were not yet ready to employ combined arms warfare. Instead, Baranov opted to use his tanks in platoon-size ambushes to disrupt and delay the German advance toward Leningrad. It took Reinhardt's panzers three days to advance 30km on the road from Kingisepp to the outskirts of Krasnogvardeysk, being engaged daily by Baranov's tankers employing 'shoot 'n scoot' ambush tactics. Höpner transferred the 8.Panzer-Division, recovered after its defeat at Soltsy, to Reinhardt's corps, where it was made the vanguard on 18 August. Spiller was tasked with defending the outskirts of Krasnogvardeysk and he deployed a platoon of five KV-1 tanks under Leytenant Zinoviy G. Kolobanov just west of the city, along the route that 8.Panzer-Division was approaching. On the morning of 19 August, Kolobanov's KV-1s, which were the '*ekranami*' model with extra 35mm-thick armour plates welded on the turret, waited hull-down in ambush.[36] Once again, the 8.Panzer-Division demonstrated a propensity for falling into enemy ambushes and a certain tactical mediocrity, as its lead kampfgruppe drove straight into the kill zone unaware. Kolobanov's five KV-1s opened fire at a range of 450 meters, engaging the lead elements of the Panzer-Aufklärungs-Abteilung 59 (reconnaissance battalion) and quickly destroyed an assortment of armoured cars, half tracks and wheeled vehicles. Panzerjäger-Abteilung 43 tried to deploy its 3.7cm and 5cm Pak into firing positions on the road, but Kolobanov easily blasted them to pieces with high explosive rounds and then hosed down the survivors with his 7.62mm coax machine-gun. The III./Panzer Regiment 10 managed to get a company or more into action, but its Pz.38(t) and Pz.IV could not defeat Kolobanov's platoon.[37] Kolobanov's tank was hit repeatedly without being knocked out, although his sights were eventually demolished and his turret jammed. He broke off the action after firing his entire basic load of ninety-eight rounds. The Soviets claimed that Kolobanov's platoon had destroyed forty-two German tanks, including twenty-two by Kolobanov himself, without a single KV-1 being lost. While Soviet kill claims were exaggerated by counting every AFV as a tank, there was little doubt that General Erich Brandenberger's 8.Panzer-Division had gotten another bloody nose. The KV had also demonstrated that it was an excellent defensive tank.[38]

Despite Baranov's efforts, the Germans managed to encircle and destroy the Luga group by 24 August. Von Manstein crushed the Soviet counterattack at Staraya Russa, inflicting heavy losses. Even worse, the OKH transferred General Rudolf Schmidt's XXXIX Armeekorps (mot.) from Heeresgruppe Mitte to Heeresgruppe Nord to reinforce the final drive on Leningrad. Schmidt's two mobile divisions, 12.Panzer-Division and 20.Infanterie-Division (mot.) quickly proved their worth by severing the main Moscow–Leningrad rail line and beginning a drive toward the vital rail-junction at Mga, to complete the isolation of Leningrad. Baranov's tankers continued to assist in repelling German panzer attacks upon Krasnogvardeysk, claiming the destruction of another thirty German tanks by the end of August, but admitted the loss of twenty-eight of their own tanks (eleven KV, four T-28, one T-34, three BT-7, nine T-26). Despite Baranov's best efforts, Höpner had a significant numerical edge in armour on the Leningrad front by late August and there were no major Red Army tank units left to stop Schmidt's steamroller advance. On 30 August, Generaloberst Josef Harpe's 12.Panzer-Division captured Mga, cutting off Leningrad's last ground link with the outside world. However, Harpe had not arrived quickly enough to prevent the machinery and thousands of workers from the Kirov plant (*Zavod 100*) from escaping through Mga by rail to Chelyabinsk, where they reestablished the KV-1 production line.[39]

After the Luga position was eliminated, Höpner and Generalfeldmarschall Wilhelm von Leeb, commander of Heeresgruppe Nord, believed that it might be possible to storm Leningrad before its defenses were fully prepared, as Harpe's 12.Panzer-Division had done at Minsk. Höpner's panzers were badly depleted and exhausted after ten weeks near-continuous fighting, but the Red Army had fewer than 100 operational tanks left defending the approaches to the city. The Soviet 42nd Army was putting up very stiff resistance at Krasnogvardeysk that stymied Reinhardt's motorized corps, but Schmidt was advancing on the east side of Leningrad against very weak opposition. Reinhardt massed the 1 and 6.Panzer-Divisionen and 36.Infanterie-Division (mot.) near Krasnogvardeysk and launched an all-out attack on 11 September that finally broke the Soviet defense near Taitsy. The remnants of Baranov's 1st Tank Division mounted a counterattack against 1.Panzer-Division near Krasnogvardeysk, including Leytenant Koloba-nov's KV-1 platoon, but could not stop the panzers. The Soviet defensive positions began to crumble, with Krasnoye Selo lost on 12 September and Krasnogvardeysk itself lost on 13 September. Baranov's tankers retreated to the last line of defense before Leningrad, the Pulkovo Heights.

While the rest of Reinhardt's forces were mopping up the Krasnogvardeysk position, a kampfgruppe from 1.Panzer-Division, consisting of II/Panzer-Regiment 1 and I/Schützen-Regiment 113, raced ahead and seized part of the Pulkovo Heights, just 7km south of Leningrad. Georgy Zhukov, who had just arrived in Leningrad to replace the incompetent Marshal Voroshilov, ordered immediate counterattacks to push the German armour back from the city. Baranov was ordered to use his last twenty-five tanks to spearhead the counter-attack, which would be supported by several battalions of militia. Kapitan Spiller, still in command of the 1st Tank Battalion, had three KV-1s and five KV-2s, but the rest of the armour consisted of light tanks. The Soviet tanks attacked around 1500 hours, with Spiller's KVs in front, lumbering out of the city and slowly climbing the heights south of the city. The German panzerjägers tried to break up the attack, but by this point they knew that their puny 3.7cm and 5cm anti-tank guns could do little to stop the KV heavy tanks. KV tanks began crushing the Pak guns under their tracks and destroying their prime movers. German infantry, witnessing the defeat of their anti-tank troops, began to pull back. Several Pz.III tanks from Panzer-Regiment I tried to intervene but were knocked out by 76.2mm fire. Eventually, the counterattack culminated in a number of Soviet tanks being immobilized by damage, but 1.Panzer-Division was forced to pull back. Afterwards, Zhukov deftly shifted the few remaining KV tanks around the shrinking Leningrad perimeter, to contest German advances on the east and west sides of the city. Zhukov also used naval gunfire from the Baltic Sea fleet to support small-scale counterattacks, which impressed the Germans.

By late September, Höpner knew that his panzers had great difficulty dealing with dug-in Soviet heavy tanks and that he lacked the firepower to fight his way into Leningrad. However, with Leningrad now surrounded, von Leeb and Höpner did not see the need to incur heavy losses in direct assault, preferring to let starvation win the battle for them. Höpner's Panzergruppe was no longer combat-ready, with most of its tanks damaged or worn out, its personnel ranks thinned by losses and the survivors exhausted. With the Leningrad campaign seemingly won, it was time to pull back the panzers in order to regroup and let the infantrymen and artillerymen of Heeresgruppe Nord handle the siege. In anticipation of the up-coming Operation Typhoon against Moscow, Höpner's

Panzergruppe 4 was transferred to Heeresgruppe Mitte on 22 September, less than a week after the German offensive crested on the Pulkovo Heights. Schmidt's XXXIX Armeekorps (mot.) was retained in Heeresgruppe Nord for the time being.

Soviet armour, as well as the self-sacrificial courage of Red Army tankers, had played a critical role in slowing the German drive on Leningrad, but every Red Army tank unit involved was burnt out in the process. The remnants of Baranov's division were disbanded at the end of September and the surviving personnel – now all experienced combat veterans – were used to form the 123rd Tank Brigade. During the autumn of 1941, as the siege began, neither side had more than a few dozen operational tanks left, which were reserved for occasional counterattacks. Höpner's conduct of the campaign deserves poor marks, since he allowed the bulk of the Northwest Front's 8th and 11th Armies to escape Lithuania, he failed to properly coordinate the operations of Reinhardt's and von Manstein's corps, and he allowed the terrain to get the better of him and set the pace of operations. He would have been better advised to send Reinhardt's corps in an end-run through Estonia to seize Narva, while using von Manstein's corps as a diversion at Luga. Once at Narva, the whole Luga line would have been flanked and, by using Lake Peipus to shield his right flank, he would have minimized the risk of Soviet counterattacks like Soltsy and Staraya Russa. Instead, Höpner's fumbling effort to overcome the Luga position cost Heeresgruppe Nord a vital month and gave the Soviets time to redeploy armour from the Finnish front and to partly rebuild their tank units with new KV heavy tanks. Despite the failure to prevent the encirclement of Leningrad, Soviet armour had achieved more on the approaches to the city than any other Red Army tank units prior to the winter of 1941–42.

Crossing the Berezina and Dnieper, July 1941

Among other mistaken assumptions, when the OKH staff developed the Barbarossa plan they had not included the Red Army's second-echelon forces deployed deeper within the Soviet Union, or the possibility of newly-raised reinforcements as important factors and, consequently, did not anticipate that the Red Army's Western Front would be able to re-form a coherent front line after its first-echelon forces were defeated in the Minsk-Bialystok salient. In fact, this planning assumption was proven wrong no fewer than four times between June and November 1941.

Although the reduction of the encircled Soviet 3rd and 10th Armies west of Minsk consumed much of Heeresgruppe Mitte's effort until 8 July, Guderian and Hoth were already moving some of their armour eastward as soon as Minsk was captured on 28 June and they attempted to seize bridgeheads across the Berezina river while part of their armour assisted with containing and reducing the trapped Soviet units west of Minsk. In Hoth's sector, only the 7.Panzer-Division was immediately available to advance eastward, but 17.Panzer-Division could assist sooner. In Guderian's sector, the bulk of von Schweppenburg's XXIV Armeekorps (mot.) was not involved in the Minsk *kessel* and was pushing toward the

Berezina, as was most of von Viettinghoff's XXXXVI Armeekorps (mot.): a total of four motorized divisions. Tank and personnel losses were not yet serious, so even these parts of Hoth's and Guderian's forces still constituted over 500 tanks. While German logistics were tenuous at this stage, Heeresgruppe Mitte was repairing two rail lines to support operations: the Brest-Baranovichi-Minsk line and the Grodno-Vilna-Minsk line.[40] By 1 July, German railroad repair troops had the line operating as far as Baranovichi and the first supply trains pulled into Minsk on 5 July. Some of the roads around Minsk were all-weather, paved-asphalt rather than the sandy tracks near the border, which made it more practical for supply trucks from the Kraftwagen-Transport-Regiment 605 (a *Großtrans-portraum* or GTR unit) to move fuel, ammunition and rations to the forward panzer units. When necessary, Luftwaffe Ju-52 transports were also being used to move emergency resupply forward to the more distant 3 and 4.Panzer-Divisionen.[41]

On the Soviet side, Marshal Semyon Timoshenko arrived at Smolensk from Moscow on 2 July to replace Pavlov and rebuild the shattered Western Front. Aside from the remnants of the 13th Army – the threadbare 20th Mechanized Corps (no tanks) and ten battered rifle divisions – Timoshenko initially had very few forces at hand. Fortunately, the Stavka had been in the process of transferring a large number of formations from the interior military districts to the West when Barbarossa began and had four armies under RVGK control. Pavlov's disaster in the Bialystok-Minsk salient bumped Timoshenko's request for rein-forcements to the top. General-leytenant Ivan S. Konev's 19th Army, with six rifle divisions, was rerouted from the Ukraine to Smolensk, while General-leytenant Pavel A. Kurochkin's 20th Army was formed with seven rifle divisions from the Moscow and Volga military districts. General-leytenant Mikhail F. Lukin's 16th Army began arriving in Smolensk on 5 July with two rifle divisions from the Ukraine and was soon joined by the independent 57th Tank Division (160 T-26 tanks) from the Transbaikal military district. All told, Timoshenko would receive a total of fifteen good-quality rifle divisions in the vicinity of Smolensk in the first half of July 1941; all these units were pre-war formations at about 84–88 per cent of authorized strength. Timoshenko also received a number of artillery regiments and anti-tank brigades from the RVGK.[42]

Furthermore, Timoshenko was fortunate in that the RVGK could quickly provide him with two nearly full-strength mechanized corps, the 5th and the 7th, to rebuild his armoured strength and four other mechanized corps later in July. General-major Ilya P. Alekseenko's 5th Mechanized Corps was in the process of transferring from the Transbaikal MR to the Kiev MR when the war began. The 109th Motorized Division had already detrained at Shepetovka and it was quickly sent to contain the German breakthrough at Ostrog, but the rest of the corps was diverted enroute to Smolensk, where it joined the 20th Army that was forming. Alekseenko was one of the most experienced senior tankers in the Red Army, having commanded a tank brigade at the Battle of Nomonhan in 1939.

Closer at hand, General-major Vasily Vinogradov's 7th Mechanized Corps was stationed around Moscow and was alerted immediately after the German invasion began. The corps moved by road and rail to Orsha, with the first elements arriving there on 26 June. Three days later, the elite 1st Moscow Motorized Division led by Polkovnik Yakov G. Kreizer was ordered to hurry toward Borisov to establish a defensive screen along the Berezina River, while the rest of the corps set up blocking positions between Orsha and Vitebsk. Kreizer's division was particularly fortunate in having four tank battalions with 225 of the latest BT-7M light tanks (with the same V-2 diesel engine as the T-34 and better sloped armour), as well as receiving ten KV heavy tanks and thirty T-34 tanks from local training units. Ammunition was still a problem and few armour-piercing rounds were available. However, Kampfgruppe Teege from General-major Walther Nehring's 18.Panzer-Division reached Borisov first, around 1300 hours on 30 June, and attempted a coup de main against the still-intact concrete road bridge. Major Willi Teege had his own II/Panzer-Regiment 18 plus the Kradschützen-Bataillon 18 and the Aufklärungs-Abteilung 88, but ran into unexpectedly heavy resistance west of the river from remnants of the 13th Army and cadre from the Borisov tank school, who shot up some of the tanks in his *vorausabteilung*. It was not until dismounted infantry from Schutzen-Regiment 52 arrived that the Kampfgruppe Teege was able to seize the bridge intact. Over the next couple of days, Nehring expanded his bridgehead and was reinforced by a kampfgruppe from 17.Panzer-Division.[43]

Kreizer's vanguard was too late to save the bridge at Borisov, but Kurochkin ordered him to assemble a counterattack to retake it as soon as possible. Even for a well-equipped division such as Kreizer's, this was a tall order. Kreizer attacked with all his armour on the morning of 3 July, by which time Nehring's division was firmly established on the east bank of the Berezina. Luftwaffe aerial recon-naissance spotted the approaching Soviet armour and provided invaluable early warning to Nehring, who was able deploy his panzers and panzerjägers in a dense patch of silver birch 8km east of the Borisov bridgehead. Amazingly, Kreizer's tanks attacked straight down the Minsk-Moscow highway, in the open, in broad daylight, and in not in any particular formation, but in small platoon and company-size gaggles of tanks. At least one KV-2, several KV-1s and a number of T-34s participated in the attack, but the bulk of Kreizer's armour consisted of the BT-7Ms. Under these conditions, the panzers and panzerjägers had little difficulty knocking out many of the attacking BT-7M light tanks, but the KV heavy tanks and T-34s managed to briefly penetrate the German defenses. At least one Pz.III was knocked out by a T-34, but the German tankers eventually concentrated their fire against the tracks of the Soviet heavy tanks, to immobilize them.[44] The intervention of German flak and heavy artillery in the battle further encouraged Kreizer's tankers to withdraw. As usual, the Soviets claimed to have inflicted heavy losses on a panzer division – some sixty–seventy tanks – but actual German losses were light. German panzer-division commanders were quick to note that seizing key terrain and then quickly switching to the tactical defensive often resulted in the Soviets mounting near-suicidal counterattacks that then opened the way for further German advances.

Thereafter, Kreizer delayed back toward Orsha, counterattacking Nehring's spearheads at Krupki on 4 July and Talachyn on 5 July. Kreizer claimed to have inflicted 1,000 casualties on the pursuing panzer units at Talachyn, but in fact his division continued to retreat. Further combat against Soviet heavy tanks revealed that in addition to shooting off their tracks to immobilize them, direct hits on their turrets could jam the traversing mechanisms. While 17 and 18.Panzer-Division were slowly pushing toward Orsha, von Schweppenburg's XXIV Armeekorps (mot.) crossed the Berezina at Bobruisk and the XXXXVI Armee-korps (mot.) soon had the *SS-Reich* and 10.Infanterie-Division (mot.) across as well. By 3 July, both German panzer groups were across the Berezina in strength and pushing against scattered resistance toward the Dnieper. Meanwhile, Hoth sent the LVII Armeekorps (mot.) to capture Polotsk, thereby guarding the left flank of the German advance, but this weakened the armour available for the up-coming Battle of Smolensk.

Timoshenko had only been in command of the Western Front for three days when he ordered the still-arriving 5th and 7th Mechanized Corps, along with infantry from the 20th Army, to counterattack the German armour advancing upon Orsha. Coordination between divisions and corps was still rudimentary, but Timoshenko believed that this mass of armour might be able to halt the relentless German advance. At 1000 hours on 6 July, Vinogradov and Alekseenko deployed their four tank divisions and one motorized division on line west of Orsha and began advancing toward Senno and Lepel. All told, both corps managed to get about 1,100 tanks, including thirty-seven KV-I and KV-II heavy tanks and sixty-nine T-34, into the operation. The Stavka had directed that a battalion of twenty-nine T-34s from the Kharkov Tank School and forty-four brand-new KV tanks from the Kirov plant be sent directly to reinforce Vinogradov's 7th Mechanized Corps, but the Soviet tankers had difficulty driving the heavy tanks and burned out the clutches on seven KVs moving just 5km from the railhead to an assembly area. Over the course of the next few days, about half of the KVs were immobilized by the same fault.[45]

Meanwhile, Schmidt's XXXIX Armeekorps (mot.) was well out in front of the rest of Hoth's Panzergruppe 3 and only had the advance units of Generalleutnant Hans Zorn's 20.Infanterie-Division (mot.) and Generalleutnant Hans Freiherr von Funck's 7.Panzer-Division screening east of Vitebsk while the rest of the corps moved up. Zorn had just occupied Beshenkovichi and Funck's lead unit, Kradschützen-Bataillon 7, was on the outskirts of Senno. Schmidt's forces were dispersed and vulnerable, but the Luftwaffe alerted them to the presence of approaching Soviet armoured units, which allowed the forward units to establish a hasty defense.

Once again, the Soviets attacked without reconnaissance and tactical com-manders had little idea of the enemy's dispositions or the nature of the terrain. Vinogradov, who had no prior experience with armour, displayed great foolish-ness in the meeting engagement phase by sending a reinforced tank company under Captain Georgy F. Haraborkin to find fording sites over the Cher-nogostitsa River east of Beshenkovichi on the morning of 6 July. Haraborkin was a very experienced tanker who had been awarded the Hero of the Soviet Union for his combat performance during the Russo-Finnish War, but Vinogradov sent him on a fool's errand. Instead of using armoured cars for reconnaissance, Vinogradov wanted a reconnaissance in force, so Haraborkin led twelve KV-1 and two BT-7 tanks to the river. In addition to the fact that the terrain around the ford site was marshland, the advance elements of Zorn's motorized division had already reached the ford and emplaced anti-tank mines. When Haraborkin attempted to cross, four KV tanks struck mines and three others became stuck. The Germans had Pak guns covering the mine obstacle and began to pound the stranded Soviet heavy tanks, while calling in artillery. The Soviet tankers managed to recover two KV tanks under fire but Haraborkin was killed and a total of seven KVs were abandoned in the river.[46]

By the end of 6 July, the Soviet 5th and 7th Mechanized Corps were in contact with the two divisions of XXXIX Armeekorps (mot.), but had not yet struck a serious blow. The actions of the two corps were not coordinated and difficulties in pushing fuel forward further desynchronized their actions. Vinogradov's corps used 75 per cent of its fuel in moving to contact and Alekseenko's 5th Corps was much the same, but Vinogradov decided to continue the advance while Alekseenko paused his advance to await more fuel. Consequently, Schmidt would only have to face one Soviet mechanized corps on 7 July, not two. Timoshenko, who often demonstrated poor situational awareness during operations, was unaware of Alekseenko's decision and confidently expected that both corps would attack and crush a single German panzer division on 7 July.

Vinogradov's attack commenced at 0800 hours on 7 July, a sunny and warm day, with the 18th Tank Division probing toward Senno with a tank battalion. However, Oberstleutnant Wolfgang Thomale's III/Pz.Regt 25 had arrived during the night to reinforce the motorcycle infantry and the Pz.38(t) and panzerjäger repulsed the first attack. After the initial attack failed, the Soviets seemed uncertain what to do and wasted precious hours until finally renewing the attack on Senno at 1630 hours. Again, Kampfgruppe Thomale repulsed this Soviet attack and a third at 1900 hours which included two KV-II and one T-34 tanks. During the course of the day, Thomale's troops destroyed a total of seventeen Soviet tanks (including both KV-II), at a cost of four of his own tanks and a 5cm Pak gun.[47] Further north, the 14th Tank Division encountered Kampfgruppe von Boineburg, which included Hauptmann Adelbert Schulz's I/Pz.Regt 25, II/Schützen Regiment 7 and 1./Panzerjäger-Abteilung 8 with six 8.8cm flak guns mounted on an Sd.Kfz.8 chassis. The Soviet attack in this sector was more powerful and included infantry support, but advanced at a slow pace which allowed the Germans time to react. While the German panzerjägers and four artillery units pounded the approaching Soviet armour, Hauptmann Schulz maneuvered his panzer battalion to strike the flank of the Soviet formation. By using fire and maneuver in the defense, Kampfgruppe von Boineburg shattered the 14th Tank Division's attack and sent it reeling with the loss of forty-three tanks. Two of the self-propelled 8.8cm flak guns, which had a very high profile, were destroyed, but otherwise proved useful against the Soviet heavy and medium tanks. By the end of the day, Funck's 7.Panzer-Division had repulsed both Soviet tank divisions and knocked out 103 Soviet tanks at a cost of eight of their own and 136 casualties.[48]

Alekseenko's armour essentially sat out the day, awaiting more fuel, while Vinogradov's armour was being demolished. By the time that Alekseenko began committing his armour on 8 July, Hoth had brought up the rest of the armour with 12 and 20.Panzer-Divisionen and Guderian had two panzer divisions from XXXXVII Armeekorps (mot.) near Orsha. The 17.Panzer-Division attacked into the flank of the 5th Mechanized Corps on 8 July and, by the next day, Hoth's and Guderian's panzers threatened to envelop both Soviet mechanized corps.[49] The Germans noted that Polkovnik Ivan P. Korchagin's 17th Tank Division performed particularly poorly and attributed this to its composition of 60 per cent Ukrainian soldiers – many of whom still remembered ill-treatment at the hands of the Soviet regime and were now unwilling to risk their necks for Mother Russia.[50] Oberst Kurt Cuno, commander of Panzer Regiment 39, used fire and maneuver tactics with his Pz.IIIs and Pz.IVs to engage Alekseenko's small number of KV and T-34 tanks:

> ... radio operator Westphal in his tank heard his commander's excited voice: 'Heavy enemy tank! Turret 10 o'clock. Armour-piercing shell. Fire!' 'Direct hit!' Unteroffizier Sarge called out. But the Russian did not even seem to feel the shell. He simply drove on. He took no notice of it whatever. Two, three, and then four tanks of 9.Kompanie were weaving around the Russian at 800–1,000 yards distance, firing. Nothing happened. Then he stopped. His turret swung around. With a bright flash his gun fired. A fountain of dirt shot up 40 yards in front of Feldwebel Hornbogen's tank of 7.Kompanie. Hornbogen swung out of the line of fire. The Russian continued to advance along a farm track.[51]

The Soviet KV-1 crushed a German 3.7cm Pak gun that tried to block its path and advanced over a dozen kilometers before finally becoming immobilized in a marsh.

Recognizing that most of Timoshenko's armour was committed to the counterattack at Senno, Hoth decided to use Schmidt's XXXIX Armeekorps (mot.) to smash in the front of the 22nd Army and then pivot to envelop Vinogradov's 7th Mechanized Corps. The 20.Panzer-Division had already captured a road bridge over the Western Dvina at Ula and had been developing a bridgehead for several days.[52] On the morning of 9 July, the 20.Panzer-Division crossed the Western Dvina into the bridgehead and conducted a superbly-executed attack that was in stark contrast to Vinogradov's debacle. Panzer-Regiment 21 made short work of the Soviet infantry, easily penetrating the front held by the 62nd Rifle Corps and advanced 60km to seize the city of Vitebsk by nightfall. Otto Carius was a loader on a Pz.38(t) tank in the I./Pz. Regt. 21 at Ula:

> We were in the lead. It was at Ula, a village that was completely burned down ...They put us out of commission just this side of the wood line on the

other side of the river. It happened like greased lightning. A hit against our tank, a metallic crack, the scream of a comrade, and that was all there was! A large piece of armour plating had been penetrated next to the radio operator's seat. No one had to tell us to get out. Not until I had run my hand across my face while crawling in the ditch next to the road did I discover that they had also got me. Our radio operator had lost his left arm. We cursed the brittle and inelastic Czech steel that gave the Russian 47-mm anti-tank gun so little trouble. The pieces of our armour plating and assembly bolts caused considerably more damage than the shrapnel of the round itself. My smashed teeth soon found their way into the trash can at the aid station.[53]

The 20.Infanterie-Division (mot.) also crossed the Dvina at a different location and supported the attack on Vitebsk. Schmidt's handling of the XXXIX Armee-korps (mot.) during the fighting along the Western Dvina amply demonstrated what well-led armour could accomplish. In contrast, the battered remnants of the 5th and 7th Mechanized Corps were in full retreat. The armoured counterattack near Orsha was a fiasco, resulting in the loss of about 832 tanks and another 100 damaged, or more than 80 per cent of the armour committed. Indeed, the scale of Soviet armoured losses in just a few days was astounding, almost as bad as if they had deliberately driven both corps off a cliff. Furthermore, a large number of Soviet tanks were simply abandoned by their crews, indicating morale problems. Perhaps the only bright spot was that at least forty-five damaged tanks (including four KV and eleven T-34) were recovered from the battlefield – a first for the Red Army in this campaign. However, instead of regrouping the survivors and repairing his damaged tanks, Timoshenko rashly ordered them and Konev's 20th Army to retake Vitebsk. Schmidt's 7 and 12.Panzer-Divisionen easily repulsed this half-hearted effort, which cost another 100 Soviet tanks. Amazingly, Timoshenko had squandered the majority of the RVGK's best armoured reserves in less than a week, before the Battle of Smolensk proper had even begun.

Seizing the Bull by the Horns: Smolensk, 10 July–5 August

In order to support the offensive toward Smolensk, Heeresgruppe Mitte quickly established a major logistics base in Minsk. By 12 July, German quartermasters had stockpiled 2,000cbm of fuel, 2,600 tons of ammunition and two days' rations of food in Minsk for Hoth's and Guderian's panzer groups, with some stockpiled as far forward as Borisov.[54] Anticipating a pursuit operation rather than heavy combat after Guderian crossed the Dnieper, German quartermasters prioritized fuel, rather than ammunition. Consequently, Guderian's panzer divisions entered the Battle of Smolensk with heavy fuel reserves – up to 5 V.S. in some divisions – but only one basic load of ammunition. Faulty logistic priorities, rather than a failure to deliver gross logistical tonnage to the front line, was more at fault in the subsequent German difficulties in the Battle of Smolensk.

Timoshenko's fumbled armoured counterattack provided the perfect segue for Hoth and Guderian's panzer groups – still full of fight – to explode across the Dnieper river on 10 July. In order to gain surprise, Guderian deliberately chose suboptimal crossing sites over the Dnieper that were relatively unguarded. The 3 and 4.Panzer-Divisionen crossed first near Staryy Bykhov on 10 July, followed by the 29.Infanterie-Division (mot.) at Kopys and the 10.Panzer-Division at Shklov on 11 July. German pioneers built a pontoon bridge at Kopys in less than eleven hours, enabling the rest of General der Artillerie Joachim Lemelsen's XXXXVII Armeekorps (mot.) to cross. On the other side of the Dnieper, the Soviet 13th Army, badly battered after the fighting around Minsk, had no mobile reserves left and its commander was mortally wounded by a Luftwaffe raid. By the end of 11 July, Guderian had all three of his motorized corps across the Dnieper and the large Soviet garrison in Mogilev was about to be encircled. The Dnieper crossing was superbly executed and it represented the third major river-crossing operation by Guderian's panzers in just three weeks. Lemelsen's XXXXVII Armeekorps (mot.), with the 29.Infanterie-Division (mot.) in the lead, followed by the 17 and 18.Panzer-Divisionen, advanced rapidly through the wreckage of the 13th Army and made a beeline for Smolensk.

Likewise, after securing Vitebsk, Hoth's panzers easily punched through the front of Ershakov's 22nd Army and Konev's 19th Army, both of which consisted entirely of rifle divisions without significant armour support. Although the Soviets had plenty of infantry in the field, the density of anti-tank guns and artillery defending this sector was very low. Soviet accounts emphasize the use of field-expedient anti-tank weapons such as Molotov cocktails during the Battle of Smolensk, but hand-thrown weapons simply could not stop massed armoured formations in open terrain. Schmidt's XXXIX Armeekorps (mot.), with General-leutnant Hans Freiherr von Funck's 7.Panzer-Division and Generalleutnant Horst Stumpff's 20.Panzer-Division in the lead, sliced through Konev's infantry like a knife through butter. Between them, these two divisions still had about 250 tanks operational and they were employed in regimental-size kampfgruppen, not company-size packets like the Red Army's armour. Consequently, there was significant panic among Konev's infantry units, causing units to retreat without orders. Funck's 7.Panzer-Division advanced over 100km in four days, shoving aside Konev's infantry, and reached the town of Demidov late on 13 July.

General-leytenant Pavel A. Kurochkin's 20th Army stood like a rock in the triangle between Smolensk-Vitebsk-Orsha, but soon found both flanks being enveloped by Hoth's and Guderian's panzers. With his Western Front crumbling just ten days after being re-established, Timoshenko was desperate to stop the German pincers, but had very little offensive power available in terms of armour, artillery or air power. Instead, he did what Soviet commanders usually did in times of defensive crisis: commit units piecemeal into the path of the German *schwerpunkt*, hoping to buy time for more of the Stavka's RVGK's reinforcements to arrive. Timoshenko was more concerned about the threat posed by Schmidt's XXXIX Armeekorps (mot.) from the north, so he ordered both the 32nd and 34th Rifle Corps to set up a new defensive front facing the 7.Panzer-Division at Demidov. Less concerned about the 29.Infanterie-Division (mot.) approaching from the south, Timoshenko decided that Polkovnik Vasiliy A. Mishulin's incomplete 57th Tank Division (only one tank regiment), just arrived in

Smolensk from Transbaikal, could stop Lemelsen's vanguard. A single rifle regiment was deployed to defend the south side of Smolensk. Mishulin, who had commanded a mechanized brigade at Nomonhan in 1939, placed his four T-26 battalions into blocking positions south of Smolensk and waited.

However, Schmidt's corps did not take the direct path toward Smolensk, instead bypassing the 32nd and 34th Rifle Corps and moving due east to Dukhovschina on 15 July. On the afternoon of 15 July, Funck detached Kampfgruppe von Boineburg to interdict the Smolensk–Moscow highway at Yartsevo, east of Smolensk. At 2030 hours, von Boineburg was able to capture the unguarded town of Yartsevo, thereby isolating the bulk of the Soviet 20th Army in the *kessel* forming west of Smolensk. Schmidt quickly redeployed his three divisions to contain Soviet troops inside the forming *kessel*, while blocking any relief attempts.

Meanwhile, Generalleutnant Walter von Boltenstern's 29.Infanterie-Division (mot.), heavily reinforced with Sturmgeschütz, flame-throwing tanks from Panzer-Abteilung (Flammpanzer) 100, Nebelwerfers and 8.8cm flak guns, approached the southern outskirts of Smolensk in the afternoon of 15 July. Mishulin's tanks and accompanying infantry were bypassed. Boltenstern used his Schutzen-Regiments 15 and 71 to clear out the city south of the Dnieper river during the rest of the day, then mounted a daring assault river-crossing operation at 0400 hours on 16 July. Rokossovsky, promoted to command the new 16th Army, arrived in Smolensk just twenty-four hours before Boltenstern's troops arrived and his headquarters had only a rifle regiment and some artillery under its direct command. The two German Schützen regiments advanced northward quickly from the river, defeating Rokossovsky's forces in detail, and Boltenstern's division had captured all of Smolensk by 2300 hours.[55] Once again, as at Minsk, German motorized forces had captured a major Soviet city 'on the bounce', before the Red Army could react.

By the morning of 17 July, the bulk of Timoshenko's Western Front was either encircled, retreating or scattered. Three tank divisions and Kreizer's 1st Motorized Rifle Division were isolated west of Smolensk, although a narrow path still existed at Solov'evo between Hoth's panzers near Yartsevo and Guderian's panzers in Smolensk. At this point, there is no doubt that the Germans made some serious operational-level mistakes that prevented an early conclusion to the Smolensk *kesselschlacht*. First, Guderian became fixated on the XXXXVI Armeekorps' (mot.) advance to Yeln'ya. Guderian believed that XXXXVII Armeekorps (mot.) had the situation in hand at Smolensk and preferred to focus on pushing east to the next obvious objective: Moscow. He believed that a *kesselschlacht* was the infantry's business and wanted to avoid more than a single one of his motorized corps from getting tangled up in a stationary battle (and falling under the authority of his rival, Generalfeldmarschall Günter von Kluge's 4.Armee). A second factor was that both von Bock at Heeresgruppe Mitte and the OKH became very nervous about the Soviet stronghold at Mogilev and the mounting Soviet threat to Guderian's right flank. Guderian was forced to employ his third corps, von Schweppenburg's XXIV Armeekorps (mot.) to contain the *kessel* at

Mogilev, which held nearly 100,000 Soviet troops, while fending off relief efforts by the 21st Army. Finally, Hitler became convinced that the Soviets were massing a major counterattack force near Velikiye Luki and ordered Hoth to divert a significant part of his forces away from Smolensk toward a secondary objective. Although Richard Stahel has argued that the declining number of operational panzers in Hoth's and Guderian's groups led to a protracted three-week battle of attrition at Smolensk, the real cause of German difficulties was the fragmentation of effort.[56] Rather than the previous unity of effort, at Smolensk each of the German motorized corps began pursuing divergent objectives, which prevented them from achieving the kind of decisive local superiorities they had heretofore employed.

Showdown at Yartsevo, 17–31 July 1941

While Heeresgruppe Mitte was trying to form a solid cordon around the isolated 20th Army west of Smolensk, the Stavka had been hurriedly forming a third echelon of armies around Vyazma and Spas-Demensk, but these were virtually all-infantry formations – including a great deal of people's militia – with no armour and few heavy weapons. On 15 July, the Stavka also issued an order abolishing all Red Army mechanized corps, even though this had already been accomplished by the Wehrmacht. Instead, the Stavka began forming the '100-series' independent tank divisions, with obsolete light tanks and a sprinkling of new construction, but woefully deficient in terms of artillery and support units. Timoshenko was provided the hurriedly raised 101st and 104th Tank Divisions to spearhead his counterattacks at Smolensk. Polkovnik Grigoriy M. Mikhailov's 101st Tank Division had seven new KV heavy tanks and seventy old light tanks, while the 104th Tank Division had twelve KV and thirty T-34 added to its mixed bag of 180 light tanks. These two formations, with a total of roughly 300 tanks, represented the only real armour reserve left to the Western Front after the fall of Smolensk. In July, the factories in Leningrad and Kharkov were producing about thirty-five KV-1 and seventy T-34 per week, but the GABTU made the mistake of doling them out to different units in company-size detachments, rather than concentrating them into a few fully-capable armour units.

Although the KV and T-34 tanks still awed the Germans whenever they appeared, by midsummer both sides had learned a great deal about the strengths and weaknesses of these tanks. One Soviet after-action report sent to the GABTU noted that the presence of 'KV tanks on the battlefield baffled enemy tanks and in all cases their tanks retreated.' However, Soviet tankers noted that enemy shell hits on the KV-1's turret could jam the traversing mechanism and both vehicles could be immobilized by damage to their tracks. The transmission on the KV-1 was a major failure and greatly reduced the mobility and mechanical reliability of the tank, but both KV and T-34 also had serious problems with their clutches and steering – which led to a high loss rate with untrained drivers.[57]

The Stavka peremptorily put Rokossovsky in charge of the effort to retake Yartsevo, although his tiny command was incapable of anything but defense until at least 18 July. Eventually, he received Mikhailov's 101st Tank Division and the

69th Motorized Division from Transbaikal, plus the burnt-out 38th Rifle Division and some artillery – all told, equivalent to eight tank and twelve infantry battalions. Funck was holding Yartsevo with the equivalent of two panzer and five infantry battalions, supported by his division's pioneers, panzerjägers and artillery regiment. After a series of probes, Group Rokossovsky began an all-out offensive to recapture Yartsevo on 21 July, but despite a 3–1 numerical superiority, the Soviet attacks were continuously repulsed. For eight days, Rokossovsky continued to hurl his armour and infantry against the 7.Panzer-Division at Yartsevo, losing most of his armour in the process. Finally, his remaining handful of KV-1 tanks were able to fight their way into the town on 29 July, but Funck counterattacked and retook Yartsevo on 31 July. Rokossovsky's beaten troops fell back, having failed to defeat the 7.Panzer-Division. While 7.Panzer-Division was easily the most battered German armoured unit in Russia, its losses up to the end of the Battle of Smolensk were far from crippling: about fifty main battle tanks destroyed and 20 per cent of its wheeled vehicles, while personnel losses were about twenty per cent. Even when damaged or inoperative equipment is included, 7.Panzer-Division still retained about 50 per cent of its combat capability after Yartsevo.[58]

Meanwhile, the XXXXVII Armeekorps fought off all efforts to retake Smolensk and helped to contain the southern side of the *kessel*. Inside the *kessel*, the Soviet 20th Army only had sixty-five tanks left by 26 July and most of their fuel and ammunition was exhausted by 29 July. The sole remaining corridor for the trapped 20th Army, through Ratchino and Solov'evo, was guarded by remnants of the 5th Mechanized Corps, which had only fifteen T-26 tanks left. It was easily within reach for Guderian to slash through this last Soviet corridor with his unengaged XXXXVII Armeekorps (mot.) and link up with the 7.Panzer-Division at Yartsevo, but he deliberately ignored direct orders to do this. Instead, he pushed the 10.Panzer-Division and SS-Reich Division toward Yelnya, which they captured on 20 July. It was not until Yelnya was secured, and with great reluctance, that Guderian redirected the 17.Panzer-Division and SS-Reich toward the vulnerable southern side of the Soviet corridor, by which point several rifle divisions had arrived to set up a defense. Guderian's forces finally linked up with Hoth's forces and sealed the pocket on 26 July. While it is true that over 40,000 Soviet troops escaped the Smolensk *kessel* before it was finally closed, they brought out only three BT and six T-26 light tanks.

The final armoured battles around Smolensk occurred on Guderian's southern flank, near Roslavl. The Soviet 28th Army formed an assault group, named Group Kachalov, which included Polkovnik Vasiliy G. Burkov's 104th Tank Division (twelve KV-1, thirty T-34, 180 BT/T-26). Group Kachalov attacked Guderian's left flank on 23 July, with Burkov's tanks initially pushing back part of Nehring's 18.Panzer-Division. However, Nehring simply fell back upon his line of artillery and panzerjägers, which stopped Burkov's tanks. Once the Smolensk pocket was finally sealed, Guderian turned to deal with Group Kachalov, by redeploying the 3 and 4.Panzer-Divisionen from von Schweppenburg's corps to conduct an enveloping attack. Guderian unleashed this attack on 1 August and, within two days, Roslavl had been captured and Group Kachalov and Burkov's tanks were encircled. Kachalov took one of Burkov's T-34 tanks and tried to fight his way out of the pocket, but was killed. Burkov was wounded, but succeeded in breaking out with some of his tankers. However by 4 August, the 4.Panzer-Division had crushed the *kessel* and another 38,500 Soviet troops were captured. After the destruction of Group Kachalov, the Western Front had been stripped of most of its armour again.

Attempts have been made in recent Eastern Front historiography, notably by David Glantz, to depict the Battle of Smolensk as a Soviet tactical victory that cost the Germans dearly in terms of casualties and time lost. It is true that the Wehrmacht suffered its heaviest losses during Operation Barbarossa during the month of July. It is also true that the protracted Battle of Smolensk ensured that the Wehrmacht would not achieve a rapid victory in the Soviet Union, although failing to accomplish a military operation on a predesignated schedule does not, in itself, equate to a defeat. Yet it is a fact that after the battle ended, all of the German panzer divisions still existed – no matter how battered – but that the last of the Red Army's mechanized corps had been eliminated and the Germans had a 2–1 or better numerical edge in tank strength on the Moscow axis for the rest of 1941. While the combat power of the panzer divisions had been reduced by 50 per cent or more, the relative combat power of the Red Army declined even more precipitously after the Battle of Smolensk, with few tanks or anti-tank guns left to stop the final phase of Operation Barbarossa. Furthermore, it is a gross over-simplification to take the number of operational tanks as the sole determinant of armoured unit combat effectiveness, which instead derived from the synergistic effect of combined arms tactics. Despite the loss of perhaps one-third of their tanks and 10 per cent of their personnel, the German combined arms teams were still intact, with the vital artillery, signals and other support units in the panzer divisions having suffered negligible losses as yet.

Velikiye Luki: Punch and Counterpunch, 17 July–26 August

While the Smolensk *kesselschlacht* was going on, von Bock, the OKH staff and Hitler were becoming increasingly concerned about the northern flank of Heeresgruppe Mitte, along the Western Dvina. Earlier, Hoth had directed General der Panzertruppen Adolf Kuntzen's LVII Armeekorps (mot.), with the 19.Panzer-Division and 18.Infanterie-Division (mot.), to seize a crossing over the Western Dvina at Disna on 4 July. German pioneers built a 195-meter long, 20-ton capacity pontoon bridge over the Western Dvina by 1830 hours on 5 July.[59] However, General-leytenant Filipp A. Ershakov's 22nd Army – with eight rifle divisions and a single tank battalion – was able to contain the German bridgehead with furious local counterattacks and constant artillery bombardment. In addition, the Polotsk fortified region, which was part of the 'Stalin line,' had T-26 tank turrets set in concrete pillboxes and proved a formidable obstacle to further expansion of the German bridgehead over the Western Dvina. As the mechanized corps from the Stavka's RVGK reserve began to arrive to reinforce the Western Front in mid-July, Hitler became convinced that Ershakov's army would be heavily reinforced and use the Polotsk fortified region as a springboard to launch an enveloping counteroffensive against von Bock's left flank, which could endanger the delicate situation around Smolensk.

Consequently, Hitler directed Hoth to use Kuntzen's LVII Armeekorps (mot.) to eliminate the Soviet fortified region at Polotsk and the bulk of Ershakov's army before it could be reinforced. This was a very tall order for just one panzer and one motorized infantry division, equipped mostly with Pz.38(t) light tanks. The 9.Armee provided some infantry to help reduce the Polotsk fortified position, but German forces committed on this axis were outnumbered in every category but tanks. Polotsk fell on 15 July and Kuntzen pushed Generalleutnant Otto von Knobelsdorff's 19.Panzer-Division up the road to Nevel, which fell late on the same day. Although the forest and lakes of the terrain were highly favorable to the defense, the German panzer attack caught Ershakov by surprise and his army was cleaved in two. However, the Stavka had indeed decided to send some armour to reinforce Ershakov's 22nd Army – Polkovnik Dmitry Y. Yakovlev's 48th Tank Division from the 23rd Mechanized Corps. Yakovlev was a forty-year-old cavalry officer and his division arrived by rail from Voronezh just before the German offensive began and was assembling at Nevel, northeast of Polotsk. The 48th Tank Division had just eighty-five tanks (seventy-eight T-26 and seven BT-7), no armoured cars and 130 ZIS-5 trucks – it was really just a regimental-size armoured group.

With Ershakov's army in disarray, Knobelsdorff boldly pushed up a forested logging trail with his panzers into Nevel and then toward Velikiye Luki. Yakovlev tried to conduct a mobile delay operation to harass Knobelsdorff and help Ershakov's rifle divisions to escape the unfolding trap. Nevertheless, Yakovlev was unable to prevent a kampfgruppe from 19.Panzer-Division from fighting its way into Velikiye Luki, a city of 30,000, and overwhelming the defense there on 17 July. Velikiye Luki was an important rail junction in northern Russia and the German vanguard succeeded in capturing a train-load of tanks at the station, intended for Yakovlev's division.

However, Ershakov's army was not defeated and the Stavka – enraged by the rapid fall of Velikiye Luki – pushed him into launching an all-out counter-attack at Kuntzen's lines of communications through Nevel. Gathering up his remaining infantry and Yakovelv's tank group, Ershakov suddenly struck the 14.Infanterie-Division (mot.) on the night of 19–20 July, causing it to stumble backward. Other Soviet rifle units counterattacked Knobelsdorff's vanguard at Velikiye Luki. Stung by the ferocity of these Soviet counterattacks, Knobelsdorff decided that his kampfgruppe in Velikiye Luki might be cut off and he ordered it to retreat southward. On the morning of 21 July, Ershakov's troops liberated Velikiye Luki – the first Russian city liberated in the Second World War.

Ershakov's triumph was short-lived. Hoth brought up the 20.Panzer-Division to reinforce 19.Panzer-Division at Nevel, as well as four infantry divisions from 9.Armee. General der Panzertruppen Georg Stumme, recently arrived from Germany, was put in charge of both panzer divisions and other assault units, designated as Gruppe Stumme. In early August, Hoth's forces gradually converged on Velikiye Luki, but Yakovlev used his armour to launch a series of spirited counterattacks that mauled a regiment from 253.Infanterie-Division. Ershakov managed to get four rifle divisions into line around the city and construct a defense-in-depth. Nevertheless, while 9.Armee gradually arrayed its infantry south and west of the city, Stumme maneuvered his two panzer divisions into assault positions southeast of the city and cut the rail line leading to Rzhev. Then he launched a set-piece attack on the morning of 22 August, kicked off by rocket bombardment from a *Nebelwerfer* battalion. It took Stumme's panzers three days to fight through the Soviet defense east of the city, but they gradually enveloped Velikiye Luki. Yakovlev's tankers and Ershakov's infantry fought a desperate two-day battle in the city, then staged a breakout on 26 August. Yakovlev managed to extract only two tanks and 2,400 troops from Velikiye Luki, but the rest of the garrison was lost and Stumme's forces took 24,109 prisoners.[60] Ignoring the outcome, Timoshenko immediately ordered Yakovlev to counterattack Gruppe Stumme and retake the city. When Yakovlev protested that his remaining troops were not capable of accomplishing this mission he was arrested and, by order of Timoshenko, executed.

The brief Soviet victory at Velikiye Luki, led by Yakovlev's tankers, demonstrates that a successful armoured operation was not dependent upon superior tanks such as KV-1 or T-34s, but on superior leadership and aggressiveness. Yakovlev performed more with his eighty-five-odd BT and T-26 light tanks than others had accomplished with entire mechanized corps equipped with modern tanks. Not only had he recaptured Velikiye Luki and held it for a month, but he had forced Hoth to divert two full panzer divisions to crush a regimental-size tank group. Unfortunately, Yakovlev received no recognition or Hero of the Soviet Union for his accomplishment, just a bullet in the back of his head from the NKVD and a shallow grave.

The Road to Kiev, 2–9 July

Even after the disastrous Battle of Dubno and the retreat to the Stalin Line in early July, Kirponos' Southwest Front still had over 1,200 tanks left. More than one-quarter of these tanks were under the command of General-major Andrey Vlasov's 4th Mechanized Corps, which had about 40 per cent of its armour. As for the rest, the 8th, 16th, 19th and 24th Mechanized Corps each had 100 tanks or more left, the 9th and 15th Mechanized Corps had about eighty each and the 22nd Mechanized Corps had about 60 tanks.[61] More than two-thirds of the Southwest Front's modern tanks were lost in the first week of the war, but the eight mechanized corps still had about 100 KV and 150 T-34 tanks left. Thus, the Southwest Front retained a numerical and qualitative advantage in armour over von Kleist's Panzergruppe 1.

Von Kleist's Panzergruppe 1 was spread out between L'vov and Rovno by 2 July, with Mackensen's III Armeekorps (mot.) fairly concentrated with his three divisions just east of Rovno. Parts of Kempf's XXXXVIII Armeekorps (mot.)

were still reducing Soviet pockets around Dubno, but Crüwell's 11.Panzer-Division and the 16.Infanterie-Division (mor.) were in a good position to resume the offensive. Only von Wietersheim's XIV Armeekorps (mot.) was not ready for further advance eastward, since it was still engaged with Soviet infantry units east of L'vov. Von Kleist had one uncommitted mobile division – the *Leibstandarte SS Adolf Hitler* (LSSAH) – which remained in reserve during the Battle of Dubno.

While Heeresgruppe Süd's AOK 6 and AOK 17 marched slowly eastward, von Kleist pondered his next move in conjunction with Generalfeldmarschall von Rundstedt, Hitler and the OKH. Despite the fact that the Southwest Front had been defeated at Dubno and L'vov, it was clear that Kirponos still had large reserves of armour, infantry and artillery with which to defend the Ukraine. Von Kleist and von Rundstedt were cautious, old-school commanders, and they favored keeping Panzergruppe 1 concentrated and focused on a single objective – namely, an operational-level envelopment against the Soviet 6th and 12th Armies retreating from the border. Hitler agreed that bagging these two armies would be a worthy objective, but he also wanted von Kleist to seize Kiev in a coup de main, as Hoth's panzers had done at Minsk. Yet splitting up Panzergruppe 1 in order to pursue multiple objectives when the Red Army in the Ukraine was undefeated seemed to be asking for trouble. Kiev was a large city of 846,000, protected by two lines of defense, which Kirponos was feverishly filling with infantry, artillery and anti-tank troops.

After a brief pause, the III and XXXXVIII Armeekorps (mot.) resumed advancing eastward on 2 July, but Major General Nikolai V. Feklenko's 19th Mechanized Corps conducted a successful mobile delay operation along the River Horyn that enabled other parts of the Soviet 5th Army to escape. Feklenko was an experienced armour officer who had served at Nomonhan and managed to properly gauge the right moment to retire. The 5th Army used the time bought by Feklenko's delay to garrison the Stalin Line positions at Novgorod Volynskiy behind the Slucz river, 83km east of Rovno. On 4 July, Mackensen's III Armeekorps (mot.) seized two division-size bridgeheads over the River Horyn with artillery and Luftwaffe support. Generalmajor Friedrich Kühn's 14.Panzer-Division reached the outskirts of Novgorod Volynskiy on 5 July, but the road bridge over the Slucz had been destroyed and all crossing sites were covered by fire from bunkers on the far side. Mackensen judged the Soviet defenses at Novgorod Volynskiy too strong for a hasty attack so he spent nearly two more days bringing up the other two divisions in his corps.

Mackensen directed Generalleutnant Walther Düvert's 13 Panzer-Division to bypass the strong defense at Novgorod Volynskiy and cross the Slucz river 8km to the south at Hulsk. At 0330 hours on 7 July, Oberstleutnant Job-Detlef von Raczeck's I/Schutzen-Regiment 93 from Düvert's division quietly slipped across the river in assault boats and surprised the Soviet troops in the bunkers covering the crossing site. Raczeck's assault troops cleared the bunkers with explosive charges and established a bridgehead, which was quickly reinforced with two more infantry battalions.[62] In this sector, the Stalin Line consisted of a dozen bunkers, which were gradually cleared out while German pioneers built a pontoon bridge over the Slucz. Kirponos decided to commit the remaining armour of the 9th, 15th, 19th and 22nd Mechanized Corps – perhaps 250–300 tanks – to eliminate Düvert's bridgehead on 8 July. However, by the time that Soviet armour began its counterattack, German panzerjägers had crossed the river and they repulsed the uncoordinated and piecemeal attacks with heavy losses. By the end of 8 July, Mackensen's corps had created a wide-scale breach in the Stalin Line and the 5th Army was in retreat. While still mopping up around Novgorod Volynskiy, Mackensen made the bold decision – the kind that German low-level commanders were empowered to make – to immediately dispatch a kampfgruppe down the road toward Kiev.

Düvert selected Raczeck to form a kampfgruppe, which included Oberleutnant Heinz Renk's 7./Pz.Regt 4, an artillery battery from AR 13 and some panzerjägers, and advance eastward as far as possible. Kampfgruppe Raczeck bypassed retreating Soviet columns and marched 80km to enter the city of Zhitomir unexpectedly on the afternoon of 8 July. Even though Raczek's force was quite small, the Red Army put up fairly weak resistance in Zhitomir – mostly snipers and a handful of BT and T-26 light tanks, which were knocked out. One German Panzer III fell into a crater and was immobilized, but Raczek secured Zhitomir at negligible cost. Deciding to continue while Soviet resistance was weak, Raczek left some troops in Zhitomir and pushed on another 110km, reaching the River Irpen at 0300 hours on 9 July. Just seventeen days after the beginning of Barbarossa, the lead element of 13.Panzer-Division was 17km from the center of Kiev.

However, Raczek could not capture a city of nearly one million people with ten tanks and a couple of infantry companies. It would take a few days for the rest of 13.Panzer-Division and the III Armeekorps (mot.) to catch up, which would give Kirponos some time to strengthen the city's defences. Nor was the XXXXVIII Armeekorps (mot.) in any immediate position to help with an impromptu assault upon Kiev. Crüwell's 11.Panzer-Division advanced from Ostrog and captured Berdichev on 7 July, but was struck by a counterattack from Vlasov's 4th Mechanized Corps the next day. With Zhukov egging him on from Moscow, Kirponos committed much of his remaining armour to interfere with the forward advance of von Kleist's panzers past Zhitomir and Berdichev, which brought the German advance to a halt for several days in order to fend off recurrent Soviet attacks. This tactic managed to delay a German assault on Kiev, but the 9th, 19th and 22nd were reduced to a total of just ninety-five tanks by the end of 13 July. The Soviet counterattacks also convinced Hitler that von Kleist's panzers could not capture Kiev without the full support of Heeresgruppe Süd's infantry and artillery, so he began to reconsider using at least one or two corps to envelope the Soviet 6th and 12th Armies in the vicinity of Uman.

Kishinev, 2–12 July 1941

While the leadership of Heeresgruppe Süd was pondering whether to go for Kiev or for envelopment of Uman, Romania made its bid to regain its lost province of

Bessarabia, which had been seized by the Red Army in 1940. The Romanian 3rd and 4th Armies were committed to the operation, with fourteen infantry divisions, six brigades and the 1st Armoured Division. Brigadier General Alecu I. Sion, a long-serving artillery officer with no prior experience commanding maneuver units, was chosen to lead the newly-formed division just six weeks before it was committed to battle. Although trained by German instructors, the Romanians chose not to commit their armour as a concentrated formation but instead detached one tank regiment with seventy-five French-built Renault R-35 tanks to act in the infantry support role for their III Army Corps. Sion led the rest of the division, which had two tank battalions (126 Skoda-built R-2 light tanks – the same as the Pz.35(t) in German service) and five motorized infantry battalions. Germany provided the 11.Armee, which was already deployed in Romania, to support the Romanian offensive with five infantry divisions and three Sturmgeschütz-Abteilungen, but no other armour. Opposing them, General Ivan Tyulenev's Southern Front relied upon the 9th Army to hold Bessarabia with seven rifle divisions, two cavalry divisions and the 2nd and 18th Mechanized Corps. The two Soviet corps had a total of 625 tanks, including a battalion of T-34s and one company of KV-1s. Unlike other front-line Red Army units, Tyulenev's Southern Front had ten days after the start of Barbarossa to prepare for combat, so they benefited from a less hectic transition to a wartime footing.

The III Army Corps of the Romanian 4th Army crossed the Prut River into central Bessarabia on 2 July with a single reserve infantry division, while the German XXX Armeekorps crossed on their left flank. The invaders advanced 8–10km on the first day, pushing aside border guard units. The Romanian advance was sluggish and it took five days for the III Army Corps to get all three of its divisions across the Prut. Initially, Tyulenev wanted to evacuate Bessarabia and withdraw the 9th Army behind the Dniester River, but he was over-ruled by the Stavka, which ordered him to use his armour to counterattack the German-Romanian units that had crossed the Prut River. Thanks to the time provided by the slow Romanian build-up, Tyulenev was able to launch a fairly coordinated attack at Lozova with the 11th Tank Division and 48th Rifle Corps on 7 July that caught the Romanians completely by surprise. The Soviet tanks overran an infantry regiment from the 35th Reserve Infantry Division, then two artillery regiments; over 2,200 Romanians and forty-four artillery pieces were captured.[63] Red Army tankers quickly learned that the Romanian Army was particularly vulnerable to Soviet armour, since it lacked the equipment or training to establish an effective anti-tank defense. Romanian light tanks were armed with low-velocity 3.7cm guns that were only suited for infantry support and the infantry divisions lacked heavy artillery or 8.8cm flak guns to stop Soviet medium or heavy tanks. Consequently, at a cost of just twenty tanks knocked out, the Red Army counterattack forced the Romanian III Army Corps onto the defensive for a week while they awaited assistance from the Germans.

The Romanian 4th Army advanced cautiously into Bessarabia, as the Soviet 9th Army continued to mount small-scale counterattacks with tanks and infantry whenever an opportunity arose. By 14 July, the German 11.Armee provided one infantry division for the drive on Kishinev and the rest of the Romanian 1st Armoured Division was committed to reinforce an all-out offensive. The Soviet forces fell back grudgingly, but Tyulenev was now authorized to withdraw behind the Dniester River. The Soviet 47th Tank Division conducted one last counterattack west of Kishinev on 15 July, with Soviet T-26 tanks engaging Romanian R-2 light tanks. By this point, with German forces threatening Kiev, the Red Army could no longer afford to have large armoured units tied up in Bessarabia and the 9th Army began withdrawing across the Dniester. Both the 2nd and 18th Mechanized Corps were ordered to move to Uman; both formations were still combat-capable and the 2nd Corps possessed most of its T-34s and KV-1s. A task force from the Romanian 1st Armoured Division entered Kishinev on the morning of 16 July on the heels of the Soviet withdrawal, over-running some Soviet rearguards. By 20 July, the last Soviet units had left Bessarabia.

The Romanian Army used its armour sparingly in the liberation of Bessarabia and it succeeded, but at the overall cost of 22,765 casualties. Romanian armour losses were light, but at least 10 per cent of the tanks involved were destroyed or damaged after two weeks of operations. In contrast, the Soviet 9th Army suffered significantly fewer losses than the Romanians and learned how poorly prepared the Romanians were to counter armoured attacks. The fighting around Kishinev demonstrated that the Red Army's armour leaders were capable of mounting effective counterattacks when given time and resources. Although a forgotten sideshow, operations around Kishinev presaged a day when Soviet armour would demonstrate the full efficacy of their Deep Battle doctrine.

Debacle at Uman, 15 July–8 August
Even as the 9th Army was withdrawing from Bessarabia, Marshal Semyon Budyonny – now placed in overall charge over both Kirponos and Tyulenev by Stalin – made the foolish decision to abandon the westernmost end of the Dniester river line, even though it had not yet been breached. The stout defense of Bessarabia convinced Budyonny that the threat from the Romanians was not serious, but Panzergruppe Kleist was a different matter. The German advance after Zhitomir was threatening to break out onto the flat steppe of the Ukraine and Budyonny wanted to build up a new front around Uman to cover the 300km-wide sector between the Dniester and Kiev. Budyonny ordered the 6th and 12th Armies – which had retreated 450km from the western Ukraine, hounded all the way by the German 17.Armee – to concentrate at Uman. To anchor the flanks of this new front, the 26th Army was assigned to defend the area south of Kiev along the Dnieper, while the 2nd Army held the area between Uman and the Dniester. Complicating matters, some of the armies were subordinate to Kirponos and others to Tyulenev, rendering any cooperation a small miracle.

Hitler was adamant that the Red Army should not reestablish a viable defensive front in the southern Ukraine or behind the Dnieper River and, in Führer Directive No. 33, issued on 19 July, he directed that, 'the most important object is, by concentric attacks, to destroy the enemy 12th and 6th Armies while they are still west of the Dnieper.'[64] Von Kleist quickly developed a plan to encircle the Soviet armies around Uman, while the 6.Armee kept up pressure on Soviet forces around Kiev. Mackensen's III Armeekorps (mot.) would strike the 26th Army before it had a chance to establish a firm defense and thereby create a breach south of Kiev. Then XIV and XXXXVIII Armeekorps (mot.) would jump off from Zhitomir with six divisions, turning southward to roll up the right flank of the 6th Army. Meanwhile, the infantry of 17.Armee would continue to act as beaters, pushing and herding both Soviet armies eastward, toward von Kleist's enveloping panzers. The German 11.Armee, which began to cross the Dniester on 20 July, would also act in a supporting role. German radio intelligence played a significant role in forming the Uman *kessel*; Soviet radio discipline deteriorated sharply during the hectic retreat from the border and the 12th Army was guilty of sending many messages in clear during this period, which provided valuable insight to von Kleist about Soviet dispositions and intentions.[65]

Although the German panzer units enjoyed a number of advantages over the Red Army at this point, Heeresgruppe Süd's logistic situation declined rapidly in early July and became increasingly critical throughout the summer. Whenever the panzers advanced quickly, they not only left much of their supporting infantry and artillery behind, but their own *Gepäcktroß* (field trains) as well. Unteroffizier Heinrich Skodell, a gunner in 1./Sturmgeschütz-Abteilung 197, noted in mid-July that, 'rations and resupply are very poor; we must take care of ourselves. Unfortunately, there was not much available.'[66]

After a brief halt to let some supplies catch up, Panzergruppe Kleist resumed its attack on 15 July, beginning with Mackensen committing the 13 and 14.Panzer-Divisionen as well as the SS-Division *Wiking* near Fastov. The 26th Army was comprised of eight rifle and two cavalry divisions, but it had few tanks and could not hope to stop Mackensen's corps in open terrain. Initially, the 26th Army fell back from Fastov and Balaya Zerkov toward the Dnieper when confronted with massed German armour. At the same time, Lemelsen's XXXXVIII Armeekorps (mot.) attacked the right flank of the 6th Army near Kazatin, with the 11 and 16.Panzer-Divisionen and two motorized infantry divisions. The remnants of the 15th and 16th Mechanized Corps were easily pushed back. Suddenly, a huge gap was appearing in the front between the 6th and 26th Armies. Von Kleist quickly sent the XIV Armeekorps (mot.) into this gap, with Generalleutnant Alfred Ritter von Hubicki's 9.Panzer-Division in the lead.

Amazingly, the 6th Army was able to respond to this crisis by quickly re-deploying the 2nd and 24th Mechanized Corps to stop the 11 and 16.Panzer-Divisionen from completely enveloping its flank. A fierce tank battle was fought around Monastryshche from 21–27 July as the Soviet 2nd and 24th Mechanized Corps tried to prop up the army's battered flank while the remainder of the 6th and 12th Armies retreated eastward toward Uman. General-major Yuri V. Novoselsky's 2nd Mechanized Corps still had about 100 operational tanks, including one KV-1 and eighteen T-34s, and gave a good account of itself – but fuel and ammunition were in very short supply. Meanwhile, the 18th Mechanized

Corps fought a delaying action against the pursuing 17.Armee, but by late July Axis forces were closing in on all sides. Although the 17.Armee had no German armour, it did include the Hungarian 'Rapid Corps' under Major General Béla Miklós. This Hungarian formation was roughly equivalent to a reinforced German motorized infantry division, with three armoured reconnaissance battalions (equipped with Swedish-designed Toldi light tanks), four motorized infantry battalions, eight bicycle infantry battalions and two cavalry regiments. Miklós, an experienced cavalry officer, led his formation with dash and élan against the flank of the retreated Soviet armies.

Despite the failure to smash in 6th Army's flank, Hubicki's 9.Panzer-Division captured Novo Archangel'sk, which threatened the Soviet lines of communication to Uman. Vlasov's 4th Mechanized Corps – reduced to perhaps thirty tanks – was tasked with retaking Novo Archangel'sk on 31 July, but the remaining T-34s were too starved of fuel and ammunition to achieve a breakthrough. Once the LSSAH moved up to take over this position, Hubicki advanced southward to seize the bridge at Pervomaysk on 2 August, where he linked up with the lead

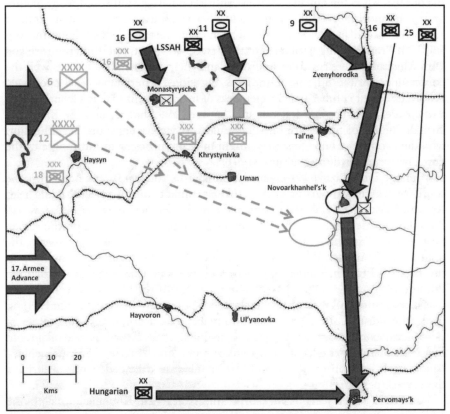

Panzergruppe 1 executes the Uman encirclement against the Soviet 6th and 12th Armies, 15 July–3 August.

element of 17.Armee – the 1.Gebirgsjäger-Division. Miklós' Hungarian 'Rapid Corps' also linked-up with 9.Panzer-Division the next day, further sealing the Uman *kessel*. Von Kleist had surrounded the bulk of the Soviet 6th and 12th Armies, including the remnants of several mechanized corps.

It is often stated that the German panzer division could encircle Soviet forces, but that they suffered heavy losses from Soviet break-out attempts while awaiting the arrival of German infantry to take over the *kesselschlacht*. This did not occur at Uman. By the time 9.Panzer-Division and LSSAH cut off the last Soviet escape route, the infantry of 17.Armee had already arrived in force on the western side of the *kessel*, which was crushed in less than a week. Since the Red Army had no significant armoured forces south of the Dnieper, von Kleist's panzers had little difficulty fending off the pin-prick counterattacks that did occur. Panzergruppe Kleist suffered 11,415 casualties between 20 July and 10 August, including 2,468 dead, which were considerable and the men could not easily be replaced. While losses of front-line junior officers and NCOs were steadily mounting, few officers above battalion level were casualties and this meant that the overall ability of German panzer units to plan and conduct operations remained fairly good. In contrast, when the Uman *kessel* was crushed on 8 August, the Red Army did not only lose another 200,000 troops, but also a large percentage of its trained command cadre in the Southwest Front. The commanders of both the 6th and 12th Armies, along with most of their staff, were captured. Both the 16th and 24th Mechanized Corps were destroyed and their commanders lost, as well the commanders of the 8th and 44th Tank Divisions. The Uman *kessel* effectively removed the last combat-worthy elements of five mechanized corps from the Red Army order of battle and left the area between the Dnieper and the Black Sea virtually bereft of Soviet armour. Some tankers were among the 11,000 troops who did escape the *kessel*, but they would only be sufficient to form three of the new tank brigades during autumn 1941.

After the Uman *kessel* was crushed, von Kleist's panzers spread out across the southern Ukraine in pursuit of the broken remnants of the Soviet 9th and 18th Armies. Most of the 2nd Army retreated into the fortified port of Odessa, which the Germans delegated to the Romanian Army to reduce. Although the Uman *kessel* was smaller than either the Minsk-Bialystok or Smolensk encirclements, the Southwest Front lacked the resources to quickly patch together a new front as the Western Front had done after each of its disasters. Consequently, neither the 9th nor 18th Armies could make a stand in front of the Dnieper River and von Kleist committed all nine of his motorized divisions to the pursuit. For the first time, in August the Red Army began to make greater use of anti-tank mines to slow German armoured advances. In some units, mines caused more damage and casualties than Soviet tank and anti-tank gun fire; one batterie of Sturmgeschütz-Abteilung 197 had five of its six StuG III assault guns damaged by mines during a three-week period.[67]

Von Macksensen's III Armeekorps (mot.) reached Kremenchug with the 13.Panzer-Division and SS-Division *Wiking* on 15 August. Further south, von Wietersheim's XIV Armeekorps (mot.) stormed Dnepropetrovsk and part of

Zaporozhe with the 14.Panzer-Division and 60.Infanterie-Division (mot.) on 17–18 August, then seized a bridgehead across the river a week later. However, the Soviets managed to blow up all the major railroad bridges across the Dniepr – at Dnepropetrovsk, Zaporozhe, Kremenchug and Kanev – which would soon cripple German logistics once they moved any distance beyond the river. Meanwhile, Lemelsen's XXXXVIII Armeekorps (mot.) eliminated Soviet forces in the port of Nikolayev with 16.Panzer-Division and the LSSAH, then cleared out the lower Dnieper River area. By late August, von Kleist's panzers had secured the entire western bank of the Dnieper River and were poised to seize bridgeheads near Kremenchug and Dnepropetrovsk that could threaten the flank of Kirponos' forces in Kiev.

Yelnya: Zhukov's Pyhrric Victory, 8 August–6 September
On 16 July, Guderian disobeyed direct orders from Generallfeldmarschall von Bock to direct his own panzer forces toward an immediate link-up with Hoth's 7.Panzer-Division at Yartsevo. Instead, Guderian figured that somebody else could attend to such details and what really mattered was pushing eastward as far and as fast as possible. Visions of Moscow's golden spires apparently twinkled in his mind's eye. Toward that end, he deliberately ordered von Vietinghoff's XXXXVI Armeekorps (mot.) to proceed east toward Yelnya, not north to Yartsevo. On 19 July, the 10.Panzer-Division captured Yelnya and gained a bridgehead across the Densa river – just 300km from Moscow. In Guderian's mind, possession of the Yelnya bridgehead was critical since it served as a springboard for a march upon Moscow. Von Bock was less than happy when he heard that Guderian had not closed the Smolensk *kessel* at Yartsevo and disregarded Guderian's claim that capture of Yelnya was a great success. Rather, von Bock wrote, 'I immediately replied that that was not what mattered, and that the only thing that did was the hermetic sealing of the Smolensk pocket while screening to the east.'[68]

Like it or not, von Bock was now forced to defend Guderian's bridgehead at Yelnya, which rapidly became a magnet for Soviet counterattacks. The 10.Panzer-Division held the salient on its own for four days, before being joined by the SS-Division *Reich* on 23 July and then Infanterie-Regiment Großdeutschland on 28 July. However, the Red Army forces arrayed around von Vietinghoff's XXXXVI Armeekorps (mot.) gathered ominously in late July. The Stavka formed the 24th Army under General-major Konstantin K. I. Rakutin, an NKVD officer, who was tasked with eliminating the salient, but his initial attacks in late July lacked the resources to overcome von Vietinghoff's defense. Armour is not well-suited to static defense and committing a motorized corps to an attritional battle was a waste of precious resources that von Bock could not tolerate for long. He ordered the XX Armeekorps to move into the salient with three infantry divisions and replace von Vietinghoff's motorized division; the first infantry division entered the salient on 30 July and by 6 August most of von Vietinghoff's forces had been replaced. The 10.Panzer-Division was placed in reserve behind the salient, to support the XX Armeekorps if needed.

In early August, Georgy Zhukov, the new commander of the Reserve Front which included Rakutin's 24th Army, decided to crush the Yelnya salient with a massive counter-offensive. Whereas Rakutin's earlier attacks had failed because he pitted a handful of Soviet rifle divisions against German panzers, Zhukov intended to mount a proper combined-arms offensive with tanks, artillery and air support – just like his triumph at Nomonhan in August 1939. Using his influence with the Stavka he received several RVGK artillery regiments, more and better-quality rifle divisions, and two tank divisons formed from incomplete mechanized corps in the Northern Caucasus and Central Asia. Polkovnik Ivan D. Illarionov's 102nd Tank Division was the strongest formation, with eight KV-1 tanks and 100 BT-series light tanks. Polkovnik Aleksei S. Beloglazov's 105th Tank Division had about 100–120 T-26 light tanks, in poor condition. Zhukov also received the 103rd and 106th Motorized Divisions, each with a battalion of 30–40 light tanks. In addition, Zhukov received a single company of nine T-34 tanks. All told, Zhukov was able to assemble a motley collection of about 300 tanks to spearhead the 24th Army's attack against the Yelnya salient.

Zhukov demonstrated little tactical finesse or operational art in planning the Yelnya counter-offensive. He formed a shock group based around Illarionov's 102nd Tank Division and three rifle divisions, supported by some 230 atillery pieces, to attack on a single axis on the northern side of the salient. The counter-offensive began at dawn on 8 August, attacking the positions held by SS-Division *Reich* and the 15.Infanterie-Division, and made only a minor advance. Fighting continued for a week, with the German 15.Infanterie-Division suffering about 2,000 casualties, but Illarionov's 102nd Tank Division lost two battalion commanders and about half his tanks. By massing his forces in just one sector rather than attempting a pincer attack, Zhukov allowed the Germans to employ the tactic of 'the central position', with all its attendant advantages for the defenders. By 18 August, Zhukov was forced to break off the counter-offensive, having achieved very little. He was particularly furious at his tank commanders and sent an angry memorandum to Polkovnik Beloglazov stating:

> 105th Tank Division, despite my categorical warning about moving forward, has marked time in one place for 10 days and, without achieving any kind of results, has suffered losses. In light of its inability to resolve independent combat missions, 105th Tank Division is disbanded and will turn its personnel and equipment over to 102nd Tank Division.[69]

Zhukov asked for and received more reinforcements from the RVGK, then resumed the Yelnya offensive on 30 August. This time, Zhukov intended to mount a concentric attack from all directions, but his main effort remained in the north. After very heavy fighting, the German defense began to give way as casualties mounted and Yelnya was captured on 5 September. Unwilling to suffer further losses, von Bock authorized the evacuation of the salient on 6 September. For the first time, the Red Army had broken a German positional defense, although no enemy units were encircled or destroyed. However, Zhukov's victory – which he went to lengths to promote – was pyrrhic in outcome. The Battle of the Yelnya salient cost the Reserve Front roughly 75,000 casualties from mid-July to early September, and both tank divisions were so depleted that they were broken up afterwards to form cadres for tank brigades.[70] In contrast, the German defenders suffered roughly 10,000 casualties in the battle, three-quarters of which were among the infantry units of 4.Armee, not Guderian's XXXXVI Armeekorps (mot.). Although efforts have been made to suggest that the defense of Yelnya sapped Guderian's armoured strength, Viettinghoff's corps had been replaced in the salient before Zhukov's counter-offensive began and did not lose a significant amount of tanks or personnel in the July defensive fighting. Instead, the main result of the Yelnya counteroffensive was to demonstrate that the Red Army did not yet have the ability to mount effective deep armoured operations, but rather, clumsy and costly battles of attrition that could only gain their objectives through profligate expenditure of blood and resources. While the loss of the Yelnya salient was a painful blow to German morale, von Bock was quick to realize that the losses suffered by the Western and Reserve Fronts increased their vulnerability when Heeresgruppe Mitte resumed its advance eastward.

Kiev: the Führer's Choice, 25 August–20 September

While von Kleist's panzers had been creating the Uman *kessel*, Kirponos had used a good portion of his remaining armour to spearhead a counterattack by the Soviet 5th Army against the left flank of 6.Armee, which was already in the suburbs of Kiev. This attack was more diversionary than a serious effort to envelope AOK 6; it was intended to divert German attention and reinforcements away from Kiev. Vlasov had been pulled out of the Uman battle before his mechanized corps was encircled and he was put in command of the newly-formed 37th Army, which barred the direct route into Kiev from the west. In order to buy time for Vlasov's defense, the 5th Army assembled a counterattack force consisting of the remnants of the 9th and 22nd Mechanized Corps as well as two rifle and one cavalry divisions. Both mechanized corps were little more than cadre formations after a month of fighting, with a total of just thirty-five tanks (including one KV-1) between them. The 5th Army's assault group attacked the German LI Armeekorps at Malyn, northwest of Kiev, on 24 July and continued attacking in this area for the next twelve days. Although the counterattack succeeded in pushing the German 262.Infanterie-Division back 10km and caused some anxiety in Heeresgruppe Süd, it failed to seriously disrupt German efforts to prepare for an all-out assault on Kiev. Furthermore, the Southwest Front's remaining armour was squandered in this effort and both the 9th and 22nd Mechanized Corps had no remaining operational tanks by mid-August. A major local attack by the German 6.Armee inflicted greater damage on the 5th Army, which finally prompted Stalin to allow the battered 5th Army to retreat behind the Dnieper River on 16 August. Vlasov's 37th Army still held a strong defense in Kiev, but German advances on his flanks left his troops in a dangerously exposed salient and Kirponos was forced to stretch out his forces to protect the northern flank along the Desna and the southern flank along the Dnieper. His only mobile reserve was the greatly-depleted 32nd Tank Division, stationed behind the Kiev salient at Priluki.

Although most of the OKH staff and the leadership of Heeresgruppe Mitte, including Guderian, had been pushing Hitler to resume the advance on Moscow after the Battle of Smolensk was concluded, the Führer was less sanguine.[71] A great deal has already been written about the internal German debates about choices of operational objectives in August 1941 and whether or not alternative decisions might have led to more favorable outcomes. I will not belabor this point – important though it is – but instead focus on those aspects that are important for assessing the conduct of armoured warfare. Hitler recognized that the 'straight-up-the-middle' approach in July through Minsk and Smolensk had been costly in terms of both equipment and personnel. Von Bock's Heeresgruppe Mitte suffered over 77,000 casualties during the month-long battle around Smolensk, including 17,000 dead. While Hitler's primary objective in Barbarossa was to destroy the Red Army, it is often missed that he wanted to do so at the lowest possible cost to his own forces. Hitler craved public support in Germany and therefore sought easy victories. By August 1941, it was apparent to Hitler that the Red Army was going to block the path to Moscow with every last soldier, tank and gun it could muster, and he became increasingly skittish about the Moscow axis as German losses mounted. He also realized that winter and the end of the campaigning season would soon be at hand and, if Barbarossa was to be presented to the German people as a success – even though a second year of fighting in Russia was now inevitable – Hitler needed another one or two large-scale victories to create the impression of triumph. The relatively quick success at Uman convinced him that the best place to find cheap victories was in the Ukraine. Führer Directive 34, issued on 30 July, had shifted Heeresgruppe Mitte to the defensive in order to provide Hoth's and Guderian's armour a brief pause and for the infantry armies to reach the front-line east of Smolensk.[72] During the pause, Guderian's panzer units had been increasingly drawn toward the south in order to deal with Soviet counterattacks from the Roslavl and Gomel areas. On 23 August, Hitler directed that two of Guderian's motorized corps near Gomel – the XXIV and XXXXVII Armeekorps (mot.) – would attack southward to link up with von Kleist's Panzergruppe 1 attacking northward out of the Kremenchug bridgehead.

Although this double envelopment looked very feasible on Hitler's map table at Rastenburg, the impact on the men and equipment in the panzer divisions would add considerable strain to units which had already been in continuous combat for nine weeks. The rough terrain did not favor rapid advances and there were numerous water obstacles to cross. Schweppenburg's XXIV Armeekorps (mot.), which would lead the advance to the south, would have difficulty keeping 100–120 tanks operational between the 3 and 4.Panzer-Divisionen.[73] Guderian's supply situation was very poor, with only a bare minimum of fuel available. Mackensen's III Armeekorps (mot.), which had the 14 and 16.Panzer-Divisionen at Dnepropetrovsk, was in better shape. Kühn's 14.Panzer-Division was able to keep ninety–100 tanks operational throughout the month of August, equivalent to 65–70 per cent of its strength at the start of Barbarossa.[74] While the Germans were initially committing just 300 tanks and seven divisions to the double envelopment operation against the Kiev salient, the Red Army had little or no armour or mobile forces left in this area to oppose them.

On 25 August, von Schweppenburg began his attack with Model's 3.Panzer-Division, while the 4.Panzer-Division and 10.Infanterie-Division (mot.) were still enroute. Guderian's *schwerpunkt* was intended to slice through the left flank of the newly-created Bryansk Front, between its 13th and 21st Armies. Von Schweppenburg's initial objective was the vital rail junction at Konotop. Kampfgruppe von Lewinski, which had about sixty tanks from Panzer-Regiment 6 and the half tracks of I/Schützen-Regiment 3, advanced 80km in thirty hours. Model was right behind this vanguard unit, aggressively leading from the front. Despite the threadbare nature of the German offensive, it began with a piece of good fortune when Kampfgruppe von Lewinski succeeded in capturing intact the 700-meter-long bridge over the Desna River near Novgorod Severskiy on the morning of 26 August. The Red Army reacted to the loss of the bridge by shelling it intensively; Model was wounded by a shell splinter and the commander of his artillery regiment was killed.[75]

However, Model's depleted panzer division was not strong enough to exploit this success on its own and rainy weather and logistical problems reduced von Schweppenburg's ability to get the rest of his corps across the Desna. In the meantime, the Stavka reacted quickly by deploying the 40th Army as a blocking force in the path of the XXIV Armeekorps (mot.) build-up on the Desna. The 40th Army was typical of the hastily-formed formations that the Red Army fielded in 1941: a grab-bag collection of three rifle divisions, 8,000 paratroop recruits – roughly 25,000 combat troops total – but very little artillery and few anti-tank guns. General-major Sergey I. Ogurtsov's 10th Tank Division, reduced to an 800-man battlegroup with about fifteen tanks, was attached as a mobile reserve for 40th Army. Yet an even bigger weakness for the Red Army at this point was the lack of radios below division level, which greatly reduced the situational awareness of Soviet commanders.

Von Schweppenburg's corps advanced very slowly in the last days of August, finally getting the 10.Infanterie-Division (mot.) across the Desna near Korop, but a strong counterattack threw them back across the river. By 1 September, von Schweppenburg had both 3 and 4.Panzer-Divisionen across the Desna with a total of just eighty-six operational tanks, and both flanks of his corps were virtually up in the air.[76] The Stavka recognized both the danger and vulnerability of Guderian's narrow thrust southward and initially tried to slow down his advance with massed air attacks by DB-3 tactical bombers on 29–31 August, but these inflicted only minor damage. While Soviet air attacks were increasing in frequency, they lacked the ability to seriously interdict German armoured movements in the manner that Allied tactical aviation demonstrated over Western Europe in 1943–45. Ogurtsov's tankers counterattacked Model's 3.Panzer-Division west of Glukhov, while minor armour units from the 21st Army struck 4.Panzer-Division near Korop. Kampfgruppe Eberbach from 4.Panzer-Division repulsed the 21st Army counterattacks, knocked out seven tanks and took over 1,200 prisoners. Model's division was brought to a halt for several days by the Soviet counterattack, as well as severe fuel shortages. Guderian had hoped to use the XXXXVII Armeekorps (mot.) in his advance to the south but continuous Soviet counterattacks from the east forced him to commit it to guard his left flank. The 10.Infanterie-Division (mot.) was used to screen the right flank of the penetration, leaving von Schweppenburg with just the much-depleted 3 and 4.Panzer-Divisionen to continue the advance. Guderian badgered von Bock to release more units to support his operation, but Heeresgruppe Mitte had its hands full containing continued counterattacks by Timoshenko's Western Front and could only promise the token addition of the Infanterie-Regiment *Grossdeutschland* on 30 August and then the SS-Division *Reich*.[77] Guderian continued to manifest a primadonna attitude throughout the Kiev operation, constantly demanding priority for reinforcements while ignoring the 'big picture.' Von Bock tried to relieve Guderian of command, but failed.[78]

Yeremenko's Attempted Deep Battle, 30 August–7 September

On 14 August, the Stavka formed the Bryansk Front from remnants of other formations and placed it under the command of General-leytenant Andrei Yeremenko, a forty-eight-year-old cavalry officer who had been recalled from the Transbaikal MD in July. Yeremenko was a rising star in the Red Army and Stalin – who was fond of officers that had served in the *Konarmia* in the Civil War – believed him to be competent and reliable, so he was often given the most difficult assignments. He played a brief but important role in the Battle of Smolensk until he was wounded. After a brief recovery, he asked for another command and the Bryansk Front was a critical post, since he would have to halt Panzergruppe Guderian.

At 0610 hours on 30 August, the Stavka issued VGK Directive No. 001428 which ordered Yeremenko to encircle and 'destroy' Panzergruppe Guderian by means of a counter-offensive toward Starodub, which was personally amended by Stalin to read: 'Guderian and his entire group must be smashed to smithereens.'[79] Such a mission was well beyond the capabilities of the Bryansk Front, but Yeremenko dutifully attempted to accomplish this mission. Lemelsen's XXXXVII Armeekorps (mot) was screening a very long stretch of Guderian's flank around Starodub, with the 17.Panzer-Division holding nearly a 60km-wide front. Yeremenko decided to attack with two rifle divisions from 3rd Army in the center, supported by flank attacks from the 13th and 50th Armies, with seven more divisions, to tie down the rest of Lemelsen's over-extended corps. In an attempt to utilize elements of the defunct Deep Battle doctrine, Yeremenko formed a mobile group under General-major Arkadiy N. Ermakov, consisting of the 108th Tank Division, the 141st Tank Brigade and the 4th Cavalry Division, to exploit the expected breakthrough. Instead of the earlier ad hoc counterattacks around Smolensk, Yeremenko hoped to mount a properly-planned attack incorporating air and artillery support, as well as adequate fuel and ammunition stockpiles, but Stalin wanted immediate results. Polkovnik Sergey A. Ivanov's

108th Tank Division had been formed in July and had sixty-five tanks (five KV, thirty-eight T-34 and twenty-two T-40), while Polkovnik Petr G. Chernov's 141st Tank Brigade had sixty-two tanks (four KV, eighteen T-34, forty BT). Given that 17.Panzer-Division was effectively reduced to only a single Panzer-Abteilung with about fifty tanks (with only half Pz.IIIs), Mobile Group Ermakov

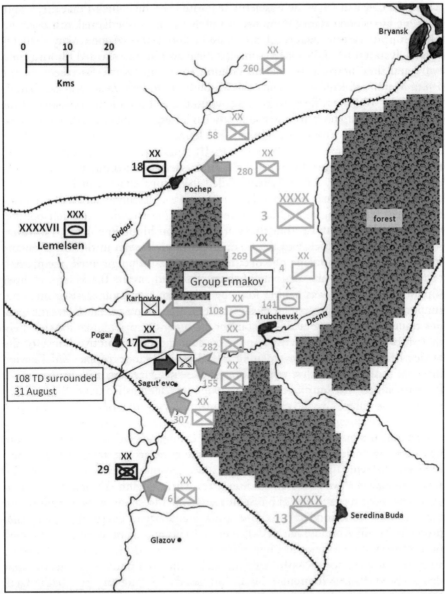

Yeremenko's Deep Battle, 30 August–7 September; Group Ermakov, including 18th Tank Division attacks Lemelsen's XXXXVII Armeekorps (mot.) in order to 'smash Panzergruppe Guderian'.

would enjoy a 2–1 numerical advantage in armour and the presence of nine KV and fifty-six T-34 tanks should have been decisive.

Hoping to appease Stalin by making an armoured probing attack on the evening of 30 August – just twelve hours after receiving the order from the Stavka – Yeremenko ordered Group Ermakov to march toward the town of Pogar and seize a crossing over the Sudost River. Apparently, Yeremenko had little idea where the German frontline was actually located and he believed that there were only enemy reconnaissance elements east of the river. Group Ermakov moved out without prior reconnaissance of the route or knowledge of the enemy's whereabouts. Ivanov's 108th Tank Division led the march and he divided his force into two parallel columns, with the left column consisting of two battalions of the 108th Motorized Rifle Regiment, a battalion of T-40 light tanks and two battalions of the 108th Artillery Regiment, while the right column consisted of his main assault group built around the 216th Tank Regiment. Some 20km northeast of Pogar, near the village of Karbovka, the leftmost column ran into an ambush by Panzer-Regiment 39, which had its Pz.III tanks hidden in a forest parallel to the road. In short order, five T-40 light tanks were knocked out and the column thrown into disarray. The Germans called in a Stuka attack which hit the two artillery battalions hard: nine artillery tractors were destroyed and half the artillery pieces were damaged. Oddly, Ivanov heard the sounds of his left column under attack just 8km away, but chose not to support his other column. However, when he tried to skirt around the German positions, he ran into another enemy blocking force at the village of Romanovka. Rashly, Ivanov ordered one platoon of three KV-1s and one platoon of three T-34s to assault the village without support. Romanovka was held in force by a detachment of Panzer-Regiment 39, supported by panzerjägers and heavy artillery. By this point, the Germans were beginning to adapt their tactics to counter the superior Soviet tanks and they held their fire until pointblank range and then concentrated upon the tracks of the Soviet heavy tanks. Amazingly, all three T-34s and one of the KV-1s were immobilized and later destroyed, forcing the two surviving KV-1s to retreat. Ivanov claimed that four German tanks were damaged in Romanovka, but they still held the village. By the end of 30 August, the vanguard of Group Ermakov's armoured spearhead was immobilized due to confusion and uncertainty.

Generalleutnant Hans-Jürgen von Arnim, commander of 17.Panzer-Division, was a strong believer in the offensive and he decided not to wait for Group Ermakov to reorganize itself and attack. On the morning of 31 August, von Arnim mounted a two-pronged counterattack with elements of Panzer-Regiment 39, his panzerjägers and one of his Schützen regiments, supported by artillery and the Luftwaffe. The sudden combined-arms counterattack caught Ivanov by surprise and his division lost one KV-1, eleven T-34s and eight T-40s, but claimed twenty-two German tanks. Strangely, Ivanov chose to dig his tanks in and formed a hedgehog in the forest – probably to shield him from further air attacks – but this allowed Panzer-Regiment 39 to surround the bulk of the 108th Tank Division by the end of the day. On 1 September, von Arnim continued to pound Ivanov's encircled division with airpower and artillery, knocking out another seven T-34s and four T-40s. Strangely, the rest of Group Ermakov and Yeremenko's Bryansk Front did little to rescue their trapped armoured spear-head, even though the German forces encircling Ivanov were grossly out-numbered. The 4th Cavalry Division was easily fended off by 17.Panzer-Division and Chernov's 141st Tank Brigade accomplished little except losses.

Yeremenko began his offensive on the morning of 2 September, with a two-hour artillery preparation, but it was a weird attack where the armoured group was already surrounded and the Germans not where they were expected. Von Arnim tried to finish off Ivanov's division with a sudden assault by a panzer battalion supported by Stukas, but this effort was repulsed after heavy fighting; the Soviets admitted the loss of six T-34s and the Germans admitted that seven panzers were knocked out. Yeremenko's counterattack was quickly falling apart and Stalin admonished him for his failures. On the night of 3–4 September, Ivanov broke out with eleven tanks and 1,200 men and reached Soviet lines, having accomplished nothing. He left most of his wounded, artillery and equip-ment behind. Yeremenko continued attacking for a few more days, but Lemelsen's over-extended XXXXVII Armeekorps (mot.) managed to repulse these uncoor-dinated pin-prick attacks. By the end of the offensive, Group Ermakov had lost seventy-five of its 127 tanks and Ivanov's tank division had been destroyed as a fighting force. Yeremenko claimed the destruction of 110 German tanks – more than double the number in von Arnim's 17.Panzer-Division – but the plain fact is that Group Ermakov's armour had failed to strike a solid blow and German tank losses were likely in the neighborhood of about twenty knocked out and five destroyed. Overall, Yeremenko's counteroffensive cost the Bryansk Front 100,000 casualties and more than half its armour.[80] The operations of Group Ermakov were also the last armoured counterattack by the Red Army involving more than 100 tanks in 1941 – including a large number of T-34s – and the last attempt to execute Deep Battle according to PU-36 for some time. The utter failure of Group Ermakov to best a depleted and over-extended panzer division represents the nadir of the Red Army's skill at armoured operations in the Second World War.

Kiev: Closing the *Kessel*, 1–20 September
While Guderian's panzers were inching southward, most of von Kleist's armour managed to get a few days of rest and refit around Krivoi Rog and Dnepro-petrovsk, while 17.Armee took over the front along the Dnieper. Von Rundstedt had already decided to make his main effort at Kremenchug, but wanted to keep von Kleist's armour near Dnepropetrovsk as long as possible until infantry arrived to take over the bridgehead there, and also to deceive Kirponos as to where the German *schwerpunkt* would fall. To some extent Kirponos was misled, focusing more on the efforts to retake Dnepropetrovsk rather than the threat of possible envelopment from Kremenchug. Instead, he sent his best remaining units to Dnepropetrovsk and left the under-resourced 38th Army to secure the area around Kremenchug; this formation had two rifle divisions formed in July from reservists and local militiamen, completely lacking in anti-tank weapons

and possessing minimal artillery support. The only mobile reserve in the Kremenchug area was the burnt-out 47th Tank Division, which had one or two dozen light tanks. After extensive preparations, on 31 August the LII Armeekorps from 17 AOK established a bridgehead 40km southeast of Kremenchug. German pioneers were able to build a pontoon bridge across the 1,200-meter-wide channel in a single night. The German bridgehead across the Dnieper was precarious, but the best that the 38th Army could do was attempt to contain it, while Kirponos beseeched the Stavka for reinforcements. Grudgingly, the Stavka agreed to provide the 132nd Tank Brigade forming at Kharkov and Generalmajor Pavel A. Belov's 2nd Cavalry Corps to reinforce the 38th Army.

The Soviet counterattacks against von Schweppenburg's XXIV Armeekorps (mot.) south of the Desna forced Guderian to narrow his axis of advance. By 4 September, he had both 3 and 4.Panzer-Divisionen on line north of Korotop, but amazingly the 293rd Rifle Division and a separate tank battalion with twenty tanks managed to hold off both divisions for two days. On the night of 5–6 September, Kampfgruppe Eberbach tried an end run to get around the 293rd Rifle Division and cross the Seym River on the bridge at Baturin, but the Soviet tankers managed to hold off his storming party until the bridge could be blown up. Oberst Eberbach contented himself with knocking out six Soviet tanks and a regiment of artillery. Model had more luck and managed to get some of his motorized infantry across the Seym at Melnya and bring up a Brücko B column, which constructed an 8-ton pontoon bridge over the river. Fuel shortages temporarily held up von Schweppenburg's exploitation of this bridgehead but then, on 10 September, Model's 3.Panzer-Division exploded southward and achieved a clear breakthrough in the Soviet front. Model formed a *Vorausabteilung* (advance guard) under Major Heinz-Werner Frank, commander of Panzerjäger-Abteilung 521, with a platoon of Pz.III tanks, a company of Panzerjäger I self-propelled 4.7cm anti-tank guns, eight reconnaissance armoured cars, an artillery battery and some infantry in SPW half tracks. Model ordered them to go all-out while the Soviets were disorganized. Oberst Günther von Manteuffel would follow with the rest of the combat elements. Despite poor roads and rainy weather, Major Frank bypassed Konotop – leaving that for 4.Panzer-Division to mop up – and advanced 70km south to seize Romny.[81]

Major Frank's *Vorausabteilung* was isolated at Romny for the next several days, with Soviet units all around them, but their deep thrust had shattered the 40th Army's front in exactly the manner in which the Germans expected Blitzkrieg operations to work. Despite the arrival of the motorized 23rd NKVD Division (which took little actual part in the fighting), the 40th Army began to retreat eastward and Soviet resistance began to evaporate. Von Manteuffel and Model were able to push to Romny and regroup most of the division, deep behind Soviet lines. Although Model could not send his supply columns back through Soviet-held territory for more fuel, he luckily captured a small Soviet fuel depot in Romny, which he used to refuel Major Frank's *Vorausabteilung*. On the morning of 13 September, Model sent Major Frank forward 45km to Lokhovitsa to meet Kleist's expected forces from the south, while he formed a hedgehog in Romny and waited for the rest of Guderian's forces to rescue him. Despite lack of experience with armoured units, Model had demonstrated that he was one of the most skillful and aggressive panzer commanders of the 1941 campaign, willing to take extreme risks – which contributed to his rapid rise in the Wehrmacht.

Meanwhile, the German AOK 17 spent the period 1–11 September expanding its bridgehead at Kremenchug by moving eight infantry divisions across the Dnieper and building a second pontoon bridge. The Soviet 38th Army's cordon around the bridgehead was gradually built up to seven rifle and three cavalry divisions, as well as the depleted 47th Tank Division. In addition, two of the newly-formed tank brigades arrived a few days before the German attack: Polkovnik Grigoriy Kuzmin's 132nd Tank Brigade (three battalions of light tanks) and Polkovnik Nikolai F. Mikhailov's 142nd Tank Brigade (seven KV-I, twenty-two T-34, fifty-seven T-26). The 38th Army attacked the German bridgehead repeatedly but failed to eliminate it; in the process the Red Army lost over 40,000 personnel and 279 tanks at Kremenchug. Nor were the Soviets expecting German armour in this sector, since von Kleist's panzers were believed to still be massed near Dnepropetrovsk. Unlike Guderian, von Kleist prepared a carefully-planned deliberate attack with General der Panzertruppen Werner Kempf's XXXXVIII Armeekorps (mot.), and he incorporated deception into his planning. On 10 September, Kempf began shifting first Hube's 16.Panzer-Division then Kuhn's 14.Panzer-Division toward Kremenchug, with 9.Panzer-Division due to follow. On the evening of 11 September, Hube's panzer division began crossing the pontoon bridge into the bridgehead.

On the morning of 12 September, Hube's 16.Panzer-Division attacked the western end of the 38th Army cordon, held by two battle-worn rifle divisions. Supported by artillery and the Luftwaffe, Hube's panzers shattered both Soviet rifle units in a matter of hours and quickly advanced to the northwest. The Soviet 38th Army's front was shattered beyond recovery. Over the next two days, von Kleist moved the bulk of the III and XXXXVIII Armeekorps (mot.) over the Dnieper and the three panzer divisions were able to create a huge bulge in Kirponos' southern flank. The 38th Army used the last of its armour to launch counterattacks into the flank of Kempf's corps, but they could not stop the German armoured juggernaut. Hube's advance elements made a tentative link-up with Model's *Vorausabteilung* at 1820 hours on 14 September, but the 9.Panzer-Division raced ahead on 15 September and made a firmer link-up with Model's division south of Lokhovitsa. When this link-up between Guderian's and von Kleist's panzers finally occurred, the bulk of the Soviet 5th, 21st, 26th and 37th Armies were encircled. Within four days, Kiev was captured, Kirponos himself was killed and 440,000 of his troops were captured in the Kiev *kessel*. Overall Soviet losses in the fighting around Kiev were over 600,000 men and 400 tanks, which left the Southwest Front gutted. Only 15,000 troops and fifty tanks escaped the *kessel*.[82] Although it took some time for Heeresgruppe Süd to mop up around Kiev and repair infrastructure across the Dnieper, the Southwest Front's surviving 38th and 40th Armies could do little but delay the inevitable German advance toward Kharkov and the Donbas region.

Sustaining the Tanks, September 1941

As the end of summer approached, the armoured units on both sides were badly depleted and exhausted by ten weeks of continuous combat. During this period, the Red Army lost over 15,000 tanks and the Wehrmacht 800 tanks. Despite German operational successes, it was clear even before 1 September that Barbarossa was not going to destroy the Red Army in a single campaign, so it was imperative for both sides to replenish their armoured forces and restore their combat capabilities.

The Stavka had abolished the pre-war mechanized corps on 15 July and employed the few remaining units as independent tank divisions. Nine new '100-series' tank divisions were hastily formed from existing units in July–August 1941 and equipped with surplus light tanks and a handful of newer models. Most of these expedient units were consumed in the Battle of Smolensk. By 1 September, there were only four intact large armoured formations left in the entire Red Army: the 61st and 111th Tank Divisions in the Transbaikal MD and the 58th and 112th Tank Divisions in the Far East. The Stavka decided to leave the two tank divisions in the Transbaikal since their combat readiness was negligible, but the two better-equipped tank divisions in the Far East were ordered to prepare for transfer to the West as soon as rail transport was available. However, the movement of Soviet industry eastward severely curtailed the amount of available rail capacity, so neither tank division could be immediately transferred. It was not until 14 October that General-major Aleksei F. Popov's 60th Tank Division, stationed on the Manchurian border, began entraining and then spent two weeks traveling over 8,600km westward by rail.

It was clear, though, that the Red Army could not rejuvenate the shattered pre-war units, and it lacked the trained personnel and equipment to create new corps or even division-size formations. In particular, the loss of command cadre and the lack of radios mandated smaller formations, so General-leytenant Yakov N. Fedorenko, head of the GABTU, successfully convinced the Stavka to concentrate on creating tank brigades for the rest of 1941. Fedorenko played an important role in rebuilding the Red Army's tank forces in 1941–43 and in guiding how they were used, but he was one of many officers whose contributions were minimized due to Zhukov's efforts to keep the spotlight on his own actions. Fedorenko combed the tank schools for officers and NCOs to act as cadres for the new tank brigades and filled them out with thousands of tankers who had lost their tanks in the early battles and survived to escape eastward. In mid-August, the first nine tank brigades began forming in Moscow, Kharkov and Stalingrad.

These first tank brigades had the pick of survivors from the pre-war formations and were supposed to consist of three tank battalions with a total of sixty-two tanks (seven KV, twenty-two T-34 and thirty-one BT/T-26) and a motorized infantry battalion. A few of these early brigades were quite good and represented a conscious effort by the Stavka to marry up the best commanders with the best available equipment. Polkovnik Mikhail E. Katukov's 4th Tank Brigade, formed at Stalingrad, was provided with thirty brand-new T-34 tanks and thirty BT-7s. Polkovnik Pavel A. Rotmistrov's 8th Tank Brigade, formed in the Urals, was also given seven new KV-1s and twenty-two T-34s. However, Soviet industry could not provide anything like the amount of equipment to outfit these brigades properly and most were provided with only light tanks and the number of tank battalions was soon reduced from three to two. Another twenty-one tank brigades began forming in September, followed by another dozen in October. Yet the diversion of all new tank production to support the formation of tank brigades meant that the remaining Soviet armoured units at the front were starved of replacements and allowed to disintegrate.

In fact, this Soviet shift to tank brigades marked a critical point in the dynamics of Eastern Front armoured warfare, since the Red Army chose to disperse all its armour into smaller units for infantry support, thereby removing any possibility of conducting decisive mobile operations until this was reversed. Each Soviet front-line army began requesting a tank brigade, which meant that the principle of concentration was set aside. This was the same mistake that the French army made with tanks in 1940. While many accounts of the Eastern Front choose to emphasize that the Soviet Union was producing more tanks than Germany in 1941, they fail to note that the Red Army was dispersing its armour to the point that it lost numerical superiority on the critical sectors. In contrast, the Germans had fewer tanks overall, but continued to mass them where it counted most. Furthermore, the new Soviet tank brigades were designed only for the infantry support role and lacked organic artillery or engineers, which put them at a major disadvantage when up against German panzer divisions.

Soviet tank production began to drop off in September 1941 as the KhPZ plant prepared to evacuate from Kharkov to Nizhny Tagil and the Kirov Plant in Leningrad was in the process of relocating to Chelyabinsk. The only major Soviet tank plant unaffected by the evacuation was the Stalingrad Tank Factory (StZ), which was producing forty T-34s per week. An alternate T-34 production line set up at Zavod 112 in Gorky managed to build only five T-34s in September and twenty in October 1941. Instead, the only tank being built in quantity in autumn 1941 was the new 5.8-ton T-60 light tank, armed with a 20mm cannon. Mass production of the T-60 began at the GAZ plant in Gorky in October, with output rising to 600 units per month in November–December, although these light tanks added very little to the Red Army's armoured capabilities. The industrial evacuation also had an impact on supplies of ammunition and other equipment necessary to outfit large armoured units. Even before the German invasion, the People's Commissariat for Munitions (Narkomat Boepripasov) had regularly failed to meet ammunition production goals and this remained one of the least efficiently-run sectors of Soviet defense industry throughout 1941. Most front-line Red Army armour units were dreadfully short of tank ammunition through-out most of the summer, but rapid efforts to increase production output led to a sudden decrease in quality control. Instead of using hardened steel for penetrators, some manufacturers began substituting other metals, which reduced the penetrative power of 45mm anti-tank shells by nearly 50 per cent. The production of 76.2mm tank and anti-tank ammunition was so low that tank gunnery training was minimal or omitted altogether. Like the Wehrmacht, Red Army tankers faced serious shortages of spare parts in the second half of 1941, which led to a high level of non-combat losses. Production of tank radios was suspended in August and did not resume until mid-1942.[83]

Despite all these problems, Stalin's war cabinet – the State Committee for Defense (*Gosudarstvenny Komitet Oborony* or GKO) – made the very critical decision to put priority on a few tank models and to build them in large quantities. A number of new models, such as the KV-II heavy tank and T-50 light tank, were discontinued. The KhPZ had already completed a prototype of an improved T-34, designated as the T-34M, which was approved for mass production just seven weeks before the start of Barbarossa. The T-34M had thicker armour and a number of other advantages over the standard T-34 Model 1941, but since it would take months to complete the design and get it into production the GKO cancelled the program. One exception was the T-34-57 equipped with the high-velocity ZiS-4 L/73 57mm gun, which was optimized for anti-tank combat. This variant was ready for production when Barbarossa began and the GABTU was keen to improve the firepower of the T-34, so a limited production run of forty-one was authorized in August, but the program was then put on hold. Furthermore, only 2,800 57mm anti-tank rounds were manufactured, making this variant little more than a field test. Afterwards, the GKO mandated that only minor, incremental changes be allowed in tank designs in order not to impact production output, even though it essentially 'froze' Soviet tank design in place for the next two years. Some aspects of the cancelled T-34M program were gradually worked into later upgraded models of the T-34.

In order to ensure that tank production goals were met by Soviet industry, Stalin made Vyacheslav Malyshev, an engineer who had proven himself in the expansion of Soviet heavy industry in the 1930s, head of the People's Commissariat of the Tank Industry of the USSR (NKTP) that was established on 11 September. Malyshev took charge of an industry that was in chaos, moving the Leningrad and Kharkov tank plants to the Urals. He rapidly began to simplify construction procedures for the T-34 and within less than a year the number of man-hours required to produce T-34s was cut in half. Malyshev encouraged the use of stamped parts and a cast turret in order to cut corners, accepting a certain temporary reduction in quality in return for much greater output of tanks. He motivated factory managers by reminding them what happened to people who didn't meet Stalin's quotas and pointedly said, 'I am responsible for the tanks with my head.' While Soviet efforts to mobilize labour and industrial resources were prodigious, it should be noted that the rapid expansion of Soviet tank production would have been handicapped without the delivery of Lend-Lease raw materials and machine tools to replace equipment lost in the hasty evacuations. After the loss of aluminum sources in the Ukraine, 80 per cent of the aluminum used in the T-34's diesel tank engine came from Lend-Lease deliveries; without Lend-Lease, there would have been significantly fewer T-34s.[84]

On the German side, in early September 1941 the Wehrmacht still had over 1,500 operational tanks on the Eastern Front, including 362 Pz.III and 193 Pz.IV. These figures meant that overall the panzer divisions still had about 48 per cent of their armour operational, but only 39 per cent of the most useful models. Yet it is important to note that the losses were not spread evenly; the 7 and 11.Panzer-Division were both reduced to about 25 per cent effectiveness, but two units – the 10 and 14.Panzer-Divisionen – still had over 70 per cent of their tanks operational. The deterioration of German operational tank strength has been used to make the case that the Wehrmacht's offensive combat power was all but gone before the summer of 1941 had even ended, but this thesis usually ignores a major game-changer: the arrival of the fresh 2 and 5.Panzer-Divisionen from Germany in mid-September.[85] Both divisions had been involved in the Balkan Campaign and had missed the first three months of Barbarossa. The divisions spent the summer resting and refitting in Germany – receiving about 160 new tanks – before being sent eastward to join the Heeresgruppe Mitte for Operation Typhoon. These two fully-equipped divisions added a total of 380 tanks to the German order of battle, including 210 Pz.III and forty Pz.IVs, and helped to restore some measure of the striking power of the panzer groups, albeit temporarily. However, the OKH made a huge mistake in not using the arrival of these two divisions to rotate at least two battle-worn panzer divisions back to Germany in autumn 1941 for refit. Personnel losses in the panzer divisions were also heavy and Panzergruppe Guderian had suffered over 32,000 casualties by the end of September 1941, including 7,200 dead. Few personnel replacements had arrived before the end of August and only enough to replace about half the casualties. Yet it is important to note that most of the casualties in panzer units were infantrymen in the Schützen-regiment and reconnaissance battalion, while tank crews accounted for only about 2.5 per cent of overall losses. Unlike the Red Army, the panzer divisions had lost very few senior leaders and the Wehrmacht had over-trained its personnel in peacetime, so the process of promoting soldiers to fill NCO and junior officer vacancies could suffice for a while.

By mid-September, the German panzer groups in the Soviet Union also had nearly 900 non-operational tanks due to battle damage or mechanical defects, of which 520 were Pz.III or Pz.IVs. Almost half the panzers awaiting repairs were in Guderian's panzer group, whereas Heeresgruppe Nord and Süd both had better success in keeping their tanks operational. Guderian's tanks had seen harder, more continual use than the other three panzer groups and operated at greater distances from their supply railhead, which resulted in higher breakdown rates. Engine failure among tanks that had driven over 2,000–3,000km within three months was common, but most could be repaired within a day or less if spare engines and parts were available. The Wehrmacht set up three main spare parts depots (Zentrales Ersatzteillager or ZEL) in the Soviet Union, located at Pleskau, Borisov and Berdichev to support the three Heeresgruppen. Over 22,000 tons of spare parts were shipped by rail to these ZEL in July–August, but the loss or breakdown of 30–50 per cent of the trucks in most panzer divisions by early September 1941 made delivery of spare parts and supplies increasingly problematic.[86] As part of the build-up for Typhoon, Hitler authorized the release of 3,500 replacement trucks to be sent to the Eastern Front in mid-September.[87]

The Eastern Front was very rough on the panzers and the thick dust degraded air filters and then engines, beginning in early July. The engine crankshaft on the Pz.IV proved to be its Achilles' Heel during extended operations, as excessive heat and metal fatigue caused it to warp and then break. Bearings for the roadwheels also wore out quickly in Russia, along with leaf springs and piston rings, all of which were in short supply. Track pins that held the track together tended to break from stress – as when the tank ran over a large object – and were always in short supply. Although the Germans managed to ship over 22,000 tons of spare parts to the Eastern Front in June–August alone, this proved to be well short of the amount required. German maintenance crews in field Werkstatt performed minor miracles to keep one-third of their tanks running week after week, but most tanks had accrued over 3,000km without real maintenance by the beginning of autumn and were operating on borrowed time.[88] Increasingly, Werkstatt crews turned to controlled substitution (aka 'cannibalization') to keep vehicles running, stripping parts from other disabled vehicles in worse condition – but this was only a quick fix that eventually turned some disabled vehicles into total losses. Occasionally, the creaking German supply system pulled off miracles, such as ensuring that Panzer-Abteilung 211, deployed at Oulu in northern Finland, continued to receive spare parts for its Hotchkiss H-39 tanks all the way from Gien in France.

Adding to the logistic inadequacies of the Wehrmacht's strained supply system, Hitler added to the tank replacement and spare parts crisis by directing that most new-build tanks and spare parts would be held back in Germany until Operation Barbarossa was completed. Hitler expected that each panzer division would disband one Panzer-Abteilung as losses mounted and send the surplus personnel back to Germany for reequipping with new tanks. This outlook was in line with the German philosophy of combat replenishment – that it was better to take whole units back and rest and reequip them in their home Wehrkreis, rather than send replacement vehicles in dribs and drabs, which resulted in units that were not refitted properly – but it did not fit the conditions of the Eastern Front. Most panzer divisions did disband one of their Panzer-Abteilung in the late summer, but they kept the personnel on hand for rear area security or other tasks. Although German industry constructed 1,890 tanks between July and December 1941, only about one-third were sent to the Eastern Front before the end of the year. At best, for every three tanks declared *totalausfall*, a panzer unit would receive only one replacement tank. Hitler authorized the OKH to release 350 new tank engines and 307 new tanks (including ninety-one Pz.38(t), 166 Pz.III and fifty Pz.IV) to reinvigorate Heeresgruppe Mitte's armour in time for Operation Typhoon, but many more tanks remained at warehouses in Magdeburg and Vienna.[89] The replacement situation was even more dire with wheeled vehicles and Guderian was forced to press captured Soviet GAZ and ZIL trucks into service to keep his supply columns functional.

Pursuit to the Donbas, September–October 1941

Once Heeresgruppe Süd was across the Dnieper River, there was little that the Red Army could do to stop von Kleist's panzers before the cold weather set in. Hitler ordered von Rundstedt to pursue the defeated Southwestern Front forces and occupy the Donbas region, which was 410km further east, as well as occupy the Crimea. In turn, von Rundstedt split up his army group, with 6.Armee to advance upon Kharkov, the 11.Armee to occupy the Crimea and Panzergruppe Kleist to head for the Donbas. The first two advances were supported by assault-gun battalions, but otherwise had no significant armoured support. Von Kleist's panzer group was still capable of mobile operations and benefited from the fact that the Red Army had few operational tank units left in the Ukraine after the debacles at Uman and Kiev. However, von Kleist was obliged to transfer nearly half his panzer strength to Heeresgruppe Mitte, including Kempf's XXXXVIII Armeekorps (mot.) with the 9.Panzer-Division, 16 and 25.Infanterie-Divisionen (mot.) and the 11.Panzer-Division. Kleist was left with just three panzer-divisions and the Waffen SS divisions *LSSAH* and *Wiking* to conquer the rest of the Ukraine.

Following Kirponos' death, Marshal Timoshenko arrived to take over the four remaining armies of the Southwest Front and he found that there were negligible amounts of armour and artillery remaining. In the words of American historian David M. Glantz, 'the Southwestern Front had to be recreated from scratch.'[90] The onset of rainy and muddy weather in early October slowed the German advance upon Kharkov, but Timoshenko could only hurl untrained rifle units into the path of the 6.Armee. Unteroffizier Heinrich Skodell, a gunner in 1./Sturmgeschütz-Abteilung 197, noted that 'that resistance was slowly giving way to flight. The Russian infantry has not been up to par for a long time. They are all older people, some of them have only been soldiers for eight days.'[91] Timoshenko's forces did buy time for the KhPZ factory to move by rail out of Kharkov, thereby saving one of the main T-34 tank-production lines, but they could not hold the city. Although desperately short of fuel and ammunition, Sturmgeschütz-Abteilung 197 fought its way into Kharkov on 22 October and the city was in German hands within two days.

The Soviet Southern Front was also in disarray, with its 9th and 12th Armies having abandoned its front on the Dnieper south of Zaporozhe. General-leytenant Ivan V.Tyulenev had been wounded in late August and replaced as front commander by General-leytenant Dmitri I. Ryabyshev, former commander of the now-defunct 8th Mechanized Corps. Ryabyshev had just received three tank brigades as reinforcements and when he saw the German 11.Armee (now under Generaloberst Erich von Manstein) split its forces, with one corps proceeding to the Perekop narrows to attack the Crimea and two other corps heading east to Melitopol, he saw an opportunity to inflict a painful defeat on his pursuers. On 26 September, rifle and tank units of the 18th Army attacked two

Romanian brigades attached to the 11.Armee and threw them back with heavy losses. Von Manstein quickly dispatched the *LSSAH* to stabilize the 11.Armee's front and the Soviet counterattack was contained within a few days. Yet Ryabyshev remained focused on pounding the vulnerable Romanian units, while oblivious to his own right flank, as Timoshenko's armies retreated. Heeresgruppe Süd was quick to notice that the boundary between Timoshenko's and Ryabyshev's fronts, which lay east of the German bridgehead at Dnepropetrovsk, was held by only two rifle divisions and one cavalry division.

Von Kleist assembled General der Infanterie Gustav von Wietersheim's XIV Armeekorps (mot.) on line on the north side of the Dnieper, with the 14 and 16.Panzer-Divisionen on line, facing east. Mackensen's III Armeekorps (mot.) was assembled behind von Wietersheim's corps, to reinforce success. Although an infantryman, the fifty-seven-year-old von Wietersheim had been in command of his corps for over three years and had led it across Poland and France – he was the oldest, but one of the most experienced motorized corps commanders in Russia. On 30 September, von Wietersheim attacked with the Soviet rifle units in front of him with both panzer divisions. Within twenty-four hours, von Wietersheim's panzers had torn a gaping hole in the boundary between the two fronts and pivoted to the southeast, rolling up the northern flank of Ryabyshev's Southern Front. Meanwhile, Ryabyshev continued to try and break through the Romanians – achieving some success – but oblivious to the approaching threat from behind. Ryabyshev's new tank brigades proved of little value in this action because they were so poorly equipped; the 15th Tank Brigade had thirty-three tanks but only three trucks, which meant that it had no support troops or logistic/ maintenance capabilities.

Von Wietersheim's panzers rolled up the 18th Army's positions around Zaporozhe on 2 October and Hube's 16.Panzer-Division plunged ahead to the southeast, overrunning the town of Orikhiv, within striking range of the Southern Front's lines of communications. Ryabyshev finally awoke to the threat of envelopment and tried to order a retreat, but von Manstein's 11.Armee pinned most of his forces with fixing attacks. A few units, such as the 130th Tank Brigade, were sent to try and check Hube's panzers at Orikhiv, but Kleist soon brought up the 13 and 14.Panzer-Divisionen to support him, giving the Germans absolute numerical superiority in armour at the critical point. The mass of von Kleist's armour began slicing across Ryabyshev's communications, heading for Berdyansk on the Sea of Azov. The cohesion of the 9th and 12th Armies began to fall apart on 5 October as units began to retreat pell-mell eastward and gaps appeared in the front line. The *LSSAH* daringly pushed into one of these gaps and advanced eastward to seize Berdyansk on 6 October. By 7 October, von Wietersheim had both his panzer divisions blocking the Soviet escape route to the east, while Mackensen's corps formed the north side of the *kessel* and von Manstein's infantry pressed in from the west. The trap had closed around both the 9th and 12th Armies. A few Soviet units escaped – without much equipment – but when the Melitopol *kessel* was crushed on 11 October, the Red Army had lost another 106,000 troops and 210 tanks. Among the dead was the commander of the 18th Army. After this debacle, Ryabyshev was replaced by General-polkovnik Yakov T. Cherevichenko. This action, dubbed the Battle of the Sea of Azov by the Germans, was a classic demonstration of the Wehrmacht's ability to conduct opportunistic mobile battles of encirclement with their panzer units slashing into the unprotected rear of larger Soviet formations. At this point, Red Army tankers had been reduced to a limited infantry support role and had no ability to conduct these kind of deep operations.

After the defeat of the Southern Front, von Kleist continued to push eastward against disorganized resistance and managed to cross the Mius River north of Taganrog with the *LSSAH* by mid-October and then seize the city by 17 October. Von Kleist split his forces, with von Wietersheim's XIV Armeekorps (mot.) advancing northeastward toward Stalin, while Mackensen's III Armeekorps (mot.) headed due east for Rostov. However, Heeresgruppe Süd was no longer able to adequately supply von Kleist's panzers so far from a railhead and rainy weather virtually immobilized his two motorized corps. By 24 October, the *LSSAH* and 13.Panzer-Division were on the approaches to Rostov, but Soviet resistance was stiffening.

Preparing for Typhoon, 6–30 September

After the fall of Kiev, Hitler was willing to consider an operational pause since Heeresgruppe Nord and Mitte had already shifted to a defensive posture and it appeared that little else could be accomplished in the remaining campaigning season aside from securing the Crimea and the Donbas region. While the Red Army was undefeated, Hitler and the OKH could still reasonably view Barbarossa as a partial success that left the Wehrmacht in a good position to finish off the Soviet Union in 1942. As a leader, Hitler was not inclined toward excessive risk-taking, particularly when he felt that he was ahead. From the beginning, Hitler viewed Moscow as a symbolic objective with little military value and he had been opposed to committing the bulk of the Wehrmacht's panzer units to seizing a geographic objective rather than carrying out their primary function as he saw it – encircling and annihilating large formations of the Red Army.

Yet even before Kirponos' Southwest Front was encircled at Kiev, Hitler came to believe that the only real Soviet combat power left lay with the Western Front defending the approaches to Moscow. Timoshenko's Western Front had launched repeated counterattacks against Heeresgruppe Mitte in August–September, particularly against the exposed Yelnya salient, but had achieved little except inflicting a bruising battle of attrition on both sides. Consequently, Hitler believed that Timoshenko's armies were exhausted from weeks of fighting and, if hit hard from the flanks, would collapse. On 6 September – the same day that von Bock evacuated the hard-pressed Yelnya salient – Hitler issued Führer Directive 35, which stated that German successes at Velikiye Luki and Kiev had created the 'prerequisites for conducting a decisive operation against Army Group Timoshenko, which is conducting unsuccessful offensive operations on Heeresgruppe Mitte's front. It must be destroyed decisively before the onset of winter.' Hitler's directive allowed for a pursuit along the Moscow axis after the destruction of Timoshenko's forces, but did not explicitly task Heeresgruppe Mitte with capturing the Soviet capital. The OKH began developing an operational plan, designated Typhoon, to smash the Soviet Western and Bryansk fronts by using most of the available German armour left on the Eastern Front. Von Bock's Heeresgruppe Mitte would become the battering ram that smashed through the last Soviet organized resistance. The OKH began shifting part of Höpner's Panzergruppe 4 from Heeresgruppe Nord to Heeresgruppe Mitte and von Kleist had to transfer four divisions from his command as well. This was a massive redeployment of armoured forces in a very short period of time; for example, Reinhardt's XXXXI Armeekorps (mot.) had to move 600km in less than a week to join von Bock's Heeresgruppe Mitte.[92] These road marches, conducted over long distances on poor road networks, resulted in a great number of breakdowns among both tracked and wheeled vehicles. A few units, such as the 1.Panzer-Division, were fortunate enough to transfer their panzers by rail to Vitebsk, thereby preserving vehicles.[93] By late September, von Bock had Guderian's Panzergruppe 2, Hoth's Panzergruppe 3 and Höpner's Panzergruppe 4 with a grand total of fourteen panzer and eight motorized infantry divisions under his control. Höpner – who had failed to pull off a single *kessel* battle during Barbarossa – was made the main effort and provided the two fresh panzer divisions as well as the still-capable 10.Panzer-Division. Operation Typhoon would be one of the largest German offensives of the war, involving about 1,800 tanks and sixty-nine divisions. An additional fourteen Sturmgeschütz-Abteilungen with 350 StuG III assault guns would support the three German infantry armies. By massing more than 80 per cent of their remaining armour along the Moscow axis, the Germans gained a substantial local numerical advantage over the Red Army for the first time in the campaign: Heeresgruppe Mitte would have a 1.7–1 superiority in the number of tanks and 1.5–1 in manpower over the Soviet Western Front. The Luftwaffe also massed half its remaining aircraft under Luftflotte 2 to support von Bock's Heeresgruppe Mitte. Although von Bock gained control over most of the Wehrmacht's remaining armour for Operation Typhoon, the army quartermasters had been unable to amass any stockpiles of fuel or ammunition in the battle zone. In particular, inter-theater fuel deliveries from Germany had been barely adequate for Heeresgruppe Mitte's defensive operations in August-September, never mind a major offensive. There simply would not be enough fuel for all of Heeresgruppe Mitte to reach Moscow even under the best circumstances.

General-leytenant Ivan Konev took over the Western Front from Timoshenko on 12 September, when the latter went south to try and stave off defeat in the Ukraine. Konev had six armies to defend the direct approach to Moscow and Marshal Semyon Budyonny commanded the Reserve Front, with six more armies echeloned directly behind him. The southern approaches to Moscow were protected by General-leytenant Andrei Yeremenko's Bryansk Front, with four more armies. The Red Army's position in front of Moscow appeared to be a strong one, since they were defending in depth and had time to construct extensive field works along the front. All told, the three Soviet fronts had a total of eighty-three rifle and nine cavalry divisions, and were supported by sixteen tank brigades and two independent tank battalions with a total of 849 tanks (including 128 T-34s and forty-seven KV-1s).[94] However, appearances were deceiving. The three Soviet fronts lacked a unified command structure and there was no significant armoured force held as a mobile reserve. Nor was there much of a defense in depth, since many of the Reserve Front units had not properly entrenched themselves and key supply and communications nodes such as Vyazma and Orel were not even garrisoned. Most of the experienced Soviet divisions were reduced to half strength or less after the fighting in August and the quality of many of the new replacement divisions was shockingly poor. Even worse, Hitler's shift toward the Ukraine had misled Stalin into believing that Moscow was no longer at great risk, so he directed the Stavka to send more replacements to Timoshenko's new command in the southern Ukraine.

Hitler had not directed that Guderian's Panzergruppe 2 should participate in Operation Typhoon since it was spread out between Konotop and Lokhovitsa after the closure of the Kiev *kessel*. Yet von Bock wanted to put every tank he could in the field to smash the Western Front in one last, mighty blow and on 15 September he ordered Guderian to reorient his forces back to the north as soon as operations around Kiev were completed, and move to assembly areas near Glukhov. The 185km road march to Glukhov put additional wear and tear on vehicles and men that were exhausted and left just two or three days for rest and refit. By 27 September Guderian had only 25 per cent of his tanks still operational, with a total of 187 tanks, including ninety-four Pz.III and thirty-six Pz.IV, between the four panzer divisions of the XXIV and XLVII Armeekorps (mot.).[95] Guderian managed to get OKH to release 149 new replacement tanks (124 Pz.III and twenty-five Pz.IV) to replenish his divisions, but these were still en route when Typhoon began and were not received until 1–2 October. Even worse, Guderian's logistic situation was the most tenuous of any of the three Panzergruppen involved in Typhoon and he would start the operation with less than two V.S. of fuel on hand, enough for a 200km advance. Moscow was 550km from Guderian's starting position.

Typhoon: Guderian's Battle, 30 September–16 October

After the defeat of Group Ermakov in Yeremenko's failed counter-offensive, General-major Arkadiy N. Ermakov and his surviving units were shifted to a relatively quiet sector to rebuild. Ermakov deployed his three rifle divisions and two cavalry divisions in a thin screen blocking the main road from Glukhov to Orel, with two tank brigades in reserve. Polkovnik Boris S. Bakharov, an experienced tank officer, commanded the 150th Tank Brigade, which sat astride the Glukhov-Orel road with twelve T-34 and eight T-50 tanks. The 14-ton T-50 was a new light tank that had just entered production as a replacement for the T-26 and it had the sloped armour and diesel engine of the T-34, but only forty-eight were completed before the GKO terminated the program in favor of the cheaper T-60. Ermakov's other armoured reserve was Polkovnik Nikolai N. Radkevich's

121st Tank Brigade, deployed near Dmitriyev with seventy tanks (six KV-1, eighteen T-34, forty-six T-26). Radkevich was also an experienced tank officer, who was a VAMM graduate and trained general staff officer. The terrain was relatively flat and open in this sector and thus did not favor the defense.

After a night of heavy rain, Guderian kicked off his part in Typhoon at 0635 hours on 30 September with a brief artillery preparation on the 283rd Rifle Division positions near Essman, followed by Stuka attacks on their artillery. Then von Schweppenburg's XXIV Armeekorps, which was designated as the main effort, attacked the center of Ermakov's line, while Lemelsen's XLVII Armee-korps (mot.) mounted a supporting attack on the boundary between Group Ermakov and the Soviet 13th Army. Kampfgruppe Eberbach from 4.Panzer-Division formed the *schwerpunkt* and easily punched through the front-line posi-tions of the Soviet 283rd Rifle Division, but ran into a company of tanks from Bakharov's 150th Tank Brigade at Essman. Eberbach's panzers from I./Pz.Regt 35 knocked out a few enemy light tanks that appeared, but were stopped for a couple of hours by two T-34 tanks in excellent hull-down positions near the town. The German tankers also encountered a substantial obstacle belt comprised of wooden TMD-40 anti-tank mines which, so far, had been rare on the Eastern Front. Eberbach sent the II/Pz.Regt 35 on a flank march to hit the T-34s from behind, but a T-34 knocked out the Pz.III belonging to Oberleutnant Arthur Wollschlaeger, commander of the 6.Kompanie. The German tankers called in air support and a flight of Bf-110 fighter-bombers strafed the Soviet positions, prompting the enemy tanks to disengage.[96]

Ermakov incorrectly reported the scale of the German attack to Yeremenko, who mistakenly assessed Guderian's attack as a mere diversion – and then directed Ermakov to resolve it with local counterattacks. However, Ermakov's C2 – shaky from the start – fell apart under the heat of battle and he lost control over his armour. After skirmishing with Kampfgruppe Eberbach, Bakharov's 150th Tank Brigade retreated eastward – leaving the road to Orel open. Radkevich's 121st Tank Brigade, which was in excellent position to conduct a flank attack against Kampfgruppe Eberbach, sat immobile for five days, doing nothing. Left unmolested by Ermakov's armour, Kampfgruppe Eberbach routed the Soviet infantry, overran Soviet artillery positions and then captured Sevsk by noon on 1 October.

On Guderian's left flank, Lemselsen's corps also enjoyed success on the western flank, punching through thinly-spread infantry positions and then defeating a counterattack by the 141st Tank Brigade. The Germans had begun to adapt their tactics to counter Soviet heavy tanks and now began attaching one medium 10.5cm howitzer and one 8.8cm flak gun to each Panzer-Abteilung. When Chernov's tanks attacked head-on into the 17 and 18.Panzer-Divisionen they managed to shoot up one German column, but ran into a deluge of fire that quickly knocked out at least one KV-I and one KV-II.[97] Lemelsen's panzers quickly pushed in the 13th Army's flank, widening the gap between it and Group Ermakov. Within forty-eight hours, Guderian had shattered Yeremenko's front, routed Group Ermakov and begun enveloping the 13th Army. For the first time in two months, Guderian's panzers had achieved a clean breakthrough and he made the most of it; Kradschützen-Abteilung 34 was sent 100km ahead up the Orel highway in the afternoon and seized the bridge over at the Oka River at Kromy by dusk. Kampfgruppe Eberbach followed, moving at maximum speed against negligible resistance.

Early on 3 October, Kampfgruppe Eberbach advanced upon Orel, a city of 110,000 people, which was defended only by a few Soviet rear service troops. Once again, German panzers were able to 'bounce' a major Soviet city and capture it before the Red Army could react. A lone panzer company, Oberleutnant Wollschlaeger's 6./Pz.Regt 35, drove into the center of Orel by 1600 hours; he lost three tanks to anti-tank fire but otherwise resistance was patchy.[98] Eberbach's panzers also engaged TB-3 bombers that were landing elements of the 5th Airborne Corps at the Orel airfield. The loss of Orel was a catastrophic blow to the Bryansk Front, since the primary communications lines ran through the city and Yeremenko quickly lost contact with many of his own units and the Stavka in Moscow.[99]

In just four days, the 4.Panzer-Division had advanced 240km and inflicted 2,200 casualties on the enemy, while capturing sixteen tanks and twenty-four artillery pieces for the loss of only forty-one killed and 120 wounded. Overall, Guderian's two corps had eliminated over 10,000 Soviet troops in this period, and mauled two tank brigades.[100] Yet Guderian's euphoric advance was short-lived, because the XXIV Armeekorps (mot.) used all its fuel to get to Orel and had none left. Eberbach made it into Orel with II/Pz.Regt 35, Schützen-Regiment 12, Kradschützen-Abteilung 34 and one artillery battalion, but the rest of the 4.Panzer-Division ran out of fuel 20–40km short of the city. Contrary to myth, Guderian's spearhead was immobilized four days prior to the first snowfall, due to lack of fuel. Ammunition stockpiles with the forward units were also very low. Guderian asked the Luftwaffe to deliver 500m^3 of fuel by Ju-52 transport to the Orel airfield, but Soviet fighters were active in this area and the Luftwaffe demurred. Instead, von Schweppenburg was forced to send his supply columns back to the rear for fuel and it would take four days to restock his two panzer divisions with one V.S. each – even though this amount was still insufficient to reach Guderian's next objective – Tula.

While von Schweppenburg's corps was immobilized at Orel, the Stavka began reacting to Guderian's breakthrough on the Bryansk Front. In Moscow, the Stavka ordered General-major Dmitri Lelyushenko to proceed immediately to Orel and take command of several RVGK reserve units that would be released to him. He was ordered to try and retake Orel or establish a new front north of the city. By chance, Polkovnik Mikhail E. Katukov's 4th Tank Brigade, en route from Stalingrad to Moscow by rail, was not far away and was rerouted to the Mtensk train station north of Orel. Katukov's brigade began unloading at Mtensk on 4 October and he had a total of sixty tanks (seven KV, twenty-two T-34, thirty-one BT-2/5/7). Polkovnik Arman P. Matisovich's 11th Tank Brigade was en route from Moscow with about fifty more tanks, including some KV-1 and T-34s. Both Lelyushenko and Katukov were very competent and experienced tank officers and, for the first time, the Red Army would have some of its best leaders and equipment in the field. Even before his brigade was fully unloaded, Katukov dispatched two tank companies with nineteen T-34s and two KV-1s under Kapetan Vladimir Gusev and Starshiy Leytenant Aleksandr F. Burda to conduct a reconnaissance in force down the road to Orel.

Meanwhile, Yeremenko was blissfully unaware of Guderian's breakthrough and instructed the 13th Army to refuse its flank, which merely gave Lemelsen the opportunity to approach Bryansk from behind. Insufficient radios and poor coordination between units robbed Yeremenko of situational awareness and enabled Guderian's forces to easily outmaneuver their opponents. Yeremenko's last mobile reserve – Chernov's 141st Tank Brigade – attempted a brief stand at Karachev against Lemelsen's two panzer divisions, but was brushed aside. The 17.Panzer-Division then dispatched a company-size kampfgruppe from I/Pz.Regt 39 under Major Hans Gradl due west, approaching Bryansk from behind. Gradl had just thirteen tanks (seven Pz.II, six Pz.III), four SPWs with a platoon of infantry and two self-propelled 2cm flak guns. Yeremenko was unaware of the threat until Gradl's panzers literally showed up outside his head-quarters and proceeded to shoot it up; Yeremenko was wounded and forced to flee.[101] Shortly thereafter, Gradl seized a bridge over the Desna River on the evening of 6 October and then advanced into Bryansk, a city of 87,000, and seized it by coup de main on the morning of 7 October. In addition to a city, Gradl captured over 1,000 Red Army soldiers, a battalion of artillery and fourteen tanks, including four KV-1.[102] At one stroke, a small German armoured force had decapitated the leadership of the Bryansk Front, seized a major Russian city and isolated the 3rd and 13th Armies with fourteen divisions. The German 2.Armee pressed in from the west, forming the Trubchevsk *kessel*. It was a remarkable success, but Guderian threw it away by refusing to allocate sufficient forces from Lemelsen's corps to properly seal off the Trubchevsk pocket. Five days later, the trapped 3rd and 13th Armies mounted a successful breakout attack that Lemelsen was unable to block, enabling elements of seven rifle divisions to slip through the loose cordon and reach Soviet lines near Tula.

Guderian was determined to maintain the initiative and did not want distractions like the Trubchevsk *kessel* to divert him from the prize of Moscow. He believed that the infantry of 2.Armee could mop up Trubchevsk. However, it was clear that Panzerarmee 2's logistic support was grossly inadequate for a further large-scale advance and Guderian was reduced to conducting a 'rock soup' style offensive, by robbing fuel and ammunition from some of his units, like 3.Panzer-Division, to give just enough resources to Kampfgruppe Eberbach to continue advancing toward Tula and then Moscow. The easy rout of Group Ermakov and capture of Bryansk convinced Guderian that the Red Army had no significant forces left in front of him – he just needed to push on as fast as possible to achieve a historic victory.

Kampfgruppe Eberbach sent a single tank company with some reconnaissance troops 15km up the Orel–Tula road on 5 October until they bumped into Gusev's and Burda's T-34s. Burda engaged the German column and knocked out some of the reconnaissance vehicles, while the rest of the German column beat a hasty retreat. A few wounded German troops were left behind and they revealed that the 4.Panzer-Division would soon advance up this road toward Mtensk. Armed with this information, Katukov pulled his armour back to the Lisiza River, where he deployed his two tank battalions on high ground overlooking the bridge. It was a perfect ambush position, since Katukov had excellent visibility from this position and the terrain would constrict any German advance.

The skirmish on 5 October alerted Eberbach to the presence of enemy heavy tanks and he acted accordingly by assigning a battery of 8.8cm flak guns, a battery of 10cm heavy artillery and a battery of 10.5cm medium field howitzers to his vanguard, which would be led by the very capable Major Meinrad von Lauchert. By 6 October, the 4.Panzer-Division had received just enough fuel to enable Lauchert to utilize five companies of tanks and Kradschützen-Abteilung 34, but there was not enough fuel for the Schützen-regiment. Although no Luftwaffe support was available, Lauchert was promised that a battalion of Nebelwerfer multiple rocket launchers and two artillery battalions would provide general support fire. At 0900 hours, von Lauchert moved out with orders to conduct a movement to contact. He moved past the site of the fighting on the previous day without spotting any Russians and it looked like the enemy had pulled back. Von Lauchert's lead tank company reached the bridge over the Lisiza River, which was curiously intact. Katukov had deployed some attached NKVD infantry and 45mm anti-tank guns, along with four of his BT light tanks, as a screening force on the north side of the bridge to deceive the Germans into thinking that this was his main defensive line. Once spotted, von Lauchert called for an artillery barrage on their position and the panzers quickly overran the hapless NKVD troops. Cautiously, von Lauchert pushed two companies of tanks across the bridge at around 1130 hours, plus some of the motorcycle infantry, two 8.8cm flak guns, a 10cm gun and the 6./Artillerie-Regiment 103 (four 10.5cm howitzers), to seize the ridge overlooking the bridge site.

Unknown to von Lauchert, Polkovnik Katukov had deployed two of his tank battalions in ambush positions about 400 meters back from the bridge on the ridgeline and when the German tanks reached the top of the grade they were struck by a barrage of 76.2mm anti-tank rounds from KV-1 and T-34 tanks concealed in stands of birch trees on both sides of the road. One German tank was knocked out, but the others returned fire. The Soviet tankers opened fire from outside the effective range of the Pz.III's low-velocity 5cm gun and the Panzergranate rounds bounced off the thickly-armoured Soviet tanks. Previous actions involving KV and T-34 tanks had usually ended in disaster due to poor choice of ground and/or poor choice of tactics, but on the road to Mtensk, Katukov reaped the benefits of a carefully planned ambush. Once the Germans realized that they were out-gunned by the T-34s and KV-1s, they pulled back into turret defilade positions at the edge of the ridgeline and brought up their 8.8cm flak guns. These flak guns required an 8-ton soft-skin Sd.Kfz.7 half track to tow them into position, which made them quite conspicuous on the battlefield, and it took ten minutes to deploy the gun into a firing position. One 8.8cm flak gun succeeded in getting into action and it hit the T-34 of Sergeant Ivan T. Lyubushkin, injuring all four crew members. However, the T-34 did not burn and another tank in his company destroyed the flak gun with a direct hit. A second 8.8cm flak gun was brought into action but fired only three rounds before it too was destroyed, along with its prime mover. Sergeant Ivan T. Lyubushkin managed to get back into action and, from his position, he methodically knocked out five German tanks at the rim of the ridgeline.

Von Lauchert had had enough and ordered his lead units to disengage and retire across the bridge. The motorcycle infantry withdrew first, but once Kapetan Vladimir Gusev noticed the German withdrawal he ordered Burda's company to attack the bridgehead. The 10cm s.K18 howitzer knocked out one T-34 with an anti-tank round but was itself destroyed. Gusev committed the rest of his battalion, some twenty-one T-34s and four KV-1s. The four 10.5cm howitzers of the 6./Artillerie-Regiment 103 stood their ground as the T-34s drove straight at them, firing on the move. Three T-34s were knocked out, but two howitzers were overrun and their crews killed. One KV-1 that drove into the German position broke down – probably a transmission defect – and several German soldiers quickly jumped up on the immobilized tank with fuel cans and set it alight. Katukov ordered his tanks to pull back to avoid further losses; they had accomplished their mission of repulsing the German river-crossing and could pound the Germans from the distance without fear of return fire. The remaining Germans quickly retreated across the bridge, abandoning knocked-out vehicles. As a fitting end to the battle, the first winter snow began falling. Von Lauchert had lost ten tanks, as well as five artillery pieces. Katukov had lost one KV-1, two T-34s and four BT tanks, plus four more T-34s damaged but recovered.[103]

The tank action near Mtensk on 6 October had a profound impact on armoured combat on the Eastern Front, even though it only involved a single tank battalion on each side. Although German tankers had been shocked by the appearance of the KV and T-34 tanks since the border battles in June, no German panzer unit had actually been defeated by these Soviet 'wonder weapons'. A special commission from the OKH sent to inspect captured T-34s and KV-1s at Raseiniai on 27 June had recommended the 8.8cm flak gun as sufficient to defeat these Soviet heavy tanks, but at Mtensk the flak guns were quickly put out of action.[104] For the first time, the Red Army was able to employ the KV and T-34 in sufficient numbers and under optimal conditions and they demonstrated a significant tactical advantage. An entire German tank company had been shot to pieces, although only seven crewmen were killed. Guderian was shocked by the battle and referred to the 4.Panzer-Division's losses as 'grievous'. He later wrote, 'the rapid advance on Tula which we had planned had therefore to be abandoned for the moment.'[105] Guderian also knew that the Battle of Mtensk signaled that at least some Red Army tank commanders were learning how to properly conduct armoured operations and that Germany's best tank, the Pz.III, was hopelessly obsolete. Guderian requested that the OKH send another special commission to examine the results of the battle and make recommendations about improving the quality of German armour. However, the OKH had its hands full directing Operation Typhoon and the commission would not be dispatched for another six weeks.

In the meantime, Guderian still had a mission to accomplish – enemy resistance, winter weather and insufficient supplies notwithstanding. The 3.Panzer-Division had to remain in Orel due to lack of fuel, so the offensive would resume with just a single panzer division. Guderian ordered von Schweppenburg to bypass Katukov's tank brigade and use outflanking maneuvers to force the Soviets to retreat. Eberbach, whose command vehicle had been destroyed in the battle on 6 October and whom Guderian found when he conferred with him to be suffering from exhaustion, sent his Kradschützen-Abteilung on a wide sweep that secured a crossing across the Oka River on 7 October and threatened to get behind Katukov.[106] Katukov merely retreated 5km and set up a new defensive line near Dumchino. Lelyushenko tasked Katukov with conducting a mobile delay – trading space for time – while he established a more solid defensive line behind the Zusha River at Mtensk. Lelyushenko provided Katukov with a tank battalion from Matisovich's 11th Tank Brigade, some NKVD border guards and two battalions of BM-13 Katyusha rocket launchers, but this was clearly an insufficient force to hold any position for very long. The lack of supporting infantry was Katukov's greatest weakness.

Von Schweppenburg spent two days restocking his fuel and ammunition for a set-piece battle. This time, German reconnaissance identified the location of Katukov's brigade and Eberbach decided upon a change of tactics: he would send his two infantry regiments, Schützen-Regiment 12 and 33, to infiltrate on foot around both flanks of Katukov's tanks and then only commit von Lauchert's tanks once the Soviets began to withdraw. The German infantry began moving forward in two groups at 0630 hours on 9 October. A single company of tanks from Pz.Regt 35 and some infantry managed to get around Katukov's left flank due to his lack of supporting infantry, but they were soon pinned by fire from T-34s in ambush positions. Eberbach called in a Stuka mission which failed to inflict significant damage, but Soviet aircraft began strafing Eberbach's columns along the road back to Orel. Katukov claimed that his tanks destroyed forty-one German tanks and thirteen guns, but the actual results in the one-sided battle were bad enough: at least five of von Lauchert's tanks were knocked out, plus an 8.8cm flak gun, a Pak gun and an SPW half track from the panzer pioneers.[107] Katukov's losses were negligible and he had stopped Guderian's best division for a full day, but he could not remain in a wooded area infested with enemy infantry at night so he pulled back to another position 3km south of Mtensk.[108]

The fighting on 9 October consumed half of Eberbach's ammunition and his Panzer-Regiment 35 had only thirty operational tanks left. A heavy snowfall on the night of 9–10 October turned the road into a muddy mess, meaning that supply trucks would not reach him anytime soon. However, the snow came to the rescue of Eberbach. German scouts had discovered a Soviet pontoon bridge over the Zusha River just southeast of Mtensk and the heavy snowfall reduced visibility to 200 meters or less. Eberbach decided on the risky tactic of sending a single tank company – Oberleutnant Arthur Wollschlaeger's 6./Pz.Regt 35 –

with a company of infantrymen from SR 33 embarked to move cross-country to seize the pontoon bridge and then take the city from the northern side. In an amazing display of tactical stupidity, the pontoon bridge was only lightly guarded and Mtensk itself had few defenders. Wollschlaeger seized the pontoon bridge without being spotted by Katukov's tankers and got his own tanks across although – proving once again that a tank can go just about anywhere, once – the pontoon bridge collapsed before an accompanying 8.8cm flak battery could cross. Undaunted, Wollschlaeger pressed on into the city at 1200 hours and overran a battery of seven BM-13 rocket launchers and an anti-aircraft battery. Although his handful of tanks and infantry were insufficient to control an entire city, Wollschlaeger seized the critical part that controlled the northern side of the main road bridge. At one stroke, Katukov's tanks were cut off.

Katukov immediately tried to counterattack across the bridge with eight tanks into the city, but the tactical situation was now changed. As Eberbach later wrote, 'Our tanks had taken up concealed and covered positions behind houses and in gardens and allowed the Soviets to approach to pointblank range. Three Russian tanks [T-34s] were knocked out; the rest pulled back...' In fact, the other Soviet tanks simply drove through the German ambush and exited the city. Only one German tank was knocked out. Despite this success, Eberbach realized that Wollschlaeger was in a tight spot and pushed the pioneers to repair the pontoon bridge and get reinforcements into Mtensk. Lelyushenko reacted to the German seizure of Mtensk by dispatching a company of six KV-1s from the 11th Tank Brigade to retake the city but, by the time they arrived, the panzer pioneers had emplaced some anti-tank mines and a 10cm howitzer had reached Wollschlaeger; three KV-1s were knocked out and the rest withdrew. In a race against time, Eberbach rushed to get more reinforcements across the Zusha into Mtensk, while Lelyushenko and Katukov tried to assemble a coordinated force. Around 1330 hours, the infantry of I/SR 33 reached Wollschlaeger, along with an 8.8cm flak gun. When Lelyushenko finally committed the rest of the 11th Tank Brigade and some infantry around 1500 hours, the Germans were dug in solidly in Mtensk. With a clear field of fire, the 8.8cm flak gun knocked out three T-34s at about 1,000 meters, causing the attackers to retreat. Cut off south of the Zusha, Katukov waited until nightfall and then conducted a wild breakout across the railroad bridge under fire. Most of Katukov's brigade reached Lelyushenko's lines north of Mtensk, but many damaged vehicles were abandoned and the 4th Tank Brigade was reduced to three KV-1, 7 T-34 and twenty-odd light tanks.

Katukov's 4th Tank Brigade had – with only limited help – limited Guderian's advance toward Tula to a crawl for nearly a week with a brilliantly-executed mobile delay. While Katukov lost about twenty-five of his sixty tanks and 300 of his personnel in this period, he destroyed eight German tanks and damaged ten more. Moreover, the 4.Panzer-Division had seized Mtensk by coup de main, but Guderian was forced to shift onto the defensive for the next two weeks until he could replenish his supplies and losses. Recognizing a winner, Stalin personally ordered that Katukov and his brigade be transferred from the now-quiet Mtensk sector to help stem the German advance on Moscow from the west. Although

Guderian did not know of it, he would have been shocked to learn that Katukov's tanks moved north on a 360km-long road march – during a period of mud that immobilized many German vehicles – without losing a single tank to mechanical breakdown.[109]

Hoth Demolishes the Western Front, 2–12 October

At 0530 hours on 2 October, the main part of Operation Typhoon began with the attacks launched by Hoth's Panzergruppe 3 and Höpner's Panzergruppe 4 against the Soviet Western and Reserve Fronts. Von Bock intended that both Panzergruppen would punch through the Soviet front lines on a narrow front, advance deep into the rear areas and then link up behind the city of Vyazma to encircle the main part of the Western and Reserve Fronts. Unlike other German panzer encirclements, this operation was conducted as a frontal attack and without operational or strategic-level surprise. On this occasion, the defending Soviet armies were alert. This time, there would be no fancy maneuvers through unexpected terrain. Yet while the Red Army had 639 tanks in these two fronts, including thirty-five KV and ninety T-34s, they were badly deployed too close to the front in infantry support roles. Half of Konev's armour was assigned to General-major Lev M. Dovator's mixed cavalry-tank group opposite the German 9.Armee. Neither front had a significant armoured reserve deployed in depth and ready to respond to a German breakthrough.

Hoth focused his XXXXI and LVI Armeekorps (mot.), which had the 1, 6 and 7.Panzer-Divisionen, on breaking the junction between the Western Front's 19th and 30th Armies. Both Soviet formations consisted entirely of rifle divisions. There were just three anti-tank guns per kilometer and no supporting armour at all along a 50km stretch of Konev's front held by these two armies. This is where Hoth decided to attack with his three panzer divisions. While many historians have pointed to the extraordinary ability of the Stavka to raise 'instant' rifle divisions in 1941, few have noted what impact this willy-nilly effort actually had on the Red Army's combat effectiveness. Whereas a pre-war Soviet rifle division had its own anti-tank battalion equipped with eighteen M1937 45mm anti-tank guns, plus a 6-gun battery in each infantry regiment and a 2-gun platoon in each infantry battalion, for a total of fifty-four anti-tank guns, the rifle divisions formed in July–August had no anti-tank battalions and were reduced to just eighteen 45mm guns. Similarly, the divisional artillery was reduced from sixty artillery pieces to just twenty-four pieces, most of which were 76.2mm F-22/USV cannons. Even worse, the artillerymen drafted during the hasty mobilization had not been trained to use indirect fire – just direct fire – which greatly reduced the ability of Soviet artillery to influence the battle beyond their own field of vision. So few radios were available that most of the new units were forced to rely upon field telephones, which were easily disrupted and useless in a mobile battle. With only two or three weeks of training, these 'instant' divisions were little more than place-holders and, after the blood-letting of Timoshenko's August counter-offensive, most of the divisions in the 19th and 30th Armies had lost 30–50 per cent of their personnel and equipment in their first month at the front. As a result, the Western Front's forward defenses were manned by depleted, poorly-trained units with minimal communications and heavy weapons support, and not much idea of how to react to a large-scale armoured attack.

General der Panzertruppen Ferdinand Schaal, having moved from command of 10.Panzer-Division to replace von Manstein as commander of the LVI Armeekorps (mot.), led Hoth's main *schwerpunkt* with the 6 and 7.Panzer-Divisionen. Altogether Schaal had about 300 tanks, mostly Czech-made Pz.35(t) and Pz.38(t), plus the StuG III assault guns of Sturmgeschütz-Abteilung 210 and the 4.7cm-armed Panzerjäger I tank destroyers of Panzerjäger-Abteilung 643. The Pz.35(t) tanks were rapidly reaching the end of their usefulness, with no spare parts left in the pipeline, and Hoth knew that Typhoon would be their last battle. Supplies of fuel and ammunition for Hoth's Panzergruppe were barely adequate for a short offensive, never mind a protracted battle.

After conducting a forward passage of lines through the 129.Infanterie-Division on the night of 1–2 October, Schaal deployed both panzer divisions abreast and designated a penetration corridor that was less than 10km wide. It was rough, hilly terrain, with more than half the area covered by forest – not particularly good tank country. After an artillery preparation that included fire from two Nebelwerfer rocket launcher battalions, Kampfgruppe Raus from 6.Panzer-Division opened the ground assault. In their path was the 91st Rifle Division from 19th Army; this was one of the very first 'Siberian divisions,' transferred from the Far East in July. Although better trained than most of its neighbors, the 91st RD proved little more than a 'speed bump' to Raus' kampfgruppe, which easily broke through the front-line defenses and advanced rapidly eastward, along with 7.Panzer-Division. On Schaal's left flank, Reinhardt's XXXXI Armeekorps (mot.) attacked with 1.Panzer-Division against the 162nd Rifle Division from 30th Army. By the end of the day, Hoth's two corps had achieved a wide breach in the Soviet frontline in this sector and they fanned out to east and west to widen the breakthrough. Hoth also had two infantry corps under his control for the offensive, the V and VI Armeekorps, which he used to launch fixing attacks against the front of the 19th and 30th Armies. Lacking armoured support, the commanders of the 19th and 30th Armies chose to fight a static battle – which is exactly what Hoth was hoping for – while awaiting Konev to send armoured reinforcements to plug the gap. By the second day of the offensive, Kampfgruppe Raus managed to capture two small wooden bridges over the Dnieper at Kholm-Zhirkovski, opening the way for a rapid advance toward Vyazma.

On the next morning a small kampfgruppe from 7.Panzer-Division began probing eastward from the Dnieper bridgehead, with a platoon of Pz.IIs, a platoon of infantry mounted in SPWs and some Panzerjager I self-propelled 4.7cm guns. The Soviets had emplaced some 'dragon's teeth' anti-tank obstacles and some dug-in T-34 tanks behind the Dnieper, but they were overcome.[110] Konev reacted quickly to Hoth's breakthrough across the Dnieper, first by ordering the 19th Army to bombard the German spearhead with three RVGK howitzer regiments – nearly 100 152mm howitzers. However, artillery has difficulty engaging a moving armoured target under the best of circumstances and the artillery failed to stop Hoth's panzers. He then directed the closest armoured unit to the breakthrough, the 143rd Tank Brigade (nine T-34, forty-four T-26), to launch a counterattack, but it mistakenly attacked the infantry of VIII Armee-korps and was repulsed. On 3 October, Konev decided to try a pincer attack from Dovator's cavalry group and other tank units from the Western Front to try and cut off Hoth's spearhead units. He designated his deputy, General-leytenant Ivan Boldin, to form an operational group, comprising the 101st Motorized Division and 126th and 128th Tank Brigades, to attack Raus' bridgehead at Kholm-Zhirkovski. Boldin had only hours to pull together these forces, which on paper had 190 tanks, including eleven KV and ten T-34. On 4 October, Operational Group Boldin attacked Kampfgruppe Raus at Kholm-Zhirkovski. Raus later wrote:

> One hundred tanks drove from the south against the road hub at Kholm. For the most part these were only medium tanks [BT and T-26], against which I dispatched a single battalion of PzKw 35ts and the 6.Kompanie of Schützen-Regiment 114. This weak force proved sufficient to contain the potentially dangerous thrust until flak and anti-tank guns could be organized into an adequate anti-tank security line between Kholm and the southern Dnieper bridge. Their tanks split up into small groups by the forest, the Russians never succeeding in organizing a powerful, unified armoured thrust. Their lead elements were eliminated piecemeal as they encountered the anti-tank front. As a result, the Soviet commander became even more timid and scattered his vehicles across the breadth and depth of the battlefield in such a manner that all subsequent tank thrusts, carried out in detail and by small groups, could be met by our anti-tank weapons and smashed ... Thus the flank attack by 100 Soviet tanks near Kholm had succeeded in delaying 6.Panzer-Division's advance for only a matter of hours.[111]

Boldin's ill-planned counterattack was defeated, with the loss of about 100 tanks. It was clear that the lack of radio communications prevented Boldin from massing his armour effectively, which enabled a far-inferior German force to defeat them. After Boldin retreated, Schaal's two panzer divisions sealed the victory by overrunning most of the unprotected Soviet artillery in the area. Konev's counter-offensive capability was eliminated in a single action and he no longer had the means to stop Hoth. In fact, Hoth's most serious problem was fuel shortages, which hampered his ability to use all his armour, and he was forced to rely upon Luftwaffe aerial resupply to keep the 7.Panzer-Division moving forward.[112] However, the Luftwaffe had committed the bulk of its transport force on the Eastern Front – 200 Ju-52s – to move the paratroopers of the 7.Flieger-Division to Leningrad during the first several days of October, leaving very few aircraft to support Typhoon.[113] This commitment of a vital transport asset to a secondary theater at the same time as the main push on Moscow began demonstrates the OKH's failure to remain focused on critical objectives.

On 6 October – the fifth day of the offensive – Kampfgruppe Manteuffel from the 7.Panzer-Division passed north of Vyazma, scattering weak Soviet units in their path, and then turned south to cut the Minsk highway around 2000 hours. Meanwhile, the 1.Panzer-Division opened the way to Rzhev for the 9.Armee by capturing Belyy, which forced Dovator's cavalry group to retreat northward. At a cost of about 1,000 casualties, Hoth's Panzergruppe had completed its mission of forming the northern pincer of the Vyazma encirclement and defeated a large portion of Konev's armour in the process.

On 5 October, all four Panzergruppen were renamed as Panzerarmee. Heretofore, the Panzergruppen had been nominally attached to one of the regular field armies, but the redesignation indicated that they were now fully independent and co-equal with the other armies. On the same day, there were significant changes in the panzer leadership ranks: Hoth left the Panzerarmee 3 to assume command of AOK 17 in Heeresgruppe Süd and his place was taken by Georg Hans Reinhardt. Walter Model, whose 3.Panzer-Division was out of fuel at Orel, was brought up to take command of Reinhardt's XXXXI Armeekorps (mot.).

Höpner Seals the Vyazma *kessel*, 2– 12 October

Generaloberst Erich Höpner's Panzergruppe 4 was given the lion's share of resources for Operation Typhoon and it was expected that his forces would be the ones to capture Moscow. His formation was completely changed from what he had commanded in Heeresgruppe Nord and now included three motorized corps: the XXXX Armeekorps (mot.) under General der Panzertruppen Georg Stumme, the XXXXVI Armeekorps (mot.) under Generaloberst Heinrich von Vietinghoff-Scheel and the LVII Armeekorps (mot.) under General der Panzertruppen Adolf Kuntzen. Altogether, Höpner had about 765 operational tanks, including over 300 Pz.III and seventy-five Pz.IV, and he received the two full-strength divisions – the 2 and 5.Panzer-Divisionen. Stumme's corps – which would be the main effort – was the strongest, with 335 tanks. In addition, Höpner had the SS-Division *Reich*, the 3.Infanterie-Division (mot.), an assault-gun battalion and two straight-leg infantry divisions. Höpner benefited from the fact that his main supply railhead, Roslavl, was only 25km from his assembly areas.

Höpner's mission was to smash through both echelons of Marshal Budyonny's Reserve Front and advance to form the southern pincer around Vyazma. Given the size of his formation, Höpner decided to attack on a fairly wide 25km attack frontage with the XXXX and XXXXVI Armeekorps (mot.) up front and Kuntzen's corps in reserve to exploit success. Opposite them, the Soviet 43rd Army had four rifle divisions thinly spread across an 85km-wide front, with a defensive density of fewer than 200 troops and 0.8 anti-tank guns per kilometer of front – meaning that Höpner's panzers would enjoy an overwhelming advantage over the defense in this sector. For example, the 10.Panzer-Division would only be opposed by a rifle regiment supported by four or five 45mm anti-tank guns. Furthermore, the 43rd Army only had eighty-eight tanks from the 145th and 148th Tank Brigades in support. Höpner kicked off his offensive at the same time as Hoth, beginning with a bombardment from Nebelwerfer rocket launchers and Stuka dive-bombers on the front-line Soviet positions. Following the preparation, Stumme's and Viettinghoff's corps quickly established bridge-heads across the Desna and punched through the thin Soviet first-echelon rifle units. The Desna River was shallow enough that the tanks of the 11.Panzer-Division were able to ford it on their own and the Soviets had failed to emplace mines at the ford sites.[114] Rather than using his armour to counterattack, the 43rd Army commander decided to use his two tank brigades to defend the vital rail junction at Spas-Demensk. Little or no effort was made to hinder Höpner's crossing of the Desna or construction of pontoon bridges. Although the infantry of the 43rd Army was quickly overrun by the German Panzerkeil, Budyonny had deployed his forces in depth and the five rifle divisions of the 33rd Army should have slowed the German advance. Instead, the Soviet rifle units were too dispersed to be mutually supporting and Stumme's corps simply massed its armoured strength against one rifle division after another, routing them. Many of Budyonny's divisions were militia units, with few heavy weapons, and they were totally unsuited to stop massed armour attacks. During the first three days of the offensive, Höpner routed much of the 33rd and 43rd Armies and created a huge breach in Budyonny's front. Budyonny made the mistake of visiting the 43rd Army headquarters and got caught up in the rout, which deprived the Reserve Front of senior leadership at a critical moment.[115] On 4 October, Viettinghoff's corps captured Spas-Demensk and encircled the 145th and 148th Tank Brigades.

On 5 October, Höpner committed Kuntzen's corps to exploit the break-through. While Stumme and Viettinghoff swung toward the north to envelope Vyazma, Kuntzen advanced boldly with the SS-Division *Reich* toward Gzhatsk and the 3.Infanterie-Division (mot.) toward Yukhnov. The next forty-eight hours went very badly for the Soviets, with one disaster after another. Budyonny's Reserve Front quickly fell apart in front of Höpner's panzers and the operation became more of a pursuit than an offensive. A lone Soviet Pe-2 light bomber on a reconnaissance mission spotted columns of German armour moving unopposed up the Warsaw–Moscow highway, but was discounted. The 10.Panzer-Division, now under General der Panzertruppen Wolfgang Fischer, conducted a bold slashing attack by sending one kampfgruppen to seize Yukhnov at 0530 hours on 6 October and another kampfgruppen toward Vyazma. When Stalin heard that Yukhnov had fallen – less than 200 km from the Kremlin – he panicked and ordered Konev and Budyonny to fall back immediately toward Mozhaisk, but it was already too late. This is when the Stavka's rapid creation of units – without adequate transportation assets – came back to haunt the Red Army; the rifle units simply lacked the mobility to outrun panzer divisions. At 1030 hours on 7 October, a kampfgruppe from the 10.Panzer-Division fought its way into Vyazma against surprisingly weak resistance – there were only militia and anti-aircraft units in the city – and linked up with Manteuffel's Kampfgruppe from 7.Panzer-Division. Rokossovsky and his staff were on hand to witness the German coup but they were powerless to stop it and beat a hasty retreat toward Moscow.[116] The jaws of the German pincers had closed around four Soviet armies inside the Vyazma *kessel*, including Boldin's Operational Group. Having plenty of practice by now in forming *kessel*, Hoth used the LVI Armeekorps (mot.) while Höpner used the XXXX and XXXXVI Armeekorps to seal the east end of the pocket, while five infantry corps pressed in from the west. Although a wet snow fell on 6 October, turning to rain on 7 October, this had little effect upon the German ability to crush the pocket. In less than a week, the Vyazma pocket was crushed, although Boldin was able to escape it with about 85,000 troops.

In ten days, the two German panzer armies conducted a series of envelopments that resulted in the Vyazma–Bryansk pockets. The Western and Reserve Fronts were demolished and the Bryansk Front scattered, having lost 855,000 troops, 830 tanks and 6,000 artillery pieces. More than thirty Soviet divisions and eight tank brigades were eliminated. Considering that von Kleist was encircling the bulk of the Southern Front at the same time as Hoth and Höpner were encircling the Western, Reserve and Bryansk Fronts, Stalin was faced with the loss of nearly one million troops and one-third of the Red Army's combat strength in just a ten-day period. German losses were significant, but Hoth's and Höpner's panzer armies were still combat effective; they had suffered about 6,000 casualties in the first ten days of Typhoon, including 1,200 dead. Overall, Heeresgruppe Mitte suffered nearly 33,000 casualties in the Vyazma–Bryansk battles, including 6,600 dead, but inflicted casualties upon the Red Army at a rate of 25–1. German tank losses from all three panzer armies amounted to only sixty tanks and five assault guns destroyed, which amounted to less than 5 per cent of their armour. In desperation, Stalin recalled Zhukov from Leningrad and he arrived in Moscow on 6 October. Stalin told him to meet with Konev and Budyonny, assess the situation and determine what the enemy was going to do next. With these vague instructions, Zhukov headed off to the front.[117]

Zhukov: Playing for Time, 7–31 October

'*Any idiot could defend the city [Moscow] with reserves.*'
Josef Stalin, October 1941

It was raining on the morning of 7 October, with low, grey clouds hanging overhead, when Polkovnik Aleksandr Druzhinina's 18th Tank Brigade began unloading its tanks from railroad flat cars just over a kilometer from the rail station at Mozhaisk. German bombers had struck the main rail station, which was wrecked, so the train unloaded Druzhinina's brigade short of the city. Druzhinina's brigade came from Vladimir, 185km east of Moscow, where the RVGK was forming three new tank brigades.[118] Even though the brigades were still incomplete, they were better equipped and trained than the slap-dash brigades sent to the field armies in August and the Stavka decided to immediately dispatch all three to provide Konev with armoured forces for his shattered Western Front. Without tanks the Germans could not be stopped. The 18th Tank Brigade had 1,400 troops in two tank and one motorized infantry battalion, with sixty-three tanks (twenty-nine T-34, thirty-three BT and one

T-26); the T-34s were newly-built models from StZ, but the light tanks were all obsolescent vehicles drawn from repair depots.

There were more tanks available but, unfortunately, not accessible. In August, Stalin had ordered the creation of a special tank reserve separate from the Stavka-controlled RVGK and to be maintained near Moscow under his personal direction. He ordered that these tanks were 'to be given to nobody.'[119] When a particular commander pleased him, he would dole out a number of tanks to him as a reward, and the RVGK then had to divert tanks to refill Stalin's personal reserve. Interestingly, both Stalin and Hitler at various times during the war tried to maintain personal tank reserves – which they alone could release – and in every case this micromanagement proved harmful.

When Zhukov finally found Konev on the evening of 7 October, he discovered that there was very little left of the Western Front and that Konev himself was in despair, expecting to be shot for his failure. In this regard he was correct – Stalin wanted his head – but Zhukov managed to defer that idea. Konev briefed him on the situation, which was awful. The SS-Division *Reich* was advancing up the Moscow–Minsk highway toward Gzhatsk, which was defended only by the 50th Rifle Division. Further south, Kuntzen's LVII Armeekorps (mot.) had captured Yukhnov and the bridge over the Ugra River; their next objective – Maloyaroslavets – was defended by two battered Moscow militia divisions. The first snow of the season had arrived but quickly turned to rain and it was getting colder, which was bound to impair German mobility, but the two main avenues to Moscow were barely guarded at all. In his memoirs, Zhukov tried to make it appear that he quickly took control of the situation and restored the front, but his role was initially advisory and much of the credit actually goes to others.

Polkovnik Semyon I. Bogdanov, a tank officer who had fought his way out of the Minsk–Bialystok pocket, was in charge of forming new tank brigades in the Moscow military district when Typhoon began. When it became apparent to the Stavka that the Western and Reserve Fronts were crumbling, Bogdanov was ordered to take command of the Mozhaisk fortified area. The Stavka also decided to reform the 5th Army – which had been destroyed in the Kiev pocket – as a command cadre at Mozhaisk for reinforcements being dispatched to restore the Western Front; Bogdanov, the man-on-the-spot, was made deputy commander. When the first two RVGK tank brigades began arriving by rail from Vladimir, Bogdanov decided to employ them as screening forces while he established a firm defense at Mozhaisk and Maloyaroslavets. He ordered Druzhinina's 18th Tank Brigade to head to Gzhatsk to block the SS-Division *Reich* and Polkovnik Ivan I. Troitsky's 17th Tank Brigade to delay Kuntzen's forces from reaching Maloyaroslavets. Three more brigades – the 9th, 19th and 20th – were en route. The decision to establish this armoured delay was made before Zhukov arrived, without Stavka approval and by a mere colonel – and it was a crucial one.

8 October 1941 proved to be another dreary, rainy, chilly day. Druzhinina and Troitsky moved their tank brigades into assembly areas near Gzhatsk and Maloyaroslavets and prepared for battle. Generalleutnant der Waffen-SS Paul Hausser's SS-Division *Reich* was one of only two major German motorized units

not involved in reducing the Vyazma-Bryansk pockets and was tasked with advancing as far down the Minsk–Moscow highway as possible. Hausser's Waffen-SS division was a strong formation with nine motorized infantry battalions, a Kradschützen-Abteilung and an Aufklärungs-Abteilung, but his only armour support was a Sturmgeschütz-Batterie with six StuG IIIs. Von Bock was so absorbed with forming the perfect *kessel* at Vyazma that he paid little attention to providing Hausser with reinforcements or supplies to sustain his advance. Likewise, Kuntzen demonstrated little drive in getting his forces up the Warsaw–Moscow highway to Maloyaroslavets, allowing the 20.Panzer-Division to lag well behind Generalleutnant Curt Jahn's 3.Infanterie-Division (mot.). Indeed, both major German spearheads advancing toward Moscow in this crucial period of 7–12 October were being led by motorized infantry divisions, with negligible armoured support.

On the morning of 9 October, the SS-Regiment *Deutschland* fought its way into Gzhatsk, only 175km west of Moscow, and secured the town by 1230 hours. Jubilant at this victory, Hausser sent his Kradschützen-Abteilung, followed by the SS-Regiment *Der Führer* to probe further down the highway toward Mozhaisk. Druzhinina had established a blocking position 10km east of Gzhatsk, with his tank concealed in ambush near the village of Budayevo.[120] At 1630 hours, Druzhinina's tankers spotted the approaching Waffen-SS vanguard, led by motorcycles and armoured cars. The Waffen-SS troops were stunned when more than fifty Soviet tanks opened fire on them, some at point-blank range. Lacking the ability to defeat T-34s, the Waffen-SS troops withdrew, after suffering 400 casualties. Hausser immediately requested that Stumme's XXXX Armeekorps (mot.) send him armoured support to counter the enemy tanks. Further south, Troitsky's 17th Tank Brigade counterattacked the lead elements of Kuntzen's corps northeast of Yukhnov. Major Nikolai Y. Klypin, who had won the HSU as a tanker in the Russo-Finnish War, led a vicious counterattack with two companies of T-34 that ripped apart Oberst Horst von Wolff's Infanterie-Regiment 478. Wolf had been moving up to reinforce Jahn's 3.Infanterie-Division (mot.), but his handful of 3.7cm Pak guns were completely useless against Klypin's T-34s. Oberst Wolff, one of the few German officers who had won both the Pour le Mérite in the First World War and the *Ritterkreuz* in the Second World War, was killed in action and his regiment routed. After days of disaster, Soviet tankers had finally gained some measure of success.

The German pursuit had been halted and the Stavka tried to make good use of this time. Polkovnik Sergey A. Kalihovich's 19th Tank Brigade arrived by rail in Mozhaisk and was sent to reinforce Druzhinina's brigade. More important, the first elements of the 32nd Rifle Division began unloading at Mozhaisk on 10 October; this was a well-trained, full-strength unit from Siberia, with 15,000 troops and a full complement of artillery. Also on this day Zhukov was finally put in overall command of the Western Front (with remnants of the Reserve Front included), with Konev as his deputy. The Germans had nearly crushed the Vyazma *kessel* by this point and the 10.Panzer-Division sent Kampfgruppe von Hauenschild (Pz.Regt 7 and SR 86) to reinforce Hausser's advance toward

Mozhaisk. Kuntzen directed the 19 and 20.Panzer-Divisionen to Yukhnov, but the vehicles of both divisions were in such poor condition that they could only advance at a crawl along the muddy roads. Command lethargy was also a factor developing among the German mid-level leaders as illness and exhaustion robbed commanders of their normal aggressiveness. German inactivity on this day was equivalent to another Soviet tactical victory.

On 11 October, General-leytenant Dmitri Lelyushenko arrived at Mozhaisk from Mtensk to take command of the 5th Army, with Bogdanov remaining as his deputy. Another RVGK tank brigade – Polkovnik Ivan F. Kirichenko's 9th Tank Brigade – arrived at the front and was sent to reinforce Troitsky's 17th Tank Brigade at Maloyaroslavets. The Western Front now had over 200 tanks, including about sixty T-34s, on the main approaches to Moscow, whereas Heeresgruppe Mitte only had a handful of assault guns up front – this asymmetry at a critical moment helped to reduce the German advance on Moscow to a crawl far more than snow, rain and mud. However, the four Soviet tank brigades were merely a screening force with very little infantry or artillery support, and the danger in a mobile delay operation is judging when the correct moment to break contact arrives. Polkovnik Druzhinina misjudged this moment. Kampfgruppe von Hauenschild arrived to reinforce Hausser's advance late on 11 October and the appearance of a battalion of Pz.III tanks from Pz.Regt 7 flanking his blocking position caught Druzhinina by surprise. The Germans did what they always did when faced with a tough enemy position – outflanked it and called in the Stukas. Under bombardment and with his brigade about to be cut off, Druzhinina fought his way out of the encirclement with seven tanks, but his deputy commander was killed and thirty-two tanks were lost. This action represented the fragility of the Soviet tank brigades, which lacked the supporting arms of a panzer division. The Germans also managed to envelop Kalihovich's 19th Tank Brigade, which was forced to withdraw after losing about a dozen tanks. Oberstleutnant Theodor Keyser's Panzer-Regiment 7, which started Typhoon with 152 tanks, had about twenty tanks knocked out while rolling back the 5th Army's armoured screening force.

One of Zhukov's first and most important decisions was to concentrate all his remaining forces to defend and hold three key positions on the Moscow periphery: that part of Rokossovsky's 16th Army that escaped the Vyazma *kessel* would defend Volokolamsk, Lelyushenko's 5th Army would hold Mozhaisk and the remnants of the 33rd and 43rd Armies would hold Maloyaroslavets. The consequence of Zhukov's decision was that the Red Army essentially abandoned less critical areas, which allowed Heeresgruppe Mitte to continue to advance into areas vacated by the Red Army despite muddy roads and supply shortages. The German infantry divisions – which were not as affected by mud or supply issues, but were vulnerable to Soviet armoured counterattacks – succeeded in capturing Kaluga on 12 October and Rzhev on 13 October. The OKH was quick to note that the Red Army appeared to be in full retreat and directed von Bock to divert the XXXXI Armeekorps (mot.) from Hoth's Panzerarmee 3 to push north, eliminate remnants of the Western's Front's 22nd and 29th Armies and then seize

Kalinin. Some in the OKH optimistically believed that Kalinin would be a useful springboard for a follow-on operation to split the junction between the Soviet Western and Northwest Fronts.

Thanks to the initial snowfall melting and a sudden dry spell, the 1.Panzer-Division – which was down to fifty tanks – dispatched *Vorausabteilung* Eckinger (initially I./SR 113 with SPWs, 3.I/Pz.Regt 1, a battalion from Artillerie-Regiment 75, a platoon of 2cm flak guns on Sd.Kfz.7 half tracks and some engineers) northward to capture Kalinin, a city of 216,000. At this point, the XXXXI Armeekorps (mot.) was extremely short of fuel and could only move a few other units to reinforce Major Josef-Franz Eckinger's small command. Oberst Hans-Christoph von Heydebrand followed with Panzer-Abteilung 101 (flame-thrower-equipped Pz.II tanks), Kradschützen-Abteilung 1 and some additional artillery and pioneers. Further back, Lehr-Brigade 900 (mot.) was also directed to proceed to Kalinin. The 36.Infanterie-Division (mot.) also contributed its own Kradschützen-Abteilung 36 and Kampfgruppe Fries with two truck-borne battalions of Infanterie-Regiment 87, but they advanced along a separate axis toward Kalinin. Given the extreme lack of fuel and the unknown enemy situation, the German drive toward Kalinin with such small forces was an extremely high-risk operation.

Shoving aside retreating Soviet units on the road to Kalinin, Eckinger was fortunate in that the Soviet defenses in Kalinin were extremely weak and initially had no armour. Nevertheless, Soviet anti-tank guns knocked out three of his tanks when he began probing into the city on the morning of 14 October. Von Heydebrand reinforced Eckinger and the flamethrower tanks proved quite useful in rooting Soviet infantry out of buildings. By 1830, Eckinger's small detachment had not only seized central Kalinin, but had also captured a large, steel highway bridge over the Volga intact. The seizure of Kalinin was the fifth time that a German panzer kampfgruppe had single-handedly seized a major Soviet city by coup de main during the 1941 campaign.

Although caught by surprise – again – the Stavka had been scrambling to get reinforcements to Kalinin. The Northwest Front's highly-competent chief-of-staff, General-leytenant Nikolai F. Vatutin, formed an operational group to head to Kalinin, consisting of two rifle and two cavalry divisions, but its primary striking element was Polkovnik Pavel A. Rotmistrov's 8th Tank Brigade with forty-nine tanks (seven KV, ten T-34, thirty-two T-40). Rotmistrov's brigade marched 250km in a single day to reach Kalinin – an amazing feat – but arrived just after the 1.Panzer-Division seized the city.[121] Rotmistrov linked up with a few battalions of Soviet infantry at Kalikino northwest of the city and hoped to launch a counterattack to retake the city once the rest of Vatutin's troops arrived, but the Germans pre-empted him. At 1145 on 15 October, the Lehr-Brigade 900, supported by a company of seventeen tanks from Pz. Regt. 1 and some assault guns from Sturmgeschütz-Abteilung 660 began advancing west along the Torzhok road, unaware that Rotmistrov's tankers were nearby. Rotmistrov's forces were exhausted after their forced march, but succeeded in launching surprise attacks against both German flanks; three German tanks were knocked out as well as eight half tracks and other vehicles, compelling the Germans to fall back into Kalinin. The Germans made a stronger push a few hours later, reinforced with a second tank company, but Rotmistrov committed his KV-1 company, which destroyed at least two German tanks with long-range 76.2mm fire. In retaliation, an 8.8cm flak battery was brought up and disabled the Soviet KV-1 tank company commander's vehicle. While Rotmistrov gained a temporary tactical victory, he was forced to shift to tactical defense due to lack of fuel. Rotmistrov had established blocking positions just outside the western outskirts of Kalinin, but he had very little infantry or artillery support. On the morning of 16 October, the Luftwaffe bombed Rotmistrov's positions and then the 1.Panzer-Division maneuvered around the Soviet right flank. Tanks from Pz.Regt 1 over-ran Rotmistrov's brigade command post and the situation was deteriorating so quickly that Rotmistrov decided to retreat – without orders. He was forced to abandon thirty-one of his damaged or out-of-fuel tanks, including six KV-1 and five T-34s. With Rotmistrov's brigade out of the way, the Lehr-Brigade 900 advanced 20km to capture Mednoye and a bridge over the River Tvertsa. Konev threatened Rotmistrov with court martial – and the explicit threat of execution – unless he immediately returned to block any further German advance along the Torzhok road. The next day, Major Eckinger did try to push further up the Torzhok road, but one of Rotmistrov's T-34s spotted his SPW command track and destroyed it with 76.2mm rounds. The death of the dynamic Major Eckinger brought the German advance to a halt and helped to redeem Rotmistrov's reputation.[122]

An even more daring Soviet effort to retake Kalinin came from the south. General-leytenant of Tank Troops Yakov N. Fedorenko, head of GABTU, personally ordered Podpolkovnik Andrei L. Lesovoi's 21st Tank Brigade – which had just arrived br rail in Moscow – to proceed to Zavidovo and then unload and prepare to assist Vatutin's effort to recapture Kalinin. Lesovoi's brigade was a fairly elite unit, equipped with nineteen T-34/76 and ten T-34-57 'tank killers', equipped with the high-velocity 57mm gun, as well as twenty BT, ten T-60 and four ZiS-30 57mm self-propelled guns. The 21st Tank Brigade also had an exceptional level of combat-experienced leadership: Major Mikhail A. Lukin, commander of the brigade's 21st Tank Regiment, had been awarded the HSU for leading a tank raid at Nomonhan in 1939, Kapetan Mikhail P. Agibalova, commander of the 1st Battalion, was also awarded the HSU for valor at Nomonhan and his deputy, Starshiy Leytenant Josif I. Makovsky, was awarded the HSU for leading tanks during the Russo-Finnish War. Once the 21st Tank Brigade detrained at Zavidovo, it marched westward to assembly areas near Turginovo, about 30km south of Kalinin. Fedorenko made little effort to co-ordinate the 21st Tank Brigade's operations with other Soviet forces in the area and Lesovoi was ordered to mount a single brigade attack on Kalinin from the south, without benefit of reconnaissance or any other external support – in essence, a tank raid.

Before dawn on 17 October, the 21st Tank Brigade began advancing north-ward toward Kalinin in two groups, one led by Lukin and the other by Agibalova.

The Germans were in the process of moving the 36.Infanterie-Division (mot) to reinforce Kampfguppe von Heydebrand in Kalinin and Lukin's force suddenly encountered a German column on the road 15km south of Kalinin. Although some German trucks were destroyed by the tanks, the 611.Artillerie-abteilung managed to get some of its 10cm howitzers into action and bring the Soviet tanks under fire.[123] A lucky shot struck Lukin's left front track, blowing off the return sprocket and causing his left track to come off. Even worse, the tank plunged nose-first off the road into soft ground and the long 57mm gun tube could not traverse properly. Lukin told his crew to abandon the tank and run for it, but he was killed by a burst of German machine-gun fire. Agibalova continued to lead the raiding force northward and some of his tanks attacked a German airfield just south of Kalinin and shot up some Ju-52 transports on the ground. Although the Soviet tank raid caught the Germans by surprise, they reacted quickly and deployed the bulk of Panzerjäger-Abteilung 36, Sturmgeschütz-abteilung 600 and Bf-109E fighter-bombers from II.(Schlacht)/LG2 to crush the Soviet tank battalion. Agibalova's T-34 was immobilized by fire near Kalinin and he committed suicide rather than surrender. Nine T-34s actually made it into Kalinin and moved individually and without coordination, since the only radios had been in Lukin's and Agibalova's T-34s. Gradually, the 36.Infanterie-Division (mot.) picked off the unsupported T-34s with a combination of artillery, anti-tank fire, mines and air attacks. Only a single T-34 made it all the way through Kalinin and reached Soviet lines northeast of the city. Lesovoi's 21st Tank Brigade was virtually wrecked after losing twenty-one of its twenty-nine T-34s and its attached motorized rifle battalion (who rode as *desant* troops on the T-34s) in the raid, as well as two Heroes of the Soviet Union, but succeeded in destroying eighty-four trucks, thirteen Sd.Kfz prime movers, two artillery pieces and eight Pak guns. At least two German Pz.III tanks from the 1.Panzer-Division and some Pz.II flamethrower tanks from Panzer-abteilung 101 were knocked out.[124] Even more significantly, twelve of the trucks destroyed were fuel tankers, which deprived Kampfguppe von Heydebrand of fuel resupply. Yet despite these accomplishments, the raid demonstrated that even large numbers of well-led T-34s could not achieve decisive results without infantry and artillery support.

By mid-October, Operation Typhoon was running out of steam even with the capture of several prominent Russian cities. The railheads supplying Heeresgruppe Mitte were well in the rear of the panzer divisions and the muddy, congested roads made movement a tortuous process for their resupply columns – it often took up to a week for supply columns to make round trips from the railhead near Vyazma to the front-line panzer divisions. Even worse, the amount of fuel reaching Vyazma was only about one-third of what was required to keep three panzer armies in motion and 3.Panzerarmee was particularly short-changed for petrol. Fuel shortages created ammunition shortages, since supply columns could not keep up with demand. At Kalinin, the hard-pressed 1.Panzer-Division had only 0.1 V.S. of fuel, only 0–5 per cent of one basic load of artillery ammunition and 10–40 per cent of one load of tank ammunition.[125] Despite these near crippling logistical shortages – alleviated only in part by emergency aerial resupply by the Luftwaffe – the OKH ordered the XXXXI Armeekorps (mot.) at Kalinin to push westward toward Torzhok. However, Kampfgruppe von Heydebrand and Lehr-Brigade 900 (mot.) advanced into a hornet's nest and became surrounded by five Soviet rifle divisions, supported by Rotmistrov's tankers, from 18–21 October. Both German units eventually managed to fight their way out of encirclement back to Kalinin, but 1.Panzer-Division lost about sixty tanks and many of its vehicles – which had to be abandoned due to lack of fuel – as well as 750 casualties. As a result of the senseless fighting around Kalinin, which diverted substantial German resources from the drive on Moscow, the XXXXI Armeekorps was badly mauled and rendered incapable of anything but static defense.

Even though the OKH was diverting a good deal of his combat power toward secondary objectives such as Kalinin and Kursk, von Bock realized that – like Zhukov – he had to focus his finite resources on the key points in order to make a decisive breakthrough before the Western Front rebuilt itself. Recognizing that time was running out, von Bock chose to emphasize the direct approach, by going straight through Mozhaisk to Moscow. Lelyushenko had four days to build an improvised defense in front of Mozhaisk at Borodino, site of the famous battle against Napoleon in 1812. Druzhinina and Kalihovich continued to fight a mobile delay on 12–13 October, which delayed the advance of the SS-Division *Reich* and 10.Panzer-Division, but cost most of their remaining tanks. Lelyushenko had managed to build two outer blocking positions at Rogachevo and Yelnya with reliable infantry from the 32nd Rifle Division and the 121st Anti-Tank Regiment, which the SS-Division *Reich* vanguards encountered on 13 October. Both German probes were repulsed and the II/Pz.Regt 7 lost six tanks knocked out at long range by concealed 76.2mm F-22 anti-tank guns. Leytenant Aleksandr V. Bodnar, commander of a dug-in KV-1 tank, cooly destroyed two German half tracks at a range of 500 meters.[126]

Although surprised by the level of Soviet resistance, Hausser and Oberst Bruno Ritter von Hauenschild decided to mount a full-scale combined arms attack the next morning. Lelyushenko's flanks were unprotected, but he lacked the troops to do much about that. While the SS-Regiment *Der Führer* and a tank battalion from Pz. Regt 7 flanked the Soviet position at Yelnya, von Hauenschild massed a brigade-size force for a frontal attack, supported by Stukas and over thirty Nebelwerfer rocket launchers. Both the Yelnya and Rogachevo positions were flanked and overrun, and Hausser committed his fresh SS-Infanterie-Regiment 11 and his assault-gun battery to exploit the collapsing Soviet front. Lelyushenko reacted by committing all the remaining elements of the 32nd Rifle Division, two battalions of 76.2mm anti-tank guns and his only armoured reserve – Polkovnik Timofei S. Orlenko's 20th Tank Brigade. The SS motorized infantry retreated at the sight of an approaching battalion of T-34 tanks, but Orlenko was shot and killed when he tried to stop a group of fleeing Soviet soldiers. Soviet morale and discipline was beginning to show signs of cracking under the pressure of repeated defeats.

By 15 October, there was an inch of snow on the battlefield as both German divisions mounted a set-piece attack that bit into the main Soviet defensive belt. Kampfgruppe von Hauenschild broke through the Soviet infantry and approached Lelyushenko's command post; Lelyushenko managed to organize a counterattack which halted the German panzers, but he was seriously wounded in the action and replaced by General-major Leonid A. Govorov, an artilleryman. The emplacement of anti-tank mines and continued effectiveness of the 76.2mm anti-tank guns limited the German advance. In consolation, a barrage of BM-13 Katyusha rockets struck Hausser's SdKfz 253 command track and severely wounded him; SS-Oberführer Wilhelm Bittrich took over the *Reich* division. The Germans mounted an even stronger attack with both divisions on 16 October, which gained more ground as the 32nd Rifle Division's defense began to crumble. Once again, it was the timely arrival of the 20th Tank Brigade, with sixty tanks including twenty-nine StZ-built T-34s and eight 57mm anti-tank guns, which counterattacked SS-Regiment *Deutschland* and prevented a breakthrough. However the respite was only temporary. At 0630 hours on 17 October, the fresh Kampfgruppe von Bulow from 10.Panzer-Division (I and II./SR 69, and Kradschützen-Abteilung 10), reinforced by the remaining tanks of Keyser's Pz.Regt 7, broke through the last defensive positions of the 32nd Rifle Division. The remaining survivors of the 5th Army conducted a fighting retreat toward Mozhaisk, but a Kampfgruppe from SS-Regiment *Deutschland* captured the town by 1500 hours on 18 October. The Kradschützen-Abteilung SS-Division *Reich* probed further down the highway toward Moscow, finding no organized resistance and Moscow only 90km away, but Stumme's XXXX Armeekorps (mot.) was too spent by the fighting at Borodino to take advantage of this fleeting opportunity.

The six-day Battle of Borodino was a very bloody affair. The 10.Panzer-Division suffered 776 casualties, including 167 killed, and about fifty tanks destroyed and many more damaged. This was the first real occasion where a German panzer unit had tried to breach a defensive zone that included a good number of Soviet anti-tank mines and 57mm and 76.2mm anti-tank guns; it was a painful preview of the PaK fronts of 1943. The SS-Division *Reich* suffered 1,242 casualties in the battle, including 270 dead, and was forced to disband one of its three motorized infantry regiments. While Lelyushenko lost most of the forces he committed at Borodino, including over 10,000 troops and most of his armour, he had purchased valuable time for Zhukov to rebuild the Western Front. The German tactical victory at Borodino did spark a brief panic in Moscow, with parts of the Soviet Government evacuating to Kuybyshev.

The rest of Zhukov's Mozhaisk Line was overrun by late October. Despite the lethargic advance of Kuntzen's LVII Armeekorps (mot.), the Soviet 43rd Army failed to build as robust a defense at Maloyaroslavets as Lelyushenko did at Borodino. The Soviets tried to build a strong defense around the 312th Rifle Division arriving from Central Asia and four tank brigades (5th, 9th, 17th and 24th), but Kuntzen finally managed to get both 19 and 20.Panzer-Divisionen into the fight and the Soviet units were defeated piecemeal. The 312th Rifle Division was encircled and crushed and Polkovnik Troitsky, commander of 17th Tank Brigade, was severely wounded in the Battle of Maloyaroslavets. Generalleutnant

Georg von Bismarck's 20.Panzer-Division had just received fifty-five new Pz.38(t) and fourteen Pz.IV tanks just before the start of Typhoon and it used them to overrun Maloyaroslavets on 18 October.

At the northern end of the Mozhaisk Line, Rokossovsky's 16th Army fought a protracted battle for the Volokolamsk crossroads against Viettinghoff's XXXXVI Armeekorps (mot.). General-major Ivan V. Panfilov's 316th Rifle Division detrained near Volokolamsk from Central Asia just a few days before the advance elements of the 2 and 11.Panzer-Divisionen arrived. Rokossovsky was also provided with the 27th and 28th Tank Brigades as well as two anti-tank regiments to stop the Germans. Viettinghoff was slow to move his divisions up – granting Rokossovsky precious time – and was not in a position to begin probing attacks until 20 October. Panfilov and the two supporting tank brigades mounted a very stubborn defense, based around dug-in T-34 tanks and 76.2mm anti-tank guns, which managed to repulse two very strong German panzer divisions for a week. As usual, the Germans tried to outflank the Soviet strongpoint, using the 10.Panzer-Division from the south, but the mud slowed this down to a crawl. Katukov's 4th Tank Brigade arrived from Mtensk late in the battle and helped to prevent Rokossovsky's defense from cracking. After much heavy fighting and losses, Viettinghoff finally captured Volokolamsk on 29 October, but failed to encircle any major units.

Even though the Mozhaisk line had finally been pierced, the Germans lacked the resources to continue the advance, with Panzerarmee 4 reporting that it was only receiving 15–20 per cent of its daily supply requirements.[127] The fighting at Mozhaisk and Volokolamsk had expended the last appreciable reserves of fuel and ammunition, so a brief lull settled over the Moscow front. Heeresgruppe Mitte had suffered 72,870 casualties in October, including 13,669 dead, as well as about 250 tanks and assault guns lost. Von Bock did have five panzer divisions within 100km of Moscow, but Zhukov had used the time gained at Borodino, Maloyaroslavets and Volokolamsk to rebuild a 50km front protecting the capital. The Red Army's tankers – from eleven different brigades – had played a major role in slowing and then stopping the German advance. Soviet losses had also been heavy and Zhukov was left with no appreciable armoured reserve, just scattered tank companies supporting knots of resistance at key points. On the German side, the pursuit operation was badly bungled by Reinhardt and Höpner, who essentially delegated authority down to corps, division and even brigade commanders. After winning big at Vyazma, von Bock violated the military principle of concentration by dispersing his armour to pursue multiple objectives, particularly Kalinin.

While Zhukov fought his intense delaying actions throughout October, the Stavka used the time to organize fresh armies that would turn the tide within a matter of weeks. Another seventeen tank brigades arrived at the front during October, replenishing some of the grievous armour losses at Vyazma-Bryansk and in the Ukraine. Most of these tank brigades had been formed in just 1–2 weeks, meaning that training and unit cohesion were minimal, but the troops were fresh and eager to do their part. On paper, these seventeen new tank brigades should have been equipped with 1,139 tanks, including 119 KV-1 and 510 T-34, but Soviet tank production was at its lowest ebb of the war in October 1941 and only 396 tanks were built that month, with just ninety-one being KV-1 and 185 T-34s. Consequently, the tank brigades were outfitted with anything available, including repaired tanks, obsolescent tanks that had been in storage or training units and the first British-built Lend-Lease tanks that were just arriving. In reality, the new tank brigades averaged thirty-one tanks – not the sixty-seven authorized – and only between none and four KV-1 and one and twenty T-34s. While the T-34 was superior to all current German tank models, many were sent to the front without basic issue items and tools, which meant that the crews could not repair simple problems like thrown track or replace damaged roadwheels – resulting in high non-operational rates due to non-combat defects.

Guderian Tries for Tula, 22 October–30 November

After two weeks of inactivity at Mtensk, Guderian struggled to get his Panzer-armee 2 back into the fight in the last days of October. Aside from a paucity of fuel and ammunition, he only had two panzer divisions from von Schweppen-burg's XXIV Armeekorps (mot.) to continue the advance toward Tula. The Bryank Front's 26th Army erected a stout defense around Mtensk based upon the 6th Guards Rifle Division and the 11th Tank Brigade. Kempf's XXXXVIIII Armeekorps (mot.) was advancing due east toward Kursk while Lemelsen's XXXXVII Armeekorps (mot.) was immobilized around Bryansk and Orel for lack of fuel. Determined to push back the Bryansk Front's 26th Army covering forces north of Mtensk, Guderian and von Schweppenburg prepared a deliberate attack to break out of the Mtensk bridgehead on 22 October. Guderian decided to mass his remaining armour in Kampfgruppe Eberbach, which was given the 6.Panzer-Regiment from 3.Panzer-Division and I./Pz.Regt 18 from the 18.Panzer-Division, giving him six Panzer-Abteilungen with about 150 tanks. After initial efforts to break out out of the Mtensk bridgehead directly failed, Guderian reverted to the standard formula of a flanking maneuver by sending Kampf-gruppe Eberbach to cross the Zusha River west of Mtensk near Roshenez. On the night of 21–22 October, several companies of *schützen* crossed the 40-meter-wide Zusha river in rubber boats to secure a bridgehead, then German pioneers began building a 16-ton bridge. The bridge was not completed until 0930 hours and it took three hours for the first German armour to get across: the III./Pz.Regt 6 (three Pz.II, sixteen Pz.III and five Pz.IV) under Hauptmann Ferdinand Schneider-Kostalski and the 1./SR 3 with infantry mounted in SPW half tracks. The Soviets had shelled the bridgehead heavily but the 26th Army missed the opportunity to launch a counterattack with the 11th Tank Brigade before the Germans got panzers across. Now, Schneider-Kostalski's small force advanced rapidly eastward to seize the village of Shelyamova. Around 1300 hours, seven T-34s from a company of the 11th Tank Brigade that had been in a nearby assembly area moved to engage the approaching German column. A brief tank battle ensued, with two T-34s and two Pz.IIIs knocked out. Inexplicably, the

Soviet tanks broke off the action and retreated, enabling the German column to capture the village and establish a defensive hedgehog for the night.[128]

During the night of 22–23 October, much of the rest of Kampfgruppe Eberbach crossed the small bridge over the Zusha, including two more Panzer-Abteilungen. When morning came, Eberbach's forces fanned out to roll up the Soviet defenses still at Mtensk from behind. Despite the successful outflanking maneuver, it still took more than a day to overwhelm the 6th Guards Rifle Divisions but, by late on 24 October, Eberbach advanced with the III/Pz.Regt 6 to reach the Mtensk–Tula road, where they caught a retreating Soviet column and engaged them in a wild night-time tank battle. Two KV-1 tanks were disabled in close combat and three other Soviet tanks knocked out. Fuel was a problem for the panzers throughout the offensive and since the normal supply trucks could not cross the muddy terrain around the Zusha River, Eberbach had directed that each panzer regiment would use tank transporters towed by Sd.Kfz.9 semi-tracks from its *Panzerwerkstattkompanie* to carry about 9,000 liters of additional fuel – enough to refuel one Panzer-Abteilung.[129]

On the morning of 25 October, Eberbach used his remaining fuel to form a *Vorausabteilung* from Schneider-Kostalski's III/Pz.Regt 6, the 1./SR3 (SPW-mounted infantry), and detachments from Panzerjager-Abteilung 521 and divisional artillery, and sent them up the road to Tula in pursuit. The 26th Army had been caught off-guard and was falling back toward Tula, but it managed to emplace a huge minefield on the main road near the town of Chern'. However, the retreating Soviets had made the amateurish mistake of not leaving a rearguard to cover the obstacle by fire and the German vanguard simply bypassed the mines and reached Chern' by dusk. It appeared that the village had been abandoned but, as Schneider-Kostalski's panzers moved in, they spotted a number of T-34 tanks. Apparently, the Soviet tankers had gone to sleep, not expecting the Germans to show up until the next morning. Schneider-Kostalski fired a parachute flare to illuminate the area and another brief night mêlée ensued. The T-34 had less of an advantage at night since combat occurred so close that the 5cm gun on the Pz.III had some chance of successfully penetrating its side armour. After several of their vehicles were hit, the Soviet tankers withdrew.

Partially refueled, Kampfgruppe Eberbach bolted north along the road to Tula in a sudden burst of speed, bypassing Soviet rifle units and forcing the 11th Tank Brigade to fall back. Despite mud and snow, Eberbach advanced about 20km per day and he attempted a broken-field play when he saw that Tula, a city of 272,000, was garrisoned only by militiamen, anti-aircraft troops and some NKVD troops. Soviet 37mm and 85mm anti-aircraft guns were used to engage Eberbach's panzers on the road south of Tula, but these were knocked out by *sprenggrenate* from the 7.5cm howitzers on the Pz.IVs. At 0530 hours on 30 October, Eberbach attacked the thin Soviet defenses in the south end of the city with about sixty panzers and several battalions of infantry. Normally, Soviet militia would have collapsed under tank attack but, in this case, they mounted a stubborn defense that inflicted significant casualties upon Eberbach's infantry – three company commanders were killed. Soviet 37mm anti-aircraft guns, fired over open sights, damaged a number of German tanks. Unwilling to advance into a city without infantry support and with his ammunition nearly exhausted, Eberbach pulled back to regroup, but his window of opportunity had closed. That night, Polkovnik Ivan Yuschuk's 32nd Tank Brigade arrived with thirty-four tanks (five KV-1, seven T-34, twenty-two T-60) and a battalion of infantry by rail, followed soon thereafter by three more rifle divisions. Yuschuk launched a counterattack the next morning on 31 October, in an effort to push Eberbach's forces back from the southern outskirts of the city, but lost two KV-1 and five T-34s knocked out by German tank and anti-tank fire. Eberbach had learned from experience to pull his panzers back when faced by Soviet heavy tanks in daylight and let the 8.8cm flak guns engage the enemy. Unable to storm Tula, Guderian's spearhead was stymied 160km south of Moscow.

Continued rain and frost made the German logistic situation in Tula even more precarious in the first week of November, with Guderian increasingly dependent upon using captured horse-drawn panje wagons and SPW half tracks to move a bare minimum of fuel and ammunition forward. Morale among Guderian's troops fell with the thermometer as soldiers were unprepared mentally or materially for living outdoors in freezing conditions. Schweppenburg's XXIV Armeekorps (mot.) was forced onto the defensive south of Tula and hit repeatedly by small company and battalion-size Soviet counterattacks.

Eventually, the ground began freezing around 11 November and von Schweppenburg's corps regained some of its mobility. However, Guderian's Panzermee 2 was scattered across a large area and he now lacked the resources to overcome Tula's defenses on his own. His nearest railhead was 130km behind his forward forces and the road from Orel to Tula was a mess, so the supply situation was not going to improve anytime soon. General-Leytenant Ivan V. Boldin's 50th Army was solidly dug in around Tula with six rifle divisions, the 11th and 32nd Tank Brigades and the 131st OTB with 21 Mk III Valentine tanks. Guderian could only commit 3, 4 and 17.Panzer-Divisionen, but he decided to have one last attempt at a pincer attack against Tula, with some help from the XLIII Armeekorps of von Kluge's 4.Armee. The Germans massed 102 operational tanks from the three panzer divisons into an armoured fist and attacked southeast of Tula at 0530 on 18 November. Panzer crews had white-washed their tanks to provide camouflage on the snow-covered battlefield. Although the first issue of winter clothing (earmuffs and greatcoats) arrived on 7 November, it was only sufficient to equip one-quarter of the troops.[130] The rest had to operate outside in −25° C (−13° F) cold in their summer uniforms. The Soviet 413th Rifle Division – one of the famed 'Siberian' units – was holding the Bolkohovo sector chosen for the German breakthrough; the Siberian troops were tough and inflicted several hundred casualties on the supporting *Schützen-Abteilungen*, but could not stop massed armour. Matisovich's 11th Tank Brigade and Yuschuk's 32nd Tank Brigade had deployed some T-34s and KV-1s forward to support the Siberians, but they were picked off individually by German 8.8cm flak guns. After penetrating the Soviet defenses, the German *schwerpunkt* fanned out, with the 3.Panzer-Division curving inward toward Tula with fifty tanks, the 17.Panzer-Division heading due north toward Venev with fifteen tanks and the 4.Panzer-Division heading towards Stalinogorsk with thirty-five tanks.[131]

After knocking out a troublesome KV-1 and some T-26 light tanks in Uzlovaya, Panzer-Regiment 35 occupied Stalinogorsk late on 22 November. Guderian had only intended that this town be occupied to screen his right flank while he enveloped Tula, but the Soviets had other ideas. They mounted a major counterattack from the east on 26 November that retook the town, forcing von Schweppenburg to divert Schneider-Kostalski's III/Pz.Regt 6 to restore the situation, but for once the ensuing tank battle went very badly for the Germans. Schneider-Kostalski was wounded and the 1.Kompanie was virtually destroyed after losing its commander and eight tanks (five Pz.III, three Pz.IV). The Red Army was learning.

The 17.Panzer-Division pushed on to the town of Venev. Unteroffizier Erich Hager, a Pz.IV driver in the 6./Pz.Regt 39, recorded his experience of the actions near Venev in his diary:

> Now the fun starts … 52-tonner [KV-1] on fire. Great to watch. A bit further on another 2 down. We attack 13 tanks. One tank destroyed. LKWs [trucks] on fire. Lots of Russian infantry destroyed. Run over by the tanks. Then the best bit. We attack two 52-tonners [KV-1] and start a real hare hunt. He couldn't turn his turret after the first direct hit and took off. We were after him with force, 20 meters behind him. Half an hour the hunt went on for until he lost a track and fell into a ditch. We fired 30 shots into him. Nothing got through. That day our vehicle fired 110 rounds … Have no more rounds.[132]

Although Hager's kampfgruppe destroyed a large number of Soviet tanks south of Venev, Soviet 85mm anti-aircraft guns knocked out several German panzers approaching the town on 24 November. There was heavy tank versus tank fighting in the town itself, with at least three KV-1 and one T-34 knocked out against two German tanks. After seizing the town, the 17.Panzer-Division pushed toward Kashira, but Panzer-Regiment 39 was down to only thirteen operational tanks and had reached the end of its combat effectiveness. Probably due to a combination of the cold and wear and tear, Hager's Pz.IV broke a torsion bar, which caused further damage to the suspension; however, due to the desperate situation, Hager's tank operated in 'degraded mode' for another week. Even more disconcerting, the 17.Panzer-Division discovered that the lead elements of Polkovnik Andrei L. Getman's 112th Tank Division, with about 200 T-26 light tanks, were arriving at Kashira from the Far East.

Boldin's defense was temporaily disrupted by Guderian's attack and the 4.Panzer-Division and Infanterie-Regiment *Grossdeutschland* managed to get behind Tula and briefly severed road and rail links to the city on 2 December. However, the offensive had over-extended Guderian's depleted forces and he was now unable to hold the terrain that had been captured. Furthermore, von Kluge's 4.Armee failed to press their part of the attack with vigor, so Guderian could not completely encircle Tula. Very few tanks were still operational by the end of November and the infantry was increasingly useless due to to the freezing temperatures. Yet it was not until 3 December that Guderian finally admitted that he could not take Tula and ordered his forces to shift to the defense. It was too late.

While the final battle for Tula was going on, Guderian received a visit from the OKH Panzerkommission he had requested to review the Battle of Mtensk over a month before. The commission included the head of the Heereswaffenamt [Army Weapons Department] Wa Pruef 6 and his senior designer, along with industry representatives from Krupp, Daimler-Benz, Henschel and MAN. Guderian allowed the commission to inspect captured T-34 tanks and stated that the Wehrmacht needed a new tank to defeat the T-34. He outlined the requirements for such a tank as having 'heavier armament' than the current Pz.III/Pz.IV, 'higher tactical mobility' and 'improved armoured protection'. Guderian emphatically told the commission that the purpose of the new tank 'should be to re-establish the previous superiority [of German tanks]'. The commission returned to Berlin and, before the end of November 1941, the *Reichsministerium für Bewaffnung und Munition* (Ministry for Armaments Production and Munitions) had issued a formal request for proposals for a new 30-ton tank outfitted with 60mm sloped armour – this became the genesis of the Pz.V Panther tank. Both MAN and Daimler-Benz began developing prototypes during the winter of 1941–42.[133]

Typhoon: the Last Roll of the Dice, 1 November–4 December

Meanwhile, after breaking through the Mozhaisk Line, the rest of Heeresgruppe Mitte had ground to a halt within 70–90km of Moscow by the end of October. Von Bock – desperate for victory before time ran out – wanted to continue the advance to Moscow, but supplies were dangerously low and the troops were exhausted. Hitler agreed to a two-week operational pause to enable Heeresegruppe Mitte to prepare for the final offensive, which would resume on 15 November. Von Kluge's 4.Armee took an inordinate time to bring up his eleven infantry divisions and he was reluctant to risk his troops in further attacks. The Russian roads were at their worst in late October and the first week of November, with many vehicles lost in the mud – the German advantage in mobility was temporarily neutralized. Curiously, von Bock squandered his primary remaining advantage – a concentrated armoured striking force – by allowing it to dissipate; he directed Hoth to commit the rest of Model's XXXXI Armeekorps (mot.) to support the 9.Armee's useless fighting around Kalinin. Consequently, Hoth's grandly-named 3.Panzerarmee was reduced to Schaal's LVI Armeekorps (mot.) with the 6 and 7.Panzer-Divisionen and 14.Infanterie-Division (mot.) – which altogether amounted to barely 150 operational tanks. The Czech-made Pz.35(t) tanks, which formed the bulk of 6.Panzer-Division's armour, were approaching the end of their useful lives. Erhard Raus estimated that most of the Pz.35(t) had over 12,000km on their odometers by the end of

October 1941 and that only ten of the remaining forty-one were repairable through cannibalization.[134]

Von Bock decided to deploy Höpner's Panzerarmee 4, which still had a total of about 400 operational tanks, with the XXXX and XXXXVI Armeekorps (mot.), on Hoth's right flank and make a combined attack from Volokolamsk toward Moscow. Höpner detached Kuntzen's dilapidated LVII Armeekorps (mot.) to operate separately under 4.Armee control near Naro-Fominsk. Consequently, von Bock's armoured fist had been reduced from five motorized corps to only four, with much less infantry support. German front-line morale declined as the freezing temperatures grew more severe, supplies were low and Soviet resistance refused to break. On the other hand, Hitler had finally agreed to release size-able tank replacements to the Eastern Front and 397 new tanks were sent east in October-November 1941.[135]

On the Soviet side, the Western Front still had 328 tanks left in thirteen tank brigades and the 1st Guards Motorized Rifle Division (1GRMD) by the end of October: thirty-three KV-1, 175 T-34, forty-three BT, fifty T-26 and thirty-two T-60. The British Arctic PQ-1 convoy had reached Archangelsk on 11 October with twenty Mark II Matilda tanks, followed by PQ-2 on 30 October with seventy-six Mark III Valentine tanks; these ninety-six tanks were rushed by rail to Moscow and used to outfit the 146th Tank Brigade and four independent tank battalions (131, 132, 136, 138 OTB).[136] Another major British Lend-Lease convoy, PQ-3, would arrive in Archangelsk on 22 November with 200 more British tanks. Red Army tank officers were not impressed with the 2-pounder (40mm) gun on the Matilda and Valentines, nor their poor cross-country mobility, but their 60–75mm-thick armour was impervious to German 3.7cm and 5cm anti-tank weapons. British-built armour plate also had a much higher nickel content – 3 per cent versus 1 per cent for Russian-made steel – which reduced the risk of armour spalling (i.e. metal splinters inside the tank) when the tank was hit by non-penetrating rounds.[137] Although designed as infantry sup-port tanks and employed in that role by the Red Army, the 2-pounder gun did not have an HE round, which reduced the value of the tanks in that role. Nevertheless, British Lend-Lease tanks helped the Red Army to restock its tank units until domestic production could catch up and are estimated to have comprised about 10 per cent of the tanks defending Moscow in November–December 1941.

Tanks were also useful for raising morale as a symbol of the Red Army's strength and Stalin decided to make them the centerpiece of the military parade celebrating the October Revolution in Moscow on 7 November; Polkovnik Andrei G. Kravchenko's newly-formed 31st Tank Brigade paraded across Red Square with its KV-1, T-34 and T-60 tanks, then headed straight to the front to join the 20th Army at Klin. In another effort to bolster morale, the Stavka decided to create the first guards units and Katukov's 4th Tank Brigade was redesignated as the 1st Guards Tank Brigade (1 GTB). Aside from the prestige associated with guards units, this began a process by the Stavka of providing the best battle-proven units with the newest tanks and keeping them up to strength.

However there were initially too few resources to create more than a few guards tank units before the end of 1941 and the Stavka was forced to form a number of independent tank battalions and company-size-detachments so that each army received at least a few tanks.

Zhukov used the respite in the German offensive to integrate fresh units into his line in front of Moscow and sent Konev to take over the new Kalinin Front. Konev was ordered to keep counterattacking the German 9.Armee in order to force von Bock to divert further forces away from Moscow. The critical area along the Lama River between Kalinin and Istra, where Höpner's panzers intended to break through to Moscow, was held by General-major Vasiliy A. Khomenko's 30th Army and Rokossovsky's 16th Army. Rokossovsky received five new rifle divisions and five tank brigades (Katukov's 4th Tank Brigade, and 23, 27, 28, 33 TB) with about 250 tanks to rebuild his battered army, but Khomenko's 30th Army was under-resourced. The other critical sector was around Naro-Fominsk, where the 5th, 33rd and 43rd Armies were provided eight tank brigades with 450 tanks. By mid-November, Zhukov's Western Front had a total of fourteen tank brigades with almost 1,000 tanks, although there were only thirty-seven KV-1 and 156 T-34s. A large part of the Red Army's remaining tank force was now comprised of light tanks that were inferior to the German Pz.III and Pz.IV.

Although the Germans were content to allow the first two weeks of November to pass quietly, Zhukov was not and he ordered his front-line units to conduct aggressive local counterattacks to hinder the German build-up. A protracted series of skirmishes occurred around the village of Skirminova, east of Volokolamsk, between Rokossovsky's tank brigades and the German 10.Panzer-Division on 8–12 November. In one skirmish, Katukov's tankers destroyed a Pz.Bef.Wg. III, killing Oberst Theodor Keyser, commander of Panzer-Regiment 7 from 10.Panzer-Division. However, a counterattack on 14–15 November by Polkovnik Aleksandr A. Kotlyarov's 58th Tank Division, recently arrived from the Far East, was less successful. Kotlyarov attacked the German 5.Infanterie-Division with over 200 light tanks, mostly BT-7 and T-26, but lost about one-third of them in less than two days of fighting. Zhukov had already executed several senior officers for battlefield failures or alleged cowardice and Kotlyarov apparently feared reporting that German infantry had defeated his tankers and opted to commit suicide instead. Zhukov's spoiling attacks accomplished very little and prevented Rokossovsky from building up any appreciable reserves. Furthermore, in addition to Kotlyarov's defeat, the new tank brigades suffered significant losses in these tank skirmishes – including about one-third of the available KV-1 and T-34 tanks. Predictably, the results of Zhukov's local counterattacks in early November were not worth the loss of troops, equipment and supplies, and only served to set the conditions for one last German tactical success.

The German plan for the second phase of Typhoon was a classic pincer attack that completed ignored terrain, weather and logistics. Hoth and Höpner would crush Rokossovsky's 16th Army and advance to Yakhroma, north of Moscow. Von Kluge, supported by Kuntzen's panzers, would break through the Soviet center at Naro-Fominsk, and Guderian would seize Tula and then approach Moscow from the south. Von Bock optimistically hoped for a link-up between the three panzer groups east of Moscow. However, Heeresgruppe Mitte was only committing thirty-six divisions to the final attack on Moscow, instead of the seventy he employed at the start of Typhoon, since nearly half of Heeresgruppe Mitte was being drawn to defend the flanks from Soviet counterattacks. Nor could von Bock rely upon the Luftwaffe, which had transferred a number of units to the Mediterranean theater and could commit only 300 aircraft to the second stage of Typhoon. Although the *Eisenbahntruppen* had regauged the rails as far forward as Gzhatsk, Volokolamsk and Kaluga, very little fuel and ammunition was arriving due to transportation issues and shortages. Due to Hitler's decision to reduce ammunition production at the start of Barbarossa, Germany was running very low on artillery ammunition at a critical moment. Most of the panzer divisions involved in the second phase of Typhoon were only able to set aside 1.0 to 1.5 V.S. of fuel for the attack.

The second phase of Typhoon began on 15 November with local actions by 1.Panzer-Division against the 30th Army around Kalinin, but the offensive proper began when Schaal's LVI Armeekorps (mot.) seized a crossing over the Lama river on 17 November. The next day, Höpner smashed in Rokossovsky's front near Volokolamsk and advanced toward Klin with the 2.Panzer-Division. Once again, German armour had made their main effort near the boundary between two Soviet armies; the breakthrough split apart the 16th and 30th armies. By late on 18 November, Rokossovsky's army was falling back under heavy pressure toward Istra, while Lelyushenko was rushed to Klin to take charge of the crumbling 30th Army from Khomenko, an incompetent NKVD general. Lelyushenko had relatively little infantry to defend Klin, but armour from three different tank brigades and the remnants of the 58th Tank Division enabled him to build a barrier around the town. The German panzers were operating better now, on the hard frozen ground, and regained a degree of their former mobility. Lelyushenko was able to hold off Hoth's panzers at Klin for five days, thanks to the presence of a handful of T-34 and KV-1 tanks. However, the 2.Panzer-Division captured Solnechnogorsk on 24 November, which threatened Lelyu-shenko with encirclement and forced him to withdraw. Stalin was worried about this German advance, which brought their panzers to within striking distance of Moscow, and asked Zhukov if the city would be held. Zhukov replied that it could be, but that it would require 200 more tanks. Stalin replied that there were no more tanks in the RVGK reserve or even his own personal reserve – Zhukov already had everything available.[138] By 25 November, the Red Army was running out of space and tanks.

Rokossovsky's 16th Army was forced to fight off Stumme's still-powerful XXXX Armeekorps (mot.) at Istra; the SS-Division *Reich* and 10.Panzer-Division continued their partnership begun at Borodino, pushing General-major Ivan V. Panfilov's stubborn 78th Rifle Division a few kilometers each day. Panfilov was killed by mortar fire on 18 November but just when it appeared that Rokos-sovsky's 16th Army could not hold, the Stavka sent him the fresh 78th Rifle

Division from Siberia. Another reinforcement provided to Rokossovsky by the Stavka was the 146th Tank Brigade with forty-two Valentine Mark III tanks – the first British Lend-Lease tanks to reach the front.[139] Although the Siberians proved a stubborn obstacle to Stumme's advance, the Germans knocked out a number of the Valentines and Höpner redeployed the 11.Panzer-Division to reinforce his *schwerpunkt*. The SS-Division *Reich* finally took Istra on 27 November after suffering 926 casualties in three days. Rokossovsky was angry with Zhukov for forcing his army to 'die in place', with his army being gradually crushed by repeated German panzer attacks. By 28 November, Rokossovsky had re-formed a line just 35km northwest of Moscow. However, the fighting at Istra and Klin had consumed most of the remaining German stocks of fuel and ammunition, while the cold weather was now impairing the fighting efficiency of German infantry units. The Soviet defenders were also plagued by ammunition shortages and few of the Soviet troops had decent winter uniforms either, but their morale was bolstered by a sense of last-ditch patriotism in defending the capital. In the last stages of the Battle of Moscow, Soviet infantry also began to receive the 14.5mm PTRD-41 anti-tank rifle. Although the weapon had entered production soon after the start of Barbarossa, the inefficiently-administered People's Commissariat for Munitions (*Narkomat Boepripasov*) did not put the 14.5mm ammunition into production until November. The PTRD-41 did not prove particularly effective in penetrating the armour on German tanks, but it did serve to boost the morale of Red Army rifle units at a critical moment by providing them with a tool to prevent them being overrun by enemy tanks.

Hoth managed to reach Yakhroma and capture an intact bridge across the Moskva-Volga canal with von Manteuffel's kampfgruppe from 7.Panzer-Division at 0410 hours on 27 November; however, von Manteuffel was only able to cross the canal with a single *Schützen-Abteilung* and a company of Pz.38(t) tanks. Just four hours later, the Soviets counterattacked with T-26 tanks from the 58th Tank Division and almost reached the bridge. The 11./Pz.Regt 25 managed to repulse the Soviet T-26s with the help of a few panzerjägers, but von Manteuffel realized that he could not hold the bridgehead as more Soviet reinforcements arrived. The Yakhroma bridgehead was evacuated by 0230 hours on 29 November.

By the end of November, Stumme's XXXX Armeekorps (mot.) had ground to a halt with the 2.Panzer-Division closest to Moscow at Krasnaya Polyana. Although temperatures were freezing, Hoth still had about eighty tanks operational in 1, 6 and 7.Panzer-Divisionen and Höpner about 170 tanks in 2, 5, 10 and 11.Panzer-Divisionen, but the fuel and ammunition were gone and the troops were past breaking point. Heeresgruppe Mitte had suffered another 45,735 casualties in November and lost another 300 tanks and assault guns, but Moscow remained beyond their grasp. The last, great offensive had failed and the troops – and commanders – knew it. On one of few occasions during the Second World War, German front-line morale collapsed. Here and there, fanatical commanders like Oberst Ludwig Fricke in 11.Panzer-Division managed to get troops to advance a little bit closer to Moscow in −40°C weather, but even these efforts fizzled out by the end of November. Von Kluge – whose 4.Armee had

mixed German armoured Kampfgruppe begins the attack into the Soviet Union. By June 1941, the ermans were well-versed in combined arms tactics, which gave them an overwhelming advantage the early border battles. (*Ian Barter*)

bandoned Soviet T-26 light tanks from Oborin's 14th Mechanized Corps in Kobrin, 23 June 1941. nzergruppe Guderian demolished this Red Army formation after crossing the Western Bug River. *uthor*)

A knocked-out T-26 light tank and a victim of the early border battles. The T-26 was the most common Soviet tank in 1941 and the German panzerjägers were well-equipped to defeat them. (*Ian Barter*)

A Pz.38(t) light tank from the 12.Panzer-Division, which was part of Hoth's Panzergruppe 3. The German dependence on Czech light tanks was an indication of Hitler's attempt to fight a total war on the cheap. (*Ian Barter*)

A German infantryman approaches a dead Soviet tanker next to his burning BT-7 fast tank, Ukraine, June 1941. The Soviet tank took a hit on the hull, probably from a 3.7cm round, which ignited the fuel tank. *(Bundesarchiv, Bild 101I-020-1268-36, Foto: Hähle, Johannes)*

A 15cm sIG 33 (sf), probably from 1.Panzer-Division, passes an abandoned KV-2 heavy tank in June 1941. The Germans were awed by the great bulk of the KV-2, even though it performed very poorly in battle. *(Author)*

During the Battle of Dubno on 26 June 1941, the Soviet 12th Tank Division attempted to attack the German-held village of Leshnev, but advancing into marshy terrain along the Syten'ka River they lost three T-34 tanks that got bogged down. Note that the tank in the foreground is a T-34 Model 1940 armed with the L-11 gun, while the other two are Model 1941 armed with the F-32 gun. The Red Army of 1941 had almost no recovery assets, so disabled or stuck tanks were simply abandoned. (*Author*)

A T-34 Model 1941 which overran and crushed a German l.FH18 10.5cm howitzer. The T-34 was a very advanced tank for 1941, but many went into battle with limited ammunition and fuel, and used ramming tactics as an expedient. (*Author*)

. StuG III assault gun crossing a river in the early stages of Operation Barbarossa. The wooden road
ridge has been damaged by the retreating Red Army, forcing the Germans to use a ford to get
cross. River-crossings dictated the tempo of armoured operations in Russia. (*Author*)

ince standard German anti-tank weapons of 1941 could not penetrate the KV-1's thick armor,
xcept at point-blank range, German units concentrated their fire against the running gear. The hull
f this KV-1 has at least four medium-caliber anti-tank round hits, which failed to penetrate, but a
rge-caliber artillery round, either 10.5cm or 15cm, has damaged the track. (*Ian Barter*)

A KV-1 heavy tank from the 124th Armored Brigade ambushed a German column northeast of Ivanovka on 9 October 1941. This burning 8.8cm flak gun and its Sd.Kfz.7 were destroyed before they had a chance to deploy. While the 8.8cm gun could defeat the KV-1, it took ten minutes to get into action – which was an eternity in tank warfare. (*Author*)

Soviet tankers examine a Pz.38(t) light tank from the 7.Panzer-Division, abandoned near Yartsevo. This tank appears to have run out of fuel, which was a common predicament for German tankers in the summer of 1941. (*Author*)

he onset of mud slowed down, but did not stop, German operations. Normally German panzer
nits were way ahead of the foot-slogging infantry, so this is probably taken during the
deployment phase prior to Operation Typhoon, in mid-September 1941. *(Ian Barter)*

oviet T-26 light tanks lead Timoshenko's counterattacks during the fighting near Smolensk in
ugust 1941. Note that it is broad daylight and that there does not appear to be any artillery
upport, which made this type of attack little more than target practice for the German panzerjägers.
uthor)

A Pz.III medium tank from 10.Panzer-Division, knocked out near Skirminova, east of Volokolamsk in mid-November 1941. Soviet resistance stiffened outside Moscow and the panzer units began to suffer their first heavy losses. This panzer crewman has suffered a tanker's fate, being burnt to death. (*RIAN Novosti, #884162*)

The last stage of Operation Typhoon began with German panzers attempting to batter their way through Rokossovsky's final layer of defense outside Moscow. Note that the German crewmen hav overcoats, but no other winter gear. (*Ian Barter*)

A Soviet white-washed T-34 in hull-down position awaits the German panzers, near Volokolamsk, November 1941. The Soviets are watching the break in the woods, which is where German armour is expected to appear. The T-34 will probably begin the engagement at a range of 500 meters. (*Author*)

olkovnik Mikhail G. Sakhno's tanks from the Moscow Proletarian Motorized Rifle Division move to a new position in the vicinity of Naro-Fominsk, December 1941. By the time that the Winter counteroffensive began, the Red Army only had small company and battalion-size tank units left, often with a mixture of models. (*RIA Novosti*)

Two overturned Matilda II tanks near Volokolamsk, 1 December 1941. Allied Lend-Lease tanks played a significant role in armoured operations on the Eastern Front in 1941–42, even though post-war Russian historians have down-played the impact of military aid from the Western Allies. (*RIAN Novosti, #881048*)

A T-34 tank moving at speed in deep snow. The T-34 had been developed to operate in winter conditions and could maneuver through areas that German tanks could not operate in. (*Author*)

The crew of a Pz.III tank from the 14.Panzer-Division watch German infantry clearing a village, mid-1942. German tank commanders were trained to operate 'unbuttoned' as much as possible, in order to improve situational awareness. This was feasible on the steppe, but not in cities or heavily wooded areas. (*Bundesarchiv, Bild 101I-748-0088-02A, Foto: Schmidt/Geyer*)

The interior of Hube's command vehicle, 16.Panzer-Division. The real secret of the panzer-division's power was based upon the use of radios for effective command and control, which repeatedly enabled them to out-fight numerically-superior foes. (*Author*)

A Pz.III tank from 11.Panzer-Division in action during the opening stages of Operation Blau, 28–30 June 1942. This photo gives a good impression of a 'tanker's-eye' view on the open steppe and the difficulty of spotting armoured vehicles in tall grass. (*Author*)

An 8.8cm flak gun employing direct fire against Soviet armour. Note that the flak gun is still limbered, which increases its height, but enables it to come into action more clearly. Unlike the British army, which eventually discovered that the best way to counter the deadly 8.8-cm flak gun was to smother it with indirect fire, Soviet armoured units had very limited organic artillery suppo in 1941–42. (*Author*)

Pz.IV tank destroyed during the Second Battle of Kharkov in May 1942. This tank, which has ffered an internal explosion, would be listed as 'totalausfall', but many tanks that were knocked t were repairable. German panzer units were expert at battlefield recovery. (*Ian Barter*)

e introduction of the Pz.III Ausf J with long 5cm gun provided the panzer-divisions with a much-eded boost in anti-tank firepower. However, most of these improved models were concentrated in e units sent to Stalingrad, which misused them in urban combat. (*Ian Barter*)

An American-built Lend-Lease M3 Lee tank, shattered by 8.8cm anti-tank fire. The Red Army did not like the high-silhouette Lee tank, which was easily spotted by German anti-tank gunners. (*Ian Barter*)

The Germans introduced the Tiger I heavy tank in August 1942, but it was only available in token numbers and initially had no significant impact on operations. The Tiger I began a trend of new German armoured fighting vehicles sacrificing mobility in favor of increased firepower and protection – which gradually deprived the panzer divisions of their ability to move long distances on their own tracks. (*Ian Barter*)

T-34 tank moving over rough terrain with infantry in *desant* role. At the tactical level, the Red rmy was beginning to learn and implement better tank-infantry cooperation in late 1942, although ue combined arms warfare was still beyond the capability of all but Guards Armoured units. *uthor)*

he arrival of the Pz.IV Ausf G with long 7.5cm cannon in mid-1942 was a game-changer for moured warfare on the Eastern Front. After a year of having a major firepower disadvantage ;ainst the T-34, the panzer-divisions finally had a tank that could engage the best Soviet armour ith confidence. *(Author)*

A KV-1 heavy tank that overran a German reconnaissance car at the Battle of Ostrov. Soviet heavy tank units aggressively plowed into German formations, with a sense of invincibility, but often came to grief against the simplest obstacles. (*Author*)

A German Tauchpanzer III in testing. These diving tanks had been developed for use in Operation Sea Lion in 1940, but they were used in the assault crossing of the Bug River in the opening hours of Barbarossa. (*Author*)

sat out most of Typhoon's second phase – made one last ridiculous gesture with part of Kuntzen's LVII Armeekorps (mot.) and three infantry divisions on 1–2 December, attacking on either side of the Soviet stronghold in the town of Naro-Fominsk. Surprisingly, the 19 and 20.Panzer-Divisionen made significant advances, but Zhukov promptly counterattacked and threw back Kuntzen's spearheads – the last significant German advance toward Moscow in the war. On 4 December, Hitler finally recognized the obvious and suspended Typhoon, optimistically hoping that Heeresgruppe Mitte could hold its positions near Moscow until another offensive became possible in spring 1942.

Gamble at Tikhvin, 16 October–18 November 1941
The bulk of Heeresgruppe Nord had settled into siege lines around Leningrad by late September and von Leeb fully expected that the garrison would quickly succumb to starvation. Yet it did not. Zhukov had flown in to reinvigorate fighting spirit among the city's defenders before leaving on 6 October, and the Red Army and Navy were quick to organize a tenuous supply line with barges across Lake Ladoga. The Soviet Volkhov Front still controlled the east side of the lake and used railheads at Volkhov and Tikhvin as staging bases for this logistic operation. Von Leeb realized that Soviet resupply operations across Lake Ladoga could prolong the siege and he decided to take a desperate risk to terminate this activity. Although Höpner's Panzergruppe 4 had already transferred to Heeresgruppe Mitte for Operation Typhoon, Schmidt's XXXIX Armeekorps (mot.) was still available near Chudovo with the 8 and 12.Panzer-Divisionen and 18 and 20.Infanterie-Divisionen (mot.). Yet Schmidt's corps was in poor condition, with its vehicles worn out and troop strength inadequate for a major offensive. Furthermore, Heeresgruppe Nord's priority for supplies was reduced to a low level after the siege began and Schmidt would have to attack with a bare minimum of fuel and ammunition. Even worse, the weather situation was deteriorating daily.

On the morning of 16 October, Schmidt attacked General-leytenant Nikolai K. Klykov's 52nd Army, which held a 60km stretch of the Volkhov river front with the 267th and 288th Rifle Divisions, both newly-raised reserve units. German pioneers built a pontoon bridge over the Volkhov at Grusino, enabling the eighty tanks of the 12.Panzer-Division to cross the river and engage the 288th Rifle Division. Snow, mixed with rain, deprived the offensive of Luftwaffe close air support and the 30cm of snow on the ground reduced all ground movement to a snail's pace. Consequently, it took Schmidt's troops four days to break through a defense that consisted of a thin line of second-rate infantry. The Soviet 52nd Army had no reserves to counter this breakthrough and the 12.Panzer-Division was able to march directly upon Tikhvin. However, the terrain was abysmal, consisting mostly of a roadless wilderness of dense forests and frozen marshlands. The 12.Panzer-Division ground forward at a meager 5km per day against negligible Soviet resistance. The 8.Panzer-Division joined the offensive on 17 October, with a supporting attack on the right flank of the 12.Panzer-Division, with two kampfgruppen; Panzer-Regiment 10 still fielded two panzer battalions with a total of ninety-one tanks.[140] All told, the Germans committed about 170 tanks to the Tikhvin operation.

Meanwhile, the Stavka recognized that the loss of Tikhvin could lead to the loss of Leningrad and allocated General-leytenant Vsevolod F. Yakovlev's 4th Army from the RVGK to defend the city. To counter the German armour, it was decided to reroute General-major Aleksei F. Popov's 60th Tank Division – currently in the process of moving by rail from the Far East to Moscow – toward Tikhvin instead. Popov's division, which began unloading at Tikhvin on 29 October, had 6,000 personnel and 179 light tanks (including thirteen BT-7, 164 T-26 and two T-37). Several other rifle units were dispatched to bolster the 4th Army at Tikhvin, including one of the first Guards Rifle Divisions and two independent tank battalions with seventy-eight light tanks. The Stavka provided Yakovlev with over 250 tanks, which made 4th Army one of the largest concentrations of Soviet armour in November 1941.

Yet rather than committing his armour as a concentrated force against Schmidt's slow-moving spearhead, Yakovlev – who was an infantryman – fell back on the Red Army's traditional method of employing tanks. He decided to split up Popov's 60th Tank Division to provide direct support to his infantry units; the entire 191st Tank Regiment was subordinated to the 4th Guards Rifle Division and another tank battalion left to protect his headquarters in Tikhvin. On top of this poor decision, Yakovlev decided to try and mount a hasty counter-offensive on 3 November before all his reinforcements had arrived. He formed an assault group with the residual 60th Tank Division, the 4th Guard Rifle Division, the 27th Cavalry Division and two other rifle divisions to attempt an overly-complicated two-pronged counter-offensive against Schmidt's panzers as they crossed the Pchyovzha River near Budogoschch. Not only did Yakovlev's plan require the armour of the 60th Tank Division to move nearly 100km along forest tracks to reach the assembly area, but tactically, the ground chosen was also very poor. Popov's tankers were expected to attack through a narrow defile surrounded by a vast marshland area – with little room for maneuver.

The poorly-planned road march proved to be the undoing of the 60th Tank Division. While most accounts of the Eastern Front stress the impact of muddy conditions upon German armoured mobility, there is little recognition that mud often impaired the Red Army's tanks as well. Popov's tanks ended up bogged down along forest tracks turned into quagmires by rain and snow and then quickly ran out of fuel. At a critical moment, this tank division was immobilized for more than a week while 4th Army conducted its counter-offensive with only infantry units. Ultimately, Yakovlev's counter-offensive proved only a minor distraction, which forced Schmidt to detach the 20.Infanterie-Division (mot.) to guard the eastern flank of his advance, but otherwise failed to stop the German push on Tikhvin.

Schmidt's panzers continued to advance slowly up the Chudovo-Tikhvin road, with his Pz.IIIs and Pz.IVs barely able to cross the rickety wooden bridges along the route. The 8.Panzer-Division was brought on line with 12.Panzer-Division. Kampfgruppe Bleicken, comprised of a motorized infantry battalion, an artillery battery and 1./Panzer-Regiment 10, led the way. Yakovlev held Tikhvin with part of the 4th Guards Division and elements of two rifle divisions, as well as a battalion from Podpolkovnik Pavel A. Garkusha's 121st Tank Regiment. By 5 November, the Germans were within 20km of Tikhvin and Garkusha was ordered to launch a spoiling attack against the flank of 8.Panzer-Division at the wooded crossroads of Zaruchev'. The next day, Garkusha's T-26s attacked out of the woods and ran straight into the Pz.38(t) tanks of 1./Pz.Regt 10. The German tankers quickly knocked out twelve of fourteen attacking T-26s and another was claimed by a 5cm Pak gun.[141] Finally, on 8 November a kampfgruppe of the 8.Panzer-Division and the 18.Infanterie-Division (mot.), fought their way into Tikhvin, while the rest of the corps fended off more Soviet local counterattacks. Within hours, Soviet resistance in the city collapsed and Tikhvin was in German hands. Schmidt then shifted Kampfgruppen from both his panzer divisions to support the stalled drive by the infantry of I.Armeekorps against Volkhov, but the attempt to envelop the town failed.

By late November, the German offensive had run its course and had achieved only partial success. However, the failure to capture Volkhov left Schmidt's XXXIX Armeekorps (mot.) in a very exposed salient and Heeresgruppe Nord was unable to establish an effective line of communications across 60km of muddy trails to Tikhvin. Quickly recovering from their setback at Tikhvin, the Soviet 4th Army launched continual attacks against the exposed flanks of the salient, which were soon close to collapse. Von Leeb's effort to speed up the siege of Leningrad not only deprived him of his only mobile reserve, but created a crisis on a front that should have been a quiet sector for the Germans in autumn 1941.

Rostov: von Kleist's Frozen Blitzkrieg, 5–20 November

The onset of winter in the Ukraine found von Kleist's 1 Panzerarmee (PzAOK 1) stuck just 22km west of Rostov, with supplies very low. Due to the destroyed railroad bridges over the Dnieper – which would not be fully repaired until 1943 – no fuel trains could proceed east of the river. Instead, supplies had to be ferried across the Dnieper and then either loaded onto the few captured Soviet trains available or moved over 300km by the trucks of the *Grosstranportraum*. Due to the poor condition of the roads, a one-way trip for a resupply column might take three to four days. By mid-October, von Kleist's forward panzer units were receiving little or no supplies at all.[142] After victory at Kiev, Kleist's forces were reduced to Mackensen's III Armeekorps (mot.) with 13.Panzer-Division, LSSAH and 60.Infanterie-Division (mot.) and von Wietersheim's XIV Armee-korps (mot.) with 14 and 16.Panzer-Divisionen and SS-Division *Wiking*. The 14.Panzer-Division still had sixty-eight operational tanks on 1 November, but overall, von Kleist could muster fewer than 200 tanks and assault guns. Further-more, he had no infantry in his sector and was obliged to hold a 100km-wide front with his own units, which meant that the panzer units had little chance to rest or refit.

In late October, General-polkovnik Yaakov T. Cherevichenko, the new Southern Front commander, managed to build a firm defense in front of Rostov with the 56th Army formed from units transferred from the Caucasus, while the rebuilt 9th Army established a defense in depth north of the city. Cherevichenko had little armour left, even though he had received six of the new tank brigades – these were quickly whittled down in defensive combat. He also had four separate tank battalions formed from repaired or recovered tanks, but altogether he had about 150 tanks, mostly light models. Cherevichenko assigned forty tanks to the 56th Army holding Rostov, sixty tanks to support the 9th Army and kept fifty in his frontal reserve. Although strictly on the defensive, Cherevichenko was forming a new 37th Army to act as a shock group for a counter-offensive once more reinforcements arrived.

With Operation Typhoon uncertain of seizing Moscow, Hitler wanted one last conquest for this campaign season and Rostov, a city of 510,000, would do nicely. He ordered von Rundstedt to use Kleist's PzAOK 1 to seize the city before the weather grew worse. While von Kleist knew that he had a slight superiority over Cherevichenko in terms of armour, he had no other material advantages. He also knew that the straight, 22km path directly into the city would be a battle of attrition which could cripple his army. Instead, von Kleist opted to gain the advantage of surprise by opting for the indirect approach. Rather than attacking due east into the teeth of Cherevichenko's defenses, von Kleist decided to mass both his motorized corps to punch a hole in the 9th Army's front, drive 60km to the northeast, then swing south to take Rostov from behind. It was a very daring plan that relied on speed and maneuver, even though autumn rains and inadequate logistics made this problematic. Von Kleist quietly began shifting two of his panzer divisions into position in early November, which was apparently missed by Soviet intelligence.

On 5 November, von Kleist attacked. While Mackensen's III Armeekorps (mot.) made a feint attack against the 56th Army positions in front of Rostov, von Wietersheim's XIV Armeekorps (mot.) struck the 30th and 136th Rifle Divisions in the center of 9th Army's front. Hube's 16.Panzer-Division spearheaded the breakthrough, which initially made good progress by advancing 20km on the first day. However, Kühn's 14.Panzer-Division ran into trouble after penetrating about 12km; a counterattack by Major Georgy Kuznetsov's 2nd Tank Brigade (eighteen tanks) struck the flank of Kühn's division and the Germans retreated to their starting positions. Even worse, the SS-Division *Wiking*, assigned to make a supporting attack on Hube's left flank, encountered a large Soviet fortified anti-tank position at D'iakovo, that was protected by thirty-seven anti-tank guns (including six 57mm ZIS-4 high-velocity anti-tank guns that could defeat all German tanks out to 1,000 meters), seven battalions of field artillery with eighty-four pieces and a rifle regiment. Normally Soviet anti-tank units had used linear defenses that were fairly easy for panzer units to defeat in detail, but the D'iakovo position was a large, well-planned hedgehog and the *Wiking*'s attack was repulsed with heavy losses. Hube soon found himself with both his flanking units having retreated and in danger of being cut off.

Amazingly, the 9th Army mounted a coordinated counterattack against Hube's exposed division from three directions on 6 November with a total of sixty to seventy tanks from the 2nd and 132nd Tank Brigades, plus two motorized rifle regiments. Hube was compelled to fall back after suffering significant losses. Despite the setback, von Wietersheim reorganized his corps and attacked in the same sector, and the 14 and 16.Panzer-Divisionen created a large bulge in the 9th Army's front. On 7 November, the 14.Panzer-Division rolled up the Soviet 339th Rifle Division, while Hube expanded the bulge eastward. Kuznetsov's 2nd Tank Brigade continued to launch aggressive counterattacks, but Soviet armoured strength in this sector was insufficient. On 8 November, the 1.Gebirgsjäger-Division – from 17.Armee – did what SS-*Wiking* could not do, and captured the D'iakovo position. Gradually, von Wietersheim's corps was chewing its way through the Soviet 9th Army and it had advanced 60km eastward by 11 November before von Kleist had to temporarily suspend his offensive due to crippling supply shortages.

Given the muddy roads and long distances involved, it took six days for von Kleist to replenish his forward panzer divisions. Cherevichenko mistakenly believed that the German offensive had culminated and sent the bulk of his reinforcements, including three tank brigades, to build up the 37th Army for a counter-offensive against von Kleist's left flank. It thus came as a surprise when Mackensen's III Armeekorps (mot.) committed the *LSSAH*, reinforced with Panzer-Regiment 4 from 13.Panzer-Division, to attack the 56th Army's outer perimeter at Sultan-Saly on 17 November. The 14.Panzer-Division and 60.Infanterie-Division joined in the final assault and the two Soviet rifle divisions in this sector were pushed back to their second line of defense. Yet even as Mackensen was closing in on Rostov, the Soviet 37th Army began its own offensive which began to threaten von Kleist's left flank. On 19 November, Kühn's 14.Panzer-Division began to fight its way into Rostov, which was defended by about 80,000 Soviet troops. This was the first and only attempt by the Germans to fight with a panzer division in a major city without infantry support and this proved a costly undertaking. By the end of 20 November, Mackensen's troops had captured most of Rostov, but his forces had finally reached their culmination point and gone well beyond it. Kühn's 14.Panzer-Division had lost twenty tanks in taking Rostov and was reduced to just thirty-six tanks (ten Pz.II, twenty Pz.III, two Pz.IV and four PzBef). Von Wietersheim's corps, although not fully involved in the final push on Rostov, were also spent and could not fend off the counter-offensive by 37th Army, even though it only consisted of six rifle divisions supported by fewer than 100 tanks. Both Hube's 16.Panzer-Division and SS-Division *Wiking* began to give ground by 21–22 November, which threatened Mackensen's position in Rostov.

Von Kleist found himself in a very difficult position, made worse by the shortage of fuel, which made it impossible for him to conduct the kind of mobile defense preferred by German commanders. The offensive to take Rostov had cost PzAOK 1 over 6,000 casualties, including 1,778 dead, and about half its remaining armour. The prospect of meaningful reinforcements was nil. By 25 November, the writing was on the wall and Mackensen's corps was slowly being squeezed as von Wietersheim's corps was continuously forced to yield ground. Von Rundstedt and von Kleist recognized that PzAOK 1 no longer had the strength to hold Rostov, but Hitler insisted that the city would be held.

Striking the Hydra's Head, 25 November–15 December

If military history teaches us anything, it is that false assumptions are at the root of all major disasters. Hitler and the OKH had begun Operation Typhoon and the armoured attacks at Tikhvin and Rostov with inadequate fuel and ammunition which – far more than the weather – caused these offensives to culminate short of their objectives. Time and again, the German panzer spearheads were forced to halt their advances because of fuel shortages. The shortage of artillery ammunition, when combined with the reduced scale of close air support, degraded the ability of the panzer groups to reduce Soviet strong points at places like Istra, Volokolamsk and Tula, which enabled the Red Army to recover from its set-backs. Operation Typhoon and the other attacks were built upon the assumption that none of these material factors would matter and that somehow the Wehrmacht would triumph through superior willpower. Yet by the time that the worst winter weather arrived in early December, each of the German panzer armies had been stopped because of material inadequacies, which precipitated a collapse of German front-line morale. Furthermore, the German panzer units on all fronts – Tikhvin, Moscow, Tula and Rostov – were all over-extended and spent, with little or no remaining offensive combat power. In each case, their attacks had left them holding positions with weakly-protected flanks and minimal infantry support.

The first to suffer from these false assumptions was von Kleist's Panzerarmee 1, which lacked the strength to hold Rostov. The Soviet South Front began its counterattack on 25 November and General-major Anton I. Lopatin's 37th Army began to push back von Wietersheim's XIV Armeekorps (mot.), which was screening von Kleist's left flank along the Tuzlov River. The area held by the Slovakian Fast Division and the SS-Division *Wiking* near Lysogorka proved to be a weak spot and Lopatin massed several rifle divisions, two cavalry divisions and three tank brigades in this sector. Von Wietersheim's defense did not collapse, but gradually fell back under pressure, which left the III Armeekorps (mot.) perilously exposed at the end of a long, thin salient in Rostov. The Soviet 56th Army committed more infantry, cavalry and a tank brigade to a direct attack from the south and east on Rostov, which added additional stress to von Kleist's position. On the night of 25–26 November, the 56th Army managed to cross the Don river with two rifle divisions and an NKVD regiment, while the 54th Tank Brigade and a cavalry division moved in on the northern side of the city – forming a pincer attack with the *LSSAH* in the middle. On 28 November, von Rundstedt authorized von Kleist to withdraw to the Mius River, which was the best course of action. However, Hitler begged to differ and relieved Rundstedt of command on 1 December. Nevertheless, Rundstedt's replacement – Generalfeldmarschall Walther von Reichenau – quickly recognized that retreat was the only option to save Panzerarmee 1 and Hitler grudgingly allowed von Kleist to fall back 70km and dig in behind the Mius River. Soviet armoured forces played a supporting role at Rostov, with only a few brigades engaged – forty-two Soviet tanks were lost in the counter-offensive to retake Rostov.[143] No German units had been lost at Rostov, but von Kleist's Panzerarmee 1 had suffered over 6,000 casualties in the November fighting and the panzer divisons were combat ineffective; the 14.Panzer-Division alone lost over fifty tanks around Rostov and had only thirteen tanks still operational when the retreat began.[144]

An even worse calamity was faced by Reinhardt's Panzerarmee 3 in the Klin bulge northwest of Moscow, where his forces held a 50km-long front along the Moscow-Volga Canal and a 60km flank stretching back to the Moscow Sea. Reinhardt had attacked and attacked until he was virtually out of fuel and ammunition, then ground to a halt within 20–40km of Moscow. Reinhardt had Walter Model's XXXXI Armeekorps (mot.) massed near Yakhroma with the 1, 6 and 7.Panzer-Divisionen, the attached 23.Infanterie-Division and four non-divisional artillery battalions. Model's corps had suffered badly in the final days of the offensive. By the first week of December, the 6.Panzer-Division only had five operational tanks left in Oberst Richard Koll's Panzer-Regiment 25 and a total of 1,061 infantry in its four *schützen* and one *Kradschützen-Abteilung*; effectively 2 per cent of its authorized armour and 25 per cent of its infantry.[145] Reinhardt's extended northern flank was screened by Schaal's LVI Armeekorps (mot.) with the 14 and 36.Infanterie-Divisionen (mot.) and the Lehr-Brigade 900, which had a handful of assault guns attached. These motorized units deployed in battalion-size *Igel* (hedgehogs) centered around villages, which were essential for housing as temperatures dropped below freezing at night, but which were not fortified. Reinhardt had part of 1.Panzer-Division in reserve, but its mobility was limited. More pertinently, he had just 10–12,000 infantrymen available to hold 100km of front. His artillery was very low on ammunition and could not be moved because most of the prime movers were non-operational and the tanks had little fuel left. A cold front moving across central Russia on 4 December pushed temperatures as low as $-40°$ C ($-40°$ F), which caused most of the troops to seek shelter, abandoning their vehicles to the frost. Very little anti-freeze had reached forward units so fuel lines froze solid and even tank tracks froze to the ground. The German advantage in tactical mobility disappeared.

Unknown to Reinhardt, Höpner or von Bock, the Stavka had been assembling three new armies to mount a major counter-offensive, which Stalin approved on 30 November. Zhukov's Western Front had General-leytenant Vasily I. Kuznetsov's 1st Shock Army and General-Leytenant Andrei A. Vlasov's 20th Army moving into position north of Moscow to strike the front of the Klin bulge. These two assault armies were plentifully equipped with infantry – roughly 60,000 – but had only limited artillery support (about thirty-six medium howitzers and fifty BM-13 Katyusha rocket launchers) and even less armour. Kuznetsov had one independent tank battalion (OTB) and Vlasov had the 24th Tank Brigade and one OTB; altogether, barely 100 tanks and no more than thirty were KV or T-34s. Kuznetsov did have one advantage, in that he held a sizeable bridgehead across the Moscow-Volga canal opposite the 6.Panzer-Division, which meant that the canal provided no real defensive benefit to the

Germans. On the northern side of the Klin bulge, Konev's Kalinin Front had General-major Dmitri D. Lelyushenko's re-formed 30th Army prepared to play a major role in the counter-offensive. Lelyushenko had a mixed force with about 30,000 infantry, 8,000 cavalry and about fifty tanks, of which no more than ten were KV or T-34s. Polkovnik Pavel A. Rotmistrov's 8th Tank Brigade, reinforced with a rifle battalion, was intended to be the 30th Army's main strike force – which was an indicator of just how depleted the Red Army's tank forces were in Decenmber 1941.

At 0600 hours on 6 December, Lelyushenko began his offensive against Reinhardt's Panzerarmee 3 from the north with a series of un-coordinated regimental-size infantry and cavalry attacks against the *Igel* of the 14 and 36.Infanterie-Divisionen (mot.). The attacks were conducted before dawn in order to minimize the effectiveness of German defensive fires. Three of Lelyushenko's rifle divisions and one cavalry division had just arrived from the Urals MD and went into battle shortly after detraining. Most of the Soviet attacks were repulsed since they were spread across a 50km-wide frontage and lacked mass. However, Rotmistrov, attacking in conjunction with the 365th Rifle Division, managed to force a German blocking detachment to evacuate the village of Zabolote, which created a gap in the 36.Infanterie-Division (mot.) sector. Rotmistrov's tankers managed to advance over 8km on the next day, driving a shallow wedge behind the German defense at Klin. On the same day, Kuznetsov's 1st Shock Army attacked the 6.Panzer-Division near Yakhroma with several rifle brigades, but failed to gain any ground. Reinhardt reacted to the Soviet counter-offensive by ordering 1.Panzer-Division to send a Panzer-Abteilung to block Rotmistrov from making any further penetration and he ordered Model's XXXXI Armeekorps (mot.) to pull back from the Dmitrov-Yakhroma area to shorten the front.

On 8 December, the Soviet counter-offensive against the Klin bulge gathered momentum as Panzerarmee 3 continued to fall back toward Klin and Solnech-nogorsk. The 14.Infanterie-Division (mot.) abandoned the important road inter-section at Rogachevo without much of a fight, abandoning a great deal of equipment and damaged vehicles. Rotmistrov's tank brigade continued to inch forward, widenening the gap in the German line, and late on 9 December he captured Yamuga, just 7km north of Klin. Reinhardt and von Bock seemed paralyzed – similar to the way Red Army commanders had reacted to the initial surprise attacks in June 1941 – and had difficulty determining whether they should try and hold fast or withdraw to defensible positions. Hitler would not approve any major retreats, but German commanders became adept at justifying minor 'line straightening' movements that were actually tactical withdrawals. Rokossovky's 16th Army had also begun attacking Höpner's Panzerarmee 4 at Krasnaya Polyana, preventing him from providing any significant aid to Reinhardt.

By 10 December, the situation around Klin was becoming very dangerous for Reinhardt, once Rotmistrov cut the Klin-Volokolamsk road and attacked the LVI Armeekorps (mot.) headquarters 4km from Klin; Schaal was forced to use a rifle to defend his command post. Reinhardt's troops kept falling back from village to village, until four of his divisions were clustered around Klin. Höpner sent part of the 2.Panzer-Division to help eject Rotmistrov's brigade, but its departure from the front enabled Rokossovsky to recapture Istra and Solnech-nogorsk on 11 December. By 12 December, it was apparent that the Soviet 30th Army and 1st Shock Army were bent on encircling the bulk of Panzer-armee 3 at Klin and that there was little that Reinhardt could do to stop it. Lelyushenko formed an operational maneuver group under Rotmistrov with the 8th and 21st Tank Brigades, an OTB and a motorcycle regiment, and instructed them to seal off Reinhardt's escape route. Rotmistrov managed to come close to surrounding the 1, 2, 6, and 7.Panzer-Divisionen and 14.Infanterie-Division (mot.) but the Germans managed to mount a small attack at Nekrasino that kept the escape route open long enough for Reinhardt's forces to escape westward, abandoning Klin on 15 December. Few if any prime movers were left, so most of the 8.8cm flak guns and artillery had to be abandoned; with few tanks or guns left, Reinhardt's divisions were reduced to little more than infantry kampfgruppen.

The Battle of the Klin bulge had been catastrophic for Panzerarmee 3, resulting in about 2,500 personnel casualties and heavy material losses, including most of the artillery and vehicles. All five of Reinhardt's motorized divisions were rendered combat-ineffective and were no longer capable even of defensive measures – instead, they continued retreating westward even though the Soviet pursuit could not keep up with them. At the same time, Konev's Kalinin Front recaptured Kalinin on 16 December and put 9.Armee to flight. Heeresgruppe Mitte's left flank was retreating in disarray. Von Bock directed Reinhardt to withdraw to the Konigsberg Line, but the retreat was more of a rout than an orderly operation. Lelyushenko managed an impressive victory at Klin despite very limited resources and time for planning, which was executed superbly at the tactical level by Rotmistrov. While far from reflective of Deep Battle doctrine, the 30th Army's attack at Klin reflected a successful hybrid mix of tanks, infantry and cavalry that was the best that the Red Army could manage until industry replaced the losses of 1941.

At Tula, Guderian's over-extended Panzerarmee 2 was quickly defeated in detail between 6–12 December as both his flanks were smashed in and he was forced to fall back again and again. The third Stavka reserve army, the 10th, suddenly appeared on Guderian's eastern flank near Mikhailov and routed Lemelsen's XXXXVII Armeekorps (mot.). The 10th Army advanced 30km in two days, slashing across Guderian's lines of communication, and threatened to link up with the 50th Army attacking out of Tula, which would have resulted in the encirclement of von Schweppenburg's XXIV Armeekorps (mot.). Guderian reacted promptly to the Soviet counter-offensive by ordering a rapid retreat and briefly created a new front between Tula and Yeifan, but when Timoshenko's Southwest Front forced the 2.Armee to retreat toward Orel, Guderian was forced to fall back as well. As with Reinhardt's Panzerarmee 3, Guderian's retreat forced him to abandon artillery and vehicles which Germany could not replace.

At Tikhvin, the XXXIX Armeekorps (mot.) had been in an untenable position since mid-November due to the impossibility of supplying a motorized corps along a single trail across frozen marshland. Generalleutnant Hans-Jürgen von Arnim took over the corps at Tikhvin after General der Panzertruppe Rudolf Schmidt reported to the OKH that his troops were 'on the brink of collapse' due to the absence of winter uniforms and supplies. However, von Arnim's arrival failed to alter the poor German situation and the Soviet 4th Army began a series of counterattacks that gradually pushed in the German flanks and interfered with ground lines of communication. The position of the Tikhvin garrison became critical and von Arnim was forced to request aerial resupply which, given the harsh weather conditions, would clearly be insufficient to keep a motorized corps in fighting trim. On 4 December, the Soviet 4th Army mounted a direct assault on the town of Tikhvin and the German lines began to buckle. On 8 December, von Arnim finally bowed to the inevitable, abandoning Tikhvin, and ordered a withdrawl to the Volkhov River. Although von Arnim's forces escaped the Soviet pincers, the 8 and 12.Panzer-Divisionen were forced to abandon a great deal of equipment in the retreat, rendering them combat-ineffective. The liberation of Tikhvin cost the 4th Army 70 tanks.[146]

Amazingly, the Red Army's counterattacks between 25 November and 15 December had resulted in the defeat of every single Geman panzer army in the Soviet Union in just three weeks. With few exceptions, the retreat caused grievous material losses to the panzer divisions, which could never be fully replaced. By the end of 1941, the Wehrmacht had lost over 2,600 tanks and assault guns on the Eastern Front and another 1,000 tanks were non-operational and in need of repairs. The losses of wheeled vehicles, artillery and 8.8cm flak guns were also very high and greatly weakened the offensive firepower and mobility of the remaining German mechanized divisions. Overall, the Wehrmacht had suffered 830,903 casualties on the Eastern Front in 1941, of which 27 per cent were in the panzer armies.

Defeat also had a price for the senior leadership of the Wehrmacht and the Panzerwaffe. In addition to von Rundstedt, Hitler relieved von Bock on 18 December and Guderian on 26 December. In each case, Hitler relieved these officers for conducting unauthorized retreats, but the real reason was that he believed that they had lost the will to win – Hitler was quick to sense defeatism in his generals. Höpner was also relieved for unauthorized retreats in January and the corps commanders von Schweppenburg and Kuntzen were replaced due to poor health. On the other hand, Hitler was quick to reward those officers, like Walter Model, who demonstrated steadfastness even in adversity. When Model complained about retreating to the Konigsberg Line in mid-December 1941, Hitler decided that he would be the perfect choice to take over the crumbling 9.Armee at Rzhev.

The Red Army came close to encircling large German panzer formations at Tikhvin, Klin and Rostov in the December counter-offensive, but lacked the strength and skill to pull this off. Indeed, despite the recovery of terrain, the Red Army failed to destroy any major German units. By the end of December 1941, the NKVD reported only 10,602 German prisoners in Soviet captivity, whereas the Germans had captured 3,355,000 Soviet soldiers in the previous six months.[147] Yet the Red Army's own tank forces were in very poor shape by the end of 1941 and only able to play a supporting role in the Winter Counter-offensive. By Christmas 1941, the armoured forces of both the Wehrmacht and the Red Army had been virtually demolished and they each had very few operational medium or heavy tanks left after six months of sustained combat. Neither side was left with any substantial armoured reserve and consequently operations degenerated into First World War-era tactics.

The main reason for the dominance of German panzer divisions throughout the armoured battles of 1941 was not due to superior doctrine, equipment or even leadership, but rather the ability of its Panzertruppen to properly employ combined arms methods at the tactical level of combat and coordinate with other friendly panzer units by radio. The lack of adequate Soviet pre-war driver and gunnery training was also a serious deficiency that often negated the mobility and firepower advantages of the KV and T-34 tanks. During 1941, in spite of the fact that the KV and T-34 tanks were superior in firepower and armoured protection to any German tanks, the Red Army managed to lose 940 of the available 1,540 KV heavy tanks (61 per cent) and 2,331 of the 3,131 available T-34 medium tanks (74 per cent). While Vyacheslav Malyshev would ensure that Soviet industry built as many tanks as possible, it was not enough to simply have more or better tanks – it was critical that General-leytenant Yakov N. Fedorenko, as head of GABTU, ensured that Soviet tankers were trained to use them. The Red Army also had to increase the number of radios in tank units in order to make command and control a practical reality – almost every Soviet armoured counter-attack in 1941 fell apart because of inadequate C2. At the operational level, German superiority was much less pronounced and the Red Army had a number of tank leaders who understood how to plan an enveloping attack and coordinate with other arms – but most Soviet tankers lacked the ability to actually conduct this on the battlefield. Both sides also failed to build logistic support structures that could adequately supply mobile operations, which seriously undermined their ability to conduct high-intensity armoured offensives for more than a few weeks.

Chapter 3

Armoured Operations in 1942

Soviet and German Armoured Forces, January-March 1942

By 1 January 1942, the nineteen German panzer divisions on the Eastern Front were in a very sorry state. The Germans had kept attacking until their panzer divisions were totally spent and then the retreats had cost them dearly. Panzer-Regiment 203 – which had only arrived in Heeresgruppe Nord on 17 December – was the strongest German armoured formation left on the Eastern Front, with about sixty operational tanks at the beginning of January. Otherwise, most of the panzer divisions were reduced to five to fifteen tanks each, for a grand total of perhaps 300 operational tanks spread across the entire Eastern Front. The *Schützen-Regiment* in most of the panzer divisions were gutted, with personnel losses between 50 and 80 per cent and vehicle losses even higher. More than half of the trucks and prime movers had been lost in the 1941 campaign, which severely reduced the mobility and logistical sustainability of many units, particularly the motorized infantry divisions. Some examples of the very limited combat effectiveness of the panzer-divisionen at the start of 1942 include:

- The 1.Panzer-Division had five operational tanks and less than two battalions of infantry.
- The 3.Panzer-Division had fifteen operational tanks in I/Pz.Regt 6 (one Pz.II, eleven Pz.III, two Pz.IV, one Pz.Bef).[1]
- The 4.Panzer-Division had one company with ten tanks, which was increased to two companies with a total of sixteen tanks by 21 January.
- The 6.Panzer-Division had no operational tanks and had lost 80 per cent of its infantry and most of its prime movers. The only combat-effective element was Kampfgruppe Zollenkopf, equivalent to a reinforced rifle battalion.[2]
- The 7.Panzer-Division had five operational tanks (four Pz.38(t) and one Pz.IV).[3]
- The 8.Panzer-Division had a mixed panzer kampfgruppe with twelve tanks (eleven Pz.38(t) and one Pz.IV) and about 15 per cent of its infantry remaining.[4]
- The 11.Panzer-Division withdrew its remaining tanks to the rear at Gzhatsk. It is not clear how many were operational, but no more than ten to fifteen.[5]
- The 18.Panzer-Division had a small number of Pz.III and Pz.IV operational.

Von Kleist's 1.Panzerarmee reported in mid-January that it still had 458 tanks, but only 166 were operational (twenty-two Pz.II, 111 Pz.III, thirty-three Pz.IV), plus fifteen StuG III assault guns – making his command the only Panzerarmee still worthy of the name on the Eastern Front. While this might sound like a combat effective force, he also reported that there was only 0.25 V.S. of fuel with the front-line units – barely enough to turn the engines over a few times a day.[6] Von Kleist did benefit from the fact that after his defeat at Rostov he did not retreat far – so little equipment was abandoned – and that the Red Army left his forces relatively unmolested for the rest of the winter. Elsewhere along the Eastern Front, most panzer regiments formed a mixed company or two with the remaining tanks, while the other panzer companies were disbanded and the personnel assigned to alarm units to deal with enemy partisans or raids. A few 'unhorsed' panzer crews were sent back to the *Ersatz-Abteilungen* (replacement battalions) in their home *Wehrkreis*, but most were pressed into the line as ad hoc infantrymen. The remaining tanks were used strictly in the infantry support role, stiffening the hard-pressed German infantry at key points. A few assault guns remained in service too, but not many. German supply services all but collapsed for a time during the winter of 1941–42, with the railroad system almost paralyzed when most German-made trains proved unable to withstand the cold in Russia and the roads blocked by snow that could be one meter or more in depth.

Although there was no major armoured combat during the winter months, German tank losses remained heavy during January–February 1942 as tanks were abandoned due to retreats and lack of recovery vehicles. Deliveries of new tanks did not begin in earnest until February 1942, by which time the Soviet Winter Counter-offensive was beginning to run out of momentum.[7] The German *Werkstatt* units were finally able to start repairing some tanks and vehicles as well, but throughout the winter the Germans had no appreciable mobile reserves on the Eastern Front.

German tankers and assault gun crews did receive one significant reinforcement in early January 1942: the first 7.5cm Gr. 38 H1 High Explosive Anti-Tank (HEAT) ammunition. The Heereswaffenamt had been experimenting with HEAT ammunition since 1939, but the weakness of conventional German anti-tank ammunition against Soviet KV-1 and T-34 tanks led to the program being accelerated in late 1941. The first batch of HEAT ammunition that reached the front suffered from temperamental fusing – the warhead had to detonate at

German Tank Strength on the Eastern Front

Month	Tanks Lost	Replacements	Number Operational on First of Month
January 1942	362	158	300
February 1942	305	582	340
March 1942	72	196	643
April 1942	125	590	736
May 1942	66	536	1,167

precisely the right moment and angle in order for the explosive to work properly, If it did, the warhead would form a gas jet that could burn through 70mm of steel plate, which could easily destroy a T-34 and inflict serious damage on a KV-1. Since the HEAT ammunition did not rely upon velocity as conventional kinetic penetrators did, the warhead was just as effective at 1,000 meters as it was at 500 meters.

On the other side, the Red Army appeared to have a huge numerical and qualitative advantage in armoured forces at the start of 1942. Ostensibly, the Red Army had 7,700 tanks on 1 January 1942, including about 600 KV heavy tanks and 800 T-34s.[8] However, about 4,400 of these tanks were stationed in the Far East, on the Turkish border or other interior military districts or in schools. There were seven tank brigades and nineteen independent tank battalions (OTB) with a total of about 880 tanks forming up or refitting in the Moscow MD. The Stavka's reserve, the RVGK, had nine tank brigades and one OTB with about 435 tanks, including about sixty KV-1 and 100 T-34s. The units in the RVGK were generally kept as close to authorized strength as possible, so that when they were committed to battle they could have the greatest impact. In the ten active fronts, from the Baltic to the Black Sea, the Red Army disposed three tank divisions, forty-three tank brigades and fifty-five OTB with approximately 2,000 tanks. The three tank divisions (21, 60 and 112) were only battle groups that would soon be converted into tank brigades. The front's tanks units were generally well understrength, with most tank brigades down to about twenty-six–thirty tanks and OTBs averaging twelve–fifteen tanks. About 30 per cent of the front-line tanks, particularly the KV-1s with their inadequate transmissions, were non-operational at any one time. Nevertheless, the Red Army's field armies enjoyed at least a 6–1 numerical advantage in armoured forces over the Panzer-waffe at the start of 1942. The question was, could the Red Army's leadership achieve anything decisive with this advantage?

Given the lack of large armoured formations and inadequate training, Zhukov and the other Soviet front commanders knew that they could not execute Deep Battle or any other fancy operational maneuvers with the forces they had available in January 1942. At best, the Red Army's nascent tank units could serve in the infantry support role and spearhead the counteroffensives in their sectors of the front. At Zhukov's recommendation, the Stavka directed each front to form shock groups, which usually consisted of a tank brigade, a rifle brigade or division, some cavalry and a ski battalion or two – perhaps 5,000 troops and thirty tanks, but with negligible artillery or logistic support. These shock groups became the basis of the Soviet Winter Counter-offensive and although they gave the Wehrmacht some bad moments, they failed to fulfill the role of a breakthrough and exploitation force.

The Winter Counter-offensive, January–March 1942

After the retreats from Moscow, Tikhvin, Tula and Rostov, it briefly seemed to the Germans on the Eastern Front that major combat operations might be suspended for the rest of the winter. The reasonable course of action for both sides was to limit their operations at the front and focus on rebuilding their badly-depleted armoured units so that they would be capable of further large-scale operations once spring arrived. However, Stalin was exuberant after the German defeat at Moscow and convinced himself – as Hitler had done about the Red Army in October 1941 – that one more major blow would cause the Wehrmacht to collapse. It is interesting how both dictators deluded themselves about the apparent weakness of their opponent, with their general staffs obsequiously feeding this delusion, and which in both cases led to catastrophic over-extension and defeat. After the German panzer armies had been pushed back from Moscow, Zhukov and a few other Red Army commanders wanted time to rebuild their armies, but Stalin was impatient. Instead, in late December 1941 Stalin informed the Stavka that he wanted a new series of counter-offensives, all along the front from Leningrad to the Crimea, to hammer the Germans mercilessly and drive the invaders out of the Soviet Union. Zhukov, realizing that the Red Army's resources were still quite limited and not capable of supporting multi-front offensives so soon, argued for concentrating at one or two points to achieve decisive results, but was over-ruled by Stalin.[9] Staffs at front-level, who had been alerted in late December to prepare for offensive action, were given at best a few days to prepare their battle plans.

The first indication that the Red Army was not going to stop after the German defeat at Moscow occurred in the Crimea, where the Soviets mounted amphibious landings at Kerch on 26 December and Feodosiya on 29 December. Von Manstein's 11.Armee was caught by surprise and the Soviets were able to land over 85,000 troops and forty-three light tanks in a matter of days. Although von Manstein was able to contain the Soviet landings, the Red Army continued to pour troops, tanks and artillery into the Kerch Peninsula in January – meaning that a test of strength would not be long in coming. There were no panzer units in the Crimea, but von Manstein's 11.Armee did have *Sturmgeschütz-Abteilungen* 190 and 197 with a handful of assault guns. Indeed, the assault-gun units proved their worth in stiffening the defense time and again during the Soviet Winter Counter-offensive.

Timoshenko was the first front commander to commit his forces into the general offensive on 1 January, when his Southwest Front began attacking the German 6.Armee near Izyum. The weather was atrocious, with temperatures of $-29°\,C$ ($-20°\,F$) and deep snow covering the ground, but Timoshenko's forces gradually overwhelmed an isolated German infantry division and achieved a significant breakthrough after two weeks of fighting, creating a 40km-wide gap between AOK 6 and AOK 17. Timoshenko's breakthrough was facilitated by a small number of KV-1 and T-34 tanks, but his Southwest Front had barely 200 tanks and was forced to rely upon cavalry as its primary exploitation force. Lacking the shock effect of armour, the Soviet cavalry spearheads were eventually halted by German and Romanian blocking detachments, but the net result was the creation of the Barvenkovo salient that drove a deep wedge in Heeresgruppe Süd's frontline.

The main component of the Soviet Winter Counter-offensive began on 6 January, with a fairly coordinated series of offensives by General Kirill A. Meretskov's Volkhov Front, General-Polkovnik Pavel A. Kurochkin's Northwest Front, Konev's Kalinin Front and Zhukov's Western Front. Zhukov employed nearly one-fifth of the Red Army's available armour in his sector, about 400 tanks, leaving less than 200 tanks for Konev, 100 for Kurochkin and 150 for Meretskov. The Volkhov Front attacked with the 4th, 59th and 2nd Shock Army against the 16.Armee and one corps of the 18.Armee. The marshy and heavily-wooded terrain along the Volkhov precluded the large use of armour by either side, although the neighboring Leningrad Front was able to use small numbers of KV-1 and T-34 tanks against the hard-pressed German *Stützpunkt* (strongpoint) at Kirishi, which quickly gained a reputation as 'the Verdun of the Volkhov'. Soviet tankers painted their KV-1s with whitewash for winter camouflage, contributing to their nickname as 'White Mammoths'. German infantrymen in front-line trenches would see the 'White Mammoths' forming up for an attack in the open, up to 1,000 meters away. The Soviets knew that their KV-1s were invulnerable to all but 8.8cm flak and heavy artillery – which could not be easily moved to the front through deep snow – and became increasingly brazen, which they hoped would undermine German morale when they realized how impotent their defenses were against the KV-1. Often, one or two KV-1s would approach German lines and, from a distance of 500 meters – beyond the effective range of the 5-cm Pak gun – they would mercilessly hammer any visible targets with high explosive rounds and machine-gun fire. This occurred day after day during the winter, when low clouds and poor visibility made it unlikely that any Luftwaffe Stukas could intervene.

On the morning of 18 January 1942, a small group of KV-1s and T-34s from Polkovnik Mikhail Rudoy's 122nd Tank Brigade began their usual demonstrations near Pogost'e, west of Kirishi. Suddenly, the Soviet tanks came under fire at a distance of about 800 meters and several of their tanks were knocked out. Lying concealed in the German positions, two StuG III assault guns from Sturmgeschütz-Batterie 667 were firing 7.5cm HEAT ammunition. Although the 'White Mammoths' broke off their attack, they apparently thought that the engagement was some kind of fluke and tried again the next day – with similar results. In two days, the German StuG IIIs managed to knock out four KV-1s and five T-34s – almost one-third of Rudoy's brigade.

The three Soviet armies encircled in Leningrad had over 100 tanks in the 124th Heavy Tank Brigade and five OTBs and made repeated efforts during the winter of 1941–42 to break out toward the rail junction at Mga in order to link-up with Meretskov's forces. In one action, the 124th Tank Brigade committed the only extant KV-3 heavy tank – an experimental version of the KV-1 that was built in Leningrad just prior to the war. The 62-ton KV-3 was intended as a 'breakthrough tank' and was given additional armour plate, making it nearly invulnerable – or so the Soviets thought. In an effort to punch through the German blockade lines around Leningrad, the single KV-3 was made the vanguard of an attack. The heavy behemoth clanked toward the German lines, but its weight greatly reduced its mobility, which gave the enemy artillery the ability to zero in on it. A well-placed German 15cm howitzer shell struck the KV-3's turret and detonated its ammunition, bringing the combat debut of the only Soviet breakthrough tank to a sudden end.

Elsewhere however, the KV-1 was more successful in creating breakthroughs. As part of Kurochkin's Northwest Front offensive, the 11th Army sent a platoon of five KV-1s under a Leytenant Astakhov and a company of T-60s across frozen Lake Il'men on the night of 7–8 January in order to outflank the German X Armeekorps at Staraya Russa. As one Soviet rider noted:

> The heavy tank on which I was riding together with a group of infantrymen cautiously lumbered forward across the ice. We were ordered to jump off and walk alongside. Old Il'men, as though annoyed by the sudden disturbance of its nocturnal peace, creaked and groaned as if shaken by a storm. The fifty-ton machines – this meant a pressure of 300 pounds per square centimetre of ice – caused the ice to crack with a strange tinkling sound, and on places where the ice did not reach the bottom, its surface could be seen palpably bending under their weight. The other heavy machines were not permitted to move along the tracks of the first ones, but branched out to the right or left. Finally the lake was left behind.[10]

Leytenant Astakhov's KV-1s crossed frozen Lake Il'men, but one tank fell through the ice and was abandoned when they crossed the River Lovat. With little left of the night, the Soviet tankers assembled in a forest and refuelled from drums brought on sledges. At daybreak, German infantrymen from the 290.Infanterie-Division were stunned when the four remaining KV-1s led an attack, along with a regiment of Soviet infantry, against a *Stutzpünkt* in the village of Yur'evo.

> Two green rockets soared into the air: the long-awaited signal calling the KV-1s into battle. Suddenly with a roar that shook the ground and the air, the giants emerged in deployed formation from the grove near the road. The Germans directed a tornado of shells upon them, but our land battleships relentlessly moved forward through the sea of fire ... The white disk of the hatch on Astakhov's tank, which was advancing on the right flank, opened and a red flag flashed three times. The message meant that the third tank was to break into the village.[11]

The third tank, commanded by a Leytenant Chilikin, was hit several times by German projectiles but burst into the village and overran the German anti-tank gun. The German defenders fell back in shock, and within two days the 11th Army was on the outskirts of Staraya Russa. This action is interesting in that Soviet tank platoon leaders were still relying upon signal flags to direct their tanks in battle and that the tanks were operating 'buttoned up' – it makes one wonder how Leytenant Chilikin could spot a signal flag at that distance in the heat of battle. Although caught by surprise, the German defences did stiffen near Staraya

Russa and a platoon of Pz.III tanks from Panzer-Regiment 203 arrived to prevent Soviet ski troops from surrounding the city.

In less than a week, three Soviet armies attacked the German front between Ostashkov and Rzhev and broke the junction of Heeresgruppe Nord and Heeresgruppe Mitte. The 9.Armee's XXIII Armeekorps was thrown back in disorder and a huge 150km-wide gap torn in the German front line. The Soviet steamroller fanned out, with the 3rd Shock Army advancing toward Kholm, the 4th Shock Army toward Velikiye Luki and the 22nd Army due south toward Yartsevo. This Soviet breakthrough was easily the worst crisis suffered during a winter filled with crises for the Germans, since it threatened the existence of Heeresgruppe Mitte. However, the Stavka had provided each of these three armies with only a single OTB and no cavalry, so their ability to exploit the victory was limited to a walking pace through deep snow. The Germans were not able to completely stop the Soviet avalanche, but they used their rail movement capability to move reinforcements to Kholm and Velikiye Luki, which became fortified strongpoints. To make matters worse for the Germans, Konev's Kalinin Front achieved a significant breakthrough with its 39th Army that isolated the German XXIII Armeekorps at Olenino and threatened to envelop the entire 9.Armee at Rzhev with the 11th Cavalry Corps.

In contrast to the Northwest and Kalinin fronts, which had limited tank and cavalry forces to exploit their victories, Zhukov ensured that the Stavka provided his Western Front with the lion's share of available armour, artillery and cavalry. However, Zhukov's fifteen tank brigades were worn out from two months of continuous combat and in poor shape for a general offensive. The strength of four of the brigades on 1 January indicates that their remaining armoured strength was 10–35 per cent of authorized strength and also that no more than one-quarter of the available tanks were T-34s:

- The 20th Tank Brigade had five operational tanks (one T-34, one T-26, one T-60 and two Valentines)
- The 23rd Tank Brigade had six operational tanks (one T-34 and five Valentines)
- The 32nd Tank Brigade had twelve operational tanks (one KV-1, five T-34, six T-60)
- The 146th Tank Brigade had sixteen operational tanks (two T-34, ten T-60, four Valentines)

After being relatively sober-minded throughout 1941, Zhukov suddenly let Stalin's vision of imminent German collapse cloud his judgment, and he believed that his Western Front could pull off a large-scale pincer attack toward Vyazma. His forces had already created a gap between 4.Panzerarmee and the 4.Armee near Borovsk and the 4.Armee's right flank had also been torn apart near Sukhinichi. Zhukov weighted his armour on his right flank, with eight tank brigades supporting the 5th, 16th and 20th Armies, while he formed another pincer on his left with the 43rd, 49th and 50th Armies, which were supported by five tank brigades. From the German point of view, with von Kluge now in charge of Heeresgruppe Mitte, the situation was awful and the only possible solution – as demanded by Hitler – was to dig in and wait for the Red Army to outrun its limited supplies. The handful of remaining German tanks were gathered in central reserve near Vyazma.

Zhukov's steamroller began on 20 January and simply shoved the German 4.Armee back along a 100km-wide front, recapturing Mozhaisk. Although the German XIII Armeekorps was nearly encircled at Yukhnov, Zhukov failed to trap any German units. His decimated tank brigades lacked the strength to conduct more than local actions and the fact that most of his armour was comprised of T-60 light tanks made it difficult for his forces to reduce a German *Stützpunkt* equipped with anti-tank guns. On 27 January, Zhukov decided to commit his own mobile group, Belov's 1st Guard Cavalry Corps, to a deep raid toward Vyazma. Belov's cavalrymen reached the outskirts of Vyazma but were turned away by a kampfgruppe from 5.Panzer-Division. Likewise, the 11th Cavalry Corps approaching from the north was prevented from cutting the Minsk– Moscow highway and Heeresgruppe Mitte's main line of communications by a kampfgruppe from 11.Panzer-Division. By 1 February, Zhukov's forces had been stopped at Gzhatsk and Yukhnov and a surprise German counterattack – led by infantry, not tanks – isolated the 33rd Army on the approaches to Vyazma. Zhukov began to display a tendency to reinforce failure by sacrificing three air-borne brigades and more troops in an effort to reenergize his offensive. However, General der Infanterie Gotthard Heinrici, the new commander of 4.Armee, fought a very cagey battle against Zhukov that prevented him from either taking Vyazma or rescuing the 33rd Army, which was eventually crushed. Likewise, Model, who took over 9.Armee, managed to repair the holes in his line, hold onto Rzhev and eventually destroy the Soviet 39th Army.

Elsewhere, the Soviet Bryansk Front managed to push the 2.Armee back towards Orel, mostly with cavalry and a few dozen light tanks. The Northwest Front also succeeded in surrounding the German II Armeekorps at Demyansk, but lacked the armour and artillery to crush the pocket. Overall, the Soviet Winter Counter-offensive stressed the Wehrmacht nearly to breaking point but failed to achieve any truly decisive results. During the winter fighting of 1941–42, neither side was able to muster more than company and battalion-size groupings of tanks, even in key sectors. Along vast stretches of front there were no tanks at all. Despite possessing an impressive numerical superiority in tanks on paper, the Red Army was never able to assemble a decent operational maneuver group due to the lack of large armoured formations. Instead, Soviet front commanders were forced to improvise mobile groups using weak tank brigades based around light tanks to support cavalry and ski troops. These ad hoc mobile groups were sufficient to outflank German positions – which caused a great deal of trouble – but lacked the firepower to reduce well-defended fortified villages and towns. Consequently, Hitler's instinctive adoption of hedgehog (*Igel*) tactics succeeded in the winter of 1941–42 due to the Red Army's temporary lack of tanks, artillery and ammunition.

Indeed, the Red Army at this point lacked the firepower or tactical skill to over-come well-defended German hedgehog positions. Two in particular – Kholm and Demyansk – held out against repeated attacks. At Kholm, Kampfgruppe Scherer, which initially started with 4,500 troops and four Pak guns, conducted an epic defense during a 105-day siege from 21 January to 5 May 1942. The Red Army repeatedly attacked the town with two rifle divisions, supported by the 146 and 170 OTB, which had a total of forty-six tanks (four KV-1, two T-34, eleven Matilda II and twenty-nine T-60). Initially, the Soviets attacked the town with only a few tanks at a time in infantry support roles, but this allowed the Germans to shift their limited number of Pak guns around the small perimeter. However, the Soviets began attacking with more tanks in February and in dif-ferent sectors simultaneously, which nearly overwhelmed the defenders. The Matildas proved impervious to the 3.7cm Pak fire, but three were lost to T-mines and their 2-pounder guns were not very effective at engaging targets in buildings due to their lack of an HE round. The Luftwaffe managed to fly in new anti-tank weapons by glider and parachute to keep the Soviets tanks at bay, including the new Stielgranate 41 HEAT rounds for the 3.7cm Pak, used for the first time on 10 March.[12] Although only 9 of 18 Stielgranate 41 rounds hit their targets and only two tanks were damaged, the introduction of HEAT warheads would slowly begin to change the anti-tank dynamic on the Eastern Front in favor of the defense, even though this would not be realized until the Panzerfaust appeared in 1944. While the two OTBs tried to break into Kholm – and nearly succeeded on several occasions – the Soviets deployed a few T-34s west of the town to block German relief efforts. During the course of the siege, over thirty Soviet tanks were destroyed around Kholm.

The first large German armoured operations in 1942 were the relief of the Kholm and Demyansk pockets in March–May 1942. The relief of Kholm was spearheaded by StuG IIIs from Sturmgeschütz-Abteilung 184 and a Kampfgrup-pen Crissoli from 8.Panzer-Division. After intense fighting on the approaches to Kholm, in which both sides lost armoured vehicles in ambush-style combat, German assault guns finally fought their way into the town and relieved Kampf-gruppe Scherer. At Demyansk, the Soviets had encircled six German divisions with 96,000 troops, but the Red Army lacked the strength to reduce the pocket or even to seriously interfere with the Luftwaffe airlift that kept the defenders in supply. On 21 March 1942, Gruppe Seydlitz began Operation *Brückenschlag*, a relief effort involving five German infantry divisions, supported by thirty tanks from I./Pz.Regt 203 and 13 StuG IIIs.[13] The going was very slow, over frozen marshlands and heavily forested, and temperatures still ranged between −20°C (−13°F) and −29°C (−20°F). The Soviets employed their only armoured reserve in this sector, the 69th Tank Brigade, to launch an attack on 27 March to try and stop the German relief effort. However, the German jägers managed to repulse the Soviet tank brigade and knocked out eight of its twenty T-34 tanks using a combination of means. The spring thaw, which began in early April, proved a bigger obstacle to the German relief effort than Soviet tanks. Never-theless, Gruppe Seydlitz finally managed to link up with the trapped German forces at Demyansk on 21 April. The use of German armour – although only a single battalion plus two assault gun batteries – had been decisive in breaking the Soviet ring around the Demyansk pocket. This episode proved to be a harbinger of many future German operations, where panzer units were used to spearhead relief efforts.

Despite a lack of decision, the winter fighting was very costly for both sides. The failed efforts to capture Rzhev and Vyazma cost Konev's and Zhukov's forces the shocking total of 776,889 casualties and 957 tanks – which was 73 per cent of their personnel strength and 150 per cent of their tank strength at the start of the operation. During the same period, Heeresgruppe Mitte suffered 150,008 combat casualties but received over 160,000 replacements. Overall, the 1941–42 Winter Counter-offensive cost the Red Army 1.854 million casualties in the first three months of 1942.[14,15]

Armoured Warfare in the Winter

German tanks were not designed with the Russian winter in mind. The tracks on the Pz.III and Pz.IV were 16–25 per cent narrower than the T-34 and both vehicles had less ground clearance than either the T-34 or KV-1, which caused them to get stuck in deep snow. In particular, the T-34 had a significant mobility advantage over the Pz.III and Pz.IV on soft ground or snow due to its superior horsepower to weight ratio and lower ground pressure. The V-2 diesel tank engine provided the T-34 with mobility, reliability and endurance that no German tank matched during the Second World War. However, the Soviet tank with the best mobility on snow and ice was actually the T-60 light tank, even though its thin armour resulted in it being dubbed the BM-2 or '*Bratskaya Mogila na dvoikh*' (a brother's grave for two) by Soviet tankers. In contrast, the British-made Valentine and Matilda tanks had very little mobility in deep snow and little traction on ice. Near Lake Seliger, when the 170th OTB was marching to the front, it lost two of its thirteen Matilda IIs when they slid off an icy road and rolled over.[16] Near Istra, the 146th Tank Brigade also lost several Valentines to roll-over incidents.

Aside from inferior mobility in deep snow, the German tanks were badly affected by the penetrating cold in Russia. Although both German and Soviet tanks had means to divert warm air from the engine exhaust to the interior of the crew compartment, this only sufficed when the engine was running. When fuel was in short supply, as in October–December 1941, they could not run their engines continuously. Lacking petrol-fired personnel heaters in their tanks (which could operate with the engines off), panzer crews retreated into nearby houses or peasant *izbas*, leaving their tanks out overnight in deep freeze. Consequently, the water inside the tank's batteries froze, cracking the cases, which then required immediate replacement – but batteries were in short supply. Even if the batteries didn't rupture, the charge they could hold dropped off rapidly below freezing. Rubber coatings on power cables could also crack at temperatures below $-29°$ C ($-20°$ F). Petrol and diesel fuels were also affected by severe cold, which could have ice crystals form in fuel lines. Below $-32°$ C ($-25°$ F), the hydraulic fluid in the main gun's recoil system would freeze, resulting in the main gun being thrown out of battery if fired. The lubricant in machine-guns froze at $-37°$ C ($-35°$ F), making the weapons unusable until cleaned. Ammunition became difficult to work with after being frozen and the main gun breech could become very 'sticky' after a frost, resulting in rounds getting stuck in the breech.[17] Even when the unit received more fuel, starting an engine that had been idle for several days in sub-zero temperatures proved very difficult for the Germans and they resorted to extreme measures, such as building a wood fire under the tank. Once heated, the frost turned to condensation inside equipment. In contrast, the Soviet T-34 had internal compressed air bottles for cold weather starting and the T-34 had been extensively tested in winter conditions. As a result, German panzer units became very vulnerable if attacked by Soviet armour early in the day, when many panzers could not start; if the German unit was forced to withdraw, non-starting tanks were abandoned.

Even when the Germans could start their tanks, they found that the cold weather seriously degraded critical systems. Radios were particularly vulnerable to freezing and condensation, as well as the gunner's primary optical sight. The optics tended to trap frost inside the lenses, which prevented effective aiming. Tank maintenance became very difficult in temperatures below $-29°$ C ($-20°$ F), with exposed skin adhering to metal surfaces and even standard oil lubricants and tank grease becoming too thick to properly use. Without lubrication, tanks quickly lost the ability to move without damaging the running gear. Tasks like changing a torsion bar or drive sprocket were all but impossible without shelters in sub-zero weather. While the Red Army could shuttle its damaged tanks back to nearby Moscow for repair in proper facilities, the Wehrmacht was at a distinct disadvantage, far from its industrial base in Germany and lacking forward repair bases. Indeed, the Russian winter reduced much of Hitler's panzer armies to frozen scrap metal in a matter of a few weeks – proving to be the most effective Soviet anti-tank weapon of 1941. This is not to say that the Russian winter defeated Hitler's panzer armies, but that it neutralized an already spent and defeated force.

Nor were German tank crews prepared for winter weather in either material or psychological terms. Most crewmen wore their black panzer uniforms throughout the winter of 1941–42, since the bulk of the available winter uniforms went to the infantry and artillery, not the panzer troops. German panzer crewmen had not been led to expect a winter campaign and when the heavy snow and deep cold began, many seemed to lapse into the idea that they would be sent home to get new tanks. Some surplus crews were sent home, but the majority were pressed into service as infantry or anti-partisan troops, for which they were ill-suited. In contrast, most Soviet tank crews were well supplied with warm winter clothing. While Soviet tankers were too thinly spread to achieve decisive results in the winter of 1941–42, they did learn a great deal during the period when their opposite numbers were laid low.

Fateful Decisions and Armoured Renewal, April–May 1942

Despite successfully surviving Operation Barbarossa and Typhoon and forcing all four German panzer armies to retreat, the Winter Counter-offensive had demonstrated that the Red Army could not inflict decisive defeats upon the Wehrmacht with a motley collection of tank brigades and separate tank battalions. In order to conduct deliberate offensives that could seize deep objectives and encircle large enemy formations, the Red Army needed to resurrect corps-size armoured formations. In February 1942, the Stavka authorized the formation of twenty-five new tank corps from existing and newly-formed tank brigades. Initially, these formations were based upon two or three tank brigades with 100–150 tanks and a motorized rifle brigade with an authorized strength of 1,900 infantry, but were provided very limited artillery, engineer, reconnaissance and air defense supporting arms. Even trucks to carry fuel and ammunition for the corps were in very short supply.

The first three tanks corps were officially formed on 31 March 1942 in the Moscow Military district, with General-major Mikhail E. Katukov commanding the 1st Tank Corps (1 TC), General-major Dmitry K. Mostovenko getting the 3 TC and General-major Vasiliy A. Mishulin getting 4 TC. Katukov's corps was based upon his own veteran 1st Guards Tank Brigade, but the other two tank brigades added to his command were newly-formed units that had not yet seen combat. Ten more tank corps were formed in mid-April and six more in May. Rotmistrov, who like Katukov had earned himself a reputation for results at the front, was given command of the 7 TC. All of the officers chosen to lead the first nine tank corps in March-April 1942 had commanded a tank brigade or division in combat during the 1941 campaign and three had been wounded in action. Thus, each corps contained a kernel of combat veterans and trained tankers, but many personnel were fresh from the tank training schools.

The Stavka and GABTU decided that the tank corps would receive the best available tanks, namely the KV-1, T-34, Matilda II and T-60. Outfitting the first nine tank corps in March-April 1942 required about 1,400 tanks, including 540 T-34s and 200 KV-1s. Equipping these tank corps should have been fairly straightforward for the GABTU, since by March Soviet industry was producing over 700 T-34s and 250 KV-1s per month. Yet while the Stavka and GABTU recognized that the new tank corps were essential to spearhead upcoming offensive operations, the Red Army's infantry commanders all demanded tank support, so the decision was made to retain and even expand the number of separate tank brigades and OTBs so that each field army would have some armour support. While most of the remaining T-26 and BT light tanks and British-made Valentines were fobbed off on the infantry support units, they too would get a share of T-34s and KV-1s. However, the Red Army was still trying to do too much, too fast and the decision to develop two separate tank forces – one for mobile warfare and one for infantry support – diluted the Soviet Union's growing advantage in tank production in early 1942 and resulted in units that often had a hodgepodge of tank models. Instead of concentrating the best armour in the tank corps, the separate brigades and battalions would divert a significant number of tanks and crews to units that would have little or no operational-level impact. The impact of this mistake was to reduce the value of the Red Army's growing numerical superiority in tanks in the early campaigning in spring and summer 1942.

Even though combat experience from the 1941 campaign indicated that the T-34 had poor visibility for its buttoned-up commanders and the KV-1 had an inadequate transmission, the GKO and GABTU decided not to make any major changes to these designs since it would reduce short-term production output. Instead, both tanks received some additional armoured protection in their 1942 models and the T-34 Model 1942 would begin using a larger hexagonal-shaped turret after May 1942 in order to help improve crew performance. New tracks and road wheels began to appear during the course of 1942, but the major defects were left uncorrected until 1943–44. Indeed, Soviet tank design became rigidly conservative for more than a year, although once Germany began to field its own improved tanks the GABTU leadership recognized that the T-34 design needed to be updated. The KV-1 was more problematic and no amount of minor improvements would change the fact that it lacked the mobility to keep up with T-34 tanks. The only new Soviet tank introduced in 1942 was the 9-ton T-70 light tank armed with a 45mm cannon, which was intended to replace the T-60, which only had a 20mm cannon. The main reason for producing the T-70 was that it could be built in quantity and would help make up the deficit of T-34s, not because it added a great deal of combat effectiveness to Soviet armoured units.

On the German side, there were a number of important developments that altered the dynamic of armoured combat. Whereas the German army had concentrated virtually all its tanks in nineteen panzer divisions in the 1941 campaign, the experience of violent Soviet tank attacks against German infantry divisions – such as the 21st Tank Brigade raid against the 36.Infanterie-Division (mot.) at Kalinin in October 1941 – convinced the OKH that the motorized infantry divisions should be provided with their own Panzer-Abteilung as soon as practical. Four of the motorized infantry divisions assigned to Heeresgruppe Süd, including the Grossdeutschland Division, were provided a tank battalion. The Waffen SS also successfully lobbied for their own panzer units, since the four divisions employed during Barbarossa were constantly forced to request armoured support from the army. A total of forty StuG III assault guns had been provided to these four Waffen-SS Divisions, but these were best suited for defensive combat, not a rapid war of movement. After much discussion, the OKH finally authorized the formation of three SS-Panzer-Abteilungen on 28 January 1942; these battalions would go to the *LSSAH*, *Reich* and *Wiking* divisions in March–April. The German army leadership had resisted giving the Waffen-SS tanks because it would make them more independent – which was regarded as a dangerous development – and it meant diverting about 150 tanks from new tank production. Not to be excluded, even the Luftwaffe managed to get authorization to form one panzer company for the new Hermann Göring Brigade. Thus, going into the 1942 campaign, the panzer divisions surrendered their previous monopoly on mobile armoured operations and conceded a role to a variety of new players. Yet the result of this change was to dilute the concentration of German armoured strength that had produced victory in the past in order to placate bureaucratic interests and eventually force the existing panzer divisions into a competition for scarce resources with the Waffen-SS and other so-called elite formations.

Hitler had been eager to form new panzer divisions for future operations and he diverted new tank production in September 1941 to begin forming the 22 and 23.Panzer-Divisionen in France. It took six months to train both divisions and they began shipment to the Eastern Front in March 1942. The 24.Panzer-Division, using the disbanded 1.Kavallerie-Division as a base, began forming in November 1941 and would be sent to the Eastern Front in May. In conjunction with these three new panzer divisions being sent eastward, the OKH ordered the badly-depleted 6, 7 and 10.Panzer-Divisionen to return by rail to Germany to refit and re-equip; it was intended that these three divisions would return in time to provide a second wave of armoured reinforcements for the later stages of the 1942 campaign. By mid-February 1942, Hitler had already decided that he wanted to make the main effort of the 1942 offensive in the south, so he directed the OKH to strengthen the panzer divisions in Heeresgruppe Süd by taking armour from the panzer divisions in Heeresgruppe Nord and Mitte; each of von Kleist's panzer divisions would be provided with three panzer battalions, but this meant that a number of the panzer divisions along the rest of the Eastern Front were now reduced to just a single panzer battalion. In the short term, this decision by Hitler quickly restored the armoured forces under the control of Heeresgruppe Süd and allowed the Wehrmacht to mount a major offensive on this part of the Eastern Front in the summer of 1942, but it reduced German armoured units on the rest of the Eastern Front to a strictly defensive capability and surrendered the initiative in these areas to the Red Army's tankers. Instead of trying to rebuild the shattered panzer armies of 1941 – which had proved doctrinally and organizationally sound – Hitler opted to direct the majority of his available armoured resources into one over-sized command, designed for a single purpose: to reach the oilfields in the Caucasus. This was a very risky and dangerous approach – although it did not appear so in Berlin in February 1942 – because if it failed, the Wehrmacht would completely lose the initiative in the East.

After spending most of a year in constant dread of the T-34 and KV-1 tanks, German panzer and panzerjäger units began to receive the first new weapons intended to counter Soviet heavy tanks in February 1942 and this process accelerated during the spring. The 7.5cm HEAT rounds had arrived in limited quantities in January and problems with quality control limited production for some time, but their appearance helped to end the Soviet predilection for raids by single KV-1s. The Germans had also captured significant quantities of Soviet 76.2mm field guns in the 1941 campaign and these were rechambered in Germany and reissued as the 7.62cm Pak 36(r) in February 1942. The Pak 36(r) was the first weapon provided to the panzerjägers that could destroy a KV-1 or T-34 tank with kinetic armour-piercing rounds out to 1,000 meters or more and helped to level the playing field in 1942 until Rheinmetall could deploy the equivalent 7.5 cm Pak 40 in quantity. Since the Pak 36(r) was double the weight of the 5 cm Pak 38, the Germans began mounting a large proportion of the Pak 36(r) guns on surplus Pz.II chassis, which entered service in April as the Marder II tank destroyer.

Production of tungsten-core 5 cm anti-tank rounds for the 5 cm Pak 38 and the 5 cm guns on the Pz.III tank was also significantly expanded in early 1942, since the Panzergranate 40 – which was the only anti-tank round that had any effect on the T-34 – had only been available in token quantities during the 1941 campaign. Additionally, a new generation of anti-tank weapons that used the Gerlach 'tapered bore' principle to produce extremely high muzzle velocities began appearing in limited numbers, such as the 4.2 cm Pak 41 and the 7.5 cm Pak 41. While tungsten penetrators and tapered bore guns led to a temporary increase in German anti-tank firepower for the 1942 campaign, Germany's supplies of tungsten – mostly imported from Portugal – were too limited to re-equip all units with this improved weaponry, or even to sustain increased production for very long. Instead, the *Heereswaffenamt* put its greatest emphasis in the short term on up-gunning the Pz.III and Pz.IV tanks to long-barreled weapons in order to increase muzzle velocities. The introduction of the Pz.III J with long 5 cm Kwk 39 L/60 in December 1941 provided Germany's main medium tank with the ability to effectively engage the T-34 at ranges up to 500 meters, although the Pz.III's inferior levels of armoured protection and mobility meant that the T-34 was still a formidable opponent, if well handled. The Pz.IVF2, equipped with the long 7.5 cm KwK 40 L/43, had the potential to become Germany's 'universal tank' that could fulfill the anti-tank and infantry support roles equally effectively, but very little effort was made to expand its production during the critical winter months. In March 1942, the Pz.IVF2 began to appear in limited numbers – usually arriving in batches of just five to ten new tanks – which meant that the barely-adequate Pz.IIIJ would be the main German battle tank for much of the 1942 campaign. Concurrently, the StuG III Aus. F assault gun began appearing with the 7.5 cm StuK 40 L/43 cannon, which provided the Sturmartillerie with a real anti-tank capability – even though their primary mission remained infantry support.

While these crash programs and ad hoc expedients significantly raised German anti-tank capabilities in 1942, the long-term plan to counter the T-34 was based upon finishing the development of the new heavy tank and medium tank designs. Henschel and Porsche were each developing heavy tank prototypes, but Hitler would not select the Henschel design for production as the Pz.VI Tiger until April. Armed with the 8.8 cm KwK 36 L/56 gun and protected by up to 120mm of armour, the Tiger would provide the Wehrmacht with a large advantage in firepower and armoured protection when it began to appear in August, but its mobility remained inferior to the T-34, as well as previous German tanks. Meanwhile, Daimler-Benz and *Maschinenfabrik Augsburg-Nurnberg* (MAN) were involved in a tight competition to produce the new medium tank, which would be equipped with the new 7.5 cm KwK 42 L/70 gun under development by

Rheinmetall. Originally, the new medium tank was supposed to be 30 tons, but the division of the *Heereswaffenamt* responsible for overseeing the new medium tank – Wa Pruef 6 – raised the requirement to 36 tons. Engineers at Daimler-Benz made a careful study of captured T-34s and developed a prototype that had a similar silhouette and was powered by a Mercedes-Benz MB 507 diesel engine. In contrast, MAN made torsion bar suspension the determining characteristic of its prototype, even though this was irrelevant to the original requirement made by Guderian in November 1941. Hitler was impressed by the Daimler-Benz design, which was shown to him in April 1942, and he favored a diesel tank engine. However, due to a variety of back-room political factors, Wa Pruef 6 favored the MAN design, which was powered by a petrol engine. Hitler was told that a diesel tank engine could not yet be manufactured in large quantities and that selecting the Daimler-Benz prototype would result in unacceptable production delays, so on 14 May he selected the MAN prototype to be the next German medium tank.[18] The decision not to equip its next main battle tank with a diesel engine proved to be one of Germany's most serious mistakes in armoured combat in the Second World War. Since fuel shortages were already crippling panzer operations by late 1941, the need for greater fuel efficiency was just as important as adding bigger guns and more armour to its tanks, but the Heereswaffenamt was oblivious to the impact that continued reliance on petrol engines would have on German mechanized operations. Hitler, who had already displayed sounder judgment than some of his engineers in pressing for a long-barreled gun on the Pz.III prior to the discovery of the T-34, regarded development of a diesel tank engine as a critical requirement for the Panzerwaffe, but the Heereswaffenamt and German industry managed to ignore his priorities. While Hitler's decisions that led to German defeats are often highlighted, those where his judgement proved correct are often overlooked. After Germany's defeat, it was convenient for German military and industrial leaders to dump all blame on Hitler's head, which helped to conceal their own egregious errors of judgment.

Clearly the most notable fault – which directly impacted the ability of the Panzerwaffe to recover from the defeats of 1941 – was that German tank production remained ridiculously weak throughout the period of January–May 1942, with an average of 240 Pz.III and sixty–eighty Pz.IV built each month – a total of just 300–320 medium tanks. In addition, 36–45 StuG III assault guns were produced each month during the same period. Much of the blame for the inadequacy of German armaments production must fall on the head of *Reichsminister* Fritz Todt, the head of the *Reichsministerium für Bewaffnung und Munition*. In addition to new tanks, German industry rebuilt sixty-seven Pz.III and twenty-four Pz.IV during January–April 1942, which was not even enough to reequip a single panzer division. This half-hearted effort by German industry enabled the Soviets to seize an impressive 3–1 or better numerical advantage in tank production output, which they never lost. Thus, Todt's death in an airplane crash on 8 February 1942 and his replacement by the capable Albert Speer can only be regarded as a lucky break for the Third Reich. While Speer's impact on

German tank production was too late to influence the 1942 campaign, his efforts to improve the efficiency of the German armaments industry would enable the Panzerwaffe to survive the losses of the 1942–43 campaigns.

Tank Skirmishes in the Crimea, 1 January–20 May

Although the Soviet Winter Counter-offensive culminated in early March, one place where the fighting continued virtually non-stop from January until the summer was in the Crimea. Both sides employed no more than a few hundred tanks and assault guns in the Crimea, but given the close-quarter fighting caused by the constrictive terrain, even small amounts of armour could make contributions well beyond the tactical level. The Soviet landings at Kerch and Feodosiya forced von Manstein to break off his attack on the fortress of Sevastopol and force-march the XXX Armeekorps eastward to contain the Soviet beachheads. This was the first time in the Second World War that the Wehrmacht had to react to a major enemy amphibious landing, but it was also the first time that the Red Army had conducted one. At the start of 1942 in the Crimea, both sides were in a race, with the Soviets trying to land more forces, including armour, to affect a breakout before the Germans could erect an impenetrable barrier across the narrow neck of the Kerch peninsula. Von Manstein requested a panzer unit to help crush the Soviet beachheads but the OKH had none to spare.

Von Manstein was at his best in a set-piece battle and, although he had no armoured support, the XXX Armeekorps had Sturmgeschütz-Abteilung 190 and the Luftwaffe still had some measure of air superiority over the Crimea, so Stuka support was available. Although the Soviet 44th Army had two weeks to fortify its position in Feodosiya and had the 79th OTB with T-26 light tanks, they were not expecting von Manstein's weaker forces to counterattack. On 15 January 1942, the XXX Armeekorps suddenly attacked Feodosiya with heavy air and artillery support and within three days they had recaptured the port. It was a stinging tactical victory and von Manstein claimed that the 44th Army lost 16,700 troops and eighty-five tanks at Feodosiya.[19]

Despite von Manstein's success at Feodosiya – the only German victory in January 1942 – the Soviets managed to establish the Crimean Front under General-leytenant Dmitri T. Kozlov in the Kerch peninsula with the 44th, 47th and 51st Armies. In order to breach the German defensive line across the 13km-wide Parpach narrows, the Stavka sent Kozlov additional armour and artillery, as well as air support. Unlike other jury-rigged Red Army operations during the Winter Counter-offensive, Kozlov was provided the resources to mount a proper set-piece attack. However, the Parpach Narrows was one of the few places on the Eastern Front where the terrain enabled the Germans to establish defensive positions in accordance with their doctrinal norms; von Manstein's infantry divisions were only required to hold 4–6km-wide fronts, not 20–25km as along much of the Eastern Front. By late February, Kozlov had nearly 200 tanks in the Kerch peninsula, including thirty-six KV-1 and twenty T-34, so he mounted a probing attack on 26 February, including the use of armour against the Romanian 18th Infantry Division. However, heavy rains, marshy terrain and German minefields made it difficult for the Soviet tanks to advance and over the course of a week's indecisive combat, Kozlov lost twenty-eight of his thirty-six KV-1 tanks and seven T-34s from the 39th and 40th Tank Brigades and 229th OTB. If ever there was a place where the KV-1 could fulfill its intended function as a break-through tank, it was in the Kerch peninsula, but it failed to deliver, despite the fact that the two opposing German infantry divisions had very limited anti-tank weaponry. Nor could von Manstein use 8.8cm flak guns in the front line, since they would be spotted in the flat terrain and destroyed by Soviet artillery. Instead, the German infantry relied upon large quantities of Tellermine 35 AT mines and the Soviet tendency to use KV-1s in small groups.

Prodded by Stalin to recommence his offensive, Kozlov decided to resume his attacks on 13 March after receiving another tank brigade and an independent tank regiment. With some 225 tanks available, as well as significant artillery support, Kozlov should have been able to dent, if not break, von Manstein's front, which was held by only two German and one Romanian infantry divisions. Yet Kozlov had learned little from his first setback and he employed his armour in the same sector with exactly the same result: between 13–19 March the 39th Tank Brigade lost twenty-three of its twenty-seven tanks, the 40th Brigade lost eighteen tanks and the 56th Tank Brigade was shattered, losing eighty-eight of its ninety T-26 light tanks. Soviet tanks tried to advance over flat, open terrain and without the element of surprise, and then cross an obstacle belt that the Germans had covered with anti-tank fire. Although von Manstein's anti-tank capabilities were modest, his troops managed to knock out more than half of Kozlov's tanks in a week. The Luftwaffe also managed to intervene on occasion and the Kerch peninsula was no place for tankers without air cover, since there was no way for a tank battalion or brigade to avoid detection on the treeless steppe.

In response to earlier pleading for armoured support, the OKH finally provided von Manstein with the newly-formed 22.Panzer-Division just as Kozlov's second offensive was smashed. Von Manstein immediately decided to mount a spoiling attack with the 22.Panzer-Division, but the operation was mounted before all of the division had arrived. Despite his reputation as a strategist, von Manstein knew very little about tank tactics and he amply demonstrated this in his imprudent employment of the 22.Panzer-Division. Oberstleutnant Wilhelm Koppenburg, commander of Panzer-Regiment 204, led two of his tank battalions in the attack which began at 0600 hours on 20 March. Koppenburg attacked with 142 tanks, mostly Pz.II and Pz.38(t), but with minimal infantry and no engineer support. A thick morning fog covered the battlefield and Koppenburg's panzers advanced blindly into the mist, with visibility down to 50–100 meters. He quickly lost control of his two battalions in the fog and the I./Pz.Regt 204 blundered into an undetected minefield. Even worse, the assembly areas of the 55th Tank Brigade and 229th OTB were nearby and the Soviets quickly committed a battalion of T-26 light tanks and four KV-1s to engage the panzers. Koppenburg's battalions split apart in the fog and Soviet tanks and anti-tank guns pounded the I./Pz.Regt 204, which suffered 40 per cent losses. After four hours of mucking about in the fog, Koppenburg's battered regiment retreated to its start position, having failed in its mission. The attack of the 22.Panzer-Division at Korpetsch was one of the most badly-bungled German armoured attacks of the entire war on the Eastern Front; thirty-two of 142 tanks had been lost (nine Pz.II, seventeen Pz.38(t) and six Pz.IV) and this new division had to immediately be pulled out of the line to refit its panzer regiment. The use of panzers without air, artillery, infantry or engineer support went completely against German combined arms doctrine and the failure to properly plan or support the attack rests squarely on von Manstein's head.

Kozlov was able to replenish his own armour and mount another offensive on 9 April with 150 tanks, but this also failed to break von Manstein's front. The Jäger-Regiment 49 of 28.Leichte Infanterie-Division had received a few of the new 2.8cm sPzB 41 tapered-bore anti-tank guns, which proved to be an excellent anti-tank weapon in the Crimea. Manning one such gun, Obergefreiter Emanuel Czernik destroyed seven T-26 tanks and one BT on 9 April, at ranges from 70–600 meters.[20] After battering his forces against a solid defense for two months, Kozlov was forced to temporarily suspend his efforts to break out of the Kerch peninsula and by early May he had over 230 tanks in four brigades and three OTBs back in service. However, the delay was fatal for the Crimea Front as warm weather had returned and the Wehrmacht intended to regain the initiative.

In order to prepare for the second German summer offensive in the Soviet Union, which the OKH had named 'Blau' (Blue), Hitler wanted two preliminary operations conducted in the spring to eliminate troublesome Soviet penetrations: Kozlov's Crimean Front in the Kerch Peninsula and Timoshenko's Southwest Front in the Barvenkovo salient. These were intended to be true 'Blitz' operations, using the proven *schwerpunkt* formula of panzer-led assaults supported by Luftwaffe dive-bombers, to quickly rip holes in the Soviet frontlines and then execute enveloping operations to encircle and eliminate entire Soviet armies. In accordance with Führer Directive 41 issued on 5 April, von Manstein was directed to eliminate Kozlov's forces first, then Heeresgruppe Süd would deal with Timoshenko and then, afterwards, von Manstein would finish off operations in the Crimea by capturing the fortress of Sevastopol. However, unlike Barbarossa, the Wehrmacht no longer had the resources to conduct simultaneous major offensives, but instead would have to shuttle its resources between the Crimea and the other armies of Heeresgruppe Süd – this might work as long as the offensives stuck to schedule and encountered no unexpected problems.

Von Manstein developed an operation plan dubbed *Trappenjad* ('Bustard Hunt') to crush Kozlov's 44th, 47th and 51st Armies in a short-term, high-intensity attack. At first glance, the odds did not appear to favor a successful German attack upon the Soviet defensive line centered upon Parpach. Even by stripping all other sectors, von Manstein was only able to concentrate the 22.Panzer-Division, five German infantry divisions and two and a half Romanian divisions to attack a total of nineteen Soviet divisions and four tank brigades (230 tanks). Kozlov had his forces deployed in depth, with General-leytenant Vladimir N. L'vov's 51st Army defending a 9km-long front in the north with eight rifle divisions, three rifle brigades and two tank brigades and General-leytenant Stepan I. Cherniak's 44th Army defending the southern sector of the front along the Black Sea with five rifle divisions and two tank brigades. In reserve, Kozlov had two rifle divisions and one cavalry division from General-major Konstantin S. Kolganov's 47th Army. Under pressure from Stalin to mount another break-out attempt soon, Kozlov intended to launch another offensive in the north and had massed the bulk of his forces to support this plan. Kozlov did not expect a major German attack given that his forces outnumbered the enemy by more than 2–1 and the marshy terrain along the Black Sea coast appeared unfavorable for offensive operations. Furthermore, the VVS-Crimean Front had controlled the skies over the eastern Crimea for months and Kozlov assumed that Soviet air superiority would deter a German offensive.

However, Soviet intelligence failed to detect the deployment of Generaloberst von Richthofen's Fliegerkorps VIII to airfields in the Crimea in early May. This elite formation had over 600 aircraft, including *Schlachtgeschwader* 1 (SchG 1) equipped with forty-three of the new Hs 129 B-1 ground attack planes; this air-craft was armed with two 20mm and one 30mm cannon. Von Manstein deliber-ately chose to place his *schwerpunkt* in the worst terrain – the southern sector held by Cherniak's 44th Army. He planned to use the three infantry divisions of Generalleutnant Fretter-Pico's XXX Armeekorps in the first echelon to breach the Soviet lines, then push the 22.Panzer-Division into the breach to exploit. Clearly von Manstein had learned from the debacle with 22.Panzer-Division in March and this time he intended to hold his armour back until Fretter-Pico's infantry created a penetration corridor through the enemy's defenses. Von Manstein skillfully provided Fretter-Pico with the tools to unlock Cherniak's defense: a total of fifty-seven StuG III assault guns from the 190, 197 and 249.Sturmgeschütz-Abteilungen, two batteries of 8.8cm flak guns and assault boats from the 902.Sturmboote Kommando to mount an amphibious landing behind Soviet lines. *Trappenjad* is an interesting use of German armour in two separate capacities – assault guns for infantry support and breakthrough, tanks for exploitation. While the German 46.Infanterie-Division and the Romanian 7th Mountain Corps fixed the strong Soviet right wing with a series of feints, von Manstein intended to smash in the weaker left wing and then pivot north with 22.Panzer-Division to trap the main Soviet forces against the Sea of Azov. Only through careful security could the 11.Armee conceal the fact that more than half of its combat forces were massed against the southernmost point of the Soviet line and that the rest of the front was only lightly held.

Operation *Trappenjad* began at 0315 hours on 8 May, with a ten-minute artillery barrage against the forward echelon of the Soviet 44th Army. Precision Stuka attacks assisted the German infantry in piercing Cherniak's first two lines of defense in just three and a half hours and reaching an 11-meter-wide anti-tank ditch that marked the boundary of the 44th Army's final line of defense. Not only had the Soviets mined the approaches to this anti-tank ditch, but they had also emplaced steel girders in it to stop tanks, although they made the amateurish error that the most formidable obstacle is of little value if not covered by fire. German infantry crossed the ditch and accompanying pioneers began to clear the obstacles. At a cost of just 388 casualties, the XXX Armeekorps ripped open the left flank of the Crimean Front. Belatedly, the 44th Army committed its 56th Tank Brigade and 126th OTB with ninety-eight tanks, including seven KV-1, to attack the 28.Jäger-Division near the breach site. However, the tanks were caught in the open by the Stukas of StG 77 and the Hs 129 Bs of SchG 1 and blasted to pieces in a hail of bombs and cannon fire; forty-eight tanks were knocked out, including all seven KV-1.

By the time that Kozlov realized how badly the 44th Army's front had been breached, German pioneers had almost completed filling in the anti-tank ditch clearing the way for 22.Panzer-Division. Kampfgruppe Groddeck, comprised of Panzer-Aufklärungs-Abteilung 22, a Panzerjäger-Abteilung, an assault-gun battery and some motorized infantry, moved out first, exploiting eastward toward Kerch. Cherniak committed the rest of his armour to local counterattacks against the German breach, which cost him twenty-six more light tanks. After midday on 9 May, the lead elements of 22.Panzer-Division began crossing the anti-tank ditch and moved northward, but a sudden heavy rain storm brought the attack to an abrupt halt by depriving the *schwerpunkt* of its air support. Despite the death of the commander of the Soviet 51st Army in a German air strike, Kozlov managed to shift the 40th Tank Brigade and 229th OTB into the path of the German panzer division, with fifty-three tanks including twenty-one KV-1. Yet when the rain stopped the next morning, the Luftwaffe easily spotted the Soviet heavy tanks and pulverized them – eleven KV-1 were knocked out and others immobilized. With the Soviet armour knocked about, the 22.Panzer-Division resumed its advance and quickly reached the Sea of Azov, cutting off the entire 51st Army. Kozlov's last armour – the 55th Tank Brigade – mounted a futile, unsupported effort to stop 22.Panzer-Division on 10 May, but lost twenty-six of forty-six tanks, including all ten KV-1. After that, the Crimean Front began to disintegrate, with many troops surrendering and others fleeing to Kerch in hope of evacuation.

By 20 May, von Manstein's forces had occupied Kerch and eliminated Kozlov's Crimean Front in less than two weeks. At a cost of just 3,397 German casualties, three Soviet armies had been smashed and 175,000 troops lost. The Red Army lost four tank brigades and three OTBs with 238 tanks, including forty-one KV-1, against only eight tanks (one Pz.II, four Pz.III, three Pz.38(t)) from 22.Panzer-Division and three assault guns. Indeed, the Germans even managed to recover six of their tanks that had been lost in March and pressed into Soviet service. Operation *Trappenjad* was an exquisitely-executed set-piece offensive, with near-perfect use of a combined-arms *schwerpunkt* to quickly achieve decisive results. Although von Manstein had to return the 22.Panzer-Division and some of the Luftwaffe units to Heeresgruppe Süd for operations around Kharkov, he could now turn confidently to reduce fortress Sevastopol with no threat of other Soviet forces at his back.

Decision at Kharkov, 12–28 May 1942
Generalfeldmarschall Fedor von Bock, who took over Heeresgruppe Süd in January 1942, had intended since February to mount a pincer attack utilizing the AOK 6 and some of von Kleist's 1.Panzerarmee to cut off Timoshenko's armies in the Barvenkovo salient, but had lacked the armour, air support or supplies to mount an enveloping operation. However, the OKH dispatched two panzer divisions and three infantry divisions to Heeresgruppe Süd in March, which restored some measure of its combat capabilities. By April, when Führer Directive 41 specified that the Barvenkovo salient had to be eliminated prior to the beginning of Operation *Blau* in June, von Bock's staff developed operational plan *Fridericus*, which expected to use these forces to cut off the 75km-wide neck of the salient. According to the original plan, General der Panzertruppen Friedrich Paulus' AOK 6 would launch the main attack from the north, while von Kleist provided Gruppe Mackensen, with the 14.Panzer-Division and 60.Infanterie-Division (mot.), to launch a supporting attack against the south side of the salient. Paulus was given the 3 and 23.Panzer-Division, which he kept in reserve near Kharkov. However, German logistics remained problematic even as warmer spring weather appeared, with Mackensen's divisions having only 0.2 V.S. of fuel on 25 April. Von Bock allowed the date for *Fridericus* to slide into May and decided to allow von Manstein to conduct *Trappenjad* first, since AOK 11's supply requirements were significantly less than the amount required for *Fridericus*. Once von Manstein crushed Kozlov's Front, Paulus and Kleist would execute *Fridericus*.

Unknown to von Bock, Timoshenko was planning his own offensive near Kharkov. Although Stalin and the Stavka expected the Germans to mount their next summer offensive against Moscow, they wanted to use the Red Army's new tank units to mount offensives in other sectors to keep the Germans off balance and divert reserves from Heeresgruppe Mitte. Since Timoshenko had achieved one of the best successes in the winter counter-offensive, Stalin favoured his proposal to mount a large-scale double envelopment to encircle and destroy Paulus' AOK 6 at Kharkov. However, Stalin was upset when Timoshenko requested 1,200 more tanks to conduct the operation, which indicates that Soviet armoured resources were still finite. Instead, Timoshenko was provided with 923 tanks, only 34 per cent of which were modern main battle tanks (eighty KV-1 and 239 T-34). Over 21 per cent of Timoshenko's armour was composed of British-made Matilda II and Valentine tanks. Not only was one-third of Timoshenko's armour comprised of T-60 light tanks of modest combat value, but he was forced to employ even obsolescent BT-2 and BT-5 light tanks in some tank brigades. Indeed, only six of Timoshenko's nineteen tank brigades were equipped according to the 10 March 1942 standard (ten KV-1, twenty T-34, twenty T-60).[21] This is very interesting because it indicates that a high-priority Red Army offensive was provided only one-third of one month's current production of KV-1 and T-34 tanks and had to make do with odds and ends, which begs the question – why didn't the Stavka provide Timoshenko with better armoured resources? The logical explanation is that the Red Army was not receiving as many tanks as Soviet industry claimed to be producing at the time. Despite a purported 3–1 Soviet advantage in output of medium/heavy tanks over German output in spring 1942, Timoshenko only had a 2–1 numerical advantage on the battlefield at Kharkov and the German panzer units had a much higher proportion of medium tanks than the opposing Soviet tank brigades. Furthermore, the Germans were able to field 112 Pz.IIIJ and seventeen Pz.IVF2 at Kharkov, which for the first time provided panzer divisions with some ability to stand up to the T-34.

Timoshenko intended to conduct the northern pincer of his offensive with the 21st, 28th and 38th Armies from the Staryi Saltov bridgehead east of Kharkov and the southern pincer with the 6th Army in the Barvenkovo salient. After breaking through the German front lines, the 6th Army would commit a mobile group comprised of the new 21st and 23rd Tank Corps to envelop AOK 6 from the south, while the northern group committed the 3rd Guards Cavalry Corps to envelop Kharkov from the other flank; Timoshenko expected the Soviet pincers to link up within four to five days of the beginning of the offensive. The Stavka hoped that Timoshenko's Kharkov operation would be the Red Army's first deliberate offensive of the Russo-German War, but Stalin was unwilling to commit the resources or time to realize this goal.

Superficially, Timoshenko tried to conduct an offensive that looked like the kind of Deep Battle operation envisioned in PU-36. However, his designated main effort – the 6th Army – was provided only 2.7 loads of fuel for its tanks, instead of the 7–8 loads that Stavka planners indicated were necessary. The amount of fuel and ammunition stockpiled in the Southwest Front was also inadequate to support a full-scale offensive for more than a few days.[22] Coordination between the four Soviet armies involved in the offensive was minimal, with no overall commander appointed over the three northern armies. Yet the most egregious error in planning the Kharkov operation was the faulty intelligence provided on German dispositions and intentions. Timoshenko was completely unaware of the presence of some of the German reinforcements and he airily dismissed the presence of Paulus' armoured reserve – the 3 and 23.Panzer-Divisionen – as irrelevant, since he claimed that the Soviet pincers would close around AOK 6 before Paulus had a chance to commit his armour to a counterattack. In essence, Timoshenko's offensive was planned on a logistical shoestring, with inadequate C2 and knowledge of the enemy, and simply assumed a static, immobile opponent.

Timoshenko did gain a certain amount of tactical and operational-level surprise when his forces attacked AOK 6 at 0630 hours on 12 May. It was a clear, sunny day with temperatures reaching 22° C (71° F). Both assault formations began the offensive in style, with powerful sixty-minute artillery preparations along large portions of Paulus' front line, followed by air strikes that struck German artillery positions further back. At 0730 hours, the attacking Soviet armies committed shock groups, each formed around a rifle division and a tank brigade with forty to forty-five tanks. All told, 300 tanks were committed in the north and 124 in the south, and front-line German infantrymen were shocked by the appearance of so many tanks. Initially, Soviet armour was used strictly in an infantry support role to help their own infantry reduce the German defences, which were based upon battalion-size *Stützpunkten* (strongpoints). The 28th and 38th Armies achieved considerable success when two of their shock groups, spearheaded by the 36th and 90th Tank Brigades, routed two kampfgruppen of the 294.Infanterie-Division and captured the town of Nepokrytaya. In this sector, the German infantry had only three 5cm Pak 38 guns to oppose more than ninety Soviet tanks; the KV-1 and Matilda II tanks quickly overwhelmed the few panzerjägers, which incited a rare 'tank panic' among the German infantrymen.[23] German artillerymen put up a stiff fight in the streets of Nepokrytaya with their 10.5cm l.FH18 howitzers firing over open sights and managing to knock out twelve Matilda II tanks, but lost two complete artillery batteries in the process. In the south, the 6th Army massed four rifle divisions and three tank brigades against two German infantry divisions, yet only managed to advance 6–8km on the first day; the flanks of both the 62.Infanterie-Division and the 454.Sicherungs-Division were pushed in, but neither division was crushed by the weight of Soviet firepower. While Paulus' infantry was severely stressed on the first day of Timoshenko's offensive – sometimes showing signs of panic – they avoided destruction by either trading space for time or entrenching themselves in fortified positions like Ternovaya.

Timoshenko's assessment that the Germans would not commit their armoured reserve in time proved wrong on the first day, when von Bock directed Paulus to move both the 3 and 23.Panzer-Divisionen up to the front to support the hard-pressed XVII Armeekorps. Neither division was prepared to launch an immediate counterstroke and von Bock instructed Paulus – who was a novice commander by German standards – to avoid committing them until he could ensure a coordinated effort with Luftwaffe support. Consequently, the shock groups of the 28th and 38th Armies crushed the remainder of the 294.Infanterie-Division on the morning of 13 May and captured Peremoga, just 18km west of Kharkov. It thus came as quite a shock when, at 1230 hours, Kampfgruppe Schmitt-Ott from 3.Panzer-Division (III/Panzer-Regiment 6 and I/Schützen Regiment 3) and the 23.Panzer-Division struck the two lead rifle divisions of the 38th Army near the Babka river. The German armour caught both Soviet rifle divisions in the open and routed them; some Soviet artillery batteries engaged the German tanks but were quickly overrun. Amazingly, only three German tanks were destroyed and nineteen disabled out of 262 committed to the counterattack. The Soviet 38th Army commander foolishly decided to combine his three tank brigades involved in infantry support into the 22nd Tank Corps to provide a counter-weight to the German armour, but the formation of this ad hoc command deprived the 38th Army's rifle units of tank support at a critical moment. Furthermore, the 22nd Tank Corps had just twenty-two T-34s and no KV-1s, the rest being light tanks and British tanks. Timoshenko reacted to the German armoured counterattack by diverting the 6th Guards Tank Brigade of 28th Army – which was still advancing – to reinforce the faltering 38th Army, thereby further weakening the northern pincer. Timoshenko also became fixated on eliminat-ing the encircled German Kampfgruppe Grüner in Stützpunkt Ternovaya and committed significant resources toward this task – a mistake the Germans would later commit themselves at Bastogne in 1944.

By the third day of the Soviet offensive, the two German panzer divisions had battered the 38th Army into a combat-ineffective state and defeated the poorly-handled 22nd Tank Corps. Overhead, Luftwaffe fighters gained air superiority and deprived the Soviet shock groups of close air support. Nevertheless, the 28th Army continued to slowly advance toward Kharkov with four rifle divisions and two tank brigades, even though its flanks were increasingly exposed. In the south, the 6th Army continued to push back the 62.Infanterie-Division, but was surprised when it bumped into the 113.Infanterie-Division and Sturmgeschütz-Abteilung 244 deployed further back. A close-quarter armoured action in the town of Efremovka on 14 May resulted in nine StuG IIIs lost against twelve Matilda II tanks knocked out.[24] The German VIII Armeekorps gradually fell back under intense pressure, but the Soviet 6th Army conducted a relatively unimaginative set-piece battle and failed to use its armour to adequately pursue retreating German units. The only clean breakthrough was made on the left flank of the 6th Army – which Timoshenko regarded as a secondary sector – where the 6th Cavalry Corps was ordered to advance toward Krasnograd. Despite the fact that he had the 269 tanks of the 21st and 23rd Tank Corps ready for the exploitation mission, Timoshenko wanted to keep them in reserve until 6th Army had achieved a clean breakthrough on the direct route to Kharkov. Timoshenko's rigid adherence to the original plan, rather than taking advantage of changed circumstances, stood in stark contrast to the flexible, opportunistic style of most senior German commanders. It was not until 16 May that Timoshenko finally decided to commit the 21st and 23rd Tank Corps to battle, by which point the repeated counterattacks of the 3 and 23.Panzer-Divisionen had completely halted the northern assault armies. Both Soviet assault groups had suffered significant losses and were running low on ammunition, without having really broken the German defences.

In the north, the 3 and 23.Panzer-Division mounted an attack on 17 May to relieve the encircled Kampfgruppe Grüner in Ternovaya. The 28th Army committed its last reserve, the 6th Guards Tank Brigade, to stop the German relief effort. A major tank battle involving about 100 tanks on each side occurred south-west of Ternovaya. The Germans lost thirteen tanks in the actions, including some of the new Pz.IIIJs, but they brought up a battery of 8.8cm flak guns which inflicted heavy losses on the Soviet tanks. Afterwards, Kampfgruppe Schmidt-Ott from 3.Panzer-Division and Kampfgruppe Soltmann from 23.Panzer-Division pushed on and relieved Grüner's encircled command. By this point in the battle, Luftwaffe air superiority was making life very difficult for Soviet tank units and the Soviet offensive in the north was reduced to uncoordinated local actions. On 20 May, the two German panzer divisions mounted another counterattack which smashed in the front of the 28th Army and brought the northern phase of Timoshenko's offensive to an abrupt end.

As the battle developed, von Bock had merely traded space for time in sectors where the AOK 6 infantry was hard-pressed, while repositioning part of von

Kleist's 1.Panzerarmee – Mackensen's III Armeekorps (mot.) and the XXXXIV Armeekorps (mot.) on the southern side of the Barvenkovo salient to execute *Fridericus*. Undetected by Soviet intelligence, von Kleist's forces moved into position opposite General-major Fedor M. Kharitonov's 9th Army, which had six rifle divisions, two tank brigades and two anti-tank regiments deployed along an extended front. Unlike the German offensives of 1941, only three of the eleven divisions von Kleist deployed for the offensive were motorized and he was obliged to attack with just a single panzer division on each attack axis. At 0500 hours on 17 May, von Kleist attacked, first with a large artillery preparation, then Stuka attacks, then two *schwerpunkten*, one led by 14.Panzer-Division and the other by 16.Panzer-Division. Despite the presence of two anti-tank regiments, Kharitonov's front-line rifle divisions were unable to stop the on-rushing German armour, were decimated and then encircled in the opening hours of von Kleist's attack. When Kharitonov's command post was bombed by the Luftwaffe, his communications were disrupted and he lost all command over his forces. Two understrength Soviet tank brigades tried to stop von Kleist from achieving a breakthrough, but at the decisive point near Barvenkovo – the *schwerpunkt* – the Red armour was outnumbered 5–1 and easily defeated. On the first day, von Kleist's panzers caused the collapse of 9th Army at a cost of just eight tanks.[25] The back door of the Barvenkovo salient was now open, with German armour pouring in.

Timoshenko was oblivious to the German counter-offensive, partly due to the evasiveness of Kharitonov in reporting the scale of the disaster suffered by his army. Instead, Timoshenko was focused on 6th Army, finally achieving some measure of success with the commitment of the 21st and 23rd Tank Corps, which pushed back both flanks of the German 113.Infanterie-Division and threatened to collapse the defense of the VIII Armeekorps. General-major Grigoriy I. Kuzmin's 21st Tank Corps was able to overrun some German infantry positions but then ran into hardened resistance in the village of Ryabukhyne, where three StuG III assault guns and an 8.8cm flak battery knocked out thirty-four Soviet tanks. General-major Efim G. Pushkin's 23rd Tank Corps had a bit more success, advancing 15km at the cost of just nine tanks, but a fresh German division – the 305.Infanterie-Division – arrived in time to prevent a complete breakthrough. Although German veterans often claimed that fresh Soviet units always seemed to appear just as their panzers were on the verge of victory, at Kharkov the boot was on the other foot. By late on 17 May, Timoshenko was aware that 9th Army was in serious trouble and, based upon recommendations from the Stavka, he decided to send Pushkin's 23rd Tank Corps back to support Kharitonov's forces. The diversion of his breakthrough force to deal with von Kleist took the wind out of 6th Army's offensive and was typical of the kind of mistakes in battle command that degraded the performance of the Red Army's armour in 1941–42.

Paulus was equally nervous about the possible collapse of his VIII Armeekorps under the hammer-blows of Soviet armour and diverted Kampfgruppe von Heydebreck (I/Pz.Regt 201) from 23.Panzer-Division and several more 8.8cm flak batteries to reinforce the faltering German infantry units. The first six of the long-awaited 7.5cm Pak40 reached the 113.Infanterie-Division, providing a counter to the KV-1 and T-34 tanks.[26]

Von Kleist completed the destruction of Kharitonov's 9th Army on 18 May, with 14 and 16.Panzer-Divisionen slicing through Soviet infantry and cavalry units. Only thirty-one hours after *Fridericus* began, the lead German armour reached the Donets and captured the southern part of Izyum. A huge bulge had been pushed into the southern side of the Barvenkovo salient and there was less than 30km separating von Kleist's spearheads from Paulus' own assault group assembling near Balakleya on the north side of the salient. The Soviet 57th Army managed to refuse its left flank to prevent von Kleist from completely rolling up the Soviet rear areas, but Timoshenko now had to divert both tank corps and most of the 6th Army reserves to try and contain the German breakthrough. Incredibly, Timoshenko ordered the 6th Army to continue its offensive, as if the threat posed by von Kleist's armour was a mere nuisance. Once the Soviet tank corps withdrew, Kampfgruppe von Heydebreck delivered a swift counterattack near Borki that caught a great deal of Soviet infantry and artillery in the open; the 6th Army offensive was halted.

With Soviet resistance disintegrating in front of him, von Kleist was able to leisurely resupply his panzers on 19 May and assemble 14 and 16.Panzer-Divisionen and 60.Infanterie-Division (mot.) into a powerful armoured fist, while his infantry divisions mopped up the 9th Army remnants. Timoshenko finally called off his own offensive on 19 May but, rather than massing his still con-siderable armoured forces to prevent von Kleist from sealing off the Barvenkovo salient, he committed the two tanks corps to a static defense near the village of Grushevakha, while clumsily trying to use the 57th Army's rifle and cavalry to try and isolate von Kleist's panzers. Von Kleist easily spotted the threat to his left flank and deftly transferred Hube's 16.Panzer-Division to mount a sudden attack on the morning of 20 May that demolished the 2nd Cavalry Corps and pushed the 57th Army back 30km. Von Kleist then returned Hube's division to his spearhead and resumed the advance northward to cut off the Barvenkovo salient. Mackensen's III Armeekorps (mot.) encountered stiff resistance near Mar'evka on 21 May, where a tank melee developed between Pushkin's 23rd Tank Corps and Hube's 16.Panzer-Division. This was one of the few large tank-vs.-tank actions of the Second Battle of Kharkov and Hube lost twenty-one tanks, but managed to capture the town and force the Soviet tankers to retreat. The Luftwaffe was out in full force and the Stukas ruthlessly pounded any concentration of Soviet armour, which forced many battalions to disperse in order to survive, but this made it easier for massed German armour to defeat them in detail. Soviet logistics in the Barvenkovo salient were also failing as von Kleist's panzers overran one Donets bridge after another. The only problem for von Bock was Paulus' dithering in moving the 3 and 23.Panzer-Division to link up with von Kleist; *Fridericus* was supposed to be a double pincer operation, but it ended up being a single envelopment until all but the end. It was not until 22 May that Paulus committed his panzers to *Fridericus*, but they rapidly tore through the Soviet infantry left holding the northern side of the salient and linked up with von Kleist's armour on 23 May, trapping the Soviet 6th and 57th Armies in the Barvenkovo *kessel*.

By May 1942 the Germans had considerable experiencing in dealing with encircled Soviet forces and von Kleist quickly brought up infantry divisions to seal off the trapped forces in the *kessel*, while his panzers were relocated to deal with the inevitable Soviet relief and breakout efforts. Timoshenko scraped together some reserve units to make an attempt to pierce the German ring, including the 114th Tank Brigade, which had American-made M-3 Stuart light tanks and M-3 Lee medium tanks. Mackensen's panzers easily turned back these puny relief efforts, while the German infantry decimated repeated Soviet efforts to break out of the *kessel*. Von Bock instructed von Kleist and Paulus to rely upon artillery and the Luftwaffe to crush the trapped forces, which they did with great relish between 24–28 May. The commanders of both the 6th and 57th Armies were killed, as well as Kuzmin, commander of the 23rd Tank Corps. Pushkin was able to escape with one brigade before the *kessel* was closed, but the rest of his corps was lost. According to the Soviets, 22,000 troops and six T-34s managed to escape the *kessel* before it was crushed, but the truth was that the Southwest Front had suffered a catastrophic defeat. Timoshenko's forces suffered 277,190 casualties or 36 per cent of the troops committed. Of the 1,200 tanks committed during the course of the battle, 775 had been lost. Kuzmin's 21st Tank Corps was annihilated – the first of the new breed to suffer that fate – and Pushkin's 23rd Tank Corps was crippled.

An interesting demonstration of the inability of Soviet armour to break through a solid German infantry defense at this time was provided by the 62.Infanterie-Division, which had been directly in the path of the Soviet 6th Army assault. During the battle from 12–24 May, the 62.Infanterie-Division suffered a total of 3,121 casualties out of 17,900 troops, including 591 dead and 1,084 missing. However, during the same period, the division claimed 162 enemy tanks knocked out and gave a detailed breakdown of how it accomplished this feat, which indicated that most Soviet tanks fell victim to either 5cm Pak 38 or 8.8cm flak guns.[27] The use of field artillery in the direct fire role against tanks occurred often during the Battle of Kharkov, but yielded a very poor 1–1 exchange ratio.

Sample Soviet Tank Losses by Cause, May 1942

Soviet tanks knocked out	Method	German losses in these actions	Exchange Ratio
61	5-cm Pak 38	25 5-cm Pak	2.4–1
60	8.8-cm Flak	10 8.8-cm Flak	6–1
17	10.5-cm l.FH18	17 l.FH18	1–1
11	Sturmgeschütz III	3 StuG III	3.6–1
6	3.7-cm Pak		
4	Tellerminen	N/A	N/A

In contrast, the Axis forces suffered 30,000 casualties during the Second Battle of Kharkov and no major units were destroyed. German infantry was becoming less helpless against Soviet armour in 1942 than it was in the previous year. Although new anti-tank weaponry only played a minor role in the final stages of the battle, the increased production of PzGr 40 anti-tank rounds greatly improved the battlefield lethality of both the 5cm Pak 38 and the 5cm guns on Pz.III; whereas these tungsten-core rounds had been in very short supply in 1941, they now comprised 17–18 per cent of the available 5cm ammunition.[28] Out of the 421 tanks committed in the four panzer divisions, 108 were lost, but this was equivalent to only one-third of monthly production and could still be replaced. Von Kleist's forces suffered the bulk of German armoured losses, since they were on the offensive. Generalmajor Hermann Breith's 3.Panzer-Division knocked out sixty-two enemy tanks, including five KV-1 and thirty-six T-34, at a cost of ten of its own panzers (seven Pz.III, three Pz.IV), while Generalmajor Hans Freiherr von Boineburg-Lengsfeld's 23.Panzer-Division knocked out 260 Soviet tanks, including fifteen KV-1 and 116 T-34, for the loss of just thirteen of its own tanks.[29,30] Additional German tanks were damaged in combat, but since they kept the battlefield, they could recover and repair them. In tactical tank-vs.-tank combat, the Germans demonstrated that they could inflict a 6–1 or better casualty ratio on Soviet armour, but the odds were more even when Soviet armour was on the defense. In strategic terms, the elimination of the Barvenkovo salient greatly shortened the German front line, thereby providing Heeresgruppe Süd with the necessary reserves to mount Operation *Blau*.

The German operational handling of their armour during the Second Battle of Kharkov was superb, and in many respects the panzer divisions were at the apogee of their capabilities. In each case, the armour-air support team had formed a successful *schwerpunkt* that broke through Soviet rifle units with relative ease. Soviet tank units were still difficult to deal with, when equipped with either KV-1 or T-34 in large numbers, but the performance of the improved German Pz.III and Pz.IV tanks and PzGr 40 ammunition indicated that the gap was closing. Another more ominous result of the battle was that von Bock and the OKH came to believe that Romanian forces could hold front-line defensive sectors if properly supported – which would lead to problems soon enough. In fact, no significant Soviet tank units were deployed against the four Romanian infantry divisions involved in the battle, so they had not really been tested. For the Stavka, Kharkov was a painful lesson about the necessity of proper intelligence and logistic preparation in order for offensives to succeed, as well as including likely German responses into planning.

Clearing up Loose Ends, 2 June–4 July

Once Timoshenko's Southwest Front was crippled by its losses in the Second Battle of Kharkov, von Bock directed his subordinate armies to clear up loose ends before Operation *Blau* began on 28 June. Von Manstein's 11.Armee began Operation *Störfang* (Sturgeon Haul) against fortress Sevastopol from 2 June, using an unprecedented amount of artillery and air support to smash the Coastal

Army's multi-layered defenses, before beginning his ground assault on 7 June. Von Manstein, who had developed the concept of the assault gun before the war, massed three Sturmgeschütz-Abteilungen with sixty-five StuG IIIs to support his infantry, but he spent two weeks battering his way through the first two Soviet lines of defense. In order to assist in reducing concrete bunkers, von Manstein also received Hauptmann Weicke's Panzer-Abteilung (FL) 300, which used radio-controlled B IV and Goliath-tracked explosive carriers to attack Soviet fortifications. Nevertheless, the reduction of Sevastopol took longer than expected and most of the Luftwaffe air support was needed elsewhere before von Manstein's assault had reached a decisive point. For their part, the Soviet Coastal Army had the 81st and 125th OTBs, with a total of one T-34 and thirty-seven T-26 tanks, which were used to support local counterattacks. Von Manstein's use of assault guns and radio-controlled tanks at Sevastopol helped to shape German thinking about how armour could be used in city-fighting, which had not occurred much in 1941.

On 10 June, Paulus' AOK 6 kicked off Operation *Wilhelm*, using four infantry divisions from VIII Armeekorps and von Mackensen's III Armeekorps (mot.) to conduct a double envelopment against the Soviet 28th Army in the Staryi Saltov bridgehead. Mackensen's armour, with 14 and 16.Panzer-Divisionen, struck at the boundary of the Soviet 28th and 38th Armies and rapidly overran a single rifle division. After resisting for a day, the 28th Army began to withdraw eastward as its flanks gave way – the Red Army had learned something from previous battles like Vyazma-Bryansk – and it used its four tank brigades to conduct self-sacrificial local counterattacks to prevent the German pincers from closing too fast. Yet within five days, the German pincers did close, trapping 24,800 Soviet troops, but two-thirds of the 28th Army escaped. Mackensen's corps accounted for more than half the prisoners and knocked out or captured 264 tanks, at a cost of 4,334 casualties.[31] Timoshenko's center was so denuded of armour after this defeat that he was obliged to transfer the 13th Tank Corps and request more armour from the RVGK. Stalin agreed to transfer the 4th and 16th Tank Corps from Bryansk Front to reinforce Timoshenko's Southwest Front, but dressed him down for losing so much armour so quickly.

A week after Operation *Wilhelm* defeated the 28th Army, von Kleist's 1.Panzerarmee launched Operation *Fridericus II* against the 9th and 38th Armies. Once again, the III Armeekorps (mot) – temporarily commanded by Geyr von Schweppenburg – formed the *schwerpunkt* which sliced through the enemy's infantry, resulting in the Battle of Kupyansk. Hube's 16.Panzer-Division bumped into determined resistance from the 9th Guards Rifle Division, supported by the 6th Guards Tank Brigade and three anti-tank brigades, which temporarily halted the panzers on 24–25 June. Hube lost four tanks to enemy mines but, once again, the Soviet forces chose to retreat rather than stand and die. By the time that *Fridericus II* concluded, the 38th Army had been badly hurt, with more than 22,000 of its troops captured and another 100 tanks sacrificed. Altogether, *Wilhelm* and *Fridericus II* further reduced the Southwest Front's ability to stop a major German offensive by severely depleting its armour and artillery.

In the Crimea, von Manstein did not achieve his big breakthrough until 29 June, when he penetrated the final defensive lines at Sevastopol. The Soviets managed to evacuate some troops by sea, but the last resistance was crushed on 4 July. The fall of Sevastopol cost the Soviets 113,000 troops, but victory did not come cheaply to von Manstein's forces, which suffered 27,000 German and 8,454 Romanian casualties.[32] Armoured units only played a supporting role at Sevastopol, but the Germans would not have been able to breach the Soviet defensive lines at an affordable cost without the assault-gun battalions. It has been implied by some historians that since the Soviet Union had greater material resources and industrial output, that somehow the losses of the Red Army did not really matter because they were replaceable, but Axis losses were less likely to be replaced *in toto*. In essence, the argument that the Red Army was best suited to win a battle of attrition tries to depict German victories as essentially empty triumphs. Yet Soviet losses did matter, and when they occurred on a grand, sudden scale as in 1941–42, they often provided the essential conditions for subsequent German operational-level success. Between10 May and 4 July, a period of just eight weeks, Heeresgruppe Süd managed to encircle and destroy major parts of nine Soviet armies in the Crimea and eastern Ukraine, inflicting over 612,000 casualties and the loss of 1,400 tanks. Von Bock's subordinate armies accomplished these victories at a cost of 67,000 German casualties and 140 tanks and assault guns, yielding an exchange ratio of 9–1 in personnel and 10–1 in armour. The lop-sided nature of these losses handed the strategic initiative back to the Wehrmacht and set the stage for Operation *Blau*, as Hitler had intended.

With the summer weather at hand, the German logistic situation improved considerably and the OKH directed most of the available new weapons, fuel and ammunition toward von Bock's Heeresgruppe Süd. The quartermasters of Heeresgruppe Süd established a large fuel depot in Stalino, with subsidiary depots close behind the German frontline.[33] From 7–19 June, Heeresgruppe Süd received a significant quantity of new anti-tank weaponry, including forty-eight Marder II and twelve Marder III tank destroyers with the Soviet-built 7.62cm Pak gun, ninety of the new 7.5cm Pak 40 (with only twenty rounds of ammunition per gun), 160 7.5-cm Pak 97/38 (with only thirty-five rounds of HEAT per gun) and 144 4.2cm Pak 41. German armoured strength was replenished in part as over 400 Pz.IIIJ and 100 more Pz.IVF2 arrived by rail from Germany and many previously damaged tanks were repaired. On 21 June, all the Armeekorps (mot.) headquarters were redesignated as 'panzerkorps'.

For the coming Operation *Blau*, Heeresgruppe Süd formed two main armoured strike groups: comprising the III and XIV Panzerkorps under von Kleist's 1.Panzerarmee and the XXIV and XXXXVIII Panzerkorps under Generaloberst Hermann Hoth's 4.Panzerarmee. However, Stumme's XXXX Panzerkorps was attached to Paulus' AOK 6 and Kirchner's LVII Panzerkorps was kept under von Bock's direct control as a reserve. Altogether, Heeresgruppe Süd managed to assemble nine panzer and six motorized infantry divisions, with a total of 1,582 tanks for Operation *Blau*. Von Bock was provided thirty-two of forty-six

Distribution of German Armour on the Eastern Front, June 1942			
	Heeresgruppe Nord	*Heeresgruppe Mitte*	*Heeresgruppe Süd*	*Total*
Panzer-Divisionen	2	8	9	19
Infanterie-Division (mot.)	3	4	6	13
Panzer-Abteilung	5	9	32	46
Sturmgeschütz Abteilung	3	5	13	21
Tanks	150	544	1,582	2,276

Panzer-Abteilungen and thirteen of twenty-one Sturmgeschütz-Abteilungen, or roughly 70 per cent of the available German armour on the Eastern Front for *Blau*, including virtually all the available new-model Pz.III and Pz.IV tanks. The rest of the German armies in the Soviet Union were left with minimal armour support – just 200–220 tanks and assault guns in Heeresgruppe Nord and 650 tanks and assault guns in Heeresgruppe Mitte. Unlike 1941, the Wehrmacht lacked the resources to mount offensives on more than one sector of the Eastern Front and was forced onto the permanent defensive along two-thirds of the front. The restoration of the German armoured force on the Eastern Front to a force with more than 2,200 tanks and 400 assault guns by 1 July was something of a mini-miracle, but committing the bulk of this force to a single offensive risked catastrophic consequences if something went wrong. As in 1941, the Wehrmacht was committing itself in *Blau* to deep-penetration mobile operations with no appreciable reserves.

Another significant factor in the revitalization of German armoured strength in early 1942 was the tripling of the production of the Sd.Kfz.251 Schützenpanzer-wagen (SPW) half tracks, including over 350 built in the period March–June 1942. The number of Schützen-Abteilung in the panzer divisions equipped with the Sd.Kfz.251 rose from just three in 1941 to twelve in 1942, which significantly improved the tactical mobility of the infantry, mortar platoons and engineers in the German combined arms team. For example, the 9.Panzer-Division in Hoth's 4.Panzerarmee received eighty-five SPWs just prior to the beginning of *Blau*.[34]

Soviet armoured strength increased dramatically during May–June, with the first tank army – although designated as 3rd Tank Army – formed at Tula on 25 May. The 5th Tank Army began forming near Moscow in June. The tank armies were intended to be the Red Army's answer to the German Panzerarmee and would be used as breakthrough armies to create major penetrations in the enemy front and then cause a collapse by exploiting deep into their rear areas. By forming the first two of four tank armies created in 1942, the Stavka indicated that it was ready to move beyond the use of armour strictly for the infantry support role and allow more mobile, independent operations for tank units. However, the tank armies had very little organic artillery support – just one regiment of BM-8/13 multiple rocket launchers – and lacked the combined arms structure of a German Panzerkorps. Nor was the equipment initially provided to the tank armies anything different from other Soviet tank units of mid-1942; the 5th Tank Army had 439 tanks, of which there were only fifty KV-1 and 132 T-34 (42 per cent), with the rest consisting of eighty-eight Matilda II and 159 T-60 tanks. Assigning tanks like the slow-moving, short-ranged Matilda II to a tank army rendered Deep Battle operations problematic.

By early July, Soviet industrial output enabled the Red Army to achieve an overall numerical superiority of about 3.4–1 over Germany's armoured forces on the Eastern Front, although the Stavka was unaware of this superiority. Soviet intelligence grossly over-estimated German tank production by nearly 400 per cent in 1942 and believed that the Germans were building almost as many tanks as the Soviet Union – thus Red Army leaders did not expect to have a large numerical superiority in armour.[35] About 48 per cent of the available Soviet armour was comprised of KV-1 and T-34 tanks that were still superior to most German tanks, but 12 per cent were foreign-built tanks (Matilda II, Valentine, Stuart, Lee) and the remaining 40 per cent were near-useless T-60 light tanks. Since Stalin was convinced that the Germans would make another attempt to capture Moscow, one-third of the Red Army's 9,100 tanks were massed around Moscow in Zhukov's Western Front or nearby in reserve. Zhukov believed that the most likely German avenue of approach to Moscow was from the south, as Guderian had tried, so Rokossovsky's Bryansk Front was also provided with an unusually large amount of armour – over 1,500 tanks – and one of the two new

Distribution of Soviet Armour on the Eastern Front, June 1942

Front	Tank Armies	Tank Corps	Tank Brigades	OTBs	Total Tanks
Leningrad			3	2	185
Volkhov			6	5	400
Northwestern			5	12	525
Kalinin		1	12	6	840
Western		6	16	4	1,720
Moscow MD			14	26	1,280
Bryansk	1	7	11		1,640
Southwestern		4	11	4	1,100
Southern			5	2	275
Stalingrad/Volga			8		360
North Caucasus			3	2	150
RVGK	1	1	3		480
Other		2			300
Total	2	22	98	63	9,260

tank armies. The Stavka expected the main tank battles of 1942 to be fought in the center of the Eastern Front and the armour possessed by Zhukov, Konev and Rokossovsky had nearly an 8–1 local superiority over Heeresgruppe Mitte's depleted armoured forces. Elsewhere, Timoshenko's armoured forces in the Southwest Front bounced back quickly from their defeats in May–June, but they were still outnumbered by Heeresgruppe Süd's concentration of armour. The other Soviet fronts, between Leningrad–Staraya Russa in the north and Rostov in the south, were provided sufficient armour for infantry support missions but not for large-scale offensive operations. It is also interesting that more than one-quarter of the Red Army's available armour – about 2,400 tanks – was in reserve and not even at the front. In contrast, the Wehrmacht had no appreciable armoured reserves on the Eastern Front or in the west – everything was committed up front.

Case *Blau*: Hoth's Advance to Voronezh, 28 June–15 July

In Führer Directive 41, issued in April, Hitler specified that the objective of the main summer offensive was 'to wipe out the entire defense potential remaining to the Soviets, and to cut them off, as far as possible, from their most important centers of war industry.'[36] Although Hitler wanted to destroy as much of the Red Army in southern Russia as possible with his next grand summer offensive, his main goal was to secure the oil fields in the Caucasus which were vital for Germany's war effort. In this regard, Hitler was correct – chronic fuel shortages had significantly reduced the combat power of the Luftwaffe and the panzer armies in 1941. Seizure of oil fields in the Soviet Union could redress this problem, while also serving to deny fuel resources to the Red Army. Three oilfields – near Maikop, Grozny and Baku – produced 82 per cent of the Soviet Union's crude oil. Without this oil, the Red Army would lose its ability to conduct sustained large-scale offensive operations with tank armies and air armies.[37] Thus, Case *Blau* was intended to be a war for oil, with victory measured by the seizure of specific geographic objectives, not a free-wheeling war of maneuver with no definite end. To some extent, Hitler and the OKH recognized that they would get better results in using their armour in operations that were tailored to available resources, in order to avoid continuous operations that ground their panzer divisions down to combat ineffectiveness. *Blau* was premised on the idea of a multi-phase operation that employed all available forces toward one objective at a time. Nor did the distances to the objectives chosen for the summer offensive seem unreasonable, compared to what the Wehrmacht accomplished in 1941. The distance from the German AOK 6 front-line positions in June 1942 to Stalingrad and the Volga River was 500km. From von Kleist's frontline on the Mius River, the distance to the oilfields in the Caucasus was 350km to Maikop, 700km to Grozny and over 1,000km to Baku. Given three months of decent weather, these distances seemed attainable to the Panzerwaffe.

The first objective of *Blau* was for Hoth's 4.Panzerarmee to smash in the left flank of General-leytenant Filipp I. Golikov's Bryansk Front with a massive armoured attack, then advance eastward to seize the city of Voronezh, a city of

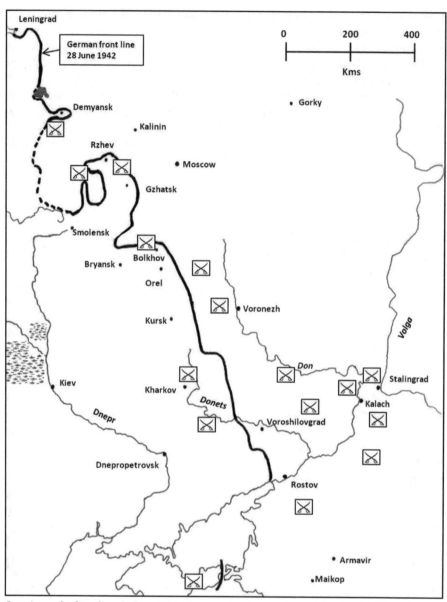

Overview – the front line, 28 June 1942. German objectives, major tank battles of 1942 on the Eastern Front.

326,000 people, on the Don.[38] Once Voronezh was seized, Hoth would pivot southward to conduct a double envelopment of Timoshenko's Southwest Front in conjunction with Paulus' AOK 6 and von Kleist's 1.Panzerarmee. The basic scheme of maneuver for *Blau* was similar to that used in Typhoon in the Battle of Vyazma-Bryansk, but it was premised that the Red Army would do as it had in

1941 – stand and fight. Hoth assembled his XXIV and XXXXVIII Panzerkorps east of Kursk, opposite the Soviet 40th Army of Bryansk Front. Hoth selected the sector north of the town of Tim, which was the boundary between the Soviet 13th and 40th Armies, for his two-corps *schwerpunkt*. The offensive opened on the morning of 28 June with a thirty-minute artillery preparation, followed by Luftwaffe air strikes on targets in the enemy rear areas. It was a warm, cloudy day, perfect for a Blitzkrieg. Although the Soviet armies were defending with two layers of rifle divisions or brigades arrayed in depth, Hoth's armour had no difficulty breaking through the front line. The XXIV Panzerkorps committed the 11.Panzer-Division against the 143rd Rifle Division from 13th Army and the 9.Panzer-Division against the 121st Rifle Division from 40th Army. Both Soviet divisions were veteran, pre-war units but lacked the defensive firepower to stand up to an attack by nearly 300 tanks; after suffering heavy losses, they retreated but lived to fight another day. The 212th Rifle Division in the path of 24.Panzer-Division from XXXXVIII Panzerkorps was less fortunate and was quickly over-run and demolished. The Sd.Kfz.251/2 half tracks mounting 8cm mortars proved particularly useful in this kind of fast-moving operation, enabling the Panzer-Abteilungen to request HE or smoke rounds to suppress enemy strongpoints in villages. Generalleutnant Johannes Baeßler's 9.Panzer-Division succeeded in quickly seizing a railroad bridge over the Tim river, which enabled the panzers to advance about 20km the first day, but the retreating Soviets managed to destroy the next bridge over the Kshen River. In its first action, Generalleutnant Bruno Ritter von Hauenschild's 24.Panzer-Division had the best first day, advancing over 30km.

After achieving their initial breakthrough, Hoth's armour spread out into a large armoured wedge, with the 9, 11 and 24.Panzer-Divisionen in the lead, followed by the 3 and 16.Infanterie-Division (mot.) and the *Grossdeutschland* Infanterie-Division (mot.). Heavy rain on 29–30 June slowed the rate of advance, but the German panzer units continued to advance. Golikov was not slow to react – he quickly committed the two tank brigades belonging to the 40th Army to delay Hoth's advance, while committing General-major Mikhail E. Katukov's 1st Tank Corps and General-major Mikhail I. Pavelkin's 16th Tank Corps to stop Hoth at the Kshen River. Nervous that Hoth's attack suggested a new push on Moscow from the southwest, as Guderian had done the previous year, the Stavka ordered Timoshenko on the night of 28–29 June to send his 4th and 24th Tank Corps to reinforce Golikov's crumbling left flank. Although some Soviet rifle units were withdrawing under pressure from Hoth's panzers, Stalin refused Golikov's request to allow his 13th and 40th Armies to retreat in order to avoid encirclement and demanded a major armoured counterattack as soon as practical. In just the first few days of *Blau*, the refitted armoured forces of both sides were committed to a major trial of strength against each other.

Despite rain, General der Panzertruppen Rudolf Veiel advanced 30km on 29 June and the 24.Panzer-Division managed to overrun the command post of the 40th Army, causing a further degradation of Soviet C2. Meanwhile, Katukov's 1st Tank Corps approached the left flank of the XXIV Panzerkorps from Livny as

Pavelkin's 16th Tank Corps moved to strike it from the east. General der Panzer-truppen Hermann Balck's 11.Panzer-Division, on the corps' left flank, was about to be squeezed between two on-rushing Soviet tank corps. However, the clash of armour – which began prematurely late on 29 June – was a disaster for the Red Army, in spite of a favorable tactical situation and a 2–1 numerical advantage. Balck's division had 110 of the improved Pz.IIIJ and 12 Pz.IVF2 tanks and had attached 8.8cm flak guns to Oberstleutnant Max Roth's Panzer-Regiment 15. Pavelkin committed only two of his three tank brigades and was roughly handled, losing about eighty tanks in two days, including most of his KV-1s. Since the two Soviet tank corps were not coordinated, Balck was able to deal first with Pavelkin, then with Katukov. Although Katukov would not admit it in his memoirs, his corps conducted a meeting engagement and apparently ran straight into a well-planned anti-armour ambush.[39] The terrain around Volovo was open agricultural land, providing Balck's troops with excellent observation and fields of fire. Katukov's corps advanced with Major Aleksandr F. Burda's battalion in the lead – these were some of the most experienced and skilled tankers in the Red Army of mid-1942. Suddenly, Burda's battalion came under intense tank and anti-tank fire – they were surprised that the new Pz.IVF2 tanks could successfully engage T-34s at ranges out to 1,000–1,200 meters. Hidden in the tall grass, the Pz.IIIJs and Pz.IVF2s methodically slaughtered Burda's tanks, while the T-34s had difficulty identifying the German tankers. The Soviet tankers were not expecting or prepared for a long-range gunnery duel. One of the casualties was Ivan T. Lyubushkin, awarded an HSU for knocking out five German tanks during the Battle of Mtensk, but now just another victim in a burning T-34. After extracting his survivors, Katukov turned his corps around and broke off the counterattack.

Golikov tried to make a stand at Kastornoye behind the Olym River, 70km west of Voronezh, by committing General-major Ivan P. Korchagin's 17th Tank Corps and the 115th and 116th Tank Brigades, which briefly halted the XXIV Panzerkorps. Elements of the 4th and 16th Tanks Corps were also nearby. General-leytenant Yakov N. Fedorenko, commander of all the Red Army's tank forces, arrived at Voronezh as Stavka representative to coordinate the armoured counterstroke. From Moscow, Stalin exhorted Golikov to smash the German penetration, noting that he had 1,000 tanks between Hoth and Voronezh, against fewer than 500 German tanks. However, the new Soviet tank corps commanders and their staffs proved unable to effectively control their own forces or coordinate with their neighbors. Korchagin's staff failed to provide enough fuel for the movement to Kastornoye, resulting in impaired tactical mobility. Rather than attack straight into a mass of Soviet armour – which was spotted by the Luftwaffe – Hoth used maneuver tactics by sending the 11.Panzer-Division to bypass Kastornoye to the north and 9.Panzer-Division to the south. Korchagin was befuddled by the German maneuvering and failed to react, allowing his corps to be defeated piece-meal; the 17th Tank Corps lost 141 tanks in a few days and fell back in disorder. Panzer-Abteilung *Grossdeutschland* had its baptism of fire, with its Pz.IVF2 tanks knocking out sixteen T-34s in the tank skirmishes around

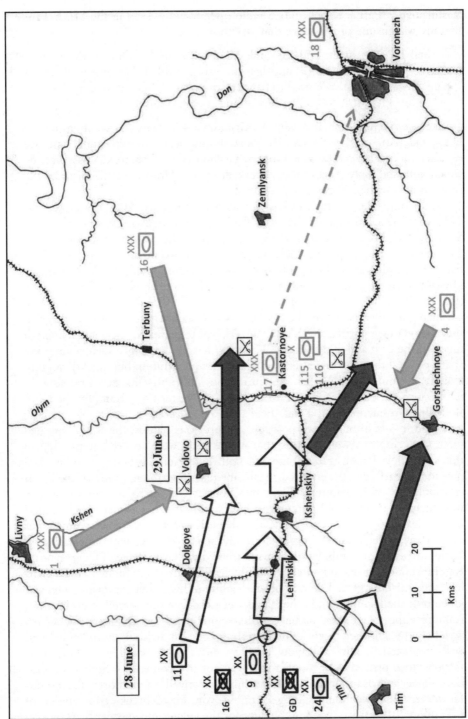

Tank battles west of Voronezh, 28 June–6 July 1942; Hoth's 4.Panzerarmee versus multiple Soviet tank corps.

Kastornoye.[40] Petr I. Kirichenko, a radio operator in a T-34 in the 116th Tank Brigade was in one of the tanks that was 'brewed up':

> A shell hit the turret, and the tank filled with smoke. One of the commander's arms was torn off and his side was shredded. He screamed with pain. It was terrible. We tried to bandage the wound, but we were unable to help him. He'd lost too much blood, and died inside the tank.[41]

Likewise, General-major Vasily A. Mishulin's 4th Tank Corps attempted to block the path of the XXXXVIII Panzerkorps near Goreshechnoe, but was repulsed by 24.Panzer-Division. Golikov's armoured counterstroke was a disaster, which inflicted only twenty-four hours delay on Hoth's 4.Panzerarmee, but resulted in four tank corps being mauled.

On 30 June, the German offensive widened as Paulus' AOK 6 attacked the 21st Army which protected the right flank of Timoshenko's Southwest Front. Stumme's XXXX Panzerkorps attacked the front of the 21st Army with the 3 and 23.Panzer-Divisionen, while AOK 6 attacked with two infantry corps on his left flank. Generalleutnant Hans Freiherr von Boineburg-Lengsfeld's 23.Panzer-Division formed Stumme's *schwerpunkt*, with Kampfgruppe von Bodenhausen (I, II./Pz.Regt 201, SR 128) and Kampfgruppe Muller (III./Pz.Regt 201, SR 126) advancing northeastward on the road to Novy Oskol, where it was intended that they would link-up with XXXXVIII Panzerkorps to complete the encirclement of much of the 21st and 40th Armies. The two German kampfgruppen, about 4km apart, crossed the start line after a brief artillery preparation but quickly ran into trouble. Kampfgruppe Muller ran into mines and anti-tank gun fire, slowing its advance to a crawl. Outside the village of Nesternoye, Kampfgruppe von Bodenhausen encountered a minefield that was covered by fire from anti-tank guns and T-34s in hull-down positions. In previous battles, the Red Army had often been sloppy about ensuring that its obstacles were covered by fire, but in this case, they demonstrated increased skill. Five German tanks were knocked out and I./Pz.Regt 201 engaged in an unequal long-range gunnery duel that consumed all of its ammunition in two hours. Eventually, Kampfgruppe von Bodenhausen maneuvered around the mines and chased a Soviet rifle battalion out of Nesternoye but due to the delay, Oberst Karl-August Pochat, commander of the Panzer-Regiment 201 ordered the advance to continue without clearing up Soviet forces on his flank. While moving toward the next village of Degtyavnoye, Kampfgruppe von Bodenhausen was hit by flanking fire from hidden Soviet artillery and anti-tank guns. Oberst Pochat, leading in his PzBef command tank, was killed by a shell splinter and other tanks were knocked out as well. Nevertheless, Kampfgruppe von Bodenhausen continued the attack on Degtyavnoye, which was held by another Soviet rifle battalion, dug in behind more mines and well-supported by anti-tank guns, artillery and T-34 tanks. The opposition at Degtyavnoye proved even tougher and was not overcome until Stukas bombed the village and Kampfgruppe Muller finally arrived to reinforce the attack. However, Oberstleutnant Georg-Henning von Heydebreck, commander of I./Pz.Regt 201, was wounded in the fight for the village and another five German tanks were lost.[42] Recognizing that the 23.Panzer-Division was encountering unusually heavy opposition, Stumme decided to halt the attack at 1200 hours in order for the two panzer kampfgruppen to resupply and more firepower to be brought to bear on this sector. However, a renewed attack up the road as evening approached met a Soviet strongpoint at Ssirotino that shot up the German vanguard and knocked out more tanks. Supporting T-34s used reverse-slope defensive positions, which allowed them to pop up, fire and then withdraw before German return fire could target them – Soviet tankers were learning. Likewise, the 3.Panzer-Division on the right flank of XXXX Panzerkorps made only slow progress against the Soviet 15th Guards Rifle Division and part of Badanov's 24th Tank Corps.

Although the 23.Panzer-Division had advanced 11km on the first day and penetrated the 21st Army's first line of defense, it had not achieved a break-through. For the first time in clear weather, the Soviets had actually stopped a German *schwerpunkt* that included panzers and Stuka close air support, and managed to inflict grievous losses. On the first day of battle, 23.Panzer-Division lost ten tanks destroyed and another fifty tanks damaged, while losing a panzer regiment commander, a battalion commander, two company commanders and several platoon leaders. The German attack had been conducted without tactical surprise along a likely avenue of approach, which the Soviets had liberally seeded with mines. Adding insult to injury, the 23.Panzer-Division had inflicted minimal damage on the enemy, who simply fell back to their second line of defense during the night.

On 1 July, the 23.Panzer-Division made another effort to storm the Soviet strongpoint at Ssirotino but, after being repulsed again, they were forced to employ a flanking maneuver. Eventually, Kampfgruppe Muller flanked the Soviet position and managed to pick off four T-34s with flank shots, causing the Soviet tank brigade to fall back a few kilometers to the next defensive position. This process was repeated for the rest of the day, with the Soviets forcing the 23.Panzer-Division to conduct time-consuming flanking maneuvers. By the end of the day, the 23.Panzer-Division had advanced another 8km, but the real breakthrough occurred on their left flank, where the infantry of VIII Armeekorps rolled up the right flank of the 21st Army. Oddly, it was the infantry that led the way in the AOK 6 sector and the panzers which had to call upon the infantry for support. Indeed, VIII Armeekorps was rolling over the 21st Army so rapidly that General-major Petr E. Shurov's 13th Tank Corps was directed to counterattack the AOK 6 infantry divisions, rather than Stumme's stalled armour. Shurov, who was known as an excellent trainer of tankers and who had been commanding the Stalingrad Tank Training facility just six weeks before, struck the German 305 and 376.Infanterie-Divisionen as they were trying to get across the Oskol River near Chernyanka. Amazingly, the panzerjägers in the infantry divisions were strong enough to repulse the attack, knocking out dozens of Soviet tanks. Shurov was mortally wounded by artillery. The fact that a German infantry division could defeat a Soviet tank corps without organic armoured support speaks volumes about the fragility of the new Soviet armoured formations. After repulsing the

13th Tank Corps, the VIII Armeekorps reached Stary Oskol the next day and linked up with XXXVIII Panzerkorps. However, the Stavka had authorized the 21st and 40th Armies to escape the forming *kessel*, so the maneuver failed to destroy any large Soviet units.

By 3 July, Soviet resistance between the Olym River and Voronezh evaporated and the defeated 17th Tank Corps retreated east, across the Don. While Balck's 11.Panzer-Division, assisted by some infantry from AOK 2, held off the 1st and 16th Tank Corps, Hoth sent the rest of his armour east toward Voronezh. The *Grossdeutschland* Division was able to capture an intact bridge over the Don at 1930 hours on 4 July and the 24.Panzer-Division seized two bridgeheads over the Don the next morning. Once again, the Red Army had failed to leave any units to garrison a major city and the 24.Panzer-Division advanced into the city on 6 July. General-major Ivan D. Chernyakhovsky's 18th Tank Corps arrived just in time to put up a fight for the city center, but quickly lost its 180th and 181st Tank Brigades with 116 tanks.[43] German video within Voronezh shows many intact T-34s, in column, which suggests that many tankers may have abandoned their tanks when they feared being cut off by the German advance. Once again, German panzers seized a major Russian city with a coup de main. However, in this case the Germans had only seized Voronezh to protect the left flank of Heeresgruppe Süd as it advanced to the Volga, and they had no intention of exploiting east across the Don, even though there was now a significant gap between the Bryansk and Southwest Fronts.

Even before Voronezh had fallen, Stalin pressured Golikov to commit his main armoured reserve – General-major Aleksandr I. Liziukov 5th Tank Army – to strike the flank of Hoth's advance to the Don. The Stavka hastily transferred General-major Pavel A. Rotmistrov's 7th Tank Corps from the Kalinin Front to join Liziukov's 5TA at the Elets railhead. In fact, Rotmistrov's corps was the first to reach its jump-off positions, while General-major Andrei G. Kravchenko's 2nd Tank Corps and General-major Aleksei F. Popov's 11th Tank Corps were slower to get into position. Despite the fact that no artillery or air support was available and that only two of nine tank brigades were ready to attack, Liziukov ordered the counterattack to begin at 0600 hours on 6 July. Thus, the first offensive operation conducted by a Soviet tank army in the Second World War was not a carefully planned action, but rather a meeting engagement where forces were fed into battle piecemeal.

Von Langermann, the XXIV Panzerkorps commander, had been alerted to the presence of Soviet armour for several days and he shifted both the 9 and 11.Panzer-Divisionen to protect 4.Panzerarmee's left flank near Bolshoy Polyana. Langerman also had time to coordinate with the neighboring XIII Armeekorps, which established a firm defensive line facing toward the threatening Soviet armour. Nevertheless, Rotmistrov's two tank brigades managed to push back 11.Panzer-Division's covering forces and advance 10km before encountering the main German defensive positions behind the Kobylia Snova river. On 7 July, one of Popov's tank brigades arrived, but the 9.Panzer-Division joined in the fight and claimed to have knocked out sixty-one tanks, which halted Rotmistrov's advance. It was not until 8 July that Popov got the rest of his corps into action and, together, the 7th and 11th Corps forced the 9 and 11.Panzer-Divisionen to fall back 6km to the Sukhaia Vereika River. Heavy fighting continued along the river on 9–10 July, with about 260 Soviet tanks opposing 200 German tanks. Although initially surprised by the weight of the Soviet armoured attack, the Germans gradually gained the upper hand as their air superiority enabled them to relentlessly hammer the Soviet formations with Stuka bombardments. Without effective artillery support, the Soviet tank corps also had difficulty suppressing the German anti-tank guns, hidden in the tall grass. On 12 July, the 11.Panzer-Division mounted a major counterattack that routed the 2nd and 7th Tank Corps, which effectively brought the 5th Tank Army's counter-offensive to an ignominious end. Between 6 and 15 July, Liziukov 5th Tank Army suffered nearly 8,000 casualties and lost 341 tanks destroyed, including 130 T-34, fifty-eight KV-1 and fifty-one Matilda II. The 5th Tank Army had just 27 per cent of its tanks, half of which were T-60 light tanks, still operational by the time the counter-offensive ended. In contrast, the 9.Panzer-Division lost only thirty-nine tanks (two Pz.II, twenty-eight Pz.III, nine Pz.IV) since the start of *Blau* and still had ninety-four operational tanks.

Hoth's advance to Voronezh was a resounding success for the Panzerwaffe, resulting in the seizure of important terrain along the Don. While no major Soviet formations were encircled and destroyed, ten Soviet tank corps were mauled in the battle and their clumsy performance indicated that the Red Army was not yet ready to conduct large-scale armoured combat toe-to-toe with the Wehrmacht. Even the best Soviet armour commanders, Katukov and Rotmistrov, had turned in very lackluster performances due to the improvised nature of Soviet operational planning. As a result of the German capture of Voronezh, the Stavka created the Voronezh Front to hold a sector along the Don. As operations wound down around Voronezh, Hitler and the OKH began to implement the next phase of their summer offensive. Heeresgruppe Süd was broken up into two smaller formations in order to pursue separate objectives at Stalingrad and in the Caucasus: Heeresgruppe A and B. Von Bock would command Heeresgruppe B, which included Hoth's PzAOK 4 and AOK 2, as well as the 2nd Hungarian, 3rd Romanian and 8th Italian Armies. Generalfeldmarschall Wilhelm List took command of Heeresgruppe A, which included von Kleist's PzAOK 1 and Paulus' AOK 6. However, Hitler wanted Hoth's 4.Panzerarmee sent south immediately after the capture of Voronezh to support the AOK 6 advance to Stalingrad, but von Bock was reluctant to release all the armour due to 5th Tank Army's counter-offensive. Hoth and von Bock effected a compromise, sending the XXXXVIII Panzerkorps south, but keeping the XXIV Panzerkorps engaged with Liziukov's armour for another week. Hitler became increasingly upset with von Bock's foot-dragging, which was justified by the tactical situation, but which threatened to upset German operational plans. Finally, Hitler relieved von Bock of command on 15 July and promoted Generaloberst Freiherr Maximilian von Weichs from command of AOK 2 to command of Heeresgruppe B. Thus, Liziukov's armoured counterattack had unforeseen consequences, in that the delay imposed upon

4.Panzerarmee in supporting the drive on Stalingrad contributed to the German failure to seize the city by coup de main as occurred at Voronezh.

Von Kleist's Panzers Head for the Oil, 9 July–6 September

Von Kleist's Panzerarmee 1 had waited behind the Donets while Hoth's panzers smashed in the Bryansk and Southwestern Fronts. By the time that von Kleist attacked at dawn on 9 July, the Southwest Front was already off-balance, with its left flank falling back under the hammer blows of AOK 6's pursuing XXXX Panzerkorps. Von Kleist deployed his III and XIV Panzerkorps on line with the 14, 16, and 22.Panzer-Division side-by-side and conducted a frontal assault against four rifle divisions of Kozlov's 37th Army. Kozlov only had a single tank brigade with forty-six tanks to oppose Kleist's 330 tanks, so the Soviets fell back rather than face encirclement and annihilation, as they had before. AOK 17 joined the offensive on 11 July, slowly pushing the Southern Front back toward Rostov. At this point, with the entire Soviet front between Voronezh and the Sea of Azov in flux, Hitler issued Führer Directive 43, which made ill-judged alterations to the *Blau* operational plan: Hoth's panzers were transferred to Heeresgruppe A for the drive into the Caucasus, rather than supporting the AOK 6 drive on Stalingrad.

Within six days, Mackensen's III Panzerkorps ended up conducting a great wheel, turning southeast and ending up behind the 12th and 37th Armies. The Soviet 12th Army was forced to abandon Voroshilovgrad and hastily retreat to avoid encirclement. Veiel's XXXXVIII Panzerkorps from Hoth's 4.Panzerarmee joined up with von Kleist's two corps, reinforcing the great armoured wheel to the southeast, with the Southern Front in full retreat. The German motorized infantry divisions, each reinforced with their own Panzer-Abteilung, proved their worth in a pursuit operation: the *Grossdeutschland* and 16 and 29.Infanterie-Divisionen (mot.) raced ahead of the panzer divisions and reached the Don river east of Rostov by 17 July. Once this occurred, the Southern Front fell back through Rostov, leaving only elements of the 56th Army to defend the city. General der Panzertruppen Friedrich Kirchner's Gruppe Kirchner (LVII Panzerkorps and XXXXIX Gebirgs-korps), which up to this point had been sitting on the sidelines, advanced 30km on 21 July and approached Rostov from the west with the 13.Panzer-Division, SS-Division *Wiking* and three infantry divisions. This action was also the combat debut of Waffen-SS armour on the Eastern Front, with SS-Sturmbannführer Johannes-Rudolf Mühlenkamp's SS-Panzer-Abteilung 5 leading the way into Rostov. Simultaneously, Mackensen's III Panzerkorps also approached Rostov from the north – four German mechanized divisions closed in on the city. Three layers of anti-tank ditches and mines slowed, but did not stop the advance of German armour into the city. A company of Brandenburg infiltration troops was attached to the 13.Panzer-Division, which assisted them in seizing key points in the city. On 22–23 July, *Wiking* and 13.Panzer-Division fought their way into western Rostov, which was burning and covered by dense clouds of smoke. The Soviets fought the battle with rearguards, enabling the Southern Front's remaining armour to escape across the Don. For the first time, German armour was involved in serious fighting in an urban environment, which made panzer commanders fearful of sticking their heads out of their cupolas due to the threat posed by Soviet snipers. Most of the streets were blocked with obstacles, which severely limited the tactical mobility of the Panzer-Abteilungen. Several centers of resistance, such as the NKVD headquarters building, required close tank-infantry coordination to reduce. After a tough fight, most of the Soviet rearguards pulled back across the Don on the night of 24–25 July, although mop-up continued in Rostov until 27 July.[44]

Despite the capture of Rostov, von Kleist's armour would not be able to reach the oil fields in the Caucasus if the 56th Army blew up the main rail bridge over the Don River at Bataysk. Without a rail bridge over the Don, Heeresgruppe Süd would not be in a position to support a deep thrust into the Caucasus for weeks, which would have given the Southern Front time to recover. The railroad bridge was not the only obstacle, but a long causeway over marshy terrain, followed by another bridge – a tailor-made blocking position. Instead, the Soviet 56th Army made the kind of horrendous error which seemed to dog the Red Army even in the second year of the war: they neglected to properly guard or destroy the railroad bridge at Bataysk. During the night of 24–25 July, a small force of motorcycle infantry from the 13.Panzer-Division and some Brandenburg infiltrators slipped across the Don in rubber boats and caught the bridge security detail by surprise. Although most of the German assault troops were killed and the bridge partly damaged, it was held long enough for a force from 13.Panzer-Division to arrive and secure the bridge, providing von Kleist with his entry point into the Caucasus. This was the place where even a single battalion of T-34 tanks might have brought Operation *Blau* to a premature halt, but the Southern Front had pulled its armour back from the river. It was a gross blunder, in a war filled with blunders.

Von Kleist sent two infantry divisions across into the Bataysk bridgehead to clear out the town and marshland, giving his panzers a brief pause. East of Rostov, the XXIV and XXXX Panzerkorps had already established four small bridgeheads with pontoon bridges across the lower Don and the 3.Panzer-Division was across in force. After Rostov fell, the German intelligence estimate of Soviet forces and dispositions in the Caucasus was vague. In fact, General-polkovnik Rodion I. Malinovsky's Southern Front had only five very beat-up armies with 112,000 troops stretched along a 300km-wide front south of the Don. Malinovsky knew that the Stavka was going to send most of its reserves to support the fighting around Voronezh and Stalingrad and that he was more or less on his own for some time. On 25 July, von Kleist began his advance into the Caucasus by probing southward with elements of XXXX and XXXVIII Panzer-korps. The 3 and 23.Panzer-Divisionen, along with 16.Infanterie-Division (mot.) easily smashed the thin defenses of the 37th Army and plunged deep into the steppe, toward the Manych River. In response, the Soviet 51st Army flung the 135th and 155th Tank Brigades against the flank of the 23.Panzer-Division at Martinovka on 28–29 July; the result was a one-sided tank battle where the Soviets lost up to seventy-seven of 100 tanks (a mix of T-34s and T-70s) against only three German tanks. Much of the action was fought at close range, under 300 meters, but Kampfgruppe Burmeister's gunnery proved far superior to that of the Russian tankers.[45]

By 28 July, Malinovsky could see his front collapsing and he ordered the 12th, 18th and 37th Armies to retreat southward. On 29 July, the LVII Panzerkorps exploded out of the Bataysk bridgehead and 13.Panzer-Division captured Ssalsk on 30 July. Von Kleist's armour shifted to full pursuit mode, with the LVII, III and XXXX Panzerkorps driving all before them. The LVII Panzerkorps took about 9,000 prisoners in four days, which – while not spectacular – was still about half the front-line strength of the opposing 18th Army. For the first time in months, German panzer divisions were advancing 20–40km per day against minimal resistance. Morale among von Kleist's tankers was sky high – pursuit of a broken foe is a heady, intoxicating feeling, while it lasts. Heeresgruppe A split into two parts, with von Kleist's 1.Panzerarmee pressing on for the oilfields while AOK 17 turned to clear the Kuban. With victory seemingly within von Kleist's grasp, two factors intervened to hobble the Blitzkrieg. First, Hitler decided to transfer the XXXXVIII Panzerkorps back to Hoth's command to support the drive on Stalingrad, which was now designated as the priority, not the Caucasus. The OKH also decided to take the Grossdeutschland Division – von Kleist's strongest motorized infantry division – and send it to Rzhev. Second, von Kleist's logistic situation deteriorated rapidly once he advanced south of the Don, away from his supply sources, and fuel shortages became endemic. As July ended, the remnants of Malinovsky's Southern Front were absorbed into Marshal Semyon Budyonny's North Caucasus Front. Budyonny tasked Malinovsky with stopping von Kleist's armour with the 12th, 37th and 51st Armies while the rest of his forces tried to stop AOK 17 in the Kuban.

As August began, von Kleist massed his three Panzerkorps into a massive wedge, with a total of about 350 tanks, and pushed due south to Armavir. Advancing across the arid steppe of the Caucasus, von Kleist's panzers encountered temperatures up to 40° C (104° F), which made water just as important for resupply as fuel. After advancing 100km, the 13.Panzer-Division captured Armavir on 3 August, while 3.Panzer-Division captured Stavropol on 5 August, which forced Malinovsky's forces to continue their retreat toward Grozny. By 7 August, von Kleist's armour was finally within range of its first objective – the oilfields at Maikop – and he directed the 13.Panzer-Division, SS-*Wiking* and 16.Infanterie-Division (mot.) to converge on the city. Although Soviet anti-tank guns put up a stiff resistance at the Laba River on 8 August and knocked out some of SS-*Wiking*'s tanks, the 12th Army had no tanks left and could not stop the III Panzerkorps. Assisted by Brandenburg infiltrators dressed in Red Army uniforms, the 13.Panzer-Division fought its way into Maikop on 9 August and occupied the oil fields by the next day. The retreating Soviets had thoroughly sabotaged the pumping equipment and set the fields alight, meaning it would be up to a year before more than a trickle of crude oil might be available to the Wehrmacht – but Maikop would be abandoned in January 1943. Nevertheless, the occupation of Maikop did deprive the Red Army of 6.8 per cent of its crude oil supplies for the duration of the war – a not inconsiderable accomplishment.

By 10 August, von Kleist had Malinovsky's forces on the run, with XXXX Panzerkorps pushing southeast down the main rail line to Grozny and Baku, while III and LVII Panzerkorps mopped up around Maikop. By this point, Malinovsky's only armoured unit was Major Vladimir Filippov's 52nd Tank Brigade – a low-quality unit equipped with a mixed group of forty-six T-34s, T-60s, Valentines and Lees. A total of 4,500 tankers who had escaped into the Caucasus after abandoning their tanks – a shocking indictment of the low state of morale and training in the Red Army's tank units in mid-1942 – were sent to the Urals to reequip with new tanks.[46] It was at this point that the Germans decided to snatch defeat from the jaws of victory. Generalfeldmarschall Wilhelm List was one of Hitler's uninspired choices to lead his main effort in the 1942 campaign, since he had limited experience with armour – just the brief Balkans campaigns – and had completely missed the first year of the war on the Eastern Front. List brought an old-school, First World War mentality to his handling of Heeresgruppe A and he was concerned when von Kleist's panzers went charging off toward Grozny and Baku, while leaving AOK 17 to clear out the Kuban and the coastline. He believed that Soviet forces in these areas posed a threat to his right flank, even though the 47th and 56th Armies had minimal combat strength remaining and just fifteen light tanks. Nevertheless, on 12 August List ordered von Kleist to divert both the III Panzerkorps and the LVII Panzerkorps to support a drive westward to Tuapse to cut off the two Soviet armies and clear the coast. During 12–18 August, SS-*Wiking*, the 13.Panzer-Division and the 16.Infanterie-Division were tied up in this ridiculous diversion, which consumed their limited fuel supplies on a secondary objective. List sent this collection of armour down a narrow road into the mountains, which was easily blocked – and they never reached Tuapse. Meanwhile, von Kleist continued toward Grozny with just 3.Panzer-Division and part of 23.Panzer-Division; even though the Wehrmacht had nineteen panzer divisions on the Eastern Front, the *schwerpunkt* aimed at the critical objectives of the entire summer offensive was reduced to less than two. List also diverted much of Heeresgruppe A's limited supplies toward his efforts to clear the Kuban and the coast, leaving von Kleist's spearhead to sputter for lack of fuel.

Nevertheless, on 15 August the 23.Panzer-Division managed to capture Georgievsk, 200km from Grozny, before its fuel began to give out. Heeresgruppe A managed to repair the rail line all the way from Rostov down to Pyatigorsk by 18 August, but it was a single-track line that could only handle very limited throughput. Given a respite from von Kleist's pursuit, the Stavka sent reinforcements to the Caucasus, including the 10th Guards Rifle Corps, which enabled Malinovsky to build a more solid defensive line behind the Terek River. Once the German drive on Tuapse stalled, List finally allowed the III Panzerkorps to rejoin von Kleist's advance toward Grozny, but the 13.Panzer-Division and 16.Infanterie-Division (mot.) ran out of fuel en route and were immobilized, then the OKH decided to transfer the latter unit to Heeresgruppe B. The XXXXIX Gebirgskorps was supposed to support von Kleist's armour, but List diverted it westward to Sochi – which was never taken. Kleist made it to the Terek river with the 3, 13 and 23.Panzer-Divisionen by 23 August, but with only two infantry divisions of LII Armeekorps in support. While von Kleist had a 3–1 numerical advantage in armour over Malinovsky, the Soviet commander had considerably more infantry. By this point, Malinovsky had scraped together three OTBs to supplement Filippov's 52nd Tank Brigade, but he had virtually no T-34s; rather, he had about forty-three Valentines, sixty-three Lees and a handful of T-60s. Due to the difficulty of shipping T-34s from the Urals on the single rail line remaining into the Caucasus, Malinovsky's forces were almost entirely dependent upon Lend-Lease American and British armour arriving through Persia. On the German side, von Kleist still had most of his armour since there had been relatively light combat in the Caucasus, and he was beginning to receive upgraded Pz.IIIL and Pz.IVG tanks. However, his fuel situation was abysmal and most of his air support had been stripped away as well.

Von Kleist realized that time was running out and he decided to try and get across the Terek River with the forces available. The 3.Panzer-Division managed to seize Mozdok on the northern side of the Terek on 25 August, but efforts to cross the wide river were repulsed. On the morning of 26 August, Generalmajor Erwin Mack, commander of the 23.Panzer-Division, and one of his battalion commanders, was killed by Soviet mortar fire while observing operations along the Terek.[47] The river proved too wide, deep and fast-flowing to cross under fire and von Kleist was stymied. In desperation, Oberst Erpo Freiherr von Bodenhausen, commander of the 23.Panzergrenadier Brigade, was selected to lead a mixed armoured kampfgruppe toward Chervlennaya on the north side of the Terek, where the junction of the Baku-Astrakhan rail line ran. Von Bodenhausen succeeded in reaching the rail junction on 31 August – only 27km from Grozny – and briefly interrupted Soviet rail traffic from Baku (still 490km distant), but his force was too small to hold this exposed position and he fell back toward the main body.[48] Von Kleist's forces were completely out of fuel and he was not able to make another attempt to get across the Terek River until 6 September. The 13.Panzer-Division succeeded in finally getting across the river, but it was too late; Malinovsky's forces had steadily been reinforced and his numerically-superior troops were too well dug in to budge. Hitler finally relieved List three days later and took personal control over Heeresgruppe A – surely one of his weirdest command decisions of the Second World War. While fighting would continue along the Terek River until early November, when the first snow arrived, von Kleist's offensive had culminated and the front became static.

The Caucasus was the kind of campaign that the panzer divisions were designed to win, using bold maneuvers across flat steppes against a disorganized foe who lacked proper air, artillery or armour support. However, Hitler and the OKH failed to provide their main effort with the resources it needed to succeed. Reduced to only five fuel-starved divisions at the tip of his spear, von Kleist's spearhead was stopped more by his own side than the Red Army. In the Caucasus, the Red Army lacked the material advantages in armour and artillery it enjoyed on other fronts. While von Kleist's panzers failed to seize a significant amount of the oil resources of the Caucasus, they did come exceedingly close to interdicting two-thirds of the Soviet Union's supply of crude oil. Oil was just as much the Red Army's strategic center of gravity as it was for the Wehrmacht. Had von Kleist's panzers reached Grozny and Baku, the Red Army would have likely found it difficult to provide fuel for the multi-front offensives of 1943–44.

Drive on Stalingrad, 16 July–23 August
When von Weichs took over Heeresgruppe B, Hoth's 4.Panzerarmee was in the midst of disengaging from the armoured battles between Bolkhov and Voronezh and Paulus' AOK 6 had begun to advance eastward with its left flank anchored on the Don. Timoshenko's forces had suffered 232,000 casualties since the start of *Blau* and had just been redesignated as the Stalingrad Front. The Stavka allowed Timoshenko to conduct a fighting withdrawal eastward, rather than the die-in-place missions of 1941. In an effort to envelop Timoshenko's retreating forces, the great pincers of Hoth's and von Kleist's panzer armies closed around Millerovo but caught very little in their net. Even worse, every time the Germans panzer armies moved distances of 100km or more, their logistic situation virtually collapsed and jury-rigged improvisations became the norm. Throughout *Blau*, fuel shortages seriously undermined the German panzer armies' ability to conduct operational-level maneuver warfare. It was only the fact that Luftflotte 4 had nearly 300 Ju-52 transports available and was willing to provide regular aerial resupply runs to the panzer spearheads that Heeresgruppe B could maintain any offensive momentum at all.[49]

Paulus' AOK 6 was ordered to advance upon Stalingrad but since the bulk of Hoth's 4.Panzerarmee had been shifted by Hitler to support Heeresgruppe A's advance into the Caucasus, Paulus did so with no appreciable armoured support. Furthermore, Hitler also accorded priority of supplies and air support to Heeresgruppe A, which meant that Paulus' AOK 6 had insufficient fuel to move all its divisions at once. Instead of Blitzkrieg, Paulus' AOK 6 waddled toward Stalingrad with only two infantry divisions of VIII Armeekorps in the lead. When the German pursuit slowed after Millerovo, Timoshenko was able to recover and began to deploy the 62nd and 64th Armies in the Don Bend to block Paulus' advance upon Stalingrad. Yet Stalin finally had enough of Timoshenko's fumbling and ineffectual operations and replaced him with General-leytenant Vasily N. Gordov on 21 July.[50] Gordov found that he had plenty of infantry to rebuild his front, but he was short of tanks since the Bryansk, Southwest and Southern Fronts may have lost as much as 2,400 tanks between 28 June and 24 July, or about three-quarters of the armour they had at the start of *Blau*. In late July, the Stavka rushed tank replacements to the Stalingrad Front to begin outfitting the 1st and 4th Tank Armies, which were intended to be used in a general counteroffensive in early August.

It was not long before Hitler, in his Wehrwolf headquarters near Vinnitsa in the western Ukraine, grew concerned that Paulus' slow advance toward Stalingrad was giving Timoshenko time to recover and ordered the transfer of von Wietersheim's XIV Panzerkorps with 16.Panzer-Division and 3 and 60.Infanterie-Divisionen to energize the AOK 6 offensive. He also issued Fuhrer Directive 45 on 22 July, which switched the main priority from the Caucasus to Stalingrad and returned Hoth's 4.Panzerarmee to Heeresgruppe B. The XIV Panzerkorps pushed the infantry of the 62nd and 64th Armies back into the Don Bend west of Stalingrad, but Paulus continued to plead for more armour support and received the XXIV Panzerkorps with the 24.Panzer-Division, which meant that he now had 300–350 tanks. Hube's 16.Panzer-Division fanned out in front of AOK 6, deployed in four kampfgruppen.[51] On 24 July, the 3 and 60.Infanterie-Divisionen (mot.) pierced the 62nd Army's thin screening forces and advanced 50km in a single day, approaching Kalach on the Don. Yet by the time that XIV Panzerkorps neared the Don, they were very low on fuel. As a result of von Wietersheim's advance, three divisions of the 62nd Army were isolated by the German breakthrough and Gordov sent General-major Trofim I. Tanaschishin's 13th Tank Corps from 1st Tank Army across the Don on 25 July to prevent Hube's panzers from completing the encirclement. A brisk tank skirmish near Manolin involving about 100 German and 150 Soviet tanks developed on 26 July between Hube's panzers and Tanaschishin's 13th Tank Corps, with losses on both sides.

Stalin was also becoming fixated on the Stalingrad axis and was worried about the rapid approach of German mechanized forces to Kalach. At this point, the smart play for Gordov's Stalingrad Front was to sit tight behind the Don river and wait for Paulus to begin crossing the river near Kalach, then hit his *schwerpunkt* with two concentrated tank armies. However, Stalin refused to wait and instead ordered Gordov to commit both of the still-forming 1st and 4th Tank Armies to an immediate counter-offensive across the Don to rescue the trapped elements of the 62nd Army. This was one of the most hair-brained Soviet armoured operations of the Second World War, with the forces involved being given just six hours to plan and prepare; at the tank battalion and tank regiment level, this meant a quick oral briefing at best. Many of the tanks in both armies were undergoing maintenance and not yet ready for action, but they were committed nonetheless.

General-major Kirill S. Moskalenko was an artilleryman but had gained considerable experience fighting German panzers since June 1941 and now led the 1st Tank Army into battle against the XIV Panzerkorps on the morning of 27 July. Initially, Moskalenko only had Tanaschishin's 13th Tank Corps in action across the Don, but he tried to feed General-major Georgi S. Rodin's 28th Tank Corps into battle as soon as possible. Altogether, Moskalenko's 1st Tank Army had seven tank brigades with 330 tanks, including 162 T-34s and thirty KV-1s, but he was unable to get more than a couple of brigades into action at once. Hube's 16.Panzer-Division was hard-pressed on 27 July, being caught with its four kampfgruppen dispersed, outnumbered and low on fuel. Tanaschishin's tankers managed to surround Kamfgruppe Witzleben from Panzer-Aufklärungs-Abteilung 16, but lost about fifty tanks to Oberst Rudolf Sieckenius' Panzer-Regiment 2 in a series of meeting engagements around Verkhne-Buzinovka. Hube requested air support from Fliegerkorps VIII, which had about eighty Ju-87D Stukas from StG 2 based at Tatsinskaya airbase.[52] The Stukas caught Tanaschishin's armour in the open and he lost thirteen T-34s and seven T-70s to air attack. Part of Georgy S. Rodin's 28th Tank Corps also crossed the Don and engaged the 3 and 60.Infanterie-Division (mot.) with some success. Yet General-major Vasily D. Kriuchenkin's 4th Tank Army, which had 370 tanks in seven tank brigades, was unable to begin crossing the Don until 28 July, which saved the XIV Panzerkorps from a serious defeat. A significant part of Kriuchenkin's tanks fell out due to mechanical difficulties on the road march to the Don, which limited his ability to feed forces into the battle. Nor did the eight OTBs in the Soviet 62nd and 64th Armies, which comprised 200 tanks, play any significant role in the counter-offensive due to lack of coordination. On 28–31 July, the tank battles continued to revolve around Verkhne-Buzinovka as the two Soviet tank armies attempted to break through the XIV Panzerkorps to the three encircled divisions of the 62nd Army. The Soviet 8th Air Army finally provided some significant air support, including a regiment of Il-2 Sturmoviks, which managed to shoot up some German columns. However, the improvised nature of the Soviet armoured counter-offensive meant that Gordov was unable to provide any significant artillery support to the two tank armies and very little motorized infantry was available.

Fliegerkorps VIII's relentless ground attack sorties helped to balance out the Soviet 2–1 numerical superiority in tanks. Kriuchenkin gradually fed General-major Aleksandr A. Shamshin's 22nd Tank Corps, General-major Abram M. Khasin's 23rd Tank Corps and Polkovnik Nikolai M. Bubnov's 133rd Heavy Tank Brigade (forty KV-1) into the battle from the northeast. Tanaschishin's 13th Tank Corps managed to break through to the encircled 62nd Army units from the south and facilitate a partly-successful breakout operation, while other Soviet tanks overran the XIV Panzerkorps command post. Gordov's armoured counter-offensive did succeed in halting AOK 6's advance on Stalingrad for a week, although German supply difficulties would have accomplished much the same result. Otherwise, the commitment of this mass of Soviet armour into open steppe terrain allowed the Germans to shoot and bomb the 1st and 4th Tank Armies to pieces over the course of a week. By 31 July, AOK 6 had halted the Soviet counteroffensive and the Stalingrad Front lost more than 600 tanks in a week. The Soviet armoured counter-offensive in the Don Bend was a virtual repeat of the 1941 Battle of Dubno – an uncoordinated, piecemeal meeting engagement that handed a tactical victory to the Germans on a silver platter. The Soviet preference for impulsive, unplanned attacks – usually instigated by Stalin – was a near-lethal tendency that the Germans continually exploited. Yet Stalin ignored his own role in the disastrous Battle of the Don Bend and issued a scathing Stavka Directive in its aftermath:

Our tank units and formations often suffer greater losses through mechanical breakdowns than they do in battle. For example, in the Stalingrad Front, when we had a significant superiority in tanks, artillery and aircraft over the enemy, during six days of battle, twelve tank brigades lost 326 out of 400 tanks, of which about 200 were lost to mechanical problems. Many of the tanks were abandoned on the battlefield. Similar instances can be observed in other fronts. Since such a high incidence of mechanical defects is implausible, the Supreme High Command sees in it covert sabotage and wrecking on the part of certain tank crews who try to exploit small mechanical problems to leave their tanks on the battlefield and avoid battle.[53]

Stalin had finally stated what many field commanders already knew: half-trained tank crews that were fed into poorly-planned battles like so much cannon fodder would often choose personal survival over mission accomplishment. Whereas German tankers usually continued to fight their tanks even after suffering one or more non-penetrating hits, many Soviet tankers abandoned tanks that were still combat effective and walked back to their assembly areas. Photographic evidence of numerous captured T-34s from mid-1942 indicates that many had little or no evidence of major damage. Stalin had already issued his 'Not One Step Backward!' [*Ni shagu nazad!*] command in Order No. 227, but tankers clearly needed more explicit guidelines. By summer 1942, Soviet tank units began to distinguish between tanks that 'burned' on the battlefield – indicating catastrophic damage – and those that were abandoned but not burned. Crews that abandoned a tank that did not burn were now sent to penal units, which served to discourage others from abandoning their tanks.[54]

While Stalin and the Stavka became fixated on the tank battles in the Don Bend, Hitler saw an opportunity for Hoth's 4.Panzerarmee to pivot north-eastward after crossing the Don and unexpectedly smash in the Stalingrad Front's left flank. Hoth's forces were relatively weak, with the main striking element being General der Panzertruppe Werner Kempf's XXXXVIII Panzerkorps with 14.Panzer-Division and 29.Infanterie-Division (mot.), with no more than 100 operational tanks, but Gordov had concentrated all his available armour on his right flank. Generalmajor Ferdinand Heim's 14.Panzer-Division achieved a spectacular breakthrough of the 51st Army's front on 1 August and advanced 40km in a single day, rolling up Gordov's flank. Supported by the 29.Infanterie-Division (mot.), Heim advanced so quickly toward the northeast that Gordov could not react quickly enough or build a new defensive line. German armour captured the railhead at Kotel'nikovo on the morning of 2 August and reached Abganerovo, only 70km southwest of Stalingrad, on 5 August. The *Vorausabteilungen* of both mechanized divisions managed to reach Tinguta station, just 60km from Stalingrad, on 6 August. As usual, an advance of this kind reduced Kempf's XXXXVIII Panzerkorps to logistical bankruptcy and the Red Army was given valuable time to recover while the Germans waited for more fuel to arrive. General-leytenant Mikhail S. Shumilov's 64th Army managed to form a new line of rifle divisions blocking the way to Stalingrad, while Gordov dispatched the decimated 13th Tank Corps and 133rd Heavy Tank Brigade to launch a counter-attack.

Shumilov counterattacked XXXXVIII Panzerkorps on the morning of 9 August. Tanaschishin's 13th Tank Corps entered the battle with only thirty T-34 and four T-70s, but was reinforced by Polkovnik Bubnov's twenty-two KV-1. It was not a particularly strong counterattack, but it caught the Germans by surprise; one German column was ambushed near Tinguta by some T-34s from the 6th Guards Tank Brigade and Leytenant Nikolai P. Andreev was able to knock-out five German tanks in quick succession. The *Vorausabteilungen* fell back in hasty retreat. After two days of tank skirmishing which cost Tanaschishin forty tanks and Heim about the same, Kempf was able to establish a stable front around Abganerovo, but lacked the strength to advance any closer to Stalingrad. Heim's 14.Panzer-Division was reduced to just twenty-four operational tanks. Despite Hitler's perception that Hoth's 4.Panzerarmee was a powerful force, by mid-August it consisted of only three mechanized divisions with less than 200 tanks and three German and four Romanian infantry divisions.

Once Soviet attention shifted to their left flank, Paulus' AOK 6 was able to finish off the elements of the 62nd Army and 1st Tank Army that were still in the Don Bend. A pincer attack begun on the morning of 7 August by Hube's 16.Panzer-Division from the north and the 24.Panzer-Division from the south quickly shattered the 62nd Army's front and achieved a link-up near Kalach by nightfall of the same day. A total of eight Soviet rifle divisions, plus the battered remnants of the 23rd and 28th Tank Corps, were trapped inside the German *kessel*. It took the Germans five days to reduce the *kessel*, but by 12 August Paulus claimed that 35,000 prisoners and 270 tanks had been taken and all the formations inside the *kessel* destroyed. In fact, about half the trapped forces escaped across the Don, but without equipment.[55] The 1st Tank Army was no more and it was officially disbanded on 17 August. Paulus then turned to finish off Kriuchenkin's 4th Tank Army, reduced to only forty-five tanks, with a sudden attack by XIV Panzerkorps on 15 August. Within two days, Kriuchenkin's army was crushed and soon disbanded, the Red Army cleared from the Don Bend except for a bridgehead at Kremenskaya.

Paulus' AOK 6 was exhausted after six weeks of continuous combat and his panzer divisions were worn down. Nevertheless, he needed to get AOK 6 across the Don in order to push into Stalingrad. At 0310 hours on 21 August, four infantry regiments from AOK 6 began crossing the Don at Vertiachii by means of the assault boats of the 902 Sturmboote Kommando. A bridgehead was rapidly seized and pioneers constructed two 20-ton pontoon bridges across the Don within twenty-four hours. During the night of 22–23 August, Hube's 16.Panzer-Division crossed the pontoon bridges, followed by the 3.Infanterie-Division (mot.). At 0430 hours on 23 August, Hube attacked out of the bridgehead with the panzers of Kampfgruppe Sieckenius in the lead followed by Kampfgruppe von Strachwitz – a broad panzerkeil (armoured wedge) of tanks and SPWs moving across the fender-high steppe grass toward the Volga. Fliegerkorps VIII mounted a maximum effort, enabling Hube's panzers to easily blast through the

Soviet 62nd Army's defenses. After a dash of 60km, the 6./Pz.Regt 2 reached the Volga north of Stalingrad at 1835 hours. One German noted that 'from the towering heights of the western shore there is a stunning view of the mighty river and the Asian steppe spreading out to infinity.'[56]

Although the rest of XIV Panzerkorps was approaching along the same route, Hube's division was in a very exposed position at the end of a long corridor, with Soviet forces ringed around him. Hube deployed his division in kampfgruppen-size hedgehogs and waited for the infantry of AOK 6 and resupply to arrive. The Germans had succeeded in reaching Stalingrad, but without the kind of coup de main that had effortlessly taken other cities – there would be no cheap victories at Stalingrad. Despite the appearance of German armour outside Stalingrad, the Stavka made the decision not to evacuate the StZ tank factory, which built 250 T-34s – or 20 per cent of Russia's total output of T-34s – in August.

Tank Battles north of Orel, 5 July–29 August

Zhukov had expected the main German summer offensive to try again for Moscow and the Stavka assessed that the most likely enemy avenue of approach was from the Bolkhov region, north of Orel. Consequently, Zhukov ensured that a great deal of the new tank production was sent to this sector and that he would have control over them. Yet when it became obvious by early July that the Germans were not going to try for Moscow again, Zhukov refused to allow his heavily-reinforced Western Front to stand idle while Heeresgruppe Süd crushed the Bryansk and Southwestern Fronts. With six tank corps under his command, Zhukov recommended to Stalin that the Western Front could mount a counter-stroke against the German 2.Panzerarmee guarding the northern part of the Orel salient. On 2 July, the Stavka authorized Zhukov to conduct a counteroffensive to help take some of the pressure off the Bryansk Front and possibly divert Hoth's armour away from Voronezh. With minimal planning, Zhukov directed General-leytenant Konstantin K. Rokossovsky's 16th Army to attack the Zhizdra sector held by General der Artillerie Joachim Lemelsen's XXXXVII Panzerkorps and General-leytenant Pavel A. Belov's 61st Army to attack the Bolkhov sector held by the German LIII Armeekorps. These two Soviet attack sectors were 90km apart and hence not mutually supporting. Zhukov was hoping to execute some-thing resembling Deep Battle, but in his eagerness to 'do something' before Voronezh fell, he opted to commit two of his armies to an operation with neg-ligible logistical preparation or coordination between units.

Belov attacked first on the morning of 5 July, committing the 12th Guards Rifle Division and the 192nd Tank Brigade as his main effort against the boundary of the German 112 and 296.Infanterie-Divisionen. Over 250 artillery pieces were available to support the attack, but most of their ammunition was fired in the initial prep bombardment. Achieving local surprise, the Soviet guardsmen managed to create a 3km-deep dent in the German security zone before being stopped by mines and well-directed artillery fire in front of the German HKL (main line of resistance). Nor was Soviet air support very helpful and the

192nd Tank Brigade lost six of its tanks to fratricidal Soviet air attacks.[57] When the Soviet attack stalled, the Germans were able to rush reinforcements, including Hauptmann Martin Buhr's Sturmgeschütz-Abteilung 202, to strengthen their HKL. Despite failing to achieve a breakthrough, Belov decided to commit his armoured exploitation force – General-major Dmitri K. Mostovenko's 3rd Tank Corps with 192 tanks – at 1400 hours on 7 July. By this point, the element of surprise was gone and the German HKL in front of Belov's shock groups had been made nearly impregnable with assault guns, 8.8cm flak batteries and additional panzerjägers. Unsurprisingly, Mostovenko's armour suffered heavy losses from anti-tank fire as they arrived on the battlefield and Belov's artillery no longer had the ammunition to suppress the enemy guns. There is an important lesson in Mostovenko's situation, in that an operational-level commander must ensure that he has sufficient fire support remaining when his exploitation force is committed. Instead, the 3rd Tank Corps was stopped cold and bloodied by determined German infantry divisions and could not advance. Although Belov continued attacking for another five days, he achieved nothing.

By waiting an extra day to attack, Rokossovsky's 16th Army was able to make a considerably stronger opening effort, with three rifle divisions, five rifle brigades and three tank brigades in the first echelon. General-major Vasily G. Burkov's 10th Tank Corps, with 152 tanks, waited to exploit the breakthrough. Rokossovsky used 400 artillery pieces to support the attack, as well as over 600 tactical air support sorties, but due to the difficult terrain in his sector he chose to attack across a fairly wide 20km frontage; this was the exact opposite of the German *schwerpunkt*, which committed all resources at a decisive point. The Zhizdra sector was also heavily wooded and marshy, which made armoured operations difficult – Zhukov apparently had not considered terrain in his decision to attack. Kicking off at 0800 hours on 6 July, Rokossovsky's infantry managed to advance 3–5km into the 208.Infanterie-Division's defenses before encountering the same determination as Belov had discovered. Even worse, the 17 and 18.Panzer-Division were both available to reinforce the front-line German infantry divisions in this sector. Unteroffizier Erich Hager, a Pz.IV driver in the 6./Pz.Regt 39, noted that his battalion had completed two days of gunnery training just prior to Rokossovsky's offensives, so the crews were well-honed.[58]

Rokossovsky's first echelon included the 94th, 112th and 146th Tank Brigades and the 519th Tank Battalion with flamethrower tanks, a total of 131 tanks, while Lemelsen decided to initially commit only small armoured kampfgruppen into battle to stabilize the front, but kept some armour in reserve to deal with the Soviet tank corps. Both panzer divisions had been forced to contribute a Panzer-Abteilung to reinforce the divisions involved in *Blau*, leaving only seventy-one tanks in the 17.Panzer-Divisionen and forty-seven tanks in the 18.Panzer-Division. Hager's 6.Kompanie was committed, but quickly lost three of its eleven Pz.IV (short-barreled) tanks. Hager noted that the Soviets had a 4–1 superiority in tanks in his sector. On 7 July, Lemelsen committed more of his armour to prevent a breakthrough of the infantry HKL, resulting in a brutal nine-hour battle between the opposing tanks and artillery. Hager's Pz.IV was hit three times, once in the hull and twice on the turret, but only one crew member was injured by spalling (splinters from the armour). Some tank-vs.-tank combat occurred as close as 200 meters. Hager noted,

> Thirty enemy tanks were destroyed and one Pak. Lots of the Russian tanks were USA (American M3 Lees). Attack continues with infantry on the HKL. Whole Abteilung shoots, shoots, shoots. Russian artillery and tanks shoot straight at us. We cannot do anything about it as they are further away than 3,000 meters ... All in all, 6 of our tanks are hit but they do not burn up so can be recovered ... Return to refuel and rearm at 2000 hours. What a day![59]

The 17 and 18.Panzer-Division managed to prevent a breakthrough and shot up most of Rokossovsky's infantry support tanks in the process. As Hager noted, German tank losses were also significant, but since they held the ground most damaged tanks could be recovered and repaired. Despite lack of a breakthrough, on the evening of 7 July Rokossovsky decided to commit Burkov's 10th Tank Corps, but their night deployment was seriously hindered by the marshy terrain in the sector. Whenever near the front, large armoured units are frequently moved at night in order to avoid detection by the enemy and thereby gain the maximum advantage of surprise. A well-trained armour unit will send a quartering party ahead to reconnoiter the route of march from the assembly areas all the way up to the front, leaving traffic control personnel along the way to ensure that vehicles stay on the correct path. However, the Red Army of mid-1942 had not yet learned these lessons and instead, tanks and vehicles of Burkov's 10th Tank Corps blundered off the road and got stuck in marshes. When daylight on 8 July arrived, Burkov's armour was still all bunched up in column formation on trails just behind the front and Lemelsen requested Luftwaffe air strikes on the mass of Soviet armour. German air superiority over the Zhizdra sector was absolute and Rokossovsky later wrote, 'before the battle I had never seen the Germans throw so many aircraft into such a small sector as the one in which the 16th Army was operating.'[60] Burkov's armour was badly knocked about by the Luftwaffe and entered battle piecemeal, not as a corps.

During the night of 7–8 July, the 17.Panzer-Division dug in a number of its tanks along the HKL to protect them from Soviet artillery fire and they awaited Burkov's armour. Hager's Pz.IV knocked out a T-34 but was hit on the hull by an HE round that damaged the track and engine. Nevertheless, Hager's Pz.IV kept firing until all ammunition was expended and remained in the fight for eight hours. One German tank platoon of three tanks knocked out ten attacking Soviet tanks and, overall, Burkov's corps lost about fifty tanks on its first day in action. Even though it was clear by 8 July that neither Belov nor Rokossovsky was going to achieve any worthwhile success, Zhukov ordered the offensive to continue and 9 July was a repeat of the previous day. Hager noted,

> The battle begins at 1200 hours. We have to stay in the same position and fire until our ammunition runs out. Russian tanks are driving around in front

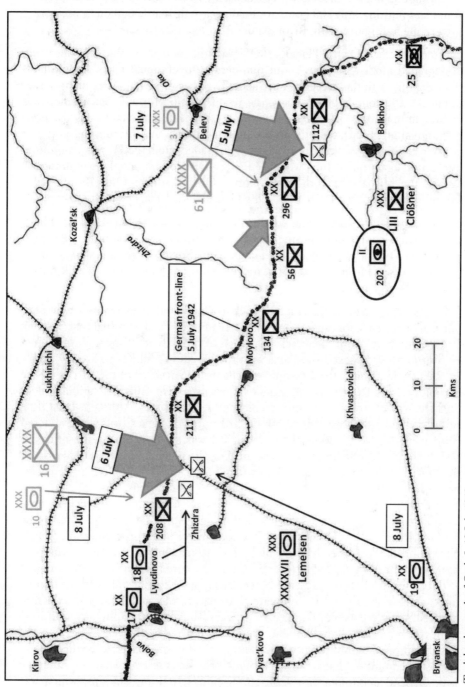

Tank battles north of Orel, 5–12 July 1942.

of us but do not see us luckily ... 35 tanks attack us and 35 tanks are knocked out and burning. At 1700 hours we finally leave the battle and make our way to refuel and rearm with 4.Kompanie. Also make repairs.

After two days of battle Hager's Pz.IV was still combat-capable, but operating in degraded mode. Statistics about numbers of 'operational tanks' should consider that many in this category were actually rather marginal. After firing something like 200 rounds in two days, the recoil system on the 7.5cm cannon was malfunctioning and finally broke down altogether. The tank's radio was also non-operational after repeated hits on the hull and turret and the running gear was in poor condition. Nevertheless, Hager's degraded-mode Pz.IV was committed into action again on 10 July, when 17.Panzer-Division mounted a counterattack against the off-balance 10th Tank Corps. Oberstleutnant Otto Büsing led a kampfgruppe from his II/Pz.Regt 39, which included Hager's 6.Kompanie:

> The same attack again. The whole Abteilung. Now the fun starts ... The regimental commander[Büsing] took a hit, bailed out. Hauptman Karen arrived. Took a hit, bailed out. Hauptmann Borsch came up, took a hit, bailed out ... Hit in the steering, move on a bit and then back. Track torn off. Have to bail out.[61]

Hager and his crew walked on foot back to their battalion assembly area – a not unusual occurrence for tankers on the Eastern Front – and admitted that 'not one Pz.IV came back' from the attack. The men of II/Pz.Regt 39 spent all of 11 July recovering their knocked-out tanks with the battalion's Sd.Kfz.9 (FAMO) semi-tracks and, amazingly, the I-Gruppe mechanics repaired six of the Pz.IVs by the end of 12 July. By that point, Zhukov's offensive had failed to seriously dent 2.Panzerarmee's front or to inconvenience German plans. Although PzAOK 2 suffered about 5,000 casualties, both the 3rd and 10th Tank Corps were rendered combat-ineffective for some time. Soviet C2 was abysmal during the offensive and inter-unit coordination non-existent. Despite much heroism and bloodshed, the Red Army had not yet learned how to break an entrenched German defensive line, particularly one supported by panzers and assault guns.

Although Zhukov's Zhizdra-Bolkhov offensive failed, he was quick to urge more offensive action in this sector as well as against the German 9.Armee in the exposed Rzhev salient. Zhukov still had four intact tank corps under his immediate control and General-leytenant Petr L. Romanenko's 3rd Tank Army was nearby in the RVGK. However, the Germans noted that the recent bungled Western Front offensive presented Heeresgruppe Mitte not only with an opportunity to mount a riposte to eliminate all or part of the Sukhinichi salient before the Red Army recovered, but also to distract Zhukov's remaining armour away from the vulnerable Rzhev salient. Despite the priority of *Blau*, Hitler and the OKH authorized a limited offensive known as *Wirbelwind*, set to begin in early August. Schmidt's 2.Panzerarmee would form the *schwerpunkt* of its offensive with General der Infanterie Heinrich Clößner's LIII Armeekorps, which was given 11 and 20.Panzer-Divisionen, the 197 and 202.Sturmgeschütz-Abteilungen and four infantry divisions. In addition, Schmidt retained Lemelsen's XXXXVII Panzerkorps with the 18.Panzer-Division and gained Generaloberst Josef Harpe's XXXXI Panzerkorps, with the 9, 17 and 19.Panzer-Divisionen. Schmidt's divisions also received their first Pz.IIIJ and Pz.IVF2 replacement tanks, putting them on a more equal footing with Zhukov's T-34s. Despite the concentration of six panzer divisions in a fairly small sector north of Bolkhov, Operation *Wirbelwind* has been overshadowed by Operation *Blau* and the Battle of Stalingrad.

Clößner's LIII Armeekorps attacked the boundary of the Soviet 61st Army north of Bolkhov on the morning of 11 August and achieved some initial success. In particular, the 11.Panzer-Division was able to advance up to 25km in heavily wooded terrain toward the intermediate objective – Sukhinichi. Thereafter, Soviet resistance hardened quickly and the Red Army was particularly formidable in forest-fighting. German tankers were wary of moving along narrow forest tracks that were usually mined and covered by anti-tank ambushes. While the 2.Panzerarmee succeeded in gaining a small bridgehead over the Zhizdra river, the 16th Army blocked any further advance toward Sukhinichi by moving Burkov's rebuilt 10th Tank Corps and General-major Aleksei V. Kurkin's 9th Tank Corps to contain the German advance. Three Soviet rifle divisions were cut off and destroyed and the two Soviet tank corps lost about 200 tanks, but *Wirbelwind* failed to seize significant terrain or seriously impair Zhukov's freedom of action. Instead, it was the German panzer units that suffered heavy losses in the ill-judged offensive and diverted resources that could have been better used elsewhere. The 9.Panzer Division, which started the operation with 110 tanks, lost forty-four tanks in *Wirbelwind*.[62] Although difficult terrain was certainly a factor in the failure of *Wirbelwind*, this was the second time since the beginning of *Blau* that a German panzer *schwerpunkt* had been stopped cold by determined Soviet resistance, which was an ominous portent of the Red Army's growing competence.

Just as Hitler decided to abort *Wirbelwind*, Zhukov made the surprise decision to commit Romanenko's 3rd Tank Army to the Bolkhov sector in an effort to cut off 2.Panzerarmee's spearhead. Romanenko's 3TA had moved by rail from Tula and assembled on the eastern flank of 2.Panzerarmee's salient, near Kozel'sk. Zhukov assembled a force of 218,000 troops and 700 tanks to crush the German forces in the salient, which were outnumbered by 3–1 in armour. Romanenko attacked at 0615 hours on 22 August, committing three rifle divisions and a rifle brigade in the first echelon to claw their way through the defenses of the German 26 and 56.Infanterie-Divisionen. After the infantry had advanced 4–6km through the outer German defenses – but not achieved a real breakthrough – Romanenko committed the 3rd, 12th and 15th Tank Corps into the battle. Once again though, the Red Army's use of large armoured formations was marred by the lack of pre-battle reconnaissance; Romanenko's tanks ran into swamps, enemy mines and generally got lost in the forest trails. Even after moving forward for twelve hours, Romanenko's tanks had not yet encountered the enemy and were behind the forward line of their own infantry. The Luftwaffe managed to gain and keep local air superiority over this sector, enabling Stukas and bombers to mercilessly hammer the stalled columns of Soviet armour. Romanenko was finally able to get some of his armour, in piecemeal fashion, into battle on 23 August, but by that time Clößner had shifted the 11 and 20.Panzer-Division to bolster the flagging German infantry. The Red Army had little experience supplying a formation of 600 tanks and Romanenko's tank corps suffered from fuel shortages, even though they never gained more than 2–3km into the German line. An effort by Rokossovsky's 16th Army to assist Romanenko by attacking the western side of the German salient was quickly snuffed out. Gradually, the combination of German panzer divisions in defense and Luftwaffe overhead reduced the immobilized 3rd Tank Army into wreckage. By the time that Zhukov finally ended the offensive in early September, the attacking Soviet forces had lost 500 of 700 tanks and Romanenko's 3rd Tank Army had been rendered hors de combat. Afterwards, both sides shifted to the defense and much of the remaining armour was transferred elsewhere.

Even though the fighting around Bolkhov-Zhizdra in July–August 1942 is not well known, it involved six of the nineteen panzer divisions and five of the twenty-two Soviet tank corps on the Eastern Front, making these battles one of the largest clashes of armour in 1942. Neither side enjoyed any real offensive success in these battles, mostly due to restrictive terrain, and German air power played a prominent role in equalizing the Soviet numerical superiority in manpower and tanks. It is also noteworthy that Zhukov's use of large armoured formations and efforts at conducting set-piece offensives had no more success than other Soviet commanders at that time. The Bolkhov-Zhizdra offensives were an amateurish waste of armour, costing the Red Army another 1,000 tanks for no gain at all. On the other hand, Hitler's willingness to commit so much armour to a secondary theater violated the principle of concentration of force, when he needed every Panzer-Abteilung, Stuka sortie and liter of petrol available to support Heeres-gruppe Süd's drive for the Caucasus.

Stalingrad: the Schwerpunkt Hits a Brick Wall, 24 August–1 November

No sooner had Hube reached the Volga River than he found that his 16.Panzer-Division was isolated from the rest of XIV Panzerkorps and under pressure from Soviet forces both north and south of his division. Von Wietersheim had to deploy the bulk of the 3 and 60.Infanterie-Divisionen (mot.) just to hold a tenuous link to Hube's division, which left nothing left to support an attack into the northern outskirts of Stalingrad. Nevertheless, Hube – easily the most aggressive and skilled panzer division commander on the Eastern Front – began attacking with three kampfgruppen into the northern outskirts of Stalingrad on 24 August. Hube only had about fifty operational tanks and was advancing into a dense urban area with just two Panzer-Abteilungen, five motorized infantry battalions and one engineer battalion – a grossly inadequate force. Yet the Germans had captured other large Soviet cities with equally small armoured forces in the past and it seemed worth a try. From their starting positions, the huge Tractor Factory was visible. At dawn on 24 August, Hube moved two kampfgruppen toward the suburbs of Spartanovka, but the Soviets were just able to rush NKVD

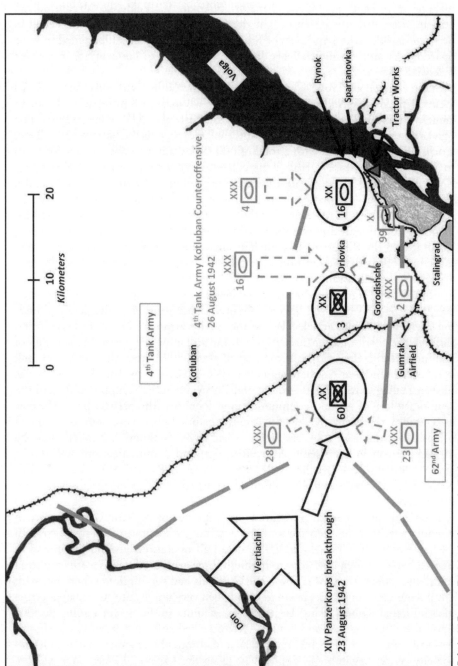

Hube's 16.Panzer-Division's drive to the Volga, 23 August, and Soviet armoured counterattack, 26 August 1942.

infantry and fifty T-34s from the StZ factory to prevent the Germans from making any headway. General-major Nikolai V. Feklenko organized an armoured counterattack that caught the Germans off-balance and succeeded in overrunning the command post of Kampfgruppe Krumpen; Hube failed to seize Spartanovka and by nightfall his division was forced to concentrate into three defensive hedgehogs.

Stalin reacted to Hube's breakthrough to the Volga with fury and ordered General-polkovnik Andrei I. Yeremenko's newly-named Southeastern Front to launch an immediate counter-offensive to crush the XIV Panzerkorps. The Stavka committed the 2nd, 4th and 16th Tank Corps, plus the battered 23rd Tank Corps, to the operation, with a total of 600 tanks, but it took two days for them to reach their assembly areas. This collection of armour included about fifty KV-1 and 250 T-34 tanks, but the rest consisted of T-60 and T-70 light tanks. Yeremenko sensibly planned for a pincer attack against both sides of the XIV Panzerkorps' narrow corridor, but the actual amount of time provided for planning and preparation was the usual inadequate five to six hours. Once again, Stalin forced the Red Army to launch its armoured forces into an uncoordinated, piecemeal effort that undermined their 10–1 local superiority in tanks. The two Soviet armoured assault groups attacked both sides of the corridor on the morning of 26 August, but encountered heavy fire from dug-in panzerjäger units. Fliegerkorps VIII harassed Soviet armoured concentrations, relentlessly pounding them with Stuka attacks. While the Soviet armour did succeed in cutting through the corridor after three days fighting and interfering with Hube's lines of communication, they did so at the cost of about 500 tanks. All four Soviet tank corps were rendered combat-ineffective. While Hube's 16.Panzer-Division was hurt, it managed to hold its ground and Luftwaffe aerial resupply mitigated the temporary loss of ground communications. Zhukov, who arrived from Moscow as a Stavka representative on 29 August, claimed that Yeremenko's counter-offensive – which he took credit for – had saved Stalingrad. Nevertheless, by 30 August von Wietersheim had restored ground communications with Hube and Yeremenko had lost the battle of the corridor. Paulus' AOK 6 and Hoth's XXXXVIII Panzerkorps then gradually pushed the Soviet forces back into Stalingrad.

Having failed to seize Stalingrad by coup de main, Paulus was forced to conduct a deliberate offensive into the city, but he was not ready to do so until 14 September. It is not my intent to detail all operations around Stalingrad in September–October 1942, but to highlight how armoured forces were employed in urban combat. Up to this point, the Germans had very limited experience with employing tanks in urban areas and it had been very unpleasant. German doctrine also militated against using large armoured units in cities, yet Paulus decided upon this course of action because AOK 6 lacked sufficient infantry and Hitler was insistent that the city be captured as soon as possible. Paulus' first assault into the city center began on 14 September, using the 14 and 24.Panzer-Divisionen, 29.Infanterie-Division (mot.) and five infantry divisions, supported by the 243 and 245 Sturmgeschütz-Abteilungen. The German armoured units were already quite depleted at the start of the fight for the city, with Generalmajor Bruno Ritter von Hauenschild's 24. Panzer-Division reduced to only thirty-four operational tanks. On 4 September, von Hauenschild was badly wounded during fighting on the outskirts of Stalingrad and replaced by Generalmajor Arno von Lenski. By the time that Paulus' offensive began on 14 September, the 24.Panzer-Division was reduced to only twenty-two operational tanks and 56 per cent of its personnel.[63]

Once sent into the city, panzer divisions were forced to commit their armour in small platoon and company-size detachments in the infantry support role – the antithesis of how the Wehrmacht wanted to use its armour. The Luftwaffe had heavily damaged large portions of Stalingrad, clogging streets with rubble that greatly limited the mobility of the German tanks. Due to enemy snipers, panzer commanders were forced to operate in 'buttoned up' mode in the city, which greatly reduced visibility and situational awareness. Soviet anti-tank guns and PTRD anti-tank rifle teams could get close to German armour that lacked effective infantry support. German infantry commanders frequently tried to use Pz.III and Pz.IV tanks as assault guns, even though the lacked the additional 30mm bolt-on armour plates that made StuG IIIs better suited for urban combat. On the Soviet side, General-leytenant Vasily I. Chuikov's 62nd Army mounted a dogged defense of the city that astounded the Germans. Chuikov's armoured support never exceeded eighty tanks and was often reduced to just a couple of dozen tanks. Most Soviet tank commanders in Stalingrad chose to dig in their tanks and integrate them into infantry fighting positions. The presence of even a few dug-in T-34s could make a Soviet battalion-size position virtually impregnable. Paulus' first assault succeeded in capturing the southern part of Stalingrad by late September and the StZ workers built their last T-34s and then joined the battle.

While AOK 6 was fighting to evict Chuikov's 62nd Army from the city, Zhukov pressured Yeremenko to mount another offensive against the German northern flank around Kotluban, held by von Wietersheim's XIV Panzerkorps. General-major Kirill S. Moskalenko, unemployed after the destruction of his 1st Tank Army, was given a new command – the 1st Guards Army – and the Stavka transferred Kravchenko's 4th Tank Corps, Rotmistrov's 7th Tank Corps and the battered 16th Tank Corps to provide armoured muscle to this strike force. By mid-September, Moskalenko had massed a force of 123,000 troops and 340 tanks (including forty-two KV-1 and 143 T-34) opposite the 60 Infanterie-Division (mot.) and 76.Infanterie-Division (mot.) near Kotluban. However, mass was not enough and Yeremenko failed to employ deception, so Paulus saw the blow coming and concentrated his anti-tank guns and 8.8cm flak guns in this sector. Moskalenko attacked on the morning of 18 September, in broad daylight, across flat terrain with good fields of fire. The German anti-tank guns and flak guns ripped the Soviet armour to pieces, inflicting 106 losses on the first day; the new 7.5cm Pak 40 was now available in quantity and could destroy either the KV-1 or T-34 at ranges up to 1,000 meters or more. The Luftwaffe also bombed the 1st Guards Army mercilessly and the impotence of Soviet air support ensured

222 Tank Warfare on the Eastern Front, 1941–1942

failure. Hube's 16.Panzer-Division launched a vicious counterattack with about fifty tanks that demolished two of Rotmistrov's tank brigades, knocking out seventy-five of his ninety-three tanks. One of Hube's panzer companies, the 7./Pz.Regt 2, had only seven operational tanks but succeeded in knocking out twenty-two of Rotmistrov's tanks. Moskalenko's 1st Guards Army suffered 46,000 casualties during the offensive and lost 341 of 384 tanks committed, including forty-eight KV-1 and 173 T-34. Rotmistrov's 7th Tank Corps was reduced to just eighteen operational tanks. German newsreels filmed after the battle depict a vast tank graveyard in the open steppe north of Stalingrad, marking another cheap German tactical victory due to the ill-considered offensive ordered by Zhukov.[64] It was not that Zhukov was incompetent – he knew better – but he had been around Stalin too long and come to accept that he could dictate a victory rather than planning one. Zhukov went back to Moscow empty-handed, but proclaimed the Kotluban offensive to have been an attritional victory.

Despite this success, von Wietersheim complained about the misuse of his armour in urban combat and Paulus relieved him of command and replaced him with Hube. On 27 September, Paulus began his second major offensive, intending to conquer the northern half of Stalingrad. The 16.Panzer-Division joined the offensive from the north, while 24.Panzer-Division advanced from the south. This time, the German *schwerpunkt* utilized four infantry divisions backed by up to 100 tanks. Attacking toward the Barrikady Gun Factory, the 24.Panzer-Division managed to advance 6km in two days – quite a feat in Stalingrad – but suffered crippling losses to its four Panzergrenadier-Abteilungen. By early October, all three of Paulus' panzer divisions were badly depleted. Many panzer crews were without tanks by October but, in a demonstration of arrant stupidity, Paulus ordered that dismounted tankers be employed as infantry in the city. The AOK 6's logistics situation was also very poor, with limited fuel, ammunition and rations reaching the remaining panzer kampfgruppen. Nevertheless, on 14 October, Paulus committed the 14.Panzer-Division and one infantry division to seize the heavily-defended Dzerzhinsky Tractor Factory. Within twenty-four hours, the Germans succeeded in capturing the tractor works, but 14.Panzer-Division suffered 138 casualties and had thirty tanks knocked out. Many of these panzers were quickly repaired, but two days later the 14.Panzer-Division was sent to attack the Barrikady Gun Factory and had seventeen tanks knocked out by dug-in T-34s.[65] Damaged German tanks were continually repaired, but only enough for limited operations. Some new replacement tanks did reach AOK 6, including two dozen Pz.IIIN, equipped with the 7.5cm KwK L/24 howitzer, which were useful for bunker-busting in the city.

At Stalingrad, Hitler and the OKH exercised insufficient oversight over Paulus and allowed him to let three of the Wehrmacht's best panzer divisions bleed to death for minimal gains. Paulus' use of armour in the city was asinine and ignored everything that von Manstein had learned under similar conditions at Sevastopol. Paulus also kept most of XIV Panzerkorps in or near the city, while his long flanks were held only by German and Romanian infantry. It was not until November that Paulus deployed part of the shattered 14.Panzer-Division to help bolster his army's left flank, but he otherwise refused to pull his armour out of the line to rest and refit.

The Rzhev Meatgrinder, 2 July–30 August

Throughout the winter and spring of 1942, Generaloberst Walter Model's 9.Armee had been precariously holding the Rzhev salient under intense pressure from Zhukov's Western Front and Konev's Kalinin Front. Gradually General-oberst Walter Model gained the upper hand and began clearing out his rear areas, which were infested with Soviet paratroopers, cavalry and partisans that were still there from the Winter Counter-offensive. Operation *Hannover*, which included kampfgruppen from both the 5 and 19.Panzer-Divisionen, eliminated this threat in May–June. During the operation, Model was badly wounded on 23 May and temporarily replaced by Generaloberst Heinrich von Viettinghoff.[66] As a result of Operation *Hannover*, the Soviet 39th Army, with seven rifle divisions, was isolated on the west flank of the salient and 9.Armee developed a more ambitious plan known as *Seydlitz* to remove this thorn from their side. Heeresgruppe Mitte sent the 1 and 20.Panzer-Divisionen to reinforce the operation, providing von Viettinghoff with a total of four panzer divisions.

Operation *Seydlitz* began on 2 July, with 1 and 2.Panzer-Divisionen mounting pincer attacks from Olenino and Belyy to link up and complete the encirclement of the 39th Army. Even though the distance to be covered was minimal – less than 30km total – the infantry of the Soviet 39th Army stopped both German panzer divisions cold and prevented the narrow corridor leading west from being closed. Admittedly, both German panzer divisions were weak in armour, with only a single Panzer-Abteilung each, but both *schwerpunkte* had failed. Even worse, the 41st Army just outside the corridor committed its 2nd Guards Motorized Division, 21st and 82nd Tank Brigades to counterattack the German panzer spearheads. Fierce tank combat ensued for several days at the mouth of the Belyy corridor, with the Soviet tankers preventing the Germans from closing the *kessel*. The German 5.Panzer-Division, attacking from Rzhev, also made no progress, but the 20.Panzer-Division, attacking from the east, found a weak spot. The 373rd Rifle Division could not hold the 20.Panzer-Division and the panzers advanced rapidly, causing the 39th Army's all-around defense to collapse. A panic ensued, allowing the 1 and 2.Panzer-Divisionen to link up on 5 July, completing the encirclement of the 39th Army. Over the next week, the Germans smashed the Soviet divisions within the *kessel*, and eventually took at least 30,000 prisoners and eliminated 218 Soviet tanks.[67]

While the 39th Army was dying on the western side of the Rzhev salient, Zhukov assembled a mass of troops and armour on the eastern side to retake Rzhev and eliminate the 9.Armee. Konev's Kalinin Front would attack with its 29th and 30th Armies from the north, while Zhukov's Western Front attacked from the east with its 20th and 31st Armies. Zhukov also ensured that there would be adequate air support for the operation – two air armies – which helps to explain why the Luftwaffe was virtually unopposed in the Bolkhov-Zhizdra sectors.

Konev's two armies attacked first, with only a few tank brigades in the infantry support role, beginning on 30 July. Yet the German infantry were well dug in north of Rzhev and Konev's own infantry could make no real progress, despite repeated efforts. Soviet artillery preparations were still undermined by limited stockpiles of ammunition and poor fire coordination, so the level of artillery support typically dropped off sharply after the first few days of an offensive. Unable to achieve a breakthrough, Konev withheld most of his armour. Zhukov waited until 4 August, hoping that Konev could divert German reserves, then committed his 20th and 31st Armies into an attack against the northeast corner of the Rzhev salient. The two Soviet armies committed a massive amount of infantry and artillery against the Pogoreloe sector, held by the German XXXXVI Panzerkorps with 36.Infanterie-Division (mot) and the 161.Infanterie-Division. Each army had a mobile group, comprised of three tank brigades, to exploit success and Zhukov had the 6th and 8th Tank Corps as front-level exploitation forces. Zhukov had a flair for pouring overwhelming resources into a battle and he simply buried these two German front-line divisions under an avalanche of firepower. Within twenty-four hours, Zhukov's forces had created a 30km-wide hole in 9.Armee's front, with penetrations varying from 12–20km. Indeed, Zhukov had succeeded in achieving a breakthrough against a strongly fortified German line – a first for the Red Army. However, Zhukov did not apparently realize the scale of his victory and allowed the 20th and 31st Armies to continue to dawdle in committing their mobile groups to exploit the victory. Indeed, the Soviet offensive made clear that the concepts of mobile warfare were still not completely understood by all Red Army senior leadership, some of whom still moved at a First World War pace of operations. In a race against time, von Viettinghoff rushed kampfgruppen from the 2 and 5.Panzer-Divisionen from Vyazma to block the advance of the 20th and 31st Armies before Soviet armour appeared in quantity on the battlefield. By the end of the second day, the 20th and 31st Armies began committing their mobile groups, but German armour was already at hand to oppose them. Yet these two panzer divisions could only put about 150–180 operational tanks into the field, while Zhukov committed 600 tanks to the Pogoreloe sector and could call upon more from the RVGK. After a rapid advance of up to 20km, both Soviet assault armies slowed to a crawl and the battle became more of a pushing and shoving match, although the Red Army still maintained the upper hand.

Frustrated that neither the 20th nor 31st Armies could push through the two incomplete panzer divisions in their path or even widen the breach, Zhukov began committing his front-level mobile group on 11 August. Zhukov put his deputy, General-major Ivan V. Galanin, in command of a mobile group comprising General-major Andrei L. Getman's 6th Tank Corps, General-major Mikhail D. Solomatin's 8th Tank Corps and General-major Vladimir V. Kriukov's 2nd Guards Cavalry Corps. Putting an infantryman with no prior experience with mechanized operations in charge of a mixed armour-cavalry mobile group with 334 tanks was probably not a sound choice, but it mattered little since the salient formed by the 20th and 31st Armies was too small for maneuver. Instead,

Galanin's mobile group simply reinforced the army-level mobile groups and proceeded to push westward. German resistance stiffened as more reinforcements arrived, including a kampfgruppe from 1.Panzer-Division and Generaloberst Walter Model, who returned to resume command of the 9.Armee.

The Germans also unveiled a new anti-tank weapon during the Rzhev battle in August: the 7.5cm Pak 41, an advanced tapered-bore weapon that fired tungsten-core Panzergranate 41 rounds that could penetrate a T-34 or KV-1 at ranges up to 1,500 meters. Panzerjäger-Abteilung 561 was equipped with twelve Pak 41s and managed to bring the 6th and 8th Tank Corps to a halt in a three-day battle around Zubtsov. The KV-1 tankers were particularly stunned to see that their previous invulnerability was now gone and forty-one out of forty-eight KV-1 tanks committed to the battle were knocked out. However, Red Army policy dicated that armour units could not disengage from an assigned mission unless all tanks were knocked out, so tank units were expected to attack until completely ineffective.[68]

Zhukov did what he always did when a battle did not go his way – he added more forces, ordering 5th Army to attack the neighboring 3.Panzerarmee at the base of the Rzhev salient on 11 August, followed by the 33rd on 13 August. Forced to divert some forces to deal with these new attacks, which stretched Heeresgruppe Mitte's limited panzer reserves, Model was forced to grudgingly give some ground against Zhukov's armoured wedges. On 23 August, the 8th Tank Corps captured Karmanovo and the 31st Army captured Zubtsov, but this was the high-water mark for Zhukov's offensive. He allowed the offensive to continue until early September, but no more significant gains were made. Overall, in a month Zhukov had advanced up to 32km, at great cost, but failed to cut off the Rzhev salient or crush the 9.Armee. To be sure, Model's 9.Armee was hurt by Zhukov's offensive, suffering 32,974 casualties in August, including 8,700 dead and missing – which was 23 per cent more than 6.Armee's casualties during the same period on the approaches to Stalingrad. The 9.Armee had been saved by the ability of Heeresgruppe Mitte to provide up to five panzer divisions to reinforce the front-line defenses before they completely collapsed, but this was an exorbitant use of armoured resources to hold a position of no strategic value. Model was quick to recognize that he could not hold the Rzhev salient without the permanent support of several panzer divisions, and he recommended evacuation of the salient as an economy of force measure, but Hitler vetoed the idea. Yet had Hitler listened to Model in September 1942, he would have had several additional panzer divisions available in reserve on the Eastern Front – which could have made a real difference when the Soviet winter counter-offensives began.

Enter the Tigers, August–December 1942
The first Pz.VI Tiger heavy tanks were completed at the Henschel factory in Kassel in August and began to equip three new separate heavy tank battalions. The 56-ton Tiger I was not a major breakthrough in tank technology because its layout was similar to the Pz.IV medium tank, it failed to incorporate sloped

armour and its Maybach HL 210 P45 engine (641hp), which still used petrol, had poor fuel efficiency and power output. The Tiger was intended to be a break-through tank, used in the forefront of any *schwerpunkt*, but it lacked the mobility for true mobile warfare. The Tiger's armour was much thicker than previous German tanks and it was impervious to 76.2mm fire from its frontal arc, but it could be successfully engaged with flank shots at ranges under 500 meters. Yet the Tiger earned its reputation – and the admiration of later generations of tank enthusiasts – due to its superior firepower. The 8.8cm Kwk 36 L/56 cannon provided the Tiger I with a very high hit/kill probability against armoured targets out to 1,000–1,200 meters; very few Second World War tank engagements occurred at ranges beyond this. After more than a year of operating in dread of the T-34, the Germans finally had a tank that could negate the Red Army's qualitative edge in armour. Unfortunately for their cause, the Tiger could only be produced in token quantities.

Within a few weeks of receiving the first production Tigers – which had many technical deficiencies that were still being addressed by the manufacturer – all three heavy tank battalions were directed to send one of their two tank companies to the front. Apparently, the OKH put no real thought into the initial operational deployment of these three Tiger I companies and it was poorly executed. The 1./502 schwere Panzer-Abteilung 502 (s.Pz.Abt. 502) was deployed by rail to the Leningrad front in August–September and eventually fielded nine Tiger tanks. The s.Pz.Abt. 501 was sent with eleven Tigers to Tunisia in November and the s.Pz.Abt. 503 was designated to reach Heeresgruppe A before the end of December with twenty Tigers. By deploying forty-odd Tiger tanks to three different areas, the OKH ensured that the new tanks would have no more than a localized, tactical impact and would prematurely expose the technical capabilities of the new weapon to both the Western Allies and the Red Army before they were available in quantity. It was an idiotic decision. Making the choice of deployment even more problematic, the OKH disregarded the difficulty of supporting a new tank type in company-size detachments. Albert Speer, as minister of armaments, warned that splitting the available Tiger tanks up into small detachments across different fronts would make logistical support virtually impossible, since very few spare parts for the Pz.VI were manufactured. Maybach only provided one spare transmission and engine for each ten Tigers, which led to a very low operational readiness rate for Tigers at the front.[69]

Nor was the combat debut of the Tiger auspicious. Shortly after receiving most of its Tigers, Heeresgruppe Nord committed 1./s.Pz.Abt. 502 in an ill-judged infantry support attack east of Leningrad on 22 September.[70] The terrain in this area was marshy, with heavy vegetation and non-existent road networks – totally unsuitable for the use of heavy tanks. In this kind of terrain, Soviet tanks and anti-tank guns had better opportunities to ambush Tigers at close range and defeat their thick armour. The Tigers were also suffering from endemic problems with their transmissions, which had not yet been perfected for field conditions. Nevertheless, four Tigers were committed to the attack, which proved to be a fiasco, with all four lost to either mechanical defects or anti-tank fire. Three damaged

Tigers were recovered, but one had to be abandoned. The 1./s.Pz.Abt. 502 continued to serve in the Leningrad area throughout the rest of 1942, but due to adverse terrain and poor operational readiness rates, it accomplished very little. The lead elements of s.Pz.Abt. 503 were sent to Heeresgruppe Don on 27 December, but arrived too late for Operation *Wintergewitter*.

The appearance of the Tiger, even in token quantities, did worry the Red Army and helped to spur qualitative improvements to Soviet armoured forces. Soviet tank design had basically frozen on 22 June 1941, with only minor improvements to the T-34, which had been sufficient for the battlefield of 1941–42. However the GABTU became concerned when the Germans introduced the long 7.5cm KwK 40 L/43 gun in spring 1942 and recognized that once German tanks with 8.8cm guns and thick armour became more common on the battlefield, the T-34 would be put at a grave disadvantage. In June 1942 the GABTU tasked the KhPZ design team, now at Nizhniy Tagil, to reexamine the pre-war T-34M in order to develop an improved T-34. By the time that the first Tigers appeared on the Eastern Front, a prototype T-43 was completed; this utilized a new larger, three-man turret, torsion-bar suspension and thicker armour, but still relied upon the same 76.2mm F-34 gun.[71] After trials indicated that the heavier T-43 had less mobility compared to current model T-34/76 tanks, the GABTU decided to defer production and continue development. Likewise, the SKB-2 team at Chelyabinsk was directed to develop a follow-on to the KV-1, designated as the KV-13. Like the T-43, the KV-13 would still employ the F-34 gun.[72] Although the development of larger 85mm, 100mm and 122mm guns was considered, the GABTU's main intent at this time was to develop a 'Universal Tank' to merge the best features of both T-34 and KV-1, not to develop an all-new tank. Impressed by the usefulness of the German StuG-III series, the GABTU also became interested in developing assault guns and tank destroyers for the Red Army. By late December, the first Su-122s would enter limited production.

Operation Uranus, 19–23 November

During the period 12–28 September, there was an intensive debate within the Stavka and GKO about planning a major counter-offensive for the autumn. In addition to Zhukov, General-polkovnik Aleksandr M. Vasilevsky, chief of the general staff, and his deputy General-leytenant Nikolai F. Vatutin, led the discussions. Zhukov, who had just returned from a two-week period at Stalingrad, recommended a major counter-offensive against the long flanks of AOK 6 along the Don. After the failed Kotluban' offensive, he recognized that a decisive success against dug-in German troops was unlikely, but the Romanian 3rd and 4th Armies were more lucrative targets. The consensus of opinion was that Soviet armour could succeed against the Romanians and that a Deep Battle attack against Paulus' lines of communication would put AOK 6 at serious risk. Stalin approved this plan, which would be called Operation Uranus. However, Zhukov also argued that the Red Army was now strong enough to mount two major counter-offensives and, in addition to Uranus, he wanted to lead a renewed attack against AOK 9 in the Rzhev salient. Stalin agreed to Zhukov's proposal, which was designated Operation Mars. Both counter-offensives were planned to begin sometime in October, giving several weeks for preparations.

While Zhukov focused on Operation Mars, the Stavka selected Vasilevsky to plan and organize Operation Uranus (Zhukov did remain involved as an overall supervisor). Although not widely recognized in the west, Vasilevsky was the Red Army's best operational-level equivalent to von Manstein and a gifted staff officer. In anticipation of the importance of the new operation, the Stavka wanted its best field commanders and assigned Vatutin to take over the Southwest Front and Rokossovsky to take over the new Don Front, while Yeremenko kept the Stalingrad Front. Vasilevsky intended to conduct a double envelopment of AOK 6 at Stalingrad, using the basic principles of the pre-war Deep Battle doctrine.[73] The main effort would be launched by Vatutin's Southwest Front, with Romanenko's 5th Tank Army attacking out of the Serafimovich bridgehead and General-leytenant Ivan M. Chistiakov's reinforced 21st Army attacking from the Kletskaya bridgehead across the Don to strike the 3rd Romanian Army. Vatutin would send Romanenko's 5th Tank Army due south toward the rail line at Oblivskaya while the mobile group from 21st Army advanced to the southeast to envelop AOK 6's left flank. Altogether, Vatutin's three tank corps and several separate tank brigades had 440 tanks, far fewer than had been committed into the Battle of the Don Bend in July. Vasilevsky based Uranus on maneuver not mass – a departure from previous Soviet counter-offensives. Rokossovsky's Don Front would conduct supporting attacks with two armies against AOK 6's left flank, but with only 103 tanks in 16th Tank Corps. The other half of the Soviet counter-offensive would begin a day later, when Yeremenko's Stalingrad Front attacked the Romanian 4th Army near Lake Sarpa, south of Stalingrad. Vasilevsky intended that Operation Uranus would be marked by a high offensive tempo and, once the Romanian defensive lines were broken, the Soviet armoured units were expected to advance 30–40km per day and a link-up occur by the end of the third day.

All told, the Red Army committed 1,560 tanks to Operation Uranus. In addition to the five tank corps involved in the counter-offensive, Uranus would also see the first employment of the newly-organized mechanized corps. Since the tank corps had proved quite fragile in combat, the Stavka wanted a formation with greater staying power. General-major Vasiliy T. Volskii's 4th Mechanized Corps, formed on 18 September, had nine motorized infantry battalions and five tank battalions, for a total of 220 tanks and 6,000 infantry. While the mechanized corps was still deficient in terms of organic artillery and support units, it demonstrated that the Red Army was learning from its mistakes and evolving its force structure to make the best of its capabilities.

General Petre Dumitrescu's 3rd Romanian Army was the primary target of Operation Uranus. Dumitrescu had over 150,000 Romanian and 11,000 German troops in the II, IV and V Corps, with seven infantry and two cavalry divisions, holding a 138km-wide front along the Don. The Romanian infantry divisions were forced to hold very wide sectors, averaging 20km wide, and were very deficient in anti-tank capability – twelve 4.7cm anti-tank guns at division-level

and twelve 37mm guns at regiment-level – and very limited artillery fire support.
Poorly-equipped and unmotivated, the Romanian infantry's ability to withstand
large-scale enemy armoured attacks was minimal. The Germans regarded the
Romanians as place-holders for their own infantry, but did not expect them to
hold off large-scale Soviet offensives on their own. Recognizing the dangers of
having both of AOK 6's flanks guarded by Romanian forces, the OKH directed
Heeresgruppe B to deploy armoured reserves behind them, ready to counterattack if necessary. Generalleutnant Ferdinand Heim's XXXXVIII Panzerkorps
was deployed 40–50km behind the Romanian 3rd Army, with Generalleutnant
Eberhard Rodt's 22.Panzer-Division and the Romanian 1st Armoured Division.
However, Rodt's division was in poor condition since it had been stripped of
one of its panzergrenadier regiments and its pioneer battalion, while its Panzer-
Regiment 204 only had forty operational tanks (including twenty-two Pz.III and
eleven Pz.IV). Although the Romanian armoured division was still equipped with
eighty-seven R-2 (Pz.35(t)) light tanks, it had recently received a major shipment
of German equipment, including eleven Pz.IIIN and eleven Pz.IVG tanks, and
nine 5cm Pak 38 and nine 7.5cm Pak 40 anti-tank guns.[74] Fuel for the entire corps
was in very short supply. Thus, Heim's XXXXVIII Panzerkorps had 150 tanks,
but limited ability to withstand large numbers of T-34s. Paulus did not expect a
major enemy counter-offensive across the Don because German intelligence
failed to identify the deployment of the 5th Tank Army, but the VIII and XI
Armeekorps commanders were so nervous about Soviet front-line activity in their
sectors, that he consented to send Major Bernhard Sauvant's kampfgruppe from
14.Panzer-Division with thirty-five tanks and some panzer-grenadiers to support
his left flank. Nor did German intelligence detect the 4th Mechanized Corps
arriving south of Stalingrad. Soviet operational-level *maskirovka* (deception)
played a major role in shaping the outcome of Uranus.

Operation Uranus began at 0720 hours on 19 November with a massive
artillery bombardment along the Southwest and Don fronts. It was snowing, with
heavy mist and a thick blanket of snow covered the ground. Visibility was very
limited and the temperature was −19° C. Vasilevsky preferred to attack in poor
weather because it preserved the element of surprise to the last moment and
prevented interference from the Luftwaffe. Dumitrescu's infantry were deployed
in field entrenchments, so the artillery barrage was only moderately effective, but
they also did not see the attacking Soviet infantry and tanks until they were within
small arms range. Minefields gave the Soviets some trouble, but Romanenko's
5th Tank Army rolled over the Romanian 9th and 14th Infantry Divisions in a
matter of hours, creating a 16km-wide breach near Bolshoy. To the east, near
Kletskaya, General-major Andrei G. Kravchenko's 4th Tank Corps smashed
through the Romanian 13th Infantry Division, but lost twenty-five of its 143
tanks knocked out in the minefields and obstacle belt. Chistiakov's 21st Army
made a 10km-wide breach in the Romanian lines and the 3rd Guards Cavalry
Corps plunged into the gap, advancing 35km on the first day. Within six hours of
the beginning of Uranus, Dumitrescu's front was pierced in two places and Soviet
armour and cavalry were advancing boldly into the breaches. Many Romanian

troops in these two sectors panicked and either surrendered or retreated without orders, widening the Soviet breakthrough.

Heim's XXXXVIII Panzerkorps began 'moving to the sound of the guns' within hours of the beginning of the Soviet offensive, but only forty-one tanks were operational and fuel limitations prevented the entire unit from moving. Instead, Kampfgruppe Oppeln was formed and dispatched toward Bolshoy. Co-ordination between XXXXVIII Panzerkorps and Heeresgruppe B, the Romanian 3rd Army or AOK 6 was virtually non-existent, so Heim was committing the sole armoured reserve into an unknown situation. Instead of advancing together, the Romanian 1st Armoured Division advanced due north, while Kampfgruppe Oppeln went to the northwest. It was already dark by 1700 hours, when the German armoured column bumped into a group of tanks from General-major Vasiliy V. Butkov's 1st Tank Corps near Petshany. A wild shoot-out occurred at close range, in the swirling snow and darkness, and the Germans were not the victor.

By 20 November it was clear that the Soviet 5th Tank Army and 21st Armies had achieved a major breakthrough of the Romanian 3rd Army front. A large *kessel* had already been formed by the Soviet armoured pincers between Bolshoy and Kletskaya, with 40,000 Romanians from Group Lascar trapped inside. Heeresgruppe B told Group Lascar to stand fast – help was on the way – but when the Romanian 1st Armoured Division tried to link up with Group Lascar it quickly became encircled within the *kessel* and only parts of it escaped. The 22.Panzer-Division tried to block Butkov's 1st Tank Corps, but it was not an effective combined arms team and lost much of its armour. This was one of the few times during the Second World War that German panzer units performed poorly and German C2 was actually worse than Soviet C2. Hitler was infuriated by the poor performance of the XXXXVIII Panzerkorps – ignoring its material deficiencies – and ordered Heim arrested and replaced by his deputy, General-major Hans Cramer. Yet Cramer was just as helpless to stop the breakthrough or the destruction of both flimsy armoured formations. Kampfgruppe Sauvant from 14.Panzer-Division managed to prevent the Don Front from smashing in AOK 6's left flank, but the German effort to support the Romanian 3rd Army was too little and too late.

South of Stalingrad, Yeremenko's Stalingrad Front began its participation in Operation Uranus on the morning of 20 November by bombarding the opposing Romanian 4th Army with 4,900 artillery pieces. In this sector near Lake Sarpa, the Romanians were spread even more thinly, with division frontages averaging 20–40km wide, meaning that it was more of a screen than a serious defensive line. General-major Vasily T. Volskii's 4th Mechanized Corps struck the Romanian VI Corps, which shattered under the weight of 200 tanks. The sector was simply too wide for a handful of anti-tank guns and minefields to seriously impede the Soviet armour. By afternoon, four Romanian divisions had been defeated and scattered. Further north, Tanaschishin's 13th Tank Corps struck the junction of the Romanian 4th Army and the German IV Armeekorps, which proved more resilient. Nevertheless, Yeremenko rapidly achieved a complete breakthrough, routing the Romanians in their path and setting the stage for an advance to Kalach. Like Vatutin and Chistiakov, Yeremenko committed a cavalry corps into the breach to reinforce the momentum of the advance, since cavalry was less dependent upon resupply. Hoth, who was with IV Armeekorps, quickly deployed the 29.Infanterie-Division (mot.) to impede Tanaschishin's armour, which prevented a complete collapse of AOK 6's right flank.

Vatutin, Chistiakov and Yeremenko all achieved breakthroughs and began to exploit into the enemy's depths within six hours of beginning their offensives, which was a first for the Red Army. These breakthroughs might still have failed if the Germans had been able to deal with them one at a time as in previous battles, but Vasilevsky, acting in the role of Stavka coordinator, played a critical role in orchestrating this complex multi-front operation. While the infantry army mopped up the Romanian 3rd and 4th Armies, three Soviet mechanized formations converged upon the town of Kalach. This was a heady time for Soviet tankers, the first where they had the operational and tactical initiative, and they

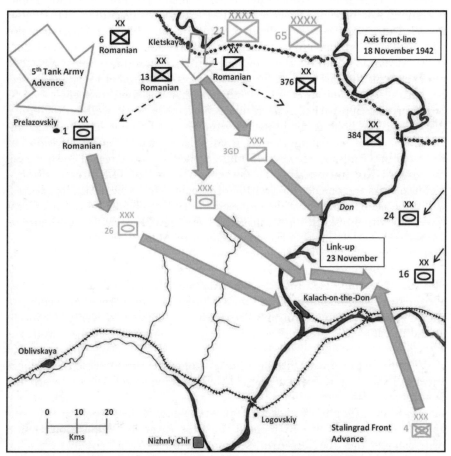

Kravchenko's 4th Tank Corps Advance to Kalach, 19–23 November 1942.

had the bit between their teeth. The 22.Panzer-Division and Romanian 1st Armoured Division continued uncoordinated skirmishing with Romanenko's 5th Tank Army, but lost almost all their tanks within two days and were forced to retreat westward.

In contrast to Soviet decisiveness, AOK 6 and Heeresgruppe B were slow to react to the developing crisis and were not fully aware of what was going on until the second day of Uranus. All three panzer divisions of Hube's XIV Panzerkorps were alerted on the evening of 19 November to pull out of the city fight and prepare to move west to support the XI Armeekorps, under attack by Rokossovsky's Don Front. Altogether, Paulus had 239 operational tanks at his disposal, including 116 Pz.IIIJ/L/M and fifty-two Pz.IVF2/G; the three panzer-divisionen had thirty to fifty-five tanks each and the motorized infantry divisions had twenty to sixty tanks each. The 29.Infanterie-Division (mot.) was in the best shape, with twenty-three Pz.III with long 5cm guns and eighteen Pz.IV with long 7.5cm guns.[75] Despite the number of tanks available – which might have made a difference at the right place – the amount of fuel available was insufficient for mobile operations. Kampfgruppe Sauvant from 14.Panzer-Division continued to support the XI Armeekorps west of Stalingrad, while 16 and 24.Panzer-Divisionen also sent small kampfgruppen to Golubinskaya, north of Kalach. Paulus focused more effort on refusing both his right and left flanks to conform to Soviet advances, rather than making an earnest effort to use his available armour to try and protect his lines of communication – he acted as if that was somebody else's job. As Soviet armour approached Kalach on 22 November, there were only German rear area troops holding the bridge over the Don and Paulus actually pulled his armour in closer to Stalingrad away from Kalach after 16.Panzer-Division lost five tanks in skirmishes. However, Kampfgruppe Sauvant retreated down the rail line toward Kotelnikovo, thereby salvaging a kernel of 14.Panzer-Division – eighteen tanks and one panzer-grenadier company – from the impending *kessel*.[76]

It came as no surprise that the lead elements of Kravchenko's 4th Tank Corps linked up with Volskii's 4th Mechanized Corps near Kalach at 1400 hours on 23 November – completing the encirclement of AOK 6. Inside the Stalingrad *kessel*, the encircled AOK 6 included Hube's XIV Panzerkorps with 14, 16 and 24.Panzer-Divisionen, as well as the 3, 29 and 60.Infanterie-Division (mot.), plus the 243 and 245.Sturmgeschütz-Abteilungen and three self-propelled Panzerjäger-Abteilungen equipped with Marder II tank destroyers. Stalingrad was an epic disaster for Germany's Panzertruppen, with six of twenty-five mechanized divisions and twelve of forty-six Panzer-Abteilungen trapped inside the *kessel*.

With the *kessel* formed, the three Soviet fronts tried to increase the distance between Paulus' AOK 6 and potential help by advancing further southward, but Romanenko's 5th Tank Army failed to get across the Chir River. Heeresgruppe B quickly formed Gruppe Hollidt with some remnants of the Romanian 3rd Army and German support troops to hold the Chir River line. Operation Uranus demonstrated that the Red Army's armoured forces could conduct complex, mobile operations if allowed time to prepare a proper offensive. Soviet victory at

Stalingrad was not due to superior numbers of tanks – that approach failed in July–August – but upon careful planning and bold tactical action, enhanced by cunning exploitation of *maskirovka* to deceive the enemy and timing during bad weather to deprive the enemy of their air support. Another reason that Operation Uranus succeeded was that Zhukov – who was preoccupied with his own Operation Mars against the Rzhev salient – had little or nothing to do with it. His command style of ruthless bullying of subordinates, reckless disregard of casualties and utter subservience to Stalin's incessant demand for immediate results could have greatly undermined the Red Army's performance at Stalingrad.

Wintergewitter, 12–19 December

Even before the Soviet armoured pincers met at Kalach, Hitler ordered Generalfeldmarschall Erich von Manstein, who was on the Leningrad Front, to proceed to Rostov and take charge of the new Heeresgruppe Don. Hitler directed von Manstein to 'bring the enemy's attacks to a standstill and recapture the positions previously occupied by us.' Unwilling to fly directly to Rostov with his staff, von Manstein did not arrive there until 26 November and Heeresgruppe Don was not operational until the next day. At that point, he took command over AOK 6 inside the Stalingrad *kessel*, General der Infanterie Karl Hollidt's scratch force on the Chir River and Hoth's shattered command, which had managed to hold onto the vital rail station at Kotelnikovo. While von Manstein was en route to Rostov, Hitler directed the Luftwaffe to begin a major airlift to sustain the AOK 6 inside the Stalingrad *kessel*. On 24 November, Generaloberst Wolfram von Richtofen's Luftflotte 4 commenced the Stalingrad airlift, using Tatsinskaya and Morozovskaya airfields as the primary operating bases for his squadrons of Ju-52 transports. The airlift rarely delivered more than 10–15 per cent of AOK 6's logistic needs, so the armoured forces within the pocket quickly declined due to lack of fuel and ammunition.[77] By late November, Paulus' AOK 6 was reduced to essentially an all-infantry force with very little mobility or organic fire support, but still capable of determined defense.

In order to provide von Manstein's new command some striking power, the OKH began transferring panzer divisions to Heeresgruppe Don. Generalmajor Erhard Raus' 6.Panzer-Division, which had just completed refitting in France, was en route when Operation Uranus began and was the first reinforcement to arrive. The 6.Panzer-Division was a superbly-equipped armoured outfit with 159 tanks (twenty-one Pz.II, seventy-three Pz.IIIL/M, thirty-two Pz.IIIN, twenty-four Pz.IVG and nine PzBef) and six Marder III tank destroyers. The lead elements of Raus' division reached Kotelnikovo on 27 November, but the first tanks of Panzer-Regiment 11 did not arrive until 3 December and they were immediately sent into action when the Soviet 51st Army conducted a spoiling attack with the 65th Tank Brigade and 81st Cavalry Division. A major tank action occurred near the village of Pokhlebin, 12km northwest of Kotelnikovo, on the morning of 5 December, involving about ninety tanks from Panzer-Regiment 11, the II (SPW)/ Panzergrenadier-Regiment 114 and anti-tank troops in a meeting engagement against about sixty tanks from the 65th Tank Brigade. First blood went to the T-34s, which ambushed Major Franz Bäke's kampfgruppe and knocked out four Pz.IVs in one company and three Pz.IIIs in another company. The Germans managed to regroup and, with the help of their artillery and panzerjägers, repulse the Soviet spoiling attack. Although about 2,000 cavalry-men were captured in mop-up operations, the tank skirmish at Pokhlebin was ample demonstration that the quality of Soviet tankers was improving. Overall, the Germans lost two Pz.III, three Pz.IV and one Marder III destroyed and ten more tanks damaged, against eleven Soviet tanks destroyed – a not very favorable exchange ratio for the Germans.[78] Raus tried to whitewash this outcome in his not-very-accurate memoirs, claiming that his Panzer-Regiment 11 'destroyed' the Soviet 4th Cavalry Corps in a masterful double envelopment at Pokhlebin and knocked out fifty-six tanks from the 65th Tank Brigade. He embellished the tale by recounting 'immortal deeds of heroism' on the part of his troops – post-war German accounts like this have helped to create a mythology about German panzer operations that obscures the fact that by late 1942 armoured battles on the Eastern Front were becoming less one-sided.[79]

Heeresgruppe Don's lateral lines of communication were awful, which, combined with winter weather, seriously hindered the German deployment of additional panzer divisions to Heeresgruppe Don. General der Panzertruppen Hermann Balck's 11.Panzer-Division, with seventy-eight tanks, departed from Roslavl and detrained near Morozovskaya airfield on 5 December. The 23.Panzer-Division, with Heeresgruppe A in the Caucasus, began moving north on 24 November, first by rail to Ssalsk, then on its own tracks to Kotelnikovo, which was hindered by snow and ice. While en route, Panzer-Regiment 201 received twenty-two new Panzer IVGs, bringing its armoured strength up to about sixty-two tanks.[80] Lastly, the OKH transferred the 17.Panzer-Division from Orel, but this unit was still en route on 10 December. Manstein assigned the 6 and 23.Panzer-Division to General der Panzertruppen Friedrich Kirchner's LVII Panzerkorps and the 11 and 17.Panzer-Divisionen to General der Panzer-truppen Otto von Knobelsdorff's XXXXVIII Panzerkorps.

While the panzer divisions were assembling, von Manstein and his staff hastily developed an operational plan to rescue Paulus' trapped AOK 6. The basic idea for Operation *Wintergewitter* (Winter Storm) was for a two-pronged attack led by Hoth, using both the XXXXVIII and LVII Panzerkorps. Previous experience in armoured operations indicated that a two-pronged offensive had the best chance of maintaining momentum, since the *schwerpunkt* could be switched between the two spearheads to keep the enemy off balance. Manstein wanted to use the German-held bridgehead across the Don at Nizhniy Chir, only 100km from Stalingrad, as the main jump-off point for XXXXVIII Panzerkorps to mount a relief operation, with LVII Panzerkorps attacking from Kotelnikovo. However, the two-pronged concept did not last long. Vatutin also recognized the importance of Nizhniy Chir and ordered Romanenko's 5th Tank Army to attack Armee-Abteilung Hollidt on the Chir River on 7 December. Butkov's 1st Tank Corps (reduced to fifty-two tanks), along with the 3rd Guards Cavalry corps and two rifle divisions, attacked the German screening positions on the Chir; the

336.Infanterie-Division held its ground against Soviet tank attacks but the 7.Luftwaffen-Feld-Division lost two of its battalions, allowing Butkov's armour to penetrate the German screen and reach Sovkhoz (State Farm) 79. Von Manstein was forced to commit the XXXXVIII Panzerkorps to restore the front and Balck's 11.Panzer-Division, which was still arriving, counterattacked into Butkov's flank on 8 December. According to von Mellenthin's well-known account in *Panzerschlachten* (1956), Balck knocked out fifty-three Soviet tanks – but there is no mention of German losses.[81] Balck's troops did find the bodies of 100 German rear-area troops who had been captured at Sovkhoz 79 and murdered by troops from the 157th Tank Brigade. Balck used this incident to raise combat morale in a statement to his troops, reminding that 'the terrible fate of Sovkhoz 79' awaited them if they were not victorious.[82] In any case, Balck prevented Romanenko's armour from getting across the Chir in strength, but Vatutin kept pressure on Hollidt's forces and eventually forced the Germans out of Nizhniy Chir, which prevented the XXXXVIII Panzerkorps from joining *Wintergewitter*.

Unable to use the XXXXVIII Panzerkorps, von Manstein was forced to adapt *Wintergewitter* to a single prong launched by LVII Panzerkorps from Kotelnikovo. From that position, the distance to Stalingrad was 145km. Although Hitler promised that von Manstein would receive a dozen divisions to conduct *Wintergewitter*, by 10 December he only had Raus' 6.Panzer-Division and part of 23.Panzer-Division in place. Although these two formations had a total of 200 tanks, there were no German infantry divisions on hand to support Hoth – just the remnants of two Romanian infantry divisions – which was an ominous sign that the operation was doomed to fail. Von Manstein wanted to wait for more reinforcements, but by this point it was clear that the Luftwaffe airlift was failing and that AOK 6's situation was becoming critical. *Wintergewitter* was based on the assumption that AOK 6 would launch a breakout effort once Hoth's armour approached close to Stalingrad, but by early December Paulus was so short of fuel and ammunition that his armoured units were all but immobilized. Consequently, von Manstein authorized Hoth to commence *Wintergewitter* on 12 December with just the 6 and part of the 23.Panzer-Divisionen, to be joined by 17.Panzer-Division when it arrived.

North of Kotelnikovo, General-major Nikolai I. Trufanov's 51st Army deployed a very thin screen of three rifle divisions, three cavalry divisions and two tank brigades (with seventy-seven tanks) in hasty blocking positions across a 150km-wide front. Most of Trufanov's units were at half-strength and had not constructed prepared defenses. When Hoth attacked with his two panzer divisions on line at 0630 hours on 12 December, they had little difficulty punching through Trufanov's thinly-spread infantry. Raus' 6.Panzer-Division overran a rifle division, then pivoted westward to overrun a cavalry division and knocked out ten Soviet tanks for no loss, then boldly advanced toward the Aksay River.[83] On their right flank, the 23.Panzer-Division was only able to make a limited attack with Kampfgruppe Illig (III./Pz.Regt 201 and I (SPW)./Pz.Gren.Regt 128), but secured its objectives and captured 250 prisoners and seventeen artillery pieces.

Fliegerkorps IV managed to provide some air support, which helped Hoth's armour in the initial actions, but as he advanced toward Stalingrad his flanks were only protected by unsteady Romanian and Luftwaffe troops.

Yeremenko reacted quickly to Hoth's rapid advance and committed Volskii's 4th Mechanized Corps, which had thirty-two T-34s and thirty-eight T-70s, to occupy blocking positions at Verkhne Kumski, while Trufanov moved Tanaschishin's 13th Tank Corps to Zutov to block the 23.Panzer-Division from getting across the Aksay.[84] Yeremenko also sought permission from the Stavka to transfer General-leytenant Rodion I. Malinovsky's 2nd Guards Army from the Don Front to reinforce Soviet defenses on the approaches to Stalingrad, but Stalin was initially reluctant since this formation was earmarked to be used in the reduction of the Stalingrad *kessel*.

Shortly after dawn on 13 December, Oberst Walther von Hünersdorff led his armoured Kampfgruppe consisting of I. and II./Pz.Regt 11, II.(SPW)/ Pz.Gren.Regt. 114, six artillery batteries, a Pioneer-Kompanie and a Panzerjäger-Kompanie across an unguarded ford at Zalivsky over the Aksay River. Kampfgruppe Hünersdorff had advanced 40km in the first twenty-four hours, although half of the 6.Panzer-Division was still engaged south of the Aksay River. After securing the Zalivsky bridgehead, Hünersdorff advanced another 12km to the village of Verkhne Kumski, a nondescript one-street Russian village. According to Raus' unreliable memoirs, Hoth had ordered 6.Panzer-Division to stop once it seized a bridgehead across the Aksay and wait for 23.Panzer-Division to catch up, but Raus allowed von Hünersdorff to move north of the river to engage and destroy Soviet armoured reserves. Shortly after von Hünersdorff occupied Verkhne Kumski, two Soviet tank brigades were spotted advancing across the open steppe toward the village from north and east. Raus goes on to describe a fanciful 'revolving battle' around the village, with von Hünersdorff's two Panzer-Abteilungen engaging a total of five Soviet brigades, which attacked piecemeal and were defeated in turn; he claims that von Hünersdorff's forces knocked out 135–140 enemy tanks in this one action, but does not mention German losses. In actuality, von Hünersdorff had advanced directly into the 4th Mechanized Corps assembly areas around Verkhne Kumski and quickly found his kampfgruppe nearly surrounded by a superior force. It is unclear why Volskii had no forces in the village itself, and his C2 was inadequate to mount a coordinated attack to crush Kampfgruppe von Hünersdorff; instead, each of his brigades attacked at the initiative of its commander. Part of Tanaschishin's 13th Tank Corps also got in the fight. While II.(SPW)/Pz.Gren.-Regt. 114 and the artillery and engineers set up a hasty defense in the tiny village, von Hünersdorff's two Panzer-Abteilungen maneuvered outside the village to engage the Soviet brigades. Soviet tank losses were heavy, but a group of T-34s managed to reach the village and overrun some of the German artillery before they were knocked out by panzer-grenadiers with the new *Hafthohlladung* hollow charge magnetic anti-tank mines. Although von Hünersdorff managed to prevent his command from being destroyed, he was forced to conduct a fighting withdrawal at dusk when it became clear that Soviet armour had cut his line of communications and his fuel and ammunition were nearly expended. Von Hünersdorff retreated to the Zalivsky bridgehead and remained there for the next three days. Contrary to Raus' lurid account, the Battle of Verkhne Kumski on 13 December was a Soviet tactical and operational victory, since Hoth's advance on Stalingrad had been halted for three critical days. Since the 4th Mechanized Corps held the ground at the end of the day, many of its knocked out tanks would be recovered and repaired. Hoth's *schwerpunkt* had been stopped and Kampfgruppe von Hünersdorff forced to retreat with heavy losses (at least thirty panzers knocked out).

Hoth consolidated his forces on the Aksay, enabling his pioneers to build a pontoon bridge across the river. Meanwhile, the 23.Panzer-Division, which was echeloned to the right of 6.Panzer-Division, engaged the 254th Tank Brigade at Ssamochin on the morning of 14 December. The Germans were alerted to the approach of the Soviet brigade due to poor communications security, with radio traffic being sent in the clear, and ambushed the two lead companies. A total of twelve Soviet tanks, including two KV-1, were knocked out by Kampfgruppe von Heydebreck, which lost two tanks and one Marder III. After this, Kampfgruppe von Heydebreck advanced to capture an intact railroad bridge over the Aksay at Kruglyakov at 1430 hours. Soviet counterattacks against both bridgeheads began on 14 December and continued the next day, forcing the panzer-grenadiers to entrench. The 23.Panzer-Division knocked out ten T-34s and two T-60s on 15 December, but lost two 8.8cm flak guns.[85] On 16 December, two companies of T-34s from the 13th Tank Corps attacked the Kruglyakov bridgehead and overran two Pak guns and three 10.5cm howitzers before being driven off. All momentum was gone from Hoth's brief advance. Reinforcements were trickling in to LVII Panzerkorps, such as Sturmgeschütz-Abteilung 228 which arrived with forty-two assault guns, but Yeremenko's forces were being reinforced as well. On 16 December, Raus tried committing Kampfgruppe von Hünersdorff again, but the 4th Mechanized Corps and other Soviet rifle units had established a defense-in-depth north of the bridgehead that could not be broken by an armour-heavy attack. Raus claimed that camouflaged Soviet PTRD anti-tank rifle teams proved too difficult to eliminate and that, 'never before had our tank crews felt so powerless.'[86] The second German armoured attack north of the Aksay had failed.

On 17 December, Raus switched tactics and used Kampfgruppe Zollenkopf with two dismounted panzer-grenadier battalions, artillery support and Luftwaffe support to expand the Zalivsky bridgehead. The 23.Panzer-Division was able to expand its own bridgehead and the lead element of 17.Panzer-Division, Kampfgruppe Seitz, arrived to reinforce the offensive. Raus massed his firepower and infantry at one point and managed to punch a hole through the 4th Mechanized Corps' front, which unhinged Volskii's defense. As the Soviet 51st Army began to fall back to the Myshkova River, Raus sent his SPW-mounted battalion to seize Verkhne Kumski in a sudden night assault. Hoth spent much of 18 December mopping up bypassed pockets of resistance and moving his forces toward the Myshkova River. By the end of 18 December, Hoth only had 101 operational tanks left and his remaining combat power was dwindling. In one last throw of the dice, Raus sent Kampfgruppe Hünersdorff in a 30km end-run on 19 December that bypassed Soviet blocking positions and managed to reach the Myshkova River, where they seized a bridge over the river at Vasilyevka at 2000 hours. The oft-repeated mythology about Stalingrad and *Wintergewitter* has made a great deal about Hünersdorff reaching a position that was just 48km from Stalingrad and how – if only Paulus had chosen to conduct a break-out effort at this point – events might have turned out differently. This is a fantasy. Stalin had released Malinovsky's 2nd Guards Army to Yeremenko on 15 December and, after a 200km road march, the lead elements of Rotmistrov's 7th Tank Corps and 2nd Guards Mechanized Corps were just reaching the Myshkova River, where they encountered scouts from Kampfgruppe Hünersdorff. Hoth's forces lacked the strength to fight their way through the 2nd Guards Army and Paulus' army lacked the mobility to even reach this area. Both of Hoth's flanks were virtually open and the closer that he came to Stalingrad, the greater the possibility that his own small strike force would be enveloped and then surrounded. In reality, Operation *Wintergewitter* failed on its second day, but the Germans did not recognize this until their *schwerpunkt* ground to a halt on the Myshkova River.

Von Manstein knew that Hoth's panzers no longer had a chance of reaching Stalingrad, but he ordered Hoth to keep Kampfgruppe Hünersdorff at the Vasilyevka bridgehead for three days, while he sought to cajole Paulus into activating the unauthorized breakout operation known as *Donnerschlag* (Thunderclap). However, Paulus refused to disobey Hitler and, as time slipped by, Malinovsky's armour began massing against Kampfgruppe Hünersdorff. Even worse, the new Soviet offensive – Operation Little Saturn – forced von Manstein to order Hoth to give up his strongest formation, 6.Panzer-Division, to support Heeresgruppe Don's collapsing left flank. *Wintergewitter* was over. In a bitter postscript, Hitler ordered that LVII Panzerkorps would hold the bridgeheads over the Aksay river 'at all costs,' which meant that 17 and 23.Panzer-Division were badly battered by Soviet counterattacks from 20–25 December. Hoth was not authorized to retreat from the Aksay River until the evening of 26 December and then LVII Panzerkorps conducted a rapid withdrawal back down the rail line, pursued by Rotmistrov's 7th Tank Corps. Soviet numerical superiority was now telling, with large numbers of T-34s threatening the retreating Germans from all directions. The 23.Panzer-Division was reduced to only five operational tanks by the time that it reached Kotelnikovo, which was then lost on 29 December.

Operation Mars, 25 November–20 December
While the Red Army had been preparing for Operation Uranus in October, Zhukov ensured that his own project – Operation Mars, the attack against Model's AOK 9 in the Rzhev salient – received priority in terms of reinforcements and supplies. The two fronts involved in the operation – Western and Kalinin – received the newly-formed 1st and 3rd Mechanized Corps as well as one of the first artillery divisions. Altogether, Zhukov committed 2,352 tanks and thirty-seven rifle divisions to Operation Mars, against Vasilevsky's 1,560 tanks and thirty-four rifle divisions earmarked for Operation Uranus.[87] Zhukov's basic

plan was to conduct a double envelopment of the Rzhev salient, with General-polkovnik Maksim A. Purkaev's Kalinin Front attacking the western side of the salient with the 22nd and 41st Armies, while Ivan S. Konev's Western Front attacked the eastern side with the 20th Army. A supporting attack would also be launched by the Kalinin Front's 39th Army against the northern side of the salient. Zhukov believed that once the German-held salient was simultaneously hit from three different directions that AOK 9 would collapse like a house of cards. Then, the Western and Kalinin Fronts would release their armour – two mechanized and two tank corps – to complete the enemy's defeat by linking up and encircling the remnants of Model's battered army. Zhukov believed that Operation Mars would lead to the disintegration of Heeresgruppe Mitte.

However, Zhukov did not put a professional effort into planning Operation Mars. He made little effort to employ *maskirovka* during the build-up phase in October, which enabled Model's intelligence officer to not only accurately assess that a Soviet major offensive was imminent, but which sectors were threatened. Model demonstrated real talent for defensive tactics in the Rzhev salient and he personally visited each sector and ensured that his front-line units had pre-planned engagement areas on likely enemy avenues of approach; anti-tank and anti-personnel mines were laid and covered by fire. Model also positioned the 5 and 9.Panzer-Divisionen, with a total of 180 tanks, as mobile reserves to support General der Panzertruppe Jürgen von Arnim's XXXIX Panzerkorps on the eastern side of the salient, and the 1.Panzer-Division to support General der Panzertruppe Josef Harpe's XXXXI Panzerkorps on the western side of the salient. Although Model's panzer divisions only had one Panzer-Abteilung each and his infantry divisions were at half-strength, his troops were well-entrenched and supported by 260 artillery pieces. Unlike the Romanian 3rd and 4th Armies near Stalingrad, Model was expecting Zhukov's offensive and well-prepared.

Operation Mars began on the morning of 25 November, with simultaneous assaults around the periphery of the Rzhev salient. The scale of the Soviet assaults was awesome – Zhukov and Konev both favored mass – but it just did not work against Model's defense. The heavily-reinforced 20th Army massed fifty-three artillery regiments to try and blast a hole through von Arnim's defenses, but fog and snow greatly reduced the accuracy of the initial Soviet artillery preparation (another example of Zhukov's inadequate planning; Operation Uranus also began in fog/snow conditions, but Vatutin ensured that his artillerymen pre-registered their guns), so the three rifle divisions that began the ground assault were repulsed with 50 per cent losses. Zhukov ignored these losses and told Konev to keep attacking in the same sector, which suited Model fine. Model relied upon his artillery to break up the massed Soviet infantry assaults, which then allowed his panzerjägers to pick off unsupported T-34s and KV-1s.

Stützpunkt Grediakino, held by Major Kurt Stieber's II/Pz.Gren. 14 from 5.Panzer-Division, proved to be an immovable roadblock for the 20th Army. Oberleutnant Hans-Siegfried Rothkirch's 2./Pz.Regt 31, equipped with a mixed group of seven tanks (one Pz.IIIN with short 7.5cm, two Pz.III with short 5cm, three Pz.III with long 5cm and one Pz.IV with short 7.5cm) and two Marder tank destroyers moved into Grediakino to support the defense. The constant Soviet artillery bombardments forced Rothkirch's panzers to remain in dead space most of the time, but they were still damaged repeatedly by near-misses and the panzer crews were forced to remain inside their vehicles for several days without resupply of food, fuel or ammunition. Nevertheless, every time Soviet armour from the 25th and 93rd Tank Brigades attacked the strongpoint, Rothkirch's panzers emerged and picked off enough enemy tanks to drive off the assault. The 42nd Guards Rifle Division managed to encircle Stützpunkt Grediakino, but the Luftwaffe provided aerial resupply drops and a lone Pz.II fought through Soviet lines with a load of Panzergranate APC ammunition. Over the course of seven days, Rothkirch's company knocked out sixteen Soviet tanks (eight T-34, two KV-1, two T-60, one Lee and three BT) at a cost of two tanks and one Marder II lost. All the German tanks were repeatedly damaged by hits from artillery and PTRD anti-tank rifle fire, but remained in action. Finally, Model recognized that Kampfgruppe Stieber was running out of defenders and organized a breakout, which succeeded at 0300 hours on 1 December. Rothkirch's 2./Pz.Regt 31 made it back to German lines.[88]

Konev's infantry finally made a small tear in von Arnim's front south of Grediakino and Zhukov prodded Konev to commit General-major Andrei L. Getman's 6th Tank Corps and 2nd Guards Cavalry Corps into the breach as a mobile group. Although Konev's mobile group managed to advance west 12km and caused a crisis for the Germans, it soon found itself in a long, thin salient. As usual, the Luftwaffe appeared and pounded Konev's tightly-packed mobile group mercilessly. Von Arnim conducted a masterful elastic defense until he was able to maneuver the 5 and 9.Panzer-Division against Konev's salient, but an initial counterattack by Kampfgruppe Hochbaum from 9.Panzer-Division at Aristovo on 27 November failed; eighteen tanks from the 6th Tank Corps were knocked out, but Panzer-Regiment 33 lost eight tanks knocked out.[89] On 29 November, von Arnim was finally able to orchestrate a counterattack the cut off Konev's mobile group, and gradually annihilated it by 4 December.

On the western side of the salient, Purkaev's Kalinin Front attacked Harpe's XXXXI Panzerkorps at two places with the 22nd and 41st Armies. The 41st Army achieved a major breakthrough south of Belyi by overrunning the 2.Luftwaffen-Feld-Division, then it pushed General-major Mikhail D. Solomatin's 1st Mechanized Corps, and 6th Rifle Corps into the breach; these forces advanced 35km eastward before being stopped by Generalleutnant Walter Krüger's 1.Panzer-Division's Kampfgruppe von Meden (one Panzer-Abteilung and three motorized infantry battalions) at the Nacha River. Solomatin started the offensive with 215 tanks, but he quickly fragmented his corps by committing one brigade against Belyi, which was held by the rest of Krüger's 1.Panzer-Division, three brigades against von Meden and his reserve brigade in a flanking maneuver. Consequently, Solomatin squandered his breakthrough by failing to mass at a single point, as the German *schwerpunkt* did. Solomatin's mechanized units eventually got across the Nacha River and began to split Kampfgruppe von Meden into two pieces, but Oberst Karl-Friedrich von der Meden was able to delay

Solomatin from finishing off his beleaguered kampfgruppe – which was down to its last two operational Pz.III tanks – until the lead elements of 12.Panzer-Division arrived to reinforce him on 1 December.

The 22nd Army also achieved a breakthrough in the Luchesa valley north of Belyi, into which it committed General-major Mikhail E. Katukov's 3rd Mechanized Corps, with 232 tanks, against the 86.Infanterie-Division. With both flanks giving way, Harpe's XXXXI Panzerkorps was on the verge of collapse. Adding to Model's problems, the 39th Army also managed to gain ground on the northern side of the Rzhev salient. Model left part of the *Grossdeutschland* Division, which had been transferred from Heeresgruppe B in August, to contain the 39th Army, but sent two kampfgruppen that included tanks from Panzer-Abteilung *Grossdeutschland* to block Katukov's tanks. The Luchesa River valley was a poor maneuver area for Katukov's tanks, since it was swampy and heavily forested, with only a single trail. By 27 November, Katukov had advanced 12km and was close to destroying Harpe's right flank, but Kampfgruppe Kohler from the *Grossdeutschland* Division was beginning to arrive. A very sharp tank battle developed on 29 November, pitting the 49th Tank Brigade against Kampfgruppe Kohler; the T-34s and KV-1s managed to overrun a battery of 5cm Pak 38 anti-tank guns, but the arrival of a battery of 8.8cm flak guns halted Katukov's tanks. By 30 November, about half of Katukov's armour had been knocked out and he had failed to break out of the Luchesa valley, but Panzer-Abteilung *Grossdeutschland* was also ground down considerably.[90]

Faced with simultaneous enemy breakthroughs all around his army's perimeter, Model acted with speed – unlike Paulus at Stalingrad – to commit local reserves to shore up the most threatened sectors while assembling his panzer reserves for a counterstroke. As a battlefield commander, Model consistently displayed the trait of *Fingerspitzengefühl* ('finger on the pulse') or 'situational awareness' in modern parlance. He worked first with von Arnim to crush Konev's mobile group, then reoriented to deal with Harpe's collapsing front. Model recognized that the depleted 1.Panzer-Division could not stop two full-strength Soviet mechanized corps on its own, so he activated a prearranged contingency plan with General-feldmarschall Günther von Kluge, commander of Heeresgruppe Mitte, to temporarily receive the 12, 19 and 20.Panzer-Divisionen, which had a heterogeneous collection of 195 tanks. While 12.Panzer-Division had received seventeen Pz.IIIJ/L/M and eighteen Pz.IVF2/G, the other two panzer divisions were still equipped with obsolete Pz.38(t) tanks and short-barreled Pz.III/Pz.IV tanks, meaning that their combat effectiveness against Soviet armour was limited.[91] While these units were en route, Harpe's troops conducted an epic defense of Belyi, which prevented the two Soviet mechanized corps from linking up. By early December, most Soviet attacks had ground to a standstill, unable to overcome German centers of resistance. On 1 December, the 19 and 20.Panzer-Divisionen launched a coordinated attack with about 120 tanks that cut off Solomatin's 1st Mechanized Corps and 6th Rifle Corps – which were demolished over the course of a week. Throughout December, Zhukov kept demanding that his subordinates continue attacking, but this only resulted in tired units becoming burnt-out wrecks and by 20 December it was clear the Operation Mars had failed.

Operation Mars cost the Western and Kalinin Fronts about 335,000 casualties in four weeks. Six elite Soviet corps were destroyed or crippled, including the 1st and 3rd Mechanized Corps and 5th and 6th Tank Corps. About 85 per cent of the Soviet armour engaged in Operation Mars was lost, with the Germans claiming 1,852 tanks knocked out.[92] At the tactical level, Zhukov's forces demonstrated poor tank-infantry cooperation and an inability to overcome German strongpoints. Model used aerial resupply to keep isolated *Stützpunkte* from running out of supplies and entrenched German infantry, when supplied with magnetic anti-tank mines and better anti-tank guns, could keep KV-1s and T-34s at bay. Although Konev and Purkaev had plenty of infantry, tanks and artillery, they consistently failed to employ them in coordinated fashion – which demonstrates that those historians who claim that the Red Army's victory was 'inevitable' are divorcing Soviet industrial output from battlefield realities. The strongest lesson of Operation Mars and Operation Uranus, when viewed together, was that the Red Army could not simply rely upon mass to win, because the kill-ratios almost always favored German defenders – the brute force approach of Timoshenko, Konev and Zhukov would result in the Red Army attacking itself to death. In order to win, the Red Army needed to employ cunning, deception and maneuver at the operational level of armoured warfare, and learn effective tank-infantry coordination at the tactical level.

Model's forces suffered heavy losses during Operation Mars, but no German units were destroyed or rendered combat ineffective. Yet despite Model's efficient battle command and defensive tactics, his forces only prevailed because Heeresgruppe Mitte was able to commit six panzer divisions to help hold the Rzhev salient – which was one-third of all the available armoured units on the Eastern Front. Even after defeating Zhukov's offensive, Model still needed thirty German divisions to hold the Rzhev salient, which was no longer affordable in light of the unfolding disaster with AOK 6 at Stalingrad. After his victory. Model recommended that AOK 9 evacuate the Rzhev salient in order to free up units for operations elsewhere, which Hitler reluctantly began to seriously consider but did not approve until February 1943.

Deep Battle, 16–30 December

Even before implementing Operation Uranus, General-polkovnik Aleksandr M. Vasilevsky, the Stavka director of operations, was developing plans for the next phase of the Soviet winter counter-offensive, which was initially designated Operation Saturn. Vasilevsky had the best skills for operational planning in the Soviet general staff and he was a student of pre-war Deep Battle theory as described by Triandafillov, Tukhachevsky and Isserson and codified in the pre-war PU-36 regulations. He believed that with proper planning, the Red Army of 1942 was capable of conducting the kind of Deep Battle operation envisioned by pre-war theory and that if successful, the next offensive could lead to the disintegration and destruction of the entire Heeresgruppe Don. Vasilevsky envisioned a two-phase offensive, with the 1st and 3rd Guards Armies from General-leytenant Nikolai Vatutin's Southwest Front smashing the Italian 8th Army, while Romanenko's 5th Tank Army defeated Armee-Abteilung Hollidt in the first phase, followed by the commitment of the 2nd Guards Army to exploit toward Rostov in the second phase. Operation Saturn was far more ambitious than any previous Soviet offensives and expected advances of up to 250km. Vatutin's main effort would be General-leytenant Vasiliy I. Kuznetsov's 1st Guards Army, which had four tank corps (17, 18, 24, 25) with 533 tanks (320 T-34, 161 T-70, fifty-two T-60) and eight rifle divisions. General-leytenant Dmitri D. Lelyushenko's 3rd Guards Army had seven rifle divisions, the 1st Guards Mechanized Corps and a tank brigade, with a total of 234 tanks.[93] Vatutin's forces would have a 10–1 superiority in armour and 7–1 superiority in artillery in the chosen attack sectors.

Due to Operation *Wintergewitter*, Vasilevsky had to send his exploitation force – Malinovsky's 2nd Guards Army – to stop Hoth's panzers and Romanenko's sub-par performance against XXXXVIII Panzerkorps on the Chir River reduced his ability to contribute to Vasilevsky's new offensive. Consequently, on 13 December Vasilevsky was forced to scale back the operation, which was redesignated Little Saturn, but his intent remained to demolish General Italo Gariboldi's (Italian) 8th Army on Heeresgruppe Don's left flank, then push strong armoured forces toward Heeresgruppe Don's lines of communication and the airfields involved in the Stalingrad airlift. The ultimate prize was Rostov, which would result in the isolation of Heeresgruppe A in the Caucasus.

Operation Uranus was a wake-up call for the Germans and von Manstein was aware of the vulnerability of Gariboldi's 8th Army, but he could send few resources other than the 298.Infanterie-Division, Sturmgeschütz-Abteilung 201 and a few 8.8cm flak guns to stiffen the Italian-held sector. Gariboldi's 8th Army had very limited armour support; just the LXVII Battaglione Bersaglieri coraz-zato (67th Bersaglieri Armoured Battalion) with fifty-eight L6/40 light tanks armed with 20mm cannon, and the XIII Gruppo Semoventi, Reggimento Caval-legeri Alessandria (Alexandria Cavalry Regiment) with nineteen Sermoventi 47/32 self-propelled guns, armed with a 47mm gun.[94] None of the Italian armoured fighting vehicles had a chance against the T-34, nor did the primary Italian anti-tank gun, the 47mm, offer an effective defense against Soviet armour. In order to make up for the weakness of Italian armour, von Manstein provided Oberst Hans Tröger's incomplete 27.Panzer-Division as an on-call mobile reserve for Gariboldi; this formation consisted of only one Panzer-Abteilung (sixty-five tanks), two Panzer-grenadier battalions, a Panzerjäger-Abteilung and two artil-lery battalions. Tröger's panzers included seven different tank types, but only ten Pz.IIIL/M and five Pz.IVG offered any real ability to stop Soviet armour.

At 0800 hours on 16 December, Kuznetsov's 1st Guards Army began a massive ninety-minute artillery preparation against the Italian II and XXXV Army Corps near the Osetrovka bridgehead. With the 6th Army launching a supporting attack with infantry across the frozen Don on his right, Kuznetsov committed two guards rifle corps against the Italian Ravenna infantry division and part of the German 298.Infanterie-Division. However, the Italo-German defense proved quite solid and Soviet infantry failed to achieve a breakthrough on the first day of Operation Little Saturn and only made limited advances of 1–2km depth. German anti-tank mines knocked out twenty-seven Soviet tanks, preventing meaningful armour support until engineers cleared lanes through the obstacle belts. During the afternoon of the first day, Tröger's 27.Panzer-Division even managed a small counterattack with twenty tanks that checked further progress. Lelyushenko's 3rd Guards Army also attacked mostly with infantry on the first day and failed to make much progress. A counterattack by remnants of the 22.Panzer-Division forced Lelyushenko's assault troops to retreat across the Don. The first day of Operation Little Saturn demonstrated that well-entrenched infantry, secure behind an obstacle belt, was just as effective at stopping an infantry assault as during the First World War.

Frustrated by the lack of progress, Vatutin ordered Kuznetsov and Lelyu-shenko to begin feeding their armour into the battle. On 17 December, Kuznetsov committed General-major Pavel P. Poluboiarov's 17th Tank Corps, General-major Boris S. Bakharov's 18th Tank Corps and General-major Petr R. Pavlov's 25th Tank Corps into an infantry support role and finally broke through the front of the Italian II Army Corps some thirty-six hours after the start of Little Saturn. Contrary to German efforts to paint the Italians as scapegoats, the Cosseria and Ravenna divisions put up unexpectedly tough resistance, forcing Vatutin to commit three of his four tank corps before he finally got his break-through. Yet while tough, the Italian defenses were thin in depth and once the Soviet armour achieved a breakthrough, there was nothing left to stop them. By late on 17 December, Vatutin alerted General-major Vasily M. Badanov's 24th Tank Corps to prepare to begin its exploitation mission on the next day. In the 3rd Guards Army sector, Lelyushenko committed General-leytenant Ivan N. Russiyanov's 1st Guards Mechanized Corps, which gained some ground before being stopped.

The boldest part of Little Saturn began at 0200 hours on 18 December, when Badanov's 24th Tank Corps passed through the penetration corridor between the shattered Ravenna and Cosseria divisions and began advancing southward. Pavlov's 25th Tank Corps had already gone through the gap in the Italian front and moved ahead of, and independent of, Badanov's corps. Vatutin directed these two corps to conduct a deep raid against the Tatsinskaya and Morozovskaya airfields, which lay 240km from the start-line on the Don. Up to this point, it was unprecedented in the history of warfare to move a large armoured formation so far behind enemy lines. However, the logistic preparations made by Vatutin's staff were inadequate to support raids of this scale and depth, which led to unanticipated dissipation of combat power prior to reaching the objectives. Aerial resupply of armoured spearheads – which the Germans had frequently utilized since the beginning of Operation Barbarossa – was not even considered by Vatutin's staff, even though transport planes were available. Badanov's and Petrov's corps each relied upon what they could carry on their own vehicles, which amounted to two loads of fuel and ammunition and five days' rations.

The Red Army had no practical experience planning this kind of Deep Battle operation and expected that the corps could advance at a steady rate of 50km per day. However, Badanov was forced to move at 25km per day in order to conserve fuel and keep his corps together. While German panzer units regularly called upon Luftwaffe aerial resupply when fuel ran out during mobile operations, the Red Army and VVS were unable to employ similar methods. Vatutin expected both corps to reach their objectives in four days, but they were unable to keep to his timetable – Clausewitz referred to this as 'friction', which needs to be factored into planning. Even the T-34s found it difficult to move cross-country through 1-meter deep snow for over 200km, and the GAZ-AA trucks carrying extra fuel and ammunition, as well as the motorized rifle brigades, fell behind before half-way to the objectives. Crews froze in their tanks and trucks, requiring frequent halts, and there were only eight and a half hours of daylight at this time of year. In short, terrain, weather and possible enemy resistance were ignored in the hasty planning process for Little Saturn, and no effort was made to get updated intelligence about the targets to the raiding forces once they were en route. Isserson's prescient pre-war calculation that a mechanized exploitation force would become vulnerable to attrition and enemy reaction after a three-day long Deep Battle operation were ignored.[95]

Badanov and Petrov's corps also found themselves moving rapidly out of Vatutin's command and control radius. Soviet armoured units were plagued throughout 1941–42 by inadequate radios, but this became particularly harmful during Deep Battle operations. Each tank corps only had a single RSB-F HF transmitter mounted on a GAZ-AAA truck, which could only communicate with higher headquarters to a maximum range of 30km while on the move. In order to achieve its maximum transmission range of 160km, the truck had to stop and put up a long whip antenna. Consequently, Badanov and Petrov were only in contact with Vatutin when they stopped at night and, when they approached the objective, not at all. Despite all these logistical problems, Badanov's and Petrov's corps plowed on through the snowy void to their objectives while the 1st and 3rd Guards Armies pushed south through the wreckage of the Italian 8th Army.

Von Manstein had little at hand to stop Vatutin's offensive and he could only guess at what was happening south of the Don. By chance, the fresh 306.Infanterie-Division was en route from Belgium to join Heeresgruppe Don and von Manstein detached part of it to protect the Stalingrad airlift airfields. Once Luftwaffe reconnaissance detected Soviet armour moving south toward Tatsinskaya and Morozovskaya airfields, the German 306.Infanterie-Division was ordered to set up hasty blocking positions along the Bystraya River. Pavlov's 25th Tank Corps encountered a regiment of the 306.Infanterie-Division at Milyutinskaya on the morning of 23 December. First blood went to a German panzerjäger platoon equipped with a few 7.5cm Pak 40 anti-tank guns, which knocked out nine of Pavlov's tanks.[96] Rather than bypassing the strongpoint, Pavlov committed his entire corps to eliminating the German infantry in his path. The German infantry regiment could not stand up to 100 Soviet tanks and a battalion was overrun with heavy loss, but it was a pyrrhic victory because Pavlov consumed a great deal of his dwindling fuel stocks in a day-long battle around the village. The beleaguered German infantrymen called upon the Stukas of I./St.G.2, which mercilessly pounded Pavlov's exposed tanks and trucks. The last twenty-five operational tanks in Pavlov's tank corps continued to crawl forward, but finally ran out of fuel 16km short of Morozovskaya airfield.

Badanov's tankers also encountered a serious roadblock at the bridge over the Bystraya at Skosyrskaya at 1700 hours on 23 December. Kampfgruppe Heinemann, composed of 200 Luftwaffe signal troops and six 8.8cm flak guns, engaged Polkovnik Stepan K. Nesterov's 130th Tank Brigade as it crossed the bridge. Nesterov's tankers managed to overrun five of the 8.8cm flak guns and chase the Germans out of the town, but many vehicles were damaged and fuel stocks were low. Badanov made the bold decision to proceed to Tatsinskaya with two tank brigades, but leave the rest of his corps in Skosyrskaya. At dawn on 24 December, about sixty tanks from Badanov's corps approached Tatsinskaya airfield, which was shrouded in fog. The Luftwaffe had not organized a ground defense of this vital airbase, which had 170 transport planes and warehouses full of supplies destined for Stalingrad – the Germans were caught totally by surprise. The 54th and 130th Tank Brigades executed a concentric attack on the airfield which caused a panic; the Ju-52s began a chaotic mass take-off that managed to save 124 transports, but Badanov's raid destroyed forty-six transports. The loss of Tatsinskaya was catastrophic for AOK 6 in Stalingrad since it brought the airlift to a virtual halt. Badanov reported to Vatutin that he had captured Tatsinskaya and still had fifty-eight tanks (thirty-nine T-34 and nineteen T-70) left, but only 0.2 loads of diesel fuel and twenty-four–forty rounds of 76.2mm ammunition for each T-34.[97]

The capture of Tatsinskaya caused a convulsion within Heeresgruppe Don. Von Manstein hastily directed both Raus' 6.Panzer-Division and Balck's 11.Panzer-Division to move west and crush the Soviet armoured raiders. The lead element of 11.Panzer-Division bumped into Badanov's 130th Tank Brigade at Babovnya, east of Tatsinskaya; seven Soviet and five German tanks were knocked out in the skirmish. A Ukrainian tank officer was captured, who under interrogation revealed the size and disposition of Badanov's forces at Tatsinskaya.[98] Both German panzer divisions converged on Tatsinskaya, encircling Badanov's fuel-starved corps. Badanov requested support from Vatutin, who told him to hold on, help was on the way. The Germans tightened the noose around Badanov on 26 December with armoured probing attacks, while Stukas pounded the immobilized Soviets. By 27 December, Badanov was surrounded by both 6 and 11.Panzer-Divisionen and it was obvious that a final assault was imminent. At 0200 hours on 28 December, Badanov conducted an unauthorized breakout with eleven tanks, thirty trucks and 927 of his men and was able to slip through the 6.Panzer-Division's lines and reach the area held by the 1st Guards Army. The two raids had succeeded in disrupting the Stalingrad airlift for a few days and inflicting significant losses upon the Luftwaffe's transport fleet, but at the cost of the 24th and 25th Tank Corps suffering crippling losses.

Vatutin called off Little Saturn on 30 December. He had succeeded in shattering the Italian 8th Army and forced Armee-Abteilung Hollidt to abandon the Chir River line, but failed to reach Rostov or cause a complete German collapse. All of the Soviet armoured units involved in the operation were in poor shape due to heavy losses and only had 10–20 per cent of their armour still operational after two weeks of Deep Battle operations.[99] Heeresgruppe Don had survived – but barely – and mostly due to inadequate Soviet logistics.

Armour on the Eastern Front at the End of 1942

During 1942, the Red Army lost over 15,000 tanks, including 1,200 KV-1, 6,600 T-34s and 7,200 T-60/70s.[100] About half of the 10,500 Lend-Lease tanks (3,000 British, 7,500 USA) delivered in 1942 were also lost.[101] Soviet industry built 24,231 tanks in 1942, including 12,535 T-34s and 2,426 KV-1s. Overall Soviet armour losses in 1942 were 62 per cent of those tanks built – which was less than the German build:loss rate and indicated that the Red Army could absorb huge losses in material. However, the overall 7–1 exchange ratio between Soviet and German tank losses was inconsistent with the Red Army gaining any kind of superiority over the Wehrmacht's panzer forces. At these loss rates, the Red Army was still far more dependent upon Lend-Lease armour than it was willing to admit, and it did not have enough excess production to fully outfit its best units with T-34s until mid-1943.

In operational terms, the Red Army mounted eleven major offensives in 1942 that employed multiple tank corps or tank armies, but only Uranus and Little Saturn could be considered successful. Despite being well-equipped, the 1st, 3rd, 4th and 5th Tank Armies had all performed poorly in battle and two of them were disbanded. The tank armies were not built as combined arms teams, being weak in organic artillery and support assets, which contributed to their failure against panzer divisions. Several tank corps were destroyed in 1942 and many more crippled at one time or another. However, the Red Army had enough large armoured units by late 1942 that it could cycle decimated units through the RVGK to rebuild, while replacing them with fresh units. In contrast, the Wehrmacht only occasionally received a rebuilt panzer division from training areas in France and its panzer divisions remained at the front until burnt out. The Wehrmacht conducted six major armoured offensives in 1942, with *Wirbelwind* and *Wintergewitter* being failures.

The Wehrmacht lost about 2,480 tanks on the Eastern Front in 1942, including about 293 Pz.II, 429 Pz.38(t), 1,261 Pz.III and 389 Pz.IV. In addition, the Germans lost another 563 tanks in North Africa during the same period, or about 18.5 per cent of their total armour losses in 1942. Although Russian historians tend to dismiss the contribution of Great Britain to defeating the Wehrmacht in 1941–42, a disproportionate share of German armour was being lost in North Africa and Rommel's Deutsche Afrika Korps (DAK) was a sink-hole for tanks that would have been better used on the Eastern Front. Altogether, Germany built 4,168 tanks in 1942 and lost 73 per cent of them; among the main types, 63 per cent of Pz.IIIs and 48 per cent of Pz.IVs were lost. German tank production remained flat throughout 1942 with negligible growth, although the proportion of assault guns being built increased to nearly one-quarter by late 1942. The increased emphasis on assault guns, plus diversion of production toward the new Pz.VI Tiger tank, cast the Panzerwaffe in an increasingly defensive role that emphasized firepower and protection over tactical mobility. Another important industrial decision was Hitler's decree in June 1942 that no more tungsten would be used for armour-piercing ammunition due to the shortage of that material, and that existing stocks had to be turned in; just as German industry was producing better tank guns, they lost access to the raw materials needed to make them most effective. Going into 1943, the Panzerwaffe and Panzerjäger would be increasingly dependent upon larger guns to increase muzzle velocity, which resulted in heavier, less mobile tanks and anti-tank guns.

While German industry was just beginning to field new tanks, it finally standardized its two main battle tanks in late 1942, enabling significant production increases in 1943. The Pz.III Ausf L and Ausf M models added only minor improvements to armoured protection and fording capability, but the Pz.IV Ausf G increased frontal armoured protection to 80mm and soon received the improved 7.5cm KwK 40 L/48 cannon. Likewise, the StuG III Ausf G, also outfitted with the L48 cannon behind 80mm thick frontal protection, began mass production in December 1942. While the Pz.IIIL/M were only modest threats to the T-34, the appearance of the up-gunned Pz.IVG and StuG IIIG signaled that the Russian policy of resisting upgrades on the T-34 in favor of increased production would carry increased costs on the battlefield. While the T-34 still had superior tactical and operational-level mobility over any German tanks, its firepower advantage was gone and its level of armoured protection increasingly inadequate. By the end of 1942, German tankers knew that they were beginning to receive tanks that gave them some measure of superiority over their opponents.

The Wehrmacht ended 1942 with nineteen panzer divisions on the Eastern Front, but three were surrounded and would be annihilated by late January 1943. The loss of these three panzer divisions, plus the three Panzergrenadier-Divisionen in the Stalingrad *kessel* was a catastrophe that had never occurred before. Far more serious than the loss of equipment – which was bad enough – was the loss of trained personnel. Some panzer cadres were flown out of the *kessel*, including Hube, or missed the *kessel* altogether by being on home leave, but the junior leaders and experienced crews could not be made good. The hard-fighting 16.Panzer-Division managed to save 4,000 of its personnel, but the remaining 9,000 would be lost.[102] The *Ersatz-Abteilungen* back in the home *Wehrkreis* found it difficult enough to train replacements to fill gaps created by normal combat losses, but it could not simply recreate experienced company commanders, platoon leaders and NCOs. Consequently, the quality of panzer crews – which was of decisive importance in the tactical success of German armoured units in 1941–42 – declined steadily after Stalingrad. Nevertheless, the Wehrmacht still had more than 1,500 operational tanks and assault guns on the Eastern Front – a far better situation than they had faced in December 1941 – and the panzer divisions still had a tactical edge over the Soviet tank corps.

Conclusions

From September 1939 until November 1941, the German use of combined arms tactics – melding armour, artillery, air power and other branches in order to produce a superior synergy of combat power at a *schwerpunkt* or decisive point, never failed. Even the failure at Moscow in November 1941 was due more to German logistical deficiencies and adverse terrain/weather considerations than any defects in German doctrine or methods. In many respects, Operation Typhoon was an aberration, where wishful thinking by the OKH led the panzer armies into a no-win situation. Yet when the German logistic situation and the weather improved in the spring of 1942, the Wehrmacht demonstrated again that it could use its combined arms tactics to pierce Soviet defensive lines at chosen points and encircle its opponents. Soviet operational-level use of tank forces was sub-par for most of 1941–42, negating much of the advantage offered by their numerical superiority. Despite the purported economic weakness of Germany in a protracted war of attrition, German armoured units retained their ability to conduct successful offensive operations until Operation *Wintergewitter* failed to break through the Soviet ring encircling AOK 6 at Stalingrad. Although there had been occasional failures by individual panzer divisions to achieve their objectives in May–July 1942, the German panzer-led *schwerpunkt* could generally penetrate or bypass Soviet linear defensive positions until *Wintergewitter*. As far as operational-level armoured warfare was concerned, the Germans lost the war in the East when their panzer–Luftwaffe combined arms teams lost the assured ability to penetrate Soviet defensive lines and, conversely, the Red Army gained the ability to break through German defenses with their tank corps.

In the German Panzerwaffe, Fascist attitudes toward war were evident in the lionizing of *Ritterkreuz* war heroes and embellishing tanks with names such as the Tiger and the Panther – which has helped to perpetuate Nazi mythology to this day. While the Germans were masters at using symbology to bolster morale on the Eastern Front, senior panzer commanders had little regard for the industrial basis behind their combat power. If they had, they would have been aware that Hitler reduced ammunition production in July 1941 and terminated the production of tungsten-core armour-piercing rounds in June 1942 and argued that they couldn't compete with the Red Army with this kind of decision-making. In contrast, the Red Army's inherent Marxist–Leninist attitude to war was evident in the total mobilization philosophy of all state resources, and the recognition that the production/labor front was just as important as the war front. Soviet tanks had no fancy names, just numbers. In the end, the Red Army's sober, material-oriented mindset proved of more value when the chips were down in

1941 as well as when Soviet industry could finally provide the means in 1942–43 to drive out the hated invaders.

Red Army tankers demonstrated increasing competence in tactical infantry support missions throughout 1941–42, but were singularly ineffective at using their armour to conduct independent Deep Battle operations. Even once the Red Army gained a significant numerical superiority in mid-1942 with its tank corps and tank armies, it lacked the ability to penetrate German defensive lines in any real depth. At Kharkov, Rzhev, Bryansk and Leningrad, Soviet tank attacks failed to crack the German defenses and suffered ruinous losses in the process. It was not until Operation Uranus offered the Red Army an opportunity to pit its armour against less-capable Romanian forces that Soviet tank units demonstrated an ability to conduct Deep Battle operations. Thus, irrespective of other strategic factors, the dynamic of armoured warfare on the Eastern Front was characterized by German superiority until November 1942, at which point the balance began to shift irrevocably toward the Red Army's tank forces.

While it was theoretically true that the Red Army could win a war of attrition with the Wehrmacht, that does not mean that it could win a lopsided war of attrition where the Germans inflicted 7–1 or more casualties in personnel and tanks. A succession of costly failures such as Kharkov, the Crimea and the Don Bend crippled the Red Army's best armoured forces for months and provided the Wehrmacht with an opportunity to reach the Volga and the Caucasus. At the heart of the Red Army's lop-sided tank losses was an amateurish and self-destructive style of decision imposed by Stalin from the top down. Generals such as Timoshenko, Budyonny, Konev and even Zhukov often abandoned military common sense in order to appease Stalin's incessant demands to attack in impulsive half-baked offensives. Without logistics, armoured operations could not be sustained and without training, armoured units performed poorly in combat and fell apart – this was the root cause of the Red Army's dysfunctional armoured operations of 1941–42.

In order to win, the Red Army needed to relearn operational maneuver art and combined arms warfare, as well as gaining a cadre of tactically-astute junior and mid-level leaders, but this did not occur until eighteen months into the war. Until the Red Army learned these lessons, it could not win, it could just avoid losing. In November 1942 there was a subtle shift in the Red Army, as months of military disasters finally caused Stalin to reduce some of his interference in military operations and allow the quiet professionals such as Vasilevsky, Vatutin and Rokossovsky to prepare proper offensives such as Uranus and Little Saturn. Nevertheless, the use of Soviet armour at the operational level remained impulsive and Zhukov and other commanders repeatedly made the same mistake of committing their armoured exploitation forces before a true breakthrough had been achieved. Both sides grappled with the problems of armoured logistics throughout the war and neither ever completely mastered the ability to sustain mobile operations for extended periods. Just as the German failure to sustain their armoured spearheads in late 1941 led to the failure of Barbarossa, the Soviet inability to sustain their tank corps in 1942 prevented Operation Little Saturn from becoming an immediate death-blow to Heeresgruppe Don.

Rank Table

U.S. Army Rank	German Army Rank	Waffen-SS Rank	Soviet Rank
General of the Army	Generalfeldmarschall	N/A	Marshal of the Soviet Union
General	Generaloberst	*SS-Oberstgruppenführer*	General Armiyi
Lieutenant General	General der Panzertruppe	*SS-Obergruppenführer*	General Polkovnik
Major General	Generalleutnant	*SS-Gruppenführer*	General Leytenant
Brigadier General	Generalmajor	*SS-Brigadeführer*	General Major
Colonel	Oberst	*SS-Standartenführer*	Polkovnik
Lieutenant Colonel	Oberstleutnant	*SS-Obersturmbannführer*	Podpolkovnik
Major	Major	*SS-Sturmbannführer*	Major
Captain	Hauptmann	*SS-Hauptsturmführer*	Kapetan
First Lieutenant	Oberleutnant	*SS-Obersturmführer*	Starshiy Leytenant
Second Lieutenant	Leutnant	*SS-Untersturmführer*	Mladshiy Leytenant

Armour Order of Battle, 22 June 1941

German

Heeresgruppe Nord (Generalfeldmarschall Wilhelm Ritter von Leeb)
Panzergruppe 4 (Generaloberst Erich Höpner)
- XXXXI Armeekorps (mot.) (General der Panzertruppen Georg-Hans Reinhardt)
  - 1.Panzer-Division (Generalleutnant Friedrich Kirchner)
  - 6.Panzer-Division (General der Panzertruppen Wilhelm Ritter von Thoma)
  - 36.Infanterie-Division (mot.) (Generalleutnant Otto-Ernst Ottenbacher)
- LVI Armeekorps (mot.) (General der Infanterie Erich von Manstein)
  - 8.Panzer-Division (General der Panzertruppen Erich Brandenberger)
  - 3.Infanterie-Division (mot.) (Generalleutnant Curt Jahn)
- Army Group Reserve
  - SS-Division "Totenkopf" (SS-Gruppenführer Theodor Eicke) WIA – 8 July 1941

Heeresgruppe Mitte (Generalfeldmarschall Fedor von Bock)
Panzergruppe 2 (Generaloberst Heinz Guderian)
- XXIV Armeekorps (mot.) (General der Panzertruppen Leo Freiherr Geyr von Schweppenburg)
  - 3.Panzer-Division (Generalleutnant Walter Model)
  - 4.Panzer-Division (Generalmajor Willibald Freiherr von Langermann und Erlencamp)
  - 10.Infanterie-Division (mot.) (Generalleutnant Friedrich-Wilhelm von Loeper)
- XXXXVI Armeekorps (Generaloberst Heinrich von Viettinghoff-Scheel)
  - 10.Panzer-Division (General der Panzertruppen Ferdinand Schaal)
  - SS-Division "Reich" (Generalleutnant der Waffen-SS Paul Hausser) WIA – 15 October 1941
  - **Infanterie-Regiment (mot) Großdeutschland (**Oberst Wilhelm-Hunold von Stockhausen)
- XXXXVII Armeekorps (General der Artillerie Joachim Lemelsen)
  - 17.Panzer-Division (Generalleutnant Hans-Jürgen von Arnim)
  - 18.Panzer-Division (General der Panzertruppen Walther Nehring)
  - 29.Infanterie-Division (mot.) (Generalmajor Walter von Boltenstern)

Panzergruppe 3 (Generaloberst Hermann Hoth)
- XXXIX Armeekorps (mot.) (General der Panzertruppe Rudolf Schmidt)
  - 7.Panzer-Division (General der Panzertruppen Hans Freiherr von Funck)
  - 20.Panzer-Division (General der Panzertruppen Horst Stumpff)
  - 14.Infanterie-Division (mot.) (Generalleutnant Friedrich Fürst)
  - 20.Infanterie-Division (mot.) (Generalleutnant Hans Zorn)
- LVII Armeekorps (mot.) (General der Panzertruppen Adolf Kuntzen)
  - 12.Panzer-Division (Generaloberst Josef Harpe)
  - 19.Panzer-Division (Generalleutnant Otto von Knobelsdorff)
  - 18.Infanterie-Division (mot.) (Generalmajor Friedrich Herrlein)

Heeresgruppe Süd (Generalfeldmarschall Gerd von Rundstedt)
Panzergruppe 1 (Generaloberst Ewald von Kleist)
- XIV Armeekorps (mot.) (General der Infanterie Gustav von Wietersheim)
  - 9.Panzer-Division (Generalleutnant Alfred Ritter von Hubicki)

○ SS-Division "Wiking" (SS-Brigadeführer Felix Steiner)
• III Armeekorps (mot.) (Generaloberst Eberhard von Mackensen)
  ○ 13.Panzer-Division (Generalleutnant Walther Düvert)
  ○ 14.Panzer-Division (General der Panzertruppen Friedrich Kühn)
• XXXXVIII Armeekorps (mot.) (General der Panzertruppen Werner Kempf)
  ○ 11.Panzer-Division (General der Panzertruppen Ludwig Crüwell)
  ○ 16.Panzer-Division (Generaloberst Hans-Valentin Hube)
• Army Group Reserve:
  ○ SS-Division (mot.) Leibstandarte SS Adolf Hitler (SS-Obergruppenführer Joseph Dietrich)
  ○ 16.Infanterie-Division (mot.) (Generalleutnant Sigfrid Henrici)
  ○ 25.Infanterie-Division (mot.) (Generalleutnant Heinrich Clößner)

Note: There were also 11 *Sturmgeschütz* battalions supporting Operation Barbarossa; 2 with Nord, 6 with Mitte and 4 with Süd.

Reinforcements:
September:
• 2.Panzer-Division (Generalleutnant Rudolf Veiel) [194 tanks]
• 5.Panzer-Division (General der Panzertruppen Gustav Fehn) [186 tanks]
December:
• Panzer-Regiment 203 (Oberst Hero Breusing) [142 tanks]

Soviet
Northern Front (General Leytenant Markian M. Popov)
14th Army (General Leytenant Valerian A. Frolov)
• 1st Tank Division (General-major Viktor I. Baranov)
23rd Army (General Leytenant Petr S. Pshennikov) KIA- 13 December 1941
• 10th Mechanized Corps (General-major Ivan G. Lazarev) Arrested – July 1941
  ○ 21st Tank Division (Polkovnik Leonid V. Bunin)
  ○ 24th Tank Division (Polkovnik Makariy I. Chesnokov)
  ○ 198th Motorized Rifle Division (General-major Vladimir V. Kryukov)

Front Assets:
• 1st Mechanized Corps (General-major Mikhail L. Cherniavsky)
  ○ 3rd Tank Division (Polkovnik Konstantin Yu. Andreev)
  ○ 163rd Motor Rifle Division (General-major Ivan M. Kuznetsov)

Northwest Front (General-Polkovnik Fedor I. Kuznetsov)
8th Army (General Leytenant Petr P. Sobennikov)
• 12th Mechanized Corps (General-major Nikolai M. Shestopalov) Captured – 28 June 1941
  ○ 23rd Tank Division (Polkovnik Timofei S. Orlenko) Died – 14 October 1941
  ○ 28th Tank Division (Polkovnik Ivan D. Chernyakhovsky)
  ○ 202nd Mechanized Division (Polkovnik Vladimir K. Gorbachev)
11th Army (General Leytenant Vasily I. Morozov)
• 3rd Mechanized Corps (General-major Aleksei V. Kurkin)
  ○ 2nd Tank Division (General-major Egor N. Solyankin) KIA – 26 June 1941
  ○ 5th Tank Division (Polkovnik Fedor F. Fedorov)
  ○ 84th Mechanized Division (General-major Petr I. Fomenko)

Western Front (General-Polkovnik Dmitry G. Pavlov) Executed – 22 July 1941
3rd Army (General Leytenant Vasily I. Kuznetsov)
• 11th Mechanized Corps – (General-major Dmitri K. Mostevenko)
  ○ 29th Tank Division (Polkovnik Nikolai P. Studnev) KIA – 14 July 1941
  ○ 33rd Tank Division (Polkovnik Mikhail F. Panov)
  ○ 204th Motor Rifle Division (Polkovnik Aleksei M. Pirov) MIA – 19 September 1941

4th Army (General-major Aleksandr A. Korobkov) Executed – 22 July 1941
- 14th Mechanized Corps (General-major Stepan I. Oborin) Executed – October 1941
  - 22nd Tank Division (General-major Vasiliy P. Puganov) KIA – 24 June 1941
  - 30th Tank Division (Polkovnik Semen I. Bogdanov)
  - 205th Motor Rifle Division (Polkovnik Filipp F. Kudyurov) KIA – 30 June 1941

10th Army (General Leytenant Konstantin D. Golubev)
- 6th Mechanized Corps (General-major Mikhail G. Khatskilevich) KIA – 25 June 1941
  - 4th Tank Division (General-major Andrei G. Potaturchev) Captured 6 July 1941
  - 7th Tank Division (General-major Semyon V. Borzilov) KIA – 28 September 1941
  - 29th Motor Rifle Division (General-major Ibrahim P. Bikzhanov) Captured 25 July 1941
- 13th Mechanized Corps (General-major Petr N. Akhliustin) KIA – 28 July 1941
  - 25th Tank Division (Polkovnik Nikolai M. Nikiforov) MIA – June 1941
  - 31st Tank Division (Polkovnik Sergey A. Kalikhovich)
  - 208th Motor Rifle Division (Polkovnik Vladimir I. Nichiporovich)

Front Assets:
- 17th Mechanized Corps (General-major Mikhail P. Petrov) Died – 10 October 1941
  - 27th Tank Division (Polkovnik Aleksei O. Akhmanov)
  - 36th Tank Division (Polkovnik Sergey Z. Miroshnikov) MIA – August 1941
  - 209th Motor Rifle Division (Polkovnik Aleksei I. Murav'ev) MIA – July 1941
- 20th Mechanized Corps (General-major Andrei G. Nikitin) WIA – June 1941
  - 26th Tank Division (General-major Viktor T. Obukhov)
  - 38th Tank Division (Polkovnik Sergey I. Kaspustin) Captured – 29 September 1941
  - 210th Motor Rifle Division (General-major Feofan A. Parkhomenko)

Southwest Front (General Leytenant Mikhail P. Kirponos) KIA – 20 September 1941
5th Army (General Leytenant Mikhail I. Potapov)
- 9th Mechanized Corps (General-major Konstantin K. Rokossovsky)
  - 20th Tank Division (Polkovnik Mikhail E. Katukov)
  - 35th Tank Division (General-major Nikolai A. Novikov)
  - 131st Motorized Division (Polkovnik Nikolai V. Kalinin)
- 22nd Mechanized Corps (General-major Semen M. Kondrusev) KIA – 24 June 1941
  - 19th Tank Division (General-major Kuzma A. Semenchenko) WIA July 1941
  - 41st Tank Division (Polkovnik Petr P. Pavlov)
  - 215th Mechanized Division (Polkovnik Pavlin A. Barabanov) Died – 9 September 1941

6th Army (General-Leytenant Ivan N. Muzychenko) Captured – 6 August 1941
- 4th Mechanized Corps (General-major Andrey A. Vlasov)
  - 8th Tank Division (Polkovnik Petr S. Fotchenkov) MIA – August 1941
  - 32nd Tank Division (Polkovnik Efim G. Pushkin)
  - 81st Motorized Division (Polkovnik Petr M. Varipaev) – MIA June 1941
- 15th Mechanized Corps (General-major Ignatii I. Karpezo) WIA – 26 June
  - 10th Tank Division (General-major Sergei I. Ogurtsov) Captured – August 1941
  - 37th Tank Division (Polkovnik Fedor G. Anikushkin)
  - 212th Motorized Division (General-major Sergei V. Baranov) Captured – 1941

12th Army (General-major Pavel G. Ponedelin) Captured – August 1941
- 16th Mechanized Corps (General-major Aleksandr D. Sokolov) Captured – August 1941
  - 15th Tank Division (Polkovnik Vasiliy I. Polozkov)
  - 39th Tank Division (Polkovnik Nikolai V. Starkov)
  - 240th Motorized Division (Polkovnik Ivan V. Gorbenko)

26th Army (General-Leytenant Fedor Ya. Kostenko)
- 8th Mechanized Corps (General-leytenant Dmitry I. Ryabyshev)
  - 12th Tank Division (General-major Timofei A. Mishanin) – KIA 29 June
  - 34th Tank Division (Polkovnik Ivan V. Vasil'ev)
  - 7th Motorized Division (Polkovnik Aleksandr G. Gerasimov)

Front Assets:
- 19th Mechanized Corps (General-major Nikolai V. Feklenko)
  o 40th Tank Division (Polkovnik Mikhail V. Shirobokov)
  o 43rd Tank Division (Polkovnik Ivan G. Tsibin)
  o 213rd Motor Rifle Division – (Polkovnik Vasiliy M. Osminskiy) Captured – August 1941
- 24th Mechanized Corps (General-major Vladimir I. Chistyakov) WIA July 1941,
  Died August 1941
  o 45th Tank Division (Polkovnik Mikhail D. Solomatin)
  o 49th Tank Division (Polkovnik Konstantin F. Shvetsov)
  o 216th Motorized Division (Polkovnik Ashot S. Sarkisyan) MIA – July 1941

Southern Front (General-Polkovnik Ivan Tyulenev)
9th Army (General-Polkovnik Yakov T. Cherevichenko)
- 2nd Mechanized Corps (General-Leytenant Yuri V. Novoselsky)
  o 11th Tank Division (Polkovnik Gregory I. Kuzmin)
  o 16th Tank Division (Polkovnik Mikhail I. Myndro) KIA – 3 August 1941
  o 15th Motorized Division (Polkovnik Nikolai N. Belov) KIA – 8 September 1941
- 18th Mechanized Corps (General-major Petr V. Volokh)
  o 44th Tank Division (Polkovnik Vasiliy P. Krymov) Captured – July 1941
  o 47th Tank Division (Polkovnik Nikolai F. Mikhailov)
  o 218th Motorized Division (Polkovnik Aleksei P. Sharagin)

RVGK
- 5th Mechanized Corps (General-major Ilya P. Alekseenko) Died – 3 August 1941
  o 13th Tank Division (Polkovnik Fedor U. Grachev) KIA – 14 July 1941
  o 17th Tank Division (Polkovnik Ivan P. Korchagin)
  o 109th Motorized Division (Polkovnik Nikolai P. Krasnoretsky) WIA – 27 June 1941
- 7th Mechanized Corps (General-major Vasiliy I. Vinogradov)
  o 14th Tank Division (Polkovnik Ivan D. Vasilyev)
  o 18th Tank Division (General-major Fedor T. Remizov)
  o 1st Motorized Division (Polkovnik Yakov G. Kreizer)
- 21st Mechanized Corps (General-major Dmitri D Lelyushenko)
  o 42nd Tank Division (Polkovnik Nikolay I. Voeikov)
  o 46th Tank Division (Polkovnik Vasiliy A. Koptsov) WIA – July 1941
  o 185th Motorized Division (General-major Petr L. Rudchuk)
- 23rd Mechanized Corps (General-major Mikhail A. Miasnikov) WIA – July 1941
  o 48th Tank Division (Polkovnik Dmitri Y. Yakovlev)
  o 51st Tank Division/110th Tank Division (Polkovnik Petr G. Chernov)
  o 220th Motorized Division (General-major Nikifor G. Khoruzhenko)
  o 25th Mechanized Corps (General-major Semen M. Krivoshein)
  o 50th Tank Division (Polkovnik Boris S. Bakharov)
  o 55th Tank Division (Polkovnik Vasiliy M. Badanov)
  o 219th Motorized Division (General-major Pavel P. Korzun)

Reinforcements:
June:
- 57th Tank Division (324x T-26) from Transbaikal MD
July:
- 69th Mechanized Division/107th Tank Division (Polkovnik Pyotr I. Domrachev) [200 BT/T-26] from Far Eastern MD
- 59th Tank Division/108th Tank Division (Polkovnik Sergey Ivanov) from Far East
- 82nd Mechanized Division/111th Tank Division (General-major Ivan V. Shevnikov) from Transbaikal MD
- 26th Mechanized Corps (General-major Nikolai I. Kirichenko) [total of 184 light tanks] from North Caucasus MD

- o 52nd Tank Division/101st Tank Division (Polkovnik Gregory M. Mikhailov)
- o 56th Tank Division/102nd Tank Division (Polkovnik Ivan D. Illarionov) KIA – October 1941
- o 103rd Motorized Division (General-major Gregory T. Timofeev)
- o 109th Tank Division (Polkovnik Semen P. Chernobai)
- Elements from 27th Mechanized Corps in Transcaucasus (re-designated 15 July 1941)
  - o 9th Tank Division/104th Tank Division (Polkovnik Vasily G. Burkov) [208 light tanks] WIA – July 1941
  - o 53rd Tank Division/105th Tank Division (Polkovnik Aleksei S. Beloglazov)
  - o 221st Motorized Division/106th Tank Division (Polkovnik Gersh M. Roytenberg)

August:
- 1st and 7th Tank Brigades

September:
- 2, 13, 15, 16, 29, 121, 123, 124, 126, 127, 128, 129, 142, 143, 147, 148, 150 Tank Brigades

October:
- 4, 8, 9, 11, 17, 18, 19, 20, 21, 22, 23, 24, 25, 26, 27, 28, 32 Tank Brigades;
- 60th Tank Divisions (General-major Aleksei F. Popov) from Far East. [179 tanks]

November:
- 31, 33, 35, 36, 37, 38, 48, 145, 146 Tank Brigades
- 58th Tank Division (General-major Aleksandr A. Kotliarov) from Far East [200 light tanks]. Suicide – 20 November 1941
- 112th Tank Division (Polkovnik Andrei L. Getman) from Far East [210 T-26].

December:
- 6, 54, 68, 69, 70, 71 Tank Brigades

Appendix III

Tanks on the Eastern Front, 1941

German Tanks

	Pz.IIF	Pz.IIIF	Pz.IIIG/H	Pz.IVF1	Pz.35(t)	Pz.38(t)
Introduced	March 1941	September 1939	April 1940	April 1941	1937	1939
Weight (metric tons)	9.5	19.5	19.5	22.3	10.5	9.8
Crew	3	5	5	5	4	4
Engine	Maybach HL 62TR	Maybach HL120TR	Maybach HL120TR	Maybach HL120TRM	Škoda T11/0	Praga Typ TNHPS/II
Horse Power	140	300	300	300	120	123
Suspension	Leaf Spring	Torsion Bar	Torsion Bar	Leaf Spring	Leaf Spring	Leaf Spring
Max Speed (kph)	40 (road)	40 (road)	40 (road)	42 (road)	34	42 (road), 15 (off)
Fuel Type	Gasoline	Gasoline	Gasoline	Gasoline	Gasoline	Gasoline
Fuel Capacity (liters)	170	320	320	470	153	220
Range (km)	190 (road)	165 (road)	165 (road)	200 (road)	190 / 115	200 (road) / 100 (C–C)
Max Fording Depth (m)	0.92	0.80	0.80	1.00	0.8	0.9
Track Width (cm)	30	36	36	40	29.3	29.3
Main Gun	2cm KwK 30 L/55	3.7cm KwK 35/36	5cm KwK 38 L/42	7.5cm KwK 37 L/24	3.7cm KwK 34(t)	3.7cm KwK 38(t)
Ammo Type	AP, HE	HE, APCBC	59 HE, 36 APCBC	APC, HE	APCBC	APCR, APCBC, HE
Ammunition	180	120	95–98	80	90	90
Frontal Armor (mm)	30–35	30	30	50	25	25
Side Armor (mm)	14	30	30	30	16	15
Radio	Fu 5	Fu 5	Fu 5	Fu 5	Fu 5	Fu 5

Soviet Tanks

	T-26	BT-7M	T-28	T-34/76	KV-1
Introduced	1937	1938	1934	1941	1941
Weight (metric tons)	9.6	14.6	32.0	28.0	45.0
Crew	3	3	6	4	5
Engine	GAZ T-26	V-2	M-17T	V-2-34	V-2-K
Horse Power	91	500	500	500	600
Suspension	Leaf Spring	Christie	Coil springs	Christie, coil springs	Torsion bars
Max Speed (kph)	31 road / 19 off-road	62 / 50	40 / 20	54 / 25	35 / 17
Fuel Type	gasoline	diesel	gasoline	diesel	diesel
Fuel Capacity (liters)	290	823	650	540	600
Range (km)	240 road / 140 off-road	700 / 600	220 / 140	300 / 210	250 / 180
Max Fording Depth (m)	0.76	1.2	0.8	1.12	1.5
Track Width (cm)	26	26	26	48	65
Main Gun	45mm 20K, mod. 1932/38	45mm 20K, mod. 1932/38	76.2mm KT-28	76.2mm F-34	76.2mm ZIS-5
Ammo Type	AP, HE-Frag	AP, HE-Frag	AP, AP-HE-Frag	APHE, HE-Frag	APHE, HE-Frag
Ammunition	122	40	70	77	114
Frontal Armor (mm)	15	22–30	20–30	45–52	75–90
Side Armor (mm)	15	13	20	45–52	75
Radio	71-TK-3	71-TK-3	71-TK-3	71-TK-3	71-TK-3

Tank Production, 1941

Germany

Month	Light	Medium			Other		
	Pz.II	*Pz.III*	*Pz.IV*	*Pz.38(t)*	*Pz.Bef*	*StuG III*	*Total*
January	0	88	31	45	16	36	216
February	0	108	26	50	20	30	234
March	7	92	28	53	24	30	234
April	15	124	36	49	22	47	293
May	12	143	29	78	14	48	324
June	15	133	38	65	5	56	312
July	21	127	38	65	13	34	298
August	25	179	44	64	0	50	362
September	25	178	46	76	2	38	365
October	38	164	51	53	0	71	377
November	40	206	52	50	0	46	394
December	35	171	61	50	16	46	379
Total	233	1,713	480	698	132	532	3,788

Manufacturing Centers: Magdeburg (Krupp-Grusonwerk AG: Pz.IV); Plauen (*Vogtlaendische Maschinenfabrik* AG: Pz.IV); Berlin (Alkett & Daimler-Benz AG: Pz.III [Alkett was a subsidiary of Rheinmetall-Borsig]); Kassel (Henschel & *Sohn* AG, Waggonfabrik Wegmann AG: Pz.III); Nurnberg (*Maschinenfabrik* Augsburg Nurnberg AG: Pz.III); Hannover (*Maschinenfabrik* Niedersachen Hannover, GmbH: Pz.III); Braunschweig (*Muehlenbau und Industrie* AG (MIAG): Pz.III); Breslau (*Fahrzeug und Motorenbau*, GmbH (FAMO): Pz.II); Pilsen (*Böhmisch-Mährische Maschinenfabrik AG*: Pz.38(t))

Tank Engines: Friedrichshafen (*Maybach Motorenbau:*Maybach HL 120 TRM); Berlin (*Norddeutsche Motorenbau*)

Main Guns: Dusseldorf (Rheinmetall-Borsig AG:) 5cm Kw.K.38 L/42, 7.5cm Kw.K.37 L/24

New tanks: Pz.III Ausf J with long 5cm KwK 39 L/60 first introduced in December 1941 (40 built)

Soviet Union

| Month | Light | | | Medium | Heavy | |
	T-60	T-50	T-26	T-34/76	KV-1/KV-2	Total
January	0	0	0	168	46	214
February	0	0	69	113	44	226
March	0	0	0	179	62	241
April	0	0	0	223	66	289
May	0	0	0	191	11/59	261
June	0	0	0	256	40/40	336
July	0	15	24	302	177	518
August	0	35	23	421	207	686
September	20	0	0	398	108	526
October	120	0	0	185	91	396
November	600	0	0	253	156	1,009
December	648	10	0	327	190	1,175
Total	1,388	60	116	3,016	1,198/99	5,877

Manufacturing Centers: Leningrad (KV-1 until October 1941, T-50 July-August); Chelyabinsk (KV-1 from July 1941); Kharkov (T-34 until October 1941); Stalingrad (T-34, T-60); Gorkiy (T-34 from September 1941, T-60), Nizhniy Tagil (T-34, from December 1941); Moscow/Kolomna (T-60)

Tank Engines: V-2 Diesel engine (Zavod 75 in Kharkov)

Main Guns: 76.2mm F-34 gun (Zavod 92 in Gorky)

New tank models:
- T-34/76 Model 1941 with 76.2mm F-34 gun introduced in February 1941
- T-50 light tank with 45mm M1938 gun introduced in July 1941
- T-60 light tank with 20mm TNSh L/107 cannon introduced in September 1941

Armour Order of Battle, 1 July 1942

German

Heeresgruppe Nord (Generalfeldmarschall Georg von Küchler)

16. Armee (Generalfeldmarschall Ernst Busch)

- XXXIX Panzerkorps (General der Panzertruppe Hans Jürgen von Arnim)
  ○ 8.Panzer-Division (General der Panzertruppen Erich Brandenberger)
  ○ Heerestruppen: Panzer-Regiment 203

18. Armee (Generaloberst Georg Lindemann)

- XXVIII Armeekorps (General der Artillerie Herbert Loch)
  ○ 12.Panzer-Division (Generalleutnant Walter Wessel)

Heeresgruppe Mitte (Generalfeldmarschall Günther von Kluge)

2. Panzerarmee (Generaloberst Rudolf Schmidt)

- XXXV Armeekorps (General der Artillerie Rudolf Kämpfe)
  ○ 4.Panzer-Division (Generalleutnant Heinrich Eberbach)
- XLVII Panzerkorps (General der Artillerie Joachim Lemelsen)
  ○ 17.Panzer-Division (Generalmajor Rudolf-Eduard Licht)
  ○ 18. Panzer-Division (Generalleutnant Karl Freiherr von Thüngen)

4.Armee (Generaloberst Gotthard Heinrici)

- LVI Panzerkorps (General der Panzertruppen Ferdinand Schaal)
  ○ 19.Panzer-Division (Generalleutnant Gustav Schmidt)

9.Armee (Generaloberst Walter Model)

- XXIII Armeekorps (General der Infanterie Albrecht Schubert)
  ○ 1.Panzer-Division (Generalleutnant Walter Krüger)
  ○ 5.Panzer-Division (General der Panzertruppen Gustav Fehn)
- XXXXVI Panzerkorps (General der Infanterie Hans Zorn)
  ○ 20.Panzer-Division (Generalleutnant Walther Düvert)
  ○ Army-control: 2.Panzer-Division (Generalleutnant Hans-Karl von Esebeck)

Heeresgruppe Süd (Generalfeldmarschall Fedor von Bock)

1.Panzerarmee (Generaloberst Ewald von Kleist)

- III Panzerkorps (General der Panzertruppen Leo Freiherr Geyr von Schweppenburg)
  ○ 16.Panzer-Division (Generaloberst Hans-Valentin Hube)
  ○ 22.Panzer-Division (Generalleutnant Wilhelm von Apell Aufstellung)
- XIV Panzerkorps (General der Infanterie Gustav von Wietersheim)
  ○ 14.Panzer-Division (Generalleutnant Ferdinand Heim)
  ○ 60.Infanterie-Division (mot.)

4.Panzerarmee (Generaloberst Hermann Hoth)

- XXIV Panzerkorps (General der Panzertruppen Wilibald Freiherr von Langermann und Erlenkamp) KIA – 3 October 1942
  ○ 9.Panzer-Division (Generalleutnant Johannes Baeßler)
  ○ 11.Panzer-Division (General der Panzertruppen Hermann Balck)
  ○ 3.Infanterie-Division (mot.) (Generalmajor Helmuth Schlömer)
- XXXXVIII Panzerkorps (General der Panzertruppen Rudolf Veiel)
  ○ 24.Panzer-Division (Generalleutnant Bruno Ritter von Hauenschild)

○ 16.Infanterie-Division (mot.) (Generalleutnant Sigfrid Henrici)
○ *Grossdeutschland* Infanterie-Division (mot.) (Generalleutnant Walter Hörnlein)
6.Armee (General der Panzertruppe Friederich Paulus)
• XXXX Panzerkorps (General der Kavallerie Georg Stumme)
○ 3.Panzer-Division (Generalleutnant Hermann Breith)
○ 23.Panzer-Division (Generalleutnant Hans Freiherr von Boineburg-Lengsfeld) – Relieved of command 20 July 1942, re-instated in August. Wounded in action 27 December.
○ 29.Infanterie-Division (mot.) (Generalmajor Max Fremerey)

Under Heeresgruppe Süd control:
• LVII Panzerkorps (General der Panzertruppen Friedrich Kirchner)
○ 13.Panzer-Division (General der Panzertruppen Traugott Herr)
○ SS-Division "Wiking" (Obergruppenführer Felix Steiner)

Reinforcements:
September
• 1./sPz.Abt. 502 (Tiger) [34 tanks]
October
• 27.Panzer-Division (Oberst Helmut Michalik) [50 Tanks]
November
• Sturmgeschütz-Abteilung 200
• 6.Panzer-Division (Generalmajor Erhard Raus) [159 tanks]
December
• Panzer-Abteilung 138 [38 tanks] (Independent Army-level unit)
• 2./s.Pz.Abt. 502 (Tiger) [18 tanks]
• s.Pz.Abt. 503 (Tiger) [51 tanks]
○ **Note:** The 6, 7 and 10.Panzer-Divisionen were withdrawn from the Soviet Union in May–June 1942 and transferred to Heeresgruppe D in France.

Soviet
Leningrad Front (General-leytenant Leonid A. Govorov)
• 23rd Army (General-major Aleksandr I. Cherepanov)
○ 152nd Tank Brigade
• 55th Army (General-major Vladimir P. Sviridov)
○ 220th Tank Brigade
• Front Forces: 1st Tank Brigade and two OTBs

Volkhov Front (General Kirill A Meretskov)
• 54th Army (General-major Aleksandr V. Sukhomlin)
○ 16, 98, 122, 124th Tank Brigades
• 59th Army (General-major Ivan T. Korovnikov)
○ 7th Guards, 29th Tank Brigades
• Front Forces: 5 OTBs

Northwestern Front (General-polkovnik Pavel A. Kurochkin)
• 11th Army (General-leytenant Vasily I. Morozov)
○ 69th Tank Brigade
• 53rd Army (General-major Aleksandr S. Ksenofontov)
○ 33, 60, 177th Tank Brigades
• Front Forces: 83rd Tank Brigade and twelve OTBs

Kalinin Front (General-polkovnik Ivan S. Konev)
• 3rd Shock Army (General-leytenant Maksim A. Purkaev)
○ 104, 184 Tank Brigades and two OTBs
• 4th Shock Army (General-leytenant Vladimir V. Kurasov)
○ 78th Tank Brigade and two OTBs

- 22nd Army (General-major Vasily A. Iushkevich)
  - 82nd Tank Brigade
- 30th Army (General-leytenant Dmitri D. Lelyushenko)
  - 28, 143rd Tank Brigades
- 31st Army (General-major Vitaly S. Polenov)
  - 92, 101 Tank Brigades
- 41st Army (General-major of NKVD German F. Tarasov)
  - 21st Tank Brigade
- 58th Army (General-major Aleksei I. Zygin)
  - 35, 81 Tank Brigades
- Front Forces:
  - 7th Tank Corps (General-major Pavel A. Rotmistrov)
    - 3rd Guards, 62nd, 87th Tank Brigades [215 tanks]
  - 71st Tank Brigade and two OTBs

Western Front (General Georgy K. Zhukov)
- 5th Army (General-major Ivan I. Fediuninsky)
  - 20th Tank Brigade and one OTB
- 10th Army (General-leytenant Vasily S. Popov)
  - 32nd Tank Brigade
- 16th Army (General-leytenant Ivan K. Bagramian)
  - 94, 112, 146th Tank Brigade and one OTB
- 20th Army (General-leytenant Maks A. Reiter)
  - 17, 120, 188 Tank Brigades
- 33rd Army (General-leytenant Mikhail S. Khozin)
  - 145th Tank Brigade and one OTB
- 43rd Army (General-leytenant Konstantin D. Golubev)
  - 18th Tank Brigade
- 49th Army (General-leytenant Ivan G. Zakharkin)
  - 34th Tank Brigade and one OTB
- 50th Army (General-leytenant Ivan V. Boldin)
  - 11, 108th Tank Brigades
- 61st Army (General-leytenant Pavel A. Belov)
  - 3rd Tank Corps (General-major Dmitri K. Mostovenko)
    - 50th, 51st, 103rd Tank Brigades) [192 tanks]
  - 68, 192nd Tank Brigades
- Front Forces:
  - 5th Tank Corps (General-major Kuzma A. Semenchenko)
    - 24th, 41st, 70th Tank Brigades
  - 6th Tank Corps (General-major Andrei L. Getman)
    - 22nd, 100th, 200th Tank Brigades [169 tanks]
  - 8th Tank Corps (General-major Mikhail D. Solomatin)
    - 25th, 31st, 93rd Tank Brigades [165 tanks]
  - 9th Tank Corps (General-major Aleksei V. Kurkin)
    - 23rd, 95th, 187th Tank Brigades
  - 10th Tank Corps (General-major Vasily G. Burkov)
    - 178th, 183rd, 186th Tank Brigades [152 tanks]
  - 6th Guards, 2nd Tank Brigades

Bryansk Front (General-leytenant Filipp I. Golikov)
- 3rd Army (General-leytenant Pavel P. Korzun)
  - 79th, 150th Tank Brigades
- 13th Army (General-major Nikolai P. Pukhov)
  - 129th Tank Brigade

- 40th Army (General-leytenant Markian M. Popov)
  - 14th, 170th Tank Brigades
- 48th Army (General-major Grigoriy A. Khaliuzin)
  - 80th, 202nd Tank Brigades
- 5th Tank Army (General-major Aleksandr I. Liziukov) KIA – 23 July 1942
  - 2nd Tank Corps (General-major Andrei G. Kravchenko)
    - 26th, 27th, 148th Tank Brigades [183 tanks total]
  - 11th Tank Corps (General-major Aleksei F. Popov)
    - 53rd, 59th 160th Tank Brigades [191 tanks total]
  - 19th Tank Brigade [65 tanks]
- Front Forces:
  - 1st Tank Corps (General-major Mikhail E. Katukov)
    - 1st Guards, 49th, 89th Tank Brigades
  - 4th Tank Corps (General-major Vasily A. Mishulin)
    - 45th, 47th, 102nd Tank Brigades [179 tanks total]
  - 16th Tank Corps (General-major Mikhail I. Pavelkin)
    - 107th, 109th, 164th Tank Brigades [181 tanks]
  - 17th Tank Corps (General-major Ivan P. Korchagin)
    - 66th, 67th, 174th Tank Brigades [145 tanks total]
  - 24th Tank Corps (General-major Vasily M. Badanov)
    - 4th Guards, 54th, 130th Tank Brigades [141 tanks total]
  - 115th, 116th, 118th, 157th, 201st Tank Brigades

Southwestern Front (Marshal Semyon K. Timoshenko)
- 9th Army (General-major Feofan A. Parkhomenko)
  - 12th Tank Brigade and two OTBs [64 tanks total]
- 21st Army (General-major Aleksei I. Danilov)
  - 13th Tank Corps (General-major Petr E. Shurov) Died of wounds – 2 July 1942
    - 85th, 167th Tank Brigades [163 tanks total]
  - 10th Tank Brigade [38 tanks]
- 28th Army (General-major Vasily D. Kriuchenkin)
  - 23rd Tank Corps (General-major Abram M. Khasin)
    - 6th Guards, 91st , 114th Tank Brigades [128 tanks total]
  - 65th, 90th Tank Brigades [87 tanks total]
- 38th Army (General-major Kirill S. Moskalenko)
  - 22nd Tank Corps (General-major Aleksandr A. Shamshin)
    - 3rd, 13th, 36th Tank Brigades [49 tanks total]
  - 133rd, 156th, 159th, 168th Tank Brigades and one OTB [94 tanks total]
- Front Forces:
  - 14th Tank Corps (General-major Nikolai N. Radkevich)
    - 138th, 139th Tank Brigades
  - 57th, 58th, 84th, 88th, 158th, 176th Tank Brigades and two OTBs

Southern Front (General-leytenant Rodion Y. Malinovsky)
- 37th Army (General-major Petr M. Kozlov)
  - 121st Tank Brigade [46 tanks]
- 56th Army (General-major Aleksandr I. Ryzhov)
  - 63rd Tank Brigade [55 tanks]
- Front Forces:
  - 5th Guards, 15th, 140th Tank Brigades and two OTBs

North Caucasus Front (Marshal Semyon M. Budyonny)
- 51st Army (General-major Nikolai I. Trufanov)
  - 40th Tank Brigade

- Front Forces:
  - 136th, 137th Tank Brigades and two OTBs

Stavka Reserve [RVGK]
- 3rd Tank Army (General-leytenant Petr L. Romanenko)
  - 12th Tank Corps (General-major Semen I. Bogdanov)
    - 30th, 97th , 106th Tank Brigades
  - 15th Tank Corps (General-major Vasily A. Koptsov)
    - 96th, 105th, 113th Tank Brigades
  - 179th Tank Brigade
- 18th Tank Corps (General-major Ivan D. Chernyakhovsky)
  - 110th, 180th, 181st Tank Brigades [181 tanks]
- 2nd, 99th, 166th Tank Brigades

Moscow Military District
- 27th Tank Corps (General-major Fedor T. Remizov) – reformed into 1st Mechanized Corps in September 1942
  - 135th, 155th, 189th Tank Brigades
  - 117th, 119th, 134th, 153rd, 154th, 161st, 163rd, 169th, 193rd, 196th Tank Brigades and 26 OTBs

Stalingrad Military District
- 6th, 39th, 55th, 56th, 173rd, 182nd, 191st Tank Brigades

Reinforcements:
July:
- 1st Tank Army (General-major Kirill S. Moskalenko), subordinated: 13 TC, 28 TC, 158 TB
- 25th Tank Corps (General-major Petr P. Pavlov)
- 111th, 162nd, 175th Tank Brigades
- 26th Tank Corps (General-major Aleksei G. Rodin)
- 28th Tank Corps (General-major Georgy S. Rodin)
August:
- 4th Tank Army (General-major Vasily D. Kriuchenkin), subordinated: 22 TC, 23 TC, 133 TB
December:
- 19th Tank Corps (Podpolkovnik S. A. Vershkovich)
- 20th Tank Corps (Polkovnik Dmitri M. Gritsenko)

Tank Production, 1942

Germany

Month	Light	Medium			Heavy	Other	
	Pz.II	*Pz.III*	*Pz.IV*	*Pz.38(t)*	*Pz.VI*	*StuG III*	*Total*
January	29	159	59	59	0	45	351
February	42	216	58	61	0	45	422
March	50	244	8	28	0	3	333
April	37	246	80	0	0	36	399
May	56	246	85	21	0	79	487
June	42	228	72	21	1	70	434
July	20	231	88	26	0	60	425
August	0	231	84	0	8	80	403
September	0	217	93	0	3	70	383
October	0	188	99	0	10	84	381
November	0	178	113	0	21	100	412
December	0	221	155	0	34	120	530
Total	276	2,605	994	216	77	792	4,960

Tank Engines: Friedrichshafen (*Maybach Motorenbau*: Maybach HL 120 TRM and Maybach HL210); Berlin (*Norddeutsche Motorenbau*).

New tanks:
- Pz.III Ausf L with 5-cm KwK 39 L/60 introduced in June 1942, improved Pz.III Ausf M introduced in October 1942.
- Pz.III Ausf N with 7.5-cm KwK 37 L/42 howitzer introduced in June 1942.
- Pz.IV Ausf F2 with 7.5-cm KwK 40 L/43 introduced in April 1942.
- Pz.IV Ausf G with 7.5-cm KwK 40 L/48 introduced in June 1942.
- Pz.VI Tiger with 8.8-cm KwK 36 L/56 introduced in August 1942.

Soviet Union

Month	Light		Medium		Heavy
	T-60	*T-70*	*T-34/76*	*KV-1*	*Total*
January	600	0	464	216	1,280
February	600	0	521	262	1,383
March	600	200	715	250	1,765
April	600	300	744	260	1,904
May	500	400	993	325	2,218
June	500	500	973	287	2,260
July	400	500	1,263	132	2,295
August	300	500	1,235	104	2,139
September	300	600	1,264	174	2,338
October	77	600	1,499	166	2,342
November	0	627	1,291	125	2,043
December	0	710	1,568	125	2,403
Total	4,477	4,883	12,535	2,426	24,321

Manufacturing Centers: CTZ, Chelyabinsk (KV-1); STZ, Stalingrad (T-34); Zavod 112, Gorky (T-34); Zavod 183, Nizhniy Tagil (T-34); Zavod 174, Omsk (T-34); GAZ, Gorky (T-60, T-70); Zavod 38, Kirov (T-60, T-70); Zavod 37, Sverdlovsk (T-60, T-70).

Tank Engines: V-2 Diesel engine (CTZ, Chelyabinsk).

New tanks:
- T-34/76 Model 1942 introduced in January 1942.
- T-70 with 45mm 20K Model 1938 L/46 introduced in March 1942.

Notes

Introduction

1. Hugh Trevor-Roper (ed.), *Hitler's War Directives 1939–1945* (London: Birlinn Ltd, 2004), p. 94.
2. Excluding machine-gun-armed Pz.I light tanks, which were no longer assigned to Panzer-Abteilungen. I also will exclude similar Soviet light tanks or tankettes such as the T-37 and T-40. By 1941 standards, these were not tanks.
3. Heinz Guderian, *Panzer Leader* (New York: Ballantine Books, 1957), pp. 31–4.
4. *The German Campaign in Russia – Planning and Operations (1940–1942)*, Historical Study No. 20-261a (Washington, D: Department of the Army, March 1955), p. 42.
5. David Kahn, *Hitler's Spies: German Military Intelligence in World War II* (Cambridge, MA: Da Capo Press, 1978), pp. 428–9 and 458–9.
6. *Die wichtigsten Panzerkampfwagen der Union der Sozialistischen Sowjetrepubliken (U.S.S.R)*, 1 June 1941, Panzerarmee 3, Ic Anlagen Band A, Teil I z. Tatigkeitsbericht Nr. 2, NAM (National Archives Microfilm), series T-313, Roll 222.
7. Richard W. Harrison, *Architect of Soviet Victory in World War II: The Life and Theories of G.S. Isserson* (Jefferson, NC: McFarland & Company, Publishers, 2010), pp. 60–121.
8. Mikhail N. Tukhachevsky, 'What is New in the Development of Red Army Tactics', in *The Soviet Art of War*, Harriet F. Scott and William F. Scott (eds.), (Boulder, CO: Westview Press, 1982), pp. 56–9.
9. Mary R. Habeck, *Storm of Steel: The Development of Armour Doctrine in Germany and the Soviet Union, 1919–1939* (Ithaca, NY: Cornell University Press, 2003).
10. Renamed GABTU in 1940.
11. Wolfgang Schneider, *Panzer Tactics: German Small-Unit Armor Tactics in World War II* (Mechanichsburg, PA: Stackpole Books, 2005), p. 293.
12. Arthur Wollschlaeger, 'The Raid on Orel', in *Knights Cross Panzers* (Mechanicsburg, PA: Stackpole Books, 2010), p. 127.
13. Artem Drabkin & Oleg Sheremet, *T-34 in Action* (Barnsley, UK: Pen & Sword Ltd, 2006), pp. 61–2.

Chapter 1: The Opposing Armoured Forces in 1941

1. To be renamed panzer armies between October 1941 and January 1942.
2. Some German armoured formations were already referring to themselves as Panzerkorps in 1941, but the change from Armeekorps (mot.) was not standardized until June 1942.
3. *Taktische Gliederung des Regiments* [Tactical Organization of the Regiment], Panzer-Regiment 18, 18.Panzer-Division, Ia, Anlage z. KTB, NAM (National Archives Microfilm), series T-315, Roll 708, Frame 258.
4. Panzergruppe 4, O.Qu., Anlagenband 3 z-KTB, NAM (National Archives Microfilm), series T-313, Roll 336, Frame 8618121.
5. Ibid.
6. A cubic meter of fuel (cbm or m³), was equivalent to 5,000 liters and weighed 739kg.
7. Hugh Trevor-Roper (ed.), *Hitler's War Directives 1939–1945* (London: Birlinn Ltd, 2004), p. 138.
8. Charles C. Sharp, *The Deadly Beginning: Soviet Tank, Mechanized, Motorized Divisions and Tank Brigades of 1940–1942*, Soviet Order of Battle World War II, Volume 1 (George F. Nafziger, 1995), pp. 10–14.
9. Excluding tankettes and obsolete foreign-built tanks.

10. *Mechanized Corps of the Red Army* website, http://mechcorps.rkka.ru/files/mechcorps/pages/12_meh.htm.
11. The same Andrey Vlasov who was captured in July 1942 and turned traitor, collaborating with the Germans to form the anti-Communist Russian Liberation Army (ROA).
12. Artem Drabkin and Oleg Sheremet, *T-34 in Action* (Barnsley, UK: Pen & Sword Books, Ltd, 2006), p. 34.
13. David Glantz, *Stumbling Colossus* (Lawrence, KS: University Press of Kansas, 1998), pp. 176–8.
14. Glantz, *Stumbling Colossus*, p. 166.

Chapter 2: The Dynamic of Armoured Operations in 1941
1. David Glantz, *The Initial Period of War on the Eastern Front, 22 June–August 1941* (London: Frank Cass & Co. Ltd, 1993), pp. 103.
2. David Glantz, *The Initial Period of War on the Eastern Front, 22 June–August 1941* (London: Frank Cass & Co. Ltd, 1993), pp. 83–5.
3. Werner Haupt, *Die 8.Panzer-Division im 2.Weltkrieg* (Eggolsheim: Podzun-Pallas Verlag, 1987), pp. 137–40.
4. Harold S. Orenstein (ed.), 'Combat Documents of the Soviet Northwestern Front, 21 June–1 July 1941', *The Journal of Soviet Military Studies*, Vol. 5, No. 2, June 1992, pp. 267–99.
5. Erhard Raus, *Panzer Operations* (Cambridge, MA: Da Capo Press, 2003), pp. 14–34.
6. Werner Haupt, *Die 8.Panzer-Division im 2.Weltkrieg* (Eggolsheim: Podzun-Pallas Verlag, 1987), p. 153.
7. Generalmajor Horst Ohrloff, 'XXXIX Motorized Corps Operations' in David M. Glantz (ed.), *The Initial Period of War on the Eastern Front, 22 June–August 1941* (Portland, OR: Frank Cass & Co. Ltd, 1997), pp. 167–83.
8. Ia, Kriegstagebuch 1 and 2, May 25–13 July 1941, XXIV Armeekorps (mot.), NAM (National Archives Microfilm), series T-314, Roll 715.
9. Korpsbefehl Nr. 1 für den Angriff, XXXXVII Armeekorps (mot.), NAM (National Archives Microfilm), series T-314, Roll 1097, frame 299.
10. Veterans of the 3rd Panzer Division, *Armored Bear: The German 3rd Panzer Division in World War II, Volume I* (Mechanichsburg, PA: Stackpole Books, 2012), pp. 147–9.
11. Ia, Kriegstagebuch Nr. 7. Jun 20–Jul 24, 1941, 8. Jäger-Division, NAM (National Archives Microfilm), series T-315, Roll 458.
12. *Bericht über Leistungen und Erfolge der II./Flakregiment 4 bei der 256. Division im der Zeit vom 22-27.6.41*, NAM (National Archives Microfilm), series T-314, Roll 653, frames 221–31.
13. 256. Infanterie-Division KTB, NAM (National Archives Microfilm), series T-315, Roll 1796.
14. Horst Slesina, *Soldaten gegen Tod und Teufel* (Giddings, TX: Preuss Publishing, 2003), pp. 28–9.
15. Ia, Kriegstagebuch Nr. 7. June 20–July 24, 1941, 8. Jäger-Division, NAM (National Archives Microfilm), series T-315, Roll 458.
16. Klaus Gerbet (ed.), *Generalfeldmarschall Fedor von Bock: The War Diary 1939–1945* (Atglen, PA: Schiffer Publishing Ltd, 1996), p. 228.
17. David Stahel, *Operation Barbarossa and Germany's Defeat in the East* (Cambridge, UK: Cambridge University Press, 2009), pp. 170–86.
18. Karlheinz Münch, *The Combat History of German Heavy Anti-tank Unit 653 in World War II* (Mechanicsburg, PA: Stackpole Books, 2005), p. 12.
19. Ia KTB, 11. Panzer-Division, NAM (National Archives Microfilm), series T-315, Roll 2320.
20. Gustav Schrodek, *Ihr Glaube galt dem Vaterland: Geschichte des Panzer-Regiments 15* (Munich: Schild-Verlag, 1976), pp. 124–9.
21. Gustav W. Schrodek, *Die 11. Panzer-Division: Gespenster-Division 1940–1945* (Eggolsheim: Dörfler Verlag GmbH, 2004), p. 132.
22. Brigadier General Edel Lingenthal, '11th Panzer Division Operations' in David M. Glantz (ed.), *The Initial Period of War on the Eastern Front, 22 June–August 1941* (Portland, OR: Frank Cass & Co. Ltd, 1997), pp. 336.
23. Victor J. Kamenir, *The Bloody Triangle: The Defeat of Soviet Armour in the Ukraine, June 1941* (Minneapolis, MN: Zenith Press, 2008), pp. 142–4.

270   *Tank Warfare on the Eastern Front, 1941–1942*

24. Brigadier General Edel Lingenthal, '11th Panzer Division Operations' in David M. Glantz (ed.), *The Initial Period of War on the Eastern Front, 22 June–August 1941* (Portland, OR: Frank Cass & Co. Ltd, 1997), p. 336.
25. Generalleutnant Albert Praun *et al.*, *German Radio Intelligence* (Washington, DC: Department of the Army, 1953).
26. Friedrich von Hake, *Der Schicksalsweg der 13. Panzer-Division 1939–1945* [The Destiny of the 13th Panzer-Division] (Eggolsheim, Germany: Dorfler im Nebel Verlag, 2006), p. 54.
27. Lieutenant General H. J. von Hoffgarten, '11th Panzer Division Operations' in David M. Glantz (ed.), *The Initial Period of War on the Eastern Front, 22 June–August 1941* (Portland, OR: Frank Cass & Co. Ltd, 1997), p. 327.
28. Richard N. Armstrong, *Red Army Tank Commanders* (Atglen, PA: Schiffer Publishing Ltd, 1994), p. 35.
29. Nikolai Popel, B., *During Difficult Times* (Moscow: Terra-Fantastica, 2001) p. 185.
30. Martin van Creveld, *Supplying War: Logistics from Wallenstein to Patton* (Cambridge: Cambridge University Press, 1977), p. 157.
31. Paul Carell, *Hitler Moves East* (Winnipeg, Canada: J. J. Fedorowicz Publishing, 1991), p. 211.
32. Ia, Anlagenband B la/b z. KTB Nr. 5, June 18–Sep 17, 1941, Panzerarmee 4, , NAM (National Archives Microfilm), series T-313, Roll 331.
33. Werner Haupt, *Die 8.Panzer-Division im 2.Weltkrieg* (Eggolsheim: Podzun-Pallas Verlag, 1987), pp. 158–60.
34. Erich von Manstein, *Lost Victories* (Novato, CA: Presidio, Press, 1982), pp. 194–7.
35. Erhard Raus, *Panzer Operations* (Cambridge, MA: Da Capo Press, 2003), p. 64.
36. Aleksei Isaev, *Inoy 1941: Ot granitsy do Leningrada* [The Other 1941: From the Border to Leningrad] (Moscow: EKSMO, 2011), pp. 326–9.
37. Werner Haupt, *Die 8.Panzer-Division im 2.Weltkrieg* (Eggolsheim: Podzun-Pallas Verlag, 1987), p. 168.
38. Robert A. Forczyk, *Panzerjäger vs. KV-1: Eastern Front 1941–43* (Oxford: Osprey Publishing, 2012), pp. 58–9.
39. Tim Bean and Will Fowler, *Russian Tanks of World War II* (St. Paul, MN' MBI Publishing Co., 20030, p. 119.
40. O. Qu., Kriegstagebuch, Panzerarmee 4, NAM (National Archives Microfilm), series T-313, Roll 330, frame 8610992.
41. Hans Schaufler, 'From the Bug to the Dnepr', in *Knights Cross Panzers* (Mechanicsburg, PA: Stackpole Books, 2010), pp. 72–3.
42. David M. Glantz, *Barbarossa Derailed: The Battle for Smolensk 10 July–10 September 1941, Volume 1* (Solihull, UK: Helion & Co. Ltd, 2010), p. 79.
43. David M. Glant, *Barbarossa Derailed: The Battle for Smolensk, 10 July–10 September 1941* (Solihull, UK: Helion & Co. Ltd, 2010), p. 65.
44. Paul Carell, *Hitler Moves East* (Winnipeg, Canada: J. J. Fedorowicz Publishing, 1991), p. 73.
45. 'Description of the fighting of the 5th and 7th Mechanized Corps in the counterattack at Senno and Lepel'] http://mechcorps.rkka.ru/files/mechcorps/pages/7_meh.htm.
46. *Journal of the Fighting of the 14th Tank Division,* http://mechcorps.rkka.ru/files/mechcorps/pages/7_meh.htm.
47. KTB, 7. Panzer-Division, NAM (National Archives Microfilm), series T-315, Roll 406, frames 0039-0041.
48. Abteilung Ic Report from Panzergruppe 3, XXXIX Armeekorps (mot.), NAM (National Archives Microfilm), series T-314, Roll 926, frame 00558.
49. David M. Glant, *Barbarossa Derailed: The Battle for Smolensk, 10 July–10 September 1941* (Solihull, UK: Helion & Co. Ltd, 2010), pp. 78–81.
50. Abteilung Ic Report from Panzergruppe 3, XXXIX Armeekorps (mot.), NAM (National Archives Microfilm), series T-314, Roll 926, frame 00558.
51. Paul Carell, *Hitler Moves East* (Winnipeg, Canada: J. J. Fedorowicz Publishing, 1991), pp. 75–6.
52. Ia Reporting, Panzerarmee 3, NAM (National Archives Microfilm), series T-313, Roll 231, frame 6176.

53. Otto Carius, *Tigers in the Mud* (Mechanichsburg, PA: Stackpole Books, 1992), pp. 7–8.
54. O.Qu., Anlagenband 2 z. KTB, May 4, 1941 – 28 April 1942, Panzerarmee 4, NAM (National Archives Microfilm), series T-313, Roll 335, Frame 8617204.
55. Bryan I. Fugate, *Operation Barbarossa: Strategy and Tactics on the Eastern Front, 1941* (Novato, CA: Presidio Press, 1984), pp. 125–8.
56. David Stahel, *Operation Barbarossa and Germany's Defeat in the East* (Cambridge, UK: Cambridge University Press, 2009), pp. 260–360
57. 'The report of the commander of the 10th Armored Division on the division's fighting from 22 June to 1 August 1941 to the Deputy People's Commissar of Defense on 2 August 1941'. http://mechcorps.rkka.ru/files/mechcorps/pages/otchet_10td.htm
58. Ib KTB der Quartiermeister-Abteilung, June 1, 1941 – May 18, 1942, 7. Panzer-Division, NAM (National Archives Microfilm), series T-315, Roll 423.
59. Ia Reporting, Panzerarmee 3, NAM (National Archives Microfilm), series T-313, Roll 231, frame 6176.
60. Ia KTB, LVII Armeekorps (mot.), NAM (National Archives Microfilm), series T-314, Roll 1,474, frame 430.
61. David Glantz, *The Initial Period of War on the Eastern Front, 22 June–August 1941* (London: Frank Cass & Co. Ltd, 1993), p. 282.
62. Friedrich von Hake, *Der Schicksalsweg der 13. Panzer-Division 1939–1945* [The Destiny of the 13th Panzer-Division] (Eggolsheim, Germany: Dorfler im Nebel Verlag, 2006), pp. 58–9.
63. Cornel I. Scafes *et al.*, *Armata romana 1941–1945* (Bucharest: Editura RAI, 1996).
64. Hugh Trevor-Roper (ed.), *Hitler's War Directives 1939–1945* (London: Birlinn Ltd, 2004), p. 139.
65. Generalleutnant Albert Praun *et al.*, *German Radio Intelligence* (Washington, DC: Department of the Army, 1953).
66. Karlheinz Münch, *The Combat History of German Heavy Anti-tank Unit 653 in World War II* (Mechanicsburg, PA: Stackpole Books, 2005), p. 5.
67. Karlheinz Münch, *The Combat History of German Heavy Anti-tank Unit 653 in World War II* (Mechanicsburg, PA: Stackpole Books, 2005), pp. 6–7.
68. Klaus Gerbet (ed), *Generalfeldmarschall Fedor von Bock: The War Diary, 1939–1945* (Atglen, PA: Schiffer Publishing Ltd, 1996), p. 255.
69. David M. Glantz, *Barbarossa Derailed: the Battle for Smolensk 10 July–10 September 1941*, Volume I (Solihull, UK: Helion & Co. Ltd, 2010), p. 545.
70. David M. Glantz, 'Forgotten Battles of the German-Soviet War 1941–1945', Volume I (22 June–4 December 1941), (self-published, 1999), pp. 88.
71. Heinz Guderian, *Panzer Leader* (New York: Ballantine Books, 1957), p. 153.
72. Hugh Trevor-Roper (ed.), *Hitler's War Directives 1939–1945* (London: Birlinn Ltd, 2004), pp. 145–6.
73. Kriegstagebuch Nr. 1, Part 2, Panzergruppe 2, August 21–October 31, 1941. NAM (National Archives Microfilm), series T-313, Roll 86.
74. Thomas L. Jentz, *Panzertruppen*, Vol. 1 (Atglen, PA: Schiffer Publishing Ltd, 1996), p. 211.
75. Konrad Leppa, *Generalfeldmarschall Walter Model: Von Genthin bis vor Moskaus Tore* (Nurnberg: Prinz-Eugen Verlag, 1962), p. 142.
76. Ia, KTB 1, Part 2, Panzergruppe 2, August 21–October 31, 1941. NAM (National Archives Microfilm), series T-313, Roll 86.
77. Klaus Gerbet (ed.), *Generalfeldmarschall Fedor von Bock: The War Diary, 1939–1945* (Atglen, PA: Schiffer Publishing Ltd, 1996), p. 298.
78. Klaus Gerbet (ed.), *Generalfeldmarschall Fedor von Bock: The War Diary, 1939–1945* (Atglen, PA: Schiffer Publishing Ltd, 1996), p. 304.
79. David M. Glantz, *Forgotten Battles of the German-Soviet War 1941–1945, Volume I* (Self-published, 1999), pp. 91–8.
80. David M. Glantz, *Forgotten Battles of the German-Soviet War 1941–1945, Volume I* (Self-published, 1999), pp. 101–2.
81. Konrad Leppa, *Generalfeldmarschall Walter Model: Von Genthin bis vor Moskaus Tore* (Nurnberg: Prinz-Eugen Verlag, 1962), pp. 145–8.

82. David M. Glantz, *Barbarossa: Hitler's Invasion of Russia 1941* (Charleston, SC: Tempus Publishing Inc., 2001), p. 132.
83. Artem Drabkin & Oleg Sheremet, *T-34 in Action* (Barnsley, UK: Pen & Sword Ltd, 2006), p. 40.
84. Albert L. Weeks, *Russia's Life-Saver: Lend-Lease Aid to the U.S.S.R. in World War II* (New York: Lexington Books, 2010), p. 9.
85. David Stahel, *Operation Barbarossa and Germany's Defeat in the East* (Cambridge, UK: Cambridge University Press, 2009).
86. Lukas Friedli, *Repairing the Panzers: German Tank Maintenance in World War 2, Volume 2* (Monroe, NY: Panzerwrecks, 2011), p. 144.
87. Franz Halder, *Kriegstagebuch: Tägliche Aufzeichnungen des Chefs des Generalstabes des Heeres 1939–1942, Band III, Der Russlandfeldzug bis zum Marsch auf Stalingrad*, edited by Hans-Adolf Jacobsen and Alfed Philippi (Stuttgart: W. Kohlhammer, 1963), p. 242.
88. Lukas Friedli, *Repairing the Panzers: German Tank Maintenance in World War 2, Volume 2* (Monroe, NY: Panzerwrecks, 2011), pp. 138–44.
89. Thomas L. Jentz, *Panzertruppen*, Vol. 1 (Atglen, PA: Schiffer Publishing Ltd, 1996), p. 205.
90. David M. Glantz, *Barbarossa: Hitler's Invasion of Russia 1941* (Charleston, SC: Tempus Publishing Inc., 2001), p. 132.
91. Karlheinz Münch, *The Combat History of German Heavy Anti-tank Unit 653 in World War II* (Mechanicsburg, PA: Stackpole Books, 2005), p. 9.
92. Franz Halder, *Kriegstagebuch: Tägliche Aufzeichnungen des Chefs des Generalstabes des Heeres 1939–1942, Band III, Der Russlandfeldzug bis zum Marsch auf Stalingrad*, edited by Hans-Adolf Jacobsen and Alfed Philippi (Stuttgart: W. Kohlhammer, 1963), p. 237.
93. Horst Reibenstahl, *The 1st Panzer Division: A Pictorial History* (West Chester, PA: Schiffer Publishing Ltd, 1990), p. 99.
94. Maksim Kolomiets, *1941 Tanki v bitve zu Moskvu [Tanks in the Battle of Moscow]* (Moscow: IAUZA, 2009), pp. 26–9.
95. Kriegstagebuch Nr. 1, Part 2, Panzergruppe 2, August 21–October 31, 1941. NAM (National Archives Microfilm), series T-313, Roll 86.
96. Hans Schäufler (ed.), *Knights Cross Panzers* (Mechanicsburg, PA: Stackpole Books, 2010), pp. 121–2.
97. David Garden and Kenneth Andrew (ed.), *The War Diaries of a Panzer Soldier* (Atglen, PA: Schiffer Military History, 2010), p. 54.
98. Hans Schäufler (ed.), *Knights Cross Panzers* (Mechanicsburg, PA: Stackpole Books, 2010), p. 124.
99. Leonid M. Sandalov, *Na Moskovskom Napravlenii* (Moscow: Nauka, 1970), p. 207.
100. Robert Forczyk, *Moscow 1941: Hitler's First Defeat* (Oxford: Osprey Publishing Ltd, 2006), p. 33.
101. Franz Kurowski, *Panzer Aces III: German Tank Commanders in Combat in World War II* (Mechanichsburg, PA: Stackpole Books, 2010), p. 113.
102. Ia, Kriegstagebuch mit Gefechtskalender, Teil III,18. Panzer-Division, NAM (National Archives Microfilm), series T-315, Roll 706.
103. Hans Schäufler (ed.), *Knights Cross Panzers* (Mechanicsburg, PA: Stackpole Books, 2010), pp. 132–3.
104. Meldung der Sonderkommission des OKH, 27 June 1941, NAM (National Archives Microfilm), series T-315, Roll 744, frame 729.
105. Heinz Guderian, *Panzer Leader* (New York: Ballantine Books, Inc., 1968), p. 179.
106. Heinz Guderian, *Panzer Leader* (New York: Ballantine Books, Inc., 1968), p. 180.
107. Richard N. Armstrong, *Red Army Tank Commanders* (Atglen, PA: Schiffer Publishing Ltd, 1994), p. 43.
108. Hans Schäufler (ed.), *Knights Cross Panzers* (Mechanicsburg, PA: Stackpole Books, 2010), pp. 134–5.
109. Richard N. Armstrong, *Red Army Tank Commanders* (Atglen, PA: Schiffer Publishing Ltd, 1994), p. 44.
110. Hasso von Manteuffel, *The 7th Panzer Division: An Illustrated History of Rommel's ‚Ghost Division' 1938–1945* (Atglen, PA: Schiffer Military History, 2000), p. 73.

111. Erhard Raus, *Panzer Operations: The Eastern Front Memoir of General Raus, 1941–45* (Cambridge, MA: Da Capo Press, 2003), p. 86.

112. Ia, Anlagen zum Kriegstagebueh Nr. 3, Part III, Sep 28, 1941–May 5, 1942, 7. Panzer-Division, NAM (National Archives Microfilm), series T-315, Roll 407.

113. Fritz Morzik, *German Air Force Airlift Operations* (Honolulu: University Press of the Pacific, 2002), pp. 76–7.

114. Gustav W. Schrodek, *Die 11. Panzer-Division: Gespenster-Division 1940–1945* (Eggolsheim: Dörfler Verlag GmbH, 2004), p. 251.

115. Georgy K. Zhukov, *The Memoirs of Marshal Zhukov* (New York: Delacorte Press, 1971), p. 324.

116. Konstantin K. Rokossovsky, *A Soldier's Duty* (Moscow: Progress Publishers, 1985), pp. 51–3.

117. Georgy K. Zhukov, *The Memoirs of Marshal Zhukov* (New York: Delacorte Press, 1971), p. 321.

118. Maksim Kolomiets, *1941 Tanki v bitve zu Moskvu* [*Tanks in the Battle of Moscow*] (Moscow: IAUZA, 2009), p. 36.

119. Simon Sebag Montefiore, *Stalin: the Court of the Red Tsar* (New York: Vintage Books, 2005), pp. 394.

120. Maksim Kolomiets, *1941 Tanki v bitve zu Moskvu* [*Tanks in the Battle of Moscow*] (Moscow: IAUZA, 2009), pp. 37–8.

121. Pavel A. Rotmistrov, *Stal'naya gvardiya* [*Steel Guards*], (Moscow: Voenizdàt, 1984), Chapter 3.

122. Jack Radey and Charles Sharp, *The Defense of Moscow 1941: The Northern Flank* (Barnsley, UK: Pen & Sword Books Ltd, 2012), pp. 90–1 and 190.

123. Jack Radey and Charles Sharp, *The Defense of Moscow 1941: The Northern Flank* (Barnsley, UK: Pen & Sword Books Ltd, 2012), p. 86.

124. Ia, Anlagenband IVb z. KTB, Verteidigung von Kalin, Oct 15– Kov 20, 1941, XXXXI Armee-korps, NAM (National Archives Microfilm), series T-314, Roll 980.

125. Ia, Anlagenband IVb z. KTB, Verteidigung von Kalin, Oct 15– Kov 20, 1941, XXXXI Armee-korps, NAM (National Archives Microfilm), series T-314, Roll 980.

126. Artem Drabkin & Oleg Sheremet, *T-34 in Action* (Barnsley, UK: Pen & Sword Ltd, 2006), p. 47.

127. Ia, Anlagenband A 1 z. KTB Nr. 6, 29 September–14 October 1941, Panzerarmee 4, NAM (National Archives Microfilm), series T-313, Roll 340.

128. Veterans of the 3rd Panzer Division, *Armored Bear: The German 3rd Panzer Division in World War II, Volume I* (Mechanichsburg, PA: Stackpole Books, 2012), pp. 249–51.

129. Ibid., p. 249.

130. David Garden and Kenneth Andrew (ed.), *The War Diaries of a Panzer Soldier* (Atglen, PA: Schiffer Military History, 2010), p. 56.

131. Veterans of the 3rd Panzer Division, *Armored Bear: The German 3rd Panzer Division in World War II, Volume I* (Mechanichsburg, PA: Stackpole Books, 2012), pp. 269–73.

132. David Garden and Kenneth Andrew (ed.), *The War Diaries of a Panzer Soldier* (Atglen, PA: Schiffer Military History, 2010), p. 58.

133. Thomas L. Jentz, *Germany's Panther Tank: The Quest for Combat Supremacy* (Atglen, PA: Schiffer Publishing Ltd, 1995), pp. 14–15.

134. Erhard Raus, *Panzer Operations: The Eastern Front Memoir of General Raus, 1941–45* (Cambridge, MA: Da Capo Press, 2003), p. 88.

135. Niklas Zetterling and Anders Frankson, *The Drive on Moscow 1941* (Philadelphia: Casemate, 2012), p. 212.

136. Alexander Hill, 'British Lend-Lease Tanks and the Battle of Moscow, November–December 1941 – Revisted', *Journal of Slavic Military Studies*, Vol. 22, No. 4 (October–December 2009), pp. 575–6.

137. Artem Drabkin and Oleg Sheremet, *T-34 in Action* (Barnsley, UK: Pen & Sword Publishers, 2006), p. 24.

138. Georgy K. Zhukov, *The Memoirs of Marshal Zhukov* (London: Jonathan Cape Ltd, 1971), pp. 339–40.

139. Alexander Hill, 'British Lend-Lease Tanks and the Battle of Moscow, November–December 1941 – Revisted', *Journal of Slavic Military Studies*, Vol. 22, No. 4 (October–December 2009), pp. 575–6.

140. Werner Haupt, *Die 8.Panzer-Division im 2.Weltkrieg* (Eggolsheim: Podzun-Pallas Verlag, 1987), p. 179.
141. Werner Haupt, *Die 8.Panzer-Division im 2.Weltkrieg* (Eggolsheim: Podzun-Pallas Verlag, 1987), pp. 192–3.
142. Martin van Creveld, *Supplying War: Logistics from Wallenstein to Patton* (Cambridge: Cambridge University Press, 1977), p. 165.
143. Grigory F. Krivosheev, *Soviet Casualties and Combat Losses in the Twentieth Century* (London: Greenhill Books, 1997), p. 261.
144. Thomas L. Jentz, *Panzertruppen*, Vol. 1(Atglen, PA: Schiffer Publishing Ltd, 1996), p. 211.
145. Erhard Raus, *Panzer Operations: The Eastern Front Memoir of General Raus, 1941–45* (Cambridge, MA: Da Capo Press, 2003), pp. 89–90.
146. Grigory F. Krivosheev, *Soviet Casualties and Combat Losses in the Twentieth Century* (London: Greenhill Books, 1997), p. 261.
147. Grigory F. Krivosheev, *Soviet Casualties and Combat Losses in the Twentieth Century* (London: Greenhill Books, 1997), p. 277.

Chapter 3: Armoured Operations in 1942

1. Veterans of the 3rd Panzer Division, *Armored Bear: The German 3rd Panzer Division in World War II, Volume I* (Mechanichsburg, PA: Stackpole Books, 2012), p. 299.
2. Erhard Raus, *Panzer Operations* (Cambridge, MA: Da Capo Press, 2003), p. 95.
3. Hasso von Manteuffel, *The 7th Panzer Division: An Illustrated History of Rommel's ,Ghost Division' 1938–1945* (Atglen, PA: Schiffer Military History, 2000), p. 101.
4. Werner Haupt, *Die 8.Panzer-Division im 2.Weltkrieg* (Eggolsheim: Podzun-Pallas Verlag, 1987), p. 205.
5. Gustav W. Schrodek, *Die 11.Panzer-Division: Gespenster-Division 1940–1945* (Eggolsheim: Dörfler Verlag GmbH, 2004), p. 306.
6. O.Qu., Anlagenband 3 z. KTB. Versorgungslagenmeldungen, Apr 1–Oct 31, 1942, Panzer-armee 1, NAM (National Archives Microfilm), series T-313, Roll 44.
7. Thomas L. Jentz, *Panzertruppen*, Vol. 1 (Atglen, PA: Schiffer Publishing Ltd, 1996), p. 252.
8. Grigory F. Krivosheev, *Soviet Casualties and Combat Losses in the Twentieth Century* (London: Greenhill Books, 1997), p. 252.
9. Simon Sebag Montefiore, *Stalin: the Court of the Red Tsar* (New York: Vintage Books, 2005), p. 407.
10. Alexander Poliakov, *White Mammoths: The Dramatic Story of Russian Tanks in Action* (New York: E. P. Dutton, 1943), pp. 71–2.
11. Alexander Poliakov, *White Mammoths: The Dramatic Story of Russian Tanks in Action* (New York: E. P. Dutton, 1943), pp. 95–6.
12. Jason D. Mark, *Besieged: the Epic Battle for Cholm* (Pymble, Australia: Leaping Horseman Books, 2011), pp. 181 and 205–6.
13. Robert A. Forczyk, *Demyansk 1942–43: The Frozen Fortress* (Oxford: Osprey Publishing, 2012), pp. 71–3.
14. Grigory F. Krivosheev, *Soviet Casualties and Combat Losses in the Twentieth Century* (London: Greenhill Books, 1997), pp. 96–7.
15. Charles C. Sharp, *School of Battle: Soviet Tank Corps and Tank Brigades, January 1942 to 1945*, Volume II (Published by George F. Nafziger, 1995), p. 1.
16. Jason D. Mark, *Besieged: the Epic Battle for Cholm* (Pymble, Australia: Leaping Horseman Books, 2011), p. 73.
17. U.S. Army, *Effects of Cold on Military Equipment*, http://www.wainwright.army.mil.
18. Thomas L. Jentz, *Germany's Panther Tank: The Quest for Combat Supremacy* (Atglen, PA: Schiffer Military History, 1995), pp. 11–18.
19. Erich von Manstein, *Lost Victories* (Novato, CA: Presidio Press, 1986), p. 228.
20. Ia, Kriegstagebuch 1 u. 2, Krim, 29 January–5 July 1942, 28. Jäger-Division, NAM (National Archives Microfilm), series T-315, Roll 834.

21. David M. Glantz, 'Prelude to German Operation Blau: Military Operations on Germany's Eastern Front, April-June 1942', Journal of Slavic Military Studies, Volume 20, No. 2, (April–June 2007), pp. 181–4.
22. David M. Glantz, *Kharkov 1942* (Chatham, UK: Ian Allen, 1998), p. 78.
23. Ia, KTB, 294. Infanterie-Division, 1 April–31 July 1942, NAM (National Archives Microfilm), Series T-315, Roll 1941.
24. Veit Scherzer, *113.Infanterie-Division: Kiew-Charkow-Stalingrad* (Jena: Scherzers Militaer-Verlag, 2007), pp. 193–5.
25. Ia, Kriegstagebuch, January–December 1942, III Armeekorps (mot.), NAM (National Archives Microfilm), series T-314, Roll 194.
26. Qu., Anlagen z. KTB. Information and reports on the supply situation, and supply statistics on the campaign in the Izyum, Kharkov, and Kastornoye areas. Mar 22–Dec 31, 1942,VIII Armeekorps, NAM (National Archives Microfilm), series T-314, Roll 385.
27. Gefechtsbericht der 62. Infanterie-Division über die kämpfe südl. Charkow in der Zeit vom 12.–25.5.42, Ia, 62. Infanterie-Division, NAM (National Archives Microfilm), series T-315, Roll 1034.
28. O.Qu., Anlagenband 3 z. KTB. Versorgungslagenmeldungen, Apr 1– Oct 31, 1942, Panzer-armee 1, NAM (National Archives Microfilm), series T-313, Roll 44.
29. Gefechtsbericht der 3. Panzer-Division (Kampfgruppe Breith) uber die Abwehrschlacht nordostw. Charkow 12.5–22.5.42, 3. Panzer-Division, NAM (National Archives Microfilm), series T-315, Roll 144.
30. Auszugsweiser Gefechtsbericht der 23. Panzer-Division für der einsatz während der schlacht um Charkow an der Nordfront vom 12.5–22.5.42 an der Südfront vom 23.5–29.5.42,23. Panzer-Division, NAM (National Archives Microfilm), series T-315, Roll 791.
31. Ia, Kriegstagebuch, January – December 1942, III Armeekorps (mot.), NAM (National Archives Microfilm), series T-314, Roll 194.
32. Ia, Zahlenmeldungen, Teil 1. Losses of personnel and ammunition, April 3 – September 15, 1942, 11. Armee, NAM (National Archives Microfilm), T-312, Roll 420.
33. O.Qu., Anlagenband B z. KTB. Versorgungskarten, Panzerarmee 1, NAM (National Archives Microfilm), series T-313, Roll 26.
34. Marek Kruk and Radoslaw Szewczyk, *9. Panzer-Division 1940–1943* (Poland: STRATUS, 2011), p. 75.
35. Arthur G. Volz, 'A Soviet Estimate of German Tank Production', *Journal of Slavic Military Studies*, Volume 21, No. 3, (July 2008), pp. 588–90.
36. Hugh Trevor-Roper (ed.), *Hitler's War Directives 1939–1945* (London: Birlinn Ltd, 2004), p. 178.
37. Dr. Peter W. Becker, 'The Role of Synthetic Fuel in World War II Germany', *Air University Review*, July–August 1981.
38. Operation *Blau* was redesignated as Operation *Braunschweig*, effective 30 June 1942. However, I will continue to use the original designation to avoid confusion.
39. Mikhail E. Katukov, *Na Ostrie glavnogo udara [At the Point of the Main Attack]* (Moscow: Voenizdat, 1974), chapter 9.
40. Hans-Joachim Jung, *Panzer Soldiers for 'God, Honor and Fatherland' The History of Panzerregiment Grossdeutschland* (Winnipeg: J. J. Fedorowicz Publishing, 2000), p. 20.
41. Artem Drabkin & Oleg Sheremet, *T-34 in Action* (Barnsley, UK: Pen & Sword Ltd, 2006), p. 113.
42. Ernst Rebentisch, *The Combat History of the 23rd Panzer Division in World War II* (Mechanicsburg, PA: Stackpole Books, 20012), p. 113.
43. David M. Glantz, *To the Gates of Stalingrad* (Lawrence, KS: University Press of Kansas, 2009), p. 154.
44. Ewald Klapdor, *Viking Panzers: the German 5th SS Tank Regiment in the East in World War II* (Mechanicsburg, PA: Stackpole Books, 2011), pp. 11–17.
45. Ernst Rebentisch, *The Combat History of the 23rd Panzer Division in World War II* (Mechanicsburg, PA: Stackpole Books, 20012), pp. 122–3.
46. David M. Glantz, *To the Gates of Stalingrad: Soviet-German Combat Operations, April–August 1942* (Lawrence, KS: Kansas University Press, 2009), p. 423.

47. Ernst Rebentisch, *The Combat History of the 23rd Panzer Division in World War II* (Mechanicsburg, PA: Stackpole Books, 20012), p. 166.
48. Ernst Rebentisch, *The Combat History of the 23rd Panzer Division in World War II* (Mechanicsburg, PA: Stackpole Books, 20012), p. 175.
49. Christer Bergstrom, *Stalingrad, The Air Battle: 1942 through January 1943* (Hersham, UK: Ian Allen Publishing Ltd, 2007), p. 62.
50. In a bizarre aftermath, Gordov was awarded the Hero of the Soviet Union in 1945, but then arrested for treason in 1947 and executed in 1950. The reason was his criticism of Stalin's conduct of the war.
51. Wolfgang Werthen, *Geschichte der 16. Panzer-Division 1939–1945* (Bad Nauheim, Germany: Podzun-Pallas-Verlag, 1958), pp. 99–103.
52. Christer Bergstrom, *Stalingrad, The Air Battle: 1942 through January 1943* (Hersham, UK: Ian Allen Publishing Ltd, 2007), pp. 60–3.
53. Stavka Directive No. 156595, dated 1930 hours 10 August 1942.
54. Artem Drabkin & Oleg Sheremet, *T-34 in Action* (Barnsley, UK: Pen & Sword Ltd, 2006), p. 53.
55. David M. Glantz, *To the Gates of Stalingrad: Soviet-German Combat Operations, April–August 1942* (Lawrence, KS: Kansas University Press, 2009), pp. 301–2.
56. Gunter Schmitz, *Die 16. PanzerDivision 1938–1945* (Eggolsheim: Dörfler Verlag GmbH, 2004), p. 105.
57. David M. Glantz, *Forgotten Battles of the German Soviet War 1941–1945, Volume III* (12 May–18 November 1942) (Self-published, 1999), p. 105.
58. David Garden and Kenneth Andrew (ed.), *The War Diaries of a Panzer Soldier* (Atglen, PA: Schiffer Military History, 2010), p. 90.
59. David Garden and Kenneth Andrew (ed.), *The War Diaries of a Panzer Soldier* (Atglen, PA: Schiffer Military History, 2010), p. 91.
60. Konstantin K. Rokossovsky, 'Soldatskii dolg' ['A Soldier's Duty'], *Voenno-istoricheskii zhurnal* [*Military Historical Journal*], No. 2 (February 1990), p. 52, and No. 7 (July 1991), pp. 4–5.
61. David Garden and Kenneth Andrew (ed.), *The War Diaries of a Panzer Soldier* (Atglen, PA: Schiffer Military History, 2010), p. 92.
62. Marek Kruk and Radoslaw Szewczyk, *9. Panzer-Division 1940–1943* (Poland: STRATUS, 2011), pp. 91–7.
63. Jason D. Mark, *Death of the Leaping Horseman: 24. Panzer-Division in Stalingrad, 12th August–20th November 1942* (Sydney: Leaping Horseman Books, 2003), p. 157.
64. David M. Glantz and Jonathan M. House, *Armageddon in Stalingrad: September-November 1942* (Lawrence, KS: University Press of Kansas, 2009), pp. 168–82.
65. Jason D. Mark, *Island of Fire: The Battle for the Barrikady Gun Factory in Stalingrad, November 1942–February 1943* (Sydney: Leaping Horseman Books, 2006), pp. 4–6.
66. Walter Gorlitz, *Strategie der Defensive Model* (Munich: Limes Verlag, 1982), p. 121.
67. Anton Detlev von Plato, *Die Geschichte Der 5. Panzerdivision 1938 bis 1945* (Regensburg: Walhalla und Praetoria verlag, 1978), p. 230.
68. Artem Drabkin & Oleg Sheremet, *T-34 in Action* (Barnsley, UK: Pen & Sword Ltd, 2006), p. 51.
69. Lukas Friedli, *Repairing the Panzers: German Tank Maintenance in World War 2, Volume 2* (Monroe, NY: Panzerwrecks, 2011), p. 151.
70. Wolfgang Schneider, *Tigers in Combat, Volume 1* (Mechanichsburg, PA: Stackpole Books, 2004), p. 73.
71. Matthew Hughes and Chris Mann, *The T-34 Russian Battle Tank* (Osceola, WI: MBI Publishing Co., 1999), p. 88.
72. Tim Bean and Will Fowler, *Russian Tanks of World War II* (St. Paul, MN' MBI Publishing Co., 20030, pp. 137–8.
73. Sergei M. Shtemenko, *The Soviet General Staff at War 1941–1945* (Hololulu, Hawaii: University Press of the Pacific, 2001), pp. 123–6.
74. George F. Nafziger, *Rumanian Order of Battle World War II* (Self-published, 1995), p. 10.
75. Thomas L. Jentz, *Panzertruppen*, Vol. II (Atglen, PA: Schiffer Publishing Ltd, 1996), p. 24.

76. R.W. Byrd, *Once I Had a Comrade: Karl Roth and the Combat History of the 36th Panzer Regiment 1939–45* (Solihull, UK: Helion & Company, 2006), pp. 94–7.

77. Fritz Morzik, *German Air Force Airlift Operations* (Honolulu: University Press of the Pacific, 2002), pp. 179–200.

78. Thomas L. Jentz, *Panzertruppen*, Vol. II (Atglen, PA: Schiffer Publishing Ltd, 1996), pp. 26–8.

79. Erhard Raus, *Panzer Operations* (Cambridge, MA: Da Capo Press, 2003), pp. 150–2.

80. Ernst Rebentisch, *The Combat History of the 23rd Panzer Division in World War II* (Mechanicsburg, PA: Stackpole Books, 20012), p. 205.

81. Friedrich W. von Mellenthin, *Panzer Battles* (New York: Ballantine Books, 1971), pp. 211–14.

82. Gustav W. Schrodek, *Die 11. Panzer-Division: Gespenster-Division 1940–1945* (Eggolsheim: Dörfler Verlag GmbH, 2004), p. 377.

83. Erhard Raus, *Panzer Operations* (Cambridge, MA: Da Capo Press, 2003), pp. 156–61.

84. John Erickson, *The Road to Berlin* (London: Cassell, 2003), p. 12.

85. Ernst Rebentisch, *The Combat History of the 23rd Panzer Division in World War II* (Mechanicsburg, PA: Stackpole Books, 20012), pp. 207–8.

86. Erhard Raus, *Panzer Operations* (Cambridge, MA: Da Capo Press, 2003), p. 176.

87. David M. Glantz, *Zhukov's Greatest Defeat: The Red Army's Epic Disaster in Operation Mars, 1942* (Lawrence, KS: The University Press of Kansas, 1999), pp. 373–7.

88. Thomas L. Jentz, *Panzertruppen*, Vol. II (Atglen, PA: Schiffer Publishing Ltd, 1996), pp. 21–6.

89. David M. Glantz, *Zhukov's Greatest Defeat: The Red Army's Epic Disaster in Operation Mars, 1942* (Lawrence, KS: The University Press of Kansas, 1999), p. 100.

90. Hans-Joachim Jung, *Panzer Soldiers for 'God, Honor and Fatherland' The History of Panzerregiment Grossdeutschland* (Winnipeg: J.J. Fedorowicz Publishing, 2000), p. 38.

91. Thomas L. Jentz, *Panzertruppen*, Vol. II (Atglen, PA: Schiffer Publishing Ltd, 1996), p. 24.

92. David M. Glantz, *Zhukov's Greatest Defeat: The Red Army's Epic Disaster in Operation Mars, 1942* (Lawrence, KS: University Press of Kansas, 1999), p. 304.

93. Aleksei Isaev et al., *Tankovyi Udar: Sovietskie tanki v boiakh 1942–1943 [Tank Attack: Soviet Tanks in Battle, 1942–1943]* (Moscow: EKSMO, 2007), pp. 78–88.

94. C. De. Franceschi and M. Mantovani, *Le Operazioni delle Unita Italiane al Fronte Russo 1941–43* (Rome: Stato Maggiore dell'Esercito, Ufficio torico, 2000), pp. 189 and 617.

95. Richard W. Harrison, *Architect of Soviet Victory in World War II: The Life and Theories of G.S. Isserson* (Jefferson, NC: McFarland & Company, Publishers, 2010), p. 146.

96. Ia, KTB 4, 306. Infanterie-Division, 20 November 1942–1 January 1943, NAM (National Archives Microfilm), Series T-315, Roll 2028.

97. Vasily M. Badanov, '*Glubokii tankovyi reid*' ['Deep Tank Raid'] in A.M. Samsonov (ed.) *Stalingradskaya epopeya* (Moscow: Nauka Publishers, 1968), pp. 625–40.

98. Ic, Tatigkeitsbericht init Kartenanlagen z. KTB 6, 1 November–31 December 1942, 11. Panzer-Division, NAM (National Archives Microfilm), Series T-315, Roll 596.

99. David M. Glantz, *From the Don to the Dnepr: Soviet Offensive Operations December 1942–August 1943* (London: Frank Cass Publisgers, 1991), p. 74.

100. Grigory F. Krivosheev, *Soviet Casualties and Combat Losses in the Twentieth Century* (London: Greenhill Books, 1997), p. 253.

101. W. K. Hancock and Margaret M. Gowing, *The British War Economy*, History of the Second World War, United Kingdom Civil Series (London: HMSO, 1949), p. 363.

102. Gunter Schmitz, *Die 16. PanzerDivision 1938–1945* (Eggolsheim: Dörfler Verlag GmbH, 2004), p. 123.

Bibliography

Department of the Army Pamphlet No. 20-290, *Terrain Factors in the Russian Campaign*, July 1951.

Richard N. Armstrong, *Red Army Tank Commanders* (Atglen, PA: Schiffer Publishing Ltd, 1994).

Vasily M. Badanov, '*Glubokii tankovyi reid*' ['Deep Tank Raid'] in A.M. Samsonov (ed.) *Stalingradskaya epopeya* (Moscow: Nauka Publishers, 1968), pp. 625–40.

Vladimir Beshanov, *Tankyi Pogrom 1941* [*Tank Pogrom*] (Moscow: AST Publishing, 2001).

Evgeni Bessonov, *Tank Rider: Into the Reich with the Red Army* (Philadelphia: Casemate, 2003).

Paul Carell, *Hitler Moves East* (Winnipeg, Canada: J.J. Fedorowicz Publishing, 1991).

Artem Drabkin & Oleg Sheremet, *T-34 in Action* (Barnsley, UK: Pen & Sword Ltd, 2006).

Lukas Friedli, *Repairing the Panzers: German Tank Maintenance in World War 2, Volume 2* (Monroe, NY: Panzerwrecks, 2011).

Robert A. Forczyk, *Panzerjäger vs. KV-1: Eastern Front 1941–43* (Oxford: Osprey Publishing, 2012).

Klaus Gerbet (ed.), *Generalfeldmarschall Fedor von Bock: The War Diary, 1939–45* (Atglen, PA: Schiffer Publishing Ltd, 1996).

David M. Glantz, *Barbarossa: Hitler's Invasion of Russia 1941* (Charleston, SC: Tempus Publishing Inc., 2001).

—— *Barbarossa Derailed: The Battle for Smolensk, 10 July–10 September 1941* (Solihull, UK: Helion & Co. Ltd, 2010).

—— *From the Don to the Dnepr* (London: Frank Cass, 1991).

—— *The Initial Period of War on the Eastern Front, 22 June–August 1941* (London: Frank Cass & Co. Ltd, 1993).

David M. Glantz and Jonathan M. House, *The Battle of Kursk* (Lawrence: University Press of Kansas, 1999).

Heinz Guderian, *Panzer Leader* (New York: Ballantine Books, Inc., 1968).

Mary R. Habeck, *Storm of Steel: The Development of Armour Doctrine in Germany and the Soviet Union, 1919–1939* (Ithaca, NY: Cornell University Press, 2003).

Werner Haupt, *Die 8. Panzer-Division im 2.Weltkrieg* (Eggolsheim: Podzun-Pallas Verlag, 1987).

Hermann Hoth, *Panzer-Operationen – Die Panzergruppe 3 und der operative Gedanke der deutschen Führung im Sommer 1941* (Heidelberg: Scharnhorst Buchkameradschaft, 1956).

Aleksei Isaev et al., *Tankovyi Udar: Sovietskie tanki v boiakh 1942–1943* [*Tank Attack: Soviet Tanks in Battle, 1942–1943*] (Moscow: EKSMO, 2007).

Victor J. Kamenir, *The Bloody Triangle: The Defeat of Soviet Armour in the Ukraine, June 1941* (Minneapolis, MN: Zenith Press, 2008).

Mikhail E. Katukov, *Na Ostrie glavnogo udara* [*At the Point of the Main Attack*] (Moscow: Voenizdat, 1974).

Ernst Klink, '*Heer und Kriegsmarine*' in Militärgeschichtliches Forschungsamt (ed.), *Das Deutsche Reich und der Zweite Weltkrieg*, Band 4: *Der Angriff auf die Sowjetunion* (Stuttgart: Deutsche Verlags-Anstalt, 1987).

Maksim Kolomiets, *1941 Tanki v bitve zu Moskvu* [*Tanks in the Battle of Moscow*] (Moscow: IAUZA, 2009).

Konrad Leppa, *Generalfeldmarschall Walter Model: Von Genthin bis vor Moskaus Tore* (Nurnberg: Prinz-Eugen Verlag, 1962)

Erich von Manstein, *Lost Victories* (Novato, CA: Presidio Press, 1982).

Hasso von Manteuffel, *The 7th Panzer Division: An Illustrated History of Rommel's Ghost Division 1938–1945* (Atglen, PA: Schiffer Military History, 2000).

Friederich W. von Mellenthin, *Panzer Battles: A Study of the Employment of Armour in the Second World War* (New York: Ballantine Books, 1971).

George M. Nipe, Jr. *Last Victory in Russia: The SS-Panzerkorps and Manstein's Counteroffensive February–March 1943* (Atglen, PA: Schiffer Military History, 2000).

Erhard Raus, *Panzer Operations: The Eastern Front Memoir of General Raus, 1941–45* (Cambridge, MA: Da Capo Press, 2003).

Gustav W. Schrodek, *Die 11. Panzer-Division: Gespenster-Division 1940–1945* (Eggolsheim: Dörfler Verlag GmbH, 2004).

Wolfgang Schneider, *Panzer Tactics: German Small-Unit Armor Tactics in World War II* (Mechanichsburg, PA: Stackpole Books, 2005).

Russell H.S. Stolfi, 'The greatest encirclement in history: Link up of the German 3rd and 9th Panzer divisions on 15 September 1941 in the Central Ukraine', *RUSI Journal*, December 1996.

Vitaliy Zhilin, *Geroi Tankisty 1941–42* [*Hero Tankers*] (Moscow: EKSMO, 2009).

Georgy K. Zhukov, *The Memoirs of Marshal Zhukov* (London: Jonathan Cape Ltd, 1971).

Index

1